General History o

Francois Guizot

Introduction

This is a comprehensive history of how civilization developed in Europe, and thus a history of how the continent was settled and formed various nation states.

From the intro:

"There are three sorts of written history:

1. A mere orderly statement of facts, unconnected in the narrative save by the order of succession. This is hardly more than a catalogue of facts and events, and does not properly constitute history. Such were the annalistic writings and the chronicles of earlier ages; some of the modern "elementary histories" belong in this group, if anywhere among historical writings.

2. A detailed recital of events and facts, so framed as to show the more immediate causes and the direct consequences and results of those events and facts. Here the causal relation between events, not widely separated in time or place, is brought into view. This is the aim of general histories, histories of individual countries, and most histories of special periods. This group includes the larger part of historical writings.

3. A study of the growth of historical ideas, of the forces that have moved men and nations, of the causes which have been operative through long periods directing the tendencies of peoples, of the development of institutions, and of their relation to the general march of history and to the advance of civilization. Such are works which trace the history of political institutions and of the ideas and forces that have shaped them. It is obvious that the aim of this last group is really the ultimate aim of all historical inquiry—not merely to know facts, but to learn the deeper purpose and meaning which run through all history, and to which each event of history is in greater or less degree contributory.

A historical study of the last class—and to this belongs in high degree the present work— presupposes on the part of the writer a thorough acquaintance with all essential facts in the period covered, and for its thorough comprehension by the reader and student, a good general knowledge of history.

In the present work the author has directed his chief attention to the external forms of political society, and has sought to trace the changes in these forms and institutions back to their causes and forward to their consequences. Both the forms themselves and their changes are traceable only in the facts of history, while the causes for the changes are the forces which have moved man to political, social, and industrial action. Such a study is not, then, a recital, but an interpretation, of facts; it is an inquiry into the meaning—the result, of external events—the philosophy of history, if I may use that high-sounding and much abused expression. It is not a history of the facts of the past fourteen centuries, nor even a substitute for such history. It is an analysis and interpretation of that history so far as it has affected the development of social and political institutions."

PREFACE.

The lectures which are comprised in this book were delivered by M. Guizot in 1828 before the students of the Sorbonne in Paris, where he occupied the chair of history. They were soon published in book form, both in French and in English, and attracted immediate attention for their grasp of facts, philosophical breadth, and clear generalizations. Their intrinsic merit and their value for the student is attested by the fact that, at the expiration of nearly seventy years, during which historical study has marvelously developed, historical methods greatly changed, and historical knowledge vastly increased, they are still widely read and studied by the general reader and by students in colleges and universities.

While no extended discussion of the lectures constituting this volume is needed, a brief statement is fitting concerning the place they occupy, the class to which they belong, among historical writings. There are three sorts of written history:

1. A mere orderly statement of facts, unconnected in the narrative save by the order of succession. This is hardly more than a catalogue of facts and events, and does not properly constitute history. Such were the annalistic writings and the chronicles of earlier ages; some of the modern "elementary histories" belong in this group, if anywhere among historical writings.

2. A detailed recital of events and facts, so framed as to show the more immediate causes and the direct consequences and results of those events and facts. Here the causal relation between events, not widely separated in time or place, is brought into view. This is the aim of general histories, histories of individual countries, and most histories of special periods. This group includes the larger part of historical writings.

3. A study of the growth of historical ideas, of the forces that have moved men and nations, of the causes which have been operative through long periods directing the tendencies of peoples, of the development of institutions, and of their relation to the general march of history and to the advance of civilization. Such are works which trace the history of political institutions and of the ideas and forces that have shaped them. It is obvious that the aim of this last group is really the ultimate aim of all historical inquiry—not merely to know facts, but to learn the deeper purpose and meaning which run through all history, and to which each event of history is in greater or less degree contributory.

A historical study of the last class—and to this belongs in high degree the present work—presupposes on the part of the writer a thorough acquaintance with all essential facts in the period covered, and for its thorough comprehension by the reader and student, a good general knowledge of history.

In the present work the author has directed his chief attention to the external forms of political society, and has sought to trace the changes in these forms and institutions back to their causes and forward to their consequences. Both the forms themselves and their changes are traceable only in the facts of history, while the causes for the changes are the forces which have moved man to political, social, and industrial action. Such a study is not, then, a recital, but an interpretation, of facts; it is an inquiry into the meaning—the result, of external events—the philosophy of history, if I may use that high-sounding and much abused expression. It is not a history of the facts of the past fourteen centuries, nor even a substitute for such history. It is an analysis and interpretation of that history so far as it has affected the development of social and political institutions.

The lectures were originally delivered before a group of students fairly well versed in the facts of history as they were then known. In the lectures, the statements of facts are therefore brief, often hardly more than mere allusions, while the generalizations are rapid, as befitted the nature of the course.

In this country, the lectures as published have found general use as a text-book in colleges, and often for those who have not had a wide preliminary knowledge of history. When so used, the book has usually been supplemented by lectures by the instructor, supplying, so far as possible, the underlying basis of fact necessary for the comprehension of the original work. Of late years, the more frequent use of the book in colleges has doubtless been in connection with or as a conclusion of an undergraduate course in general mediæval and modern history. While the place accorded these lectures in a historical course has thus slightly changed, there has been, at the same time, during the seventy years since they were delivered a great advance in knowledge of the period covered by the lectures. During that time the unwearied researches of scholars have brought to view many hitherto unknown or obscure facts in mediæval history and institutions; for example, touching the origin of the feudal system or the relation of the trade gilds to the mediæval cities. Some of these results have an important bearing on the verification or modification of views presented in the lectures of M. Guizot.

The object had constantly in view in the making of the present edition and in the preparation of the notes has been twofold: To furnish such brief historical data as may be helpful in recalling to the reader the fuller significance of the facts on which the lectures are based, and to note the opinions of modern scholars and the results of later researches where they seem to supplement or to controvert the conclusions of the author. It will be found that the notes fall into three groups: historical, critical, and supplementary. At the end of several of the lectures an extended note has been inserted, giving a rapid summary of events during the historical period whose institutions and tendencies are discussed in the lecture. Wherever a special point has seemed worthy of notice beyond the scope of a note, or wherever it has seemed probable that further information than that given in a note would be desired, references have been made to authorities usually accessible in reference libraries. The constant aim has been, without desecrating the lectures by a mutilation of the original form, to make the book more useful for all classes of readers. It is not intended as a revision of M. Guizot's work. I have not presumed to rewrite, restate, or even to modernize the lectures. The work has been strictly that of annotation for the purposes mentioned. I have been increasingly surprised, as the work progressed, to find how well the lectures have stood the test of three quarters of a century, and how few of the statements are noticeably at variance with modern knowledge or opinion.

It is assumed that those into whose hands this volume comes are familiar with the general facts of history. When that is not the case, general outlines may be used in connection with this work, such as Duruy's History of the Middle Ages, Duruy's History of Modern Times, and Fisher's Outlines of Universal History.

The present edition is based on the edition of 1842, annotated by Professor C. S. Henry. The text of that edition has been retained, save that a few errors of translation and an occasional bad English sentence have been corrected. A considerable number of Professor Henry's notes have been retained, while several have been omitted as unnecessary or have been replaced by others. In one case, a long note of the former edition has been broken into parts which now appear as unconnected notes on separate passages. To all of Professor Henry's notes the initial "H." has been appended, thus distinguishing them from those which now appear for the first time. For all

not so indicated the present editor is responsible. My thanks are due to my colleague, Dr. F. C. Clark, for his assistance in the annotation of the last three lectures.
G. W. K.
Ohio State University, May 27, 1896.

BIOGRAPHICAL SKETCH.

François Pierre Guillaume Guizot was born of Protestant parentage at Nîmes, France, on October 4, 1787. His father, a prominent advocate, became a victim of the French Revolution during the Reign of Terror, dying on the scaffold in 1794. Madame Guizot removed to Geneva, where her son received a classical education under Protestant influences. It is stated that before he left Geneva, at the age of eighteen, he was able to read Greek, Latin, German, Italian, and English. Spanish he learned when he was seventy-two years of age, in order that he might write a history of Spain. In 1805 he removed to Paris to enter upon the study of law. He soon obtained a position as tutor in the family of M. Stapfer, the Swiss minister to France, supporting himself in this way while pursuing his studies. The study of law he soon abandoned for literary and historical work. Within a few years he began writing for the press, his first articles appearing in Le Publiciste, then controlled by M. Suard. Through his connection with M. Suard he became acquainted with Mademoiselle Pauline de Meulan, who was also a contributor to the paper. Though she was fourteen years his senior, their common occupation and mutual tastes led to their marriage in 1812. M. Guizot published in 1809 a dictionary of French synonyms, in 1810 an essay on the Fine Arts in France, and in 1813 an annotated translation of Gibbon's Decline and Fall of the Roman Empire. In 1812 he was chosen assistant professor of history in the Faculty of Letters at the Sorbonne in Paris, and a little later was made professor of modern history. His professorship gave him the acquaintance of M. Royer-Collard, then professor of philosophy at the Sorbonne, to whom he was indebted for his first public position under the later restored government of Louis XVIII. His writings during this period were mainly philosophical and literary. Politically he was an advocate of legitimate monarchy as against Napoleon, and desired the restoration of the Bourbons, with such constitutional limitations as would secure the rights of the people against the recurrence of prerevolutionary absolutism.

In 1814, on the downfall of Napoleon, he was given the position of Secretary-General in the Department of the Interior under the monarchy of Louis XVIII. After the return of Napoleon, the Hundred Days, and the second restoration of Louis XVIII, he became Secretary-General of the Department of Justice, and in 1817 was made a member of the Council of State, and Director-General of the departmental and communal administration. He was identified at this time with the political party or faction known as the Doctrinaires, of which M. Royer-Collard was a prominent exponent. This group desired constitutional monarchy based on suffrage in the hands of the middle classes; they were thus opposed on the one hand to the radical democratic spirit growing out of the Revolution, and on the other to the growing absolutism of Louis XVIII and his court. During this period he wrote several political pamphlets in exposition of these general views.

In 1820 the royalist reaction consequent upon the murder of the Duc de Berri caused the downfall of the ministry, and Guizot resigned all his offices. He immediately resumed his lectures at the Sorbonne. It was at this time that he delivered the celebrated course of lectures on the History of Representative Government. His lectures and writings did not accord with the reactionary spirit of the reign of Charles X, and in 1825 he was forbidden to continue his lectures. During the next few years he was active among the opposition to the policy of the government, but devoted himself principally to historical writing. In rapid succession he published a collection of Memoirs on the English Revolution, Memoirs relating to the History of France, and an Introduction to a revised translation of Shakespeare. The most important work was the History of the English Revolution, of which only the first two volumes were completed at this time.

In 1825 his wife died, and in the following year he married Mademoiselle Dillon, the niece of his first wife. In 1828, upon a change of the ministry, M. Guizot was restored to his professorial chair. In that year he delivered the lectures on the History of Civilization in Europe which form the present volume; in the following year he gave a course on the History of Civilization in France. These lectures not only attracted immediate attention, but they marked an epoch in historical writing. The careful research, the profundity of reasoning, the skill and rapidity of generalization, and the breadth of view displayed take these lectures out of the rank of ordinary historical productions. The influence of the spirit in which M. Guizot undertook the consideration of historical material and of the development of political institutions was unquestionably productive of an important result upon historical method. From this time forth, in the intervals of political service and after his retirement from public life, he gave himself to historical writing in the broad, scholarly, philosophical spirit which he here displayed.

In 1830 he was elected to the Chamber of Deputies, and from that time until 1848 he was almost constantly engaged in public position. He took a prominent part in the protest against the arbitrary acts of Charles X which led to the July Revolution of 1830, and to the accession of Louis Philippe to the throne of the French. Under the new government M. Guizot was made Provisional Minister of the Interior, but retired after a short incumbency. In 1832, under the ministry of Marshal Soult, he became Minister of Public Instruction. He reorganized the work of public instruction in France, and originated and carried through the Chambers the law of June 28, 1833, which was the basis of the system of popular primary instruction that was rapidly extended over France. Into all the details of organizing this work the minister went with the most careful attention and interest, furnishing to the directors, subordinates, and teachers kindly instructions which show in every phase his deep concern in the work. Secondary and higher instruction also received careful attention.

In 1836 the ministry fell, and Guizot retired from his position, retaining his seat in the Chamber of Deputies. In 1840 he was sent to England as ambassador, where he was warmly welcomed because of his literary reputation, his admiration for the British Constitution, and his friendliness for England in the then existing European situation. In the same year he was recalled, and on October 29th became Minister of Foreign Affairs. Until 1848 he was the real head of the ministry. His policy was the maintenance of constitutional government at home, against the radical tendencies of the Republicans, and peace abroad, against the war-loving spirit of the French people.

In the latter part of his ministry he yielded more and more to the king, and was led to meet the rising spirit of democracy and the cry for electoral reform by measures that were reactionary and extraconstitutional, if not unconstitutional. His devotion to law and order were at this time transforming him into an ultra-conservative. In 1848 the ministry fell, and with it the monarchy of Louis Philippe. During the eight years of its continuance the ministry of which Guizot was the chief spirit gave peace and prosperity to France; industry and commerce flourished; popular instruction was improved; the penal code was revised, and internal improvements on a large scale undertaken. The ministry failed, largely because of Guizot's lack of knowledge and appreciation of the practical side of political and governmental life. He was of the closet, not of the people, and in the zeal of his Doctrinaire policy he failed to appreciate the necessity of keeping in fairly close touch with popular feeling. Concession of principle he could never make, and by refusing to yield anything to the opposition, he, and the monarchy whose destinies he was seeking to guide, lost all.

After the Revolution of 1848 he retired to England, and, with the exception of a single unsuccessful candidacy for the Chamber of Deputies, never again took part in French politics. In 1851 he returned to France, and spent the remaining twenty-three years of his life in literary pursuits on his estate at Val Richer, in Normandy. While in England, he wrote and published the History of the English Republic and the Protectorate of Cromwell, and later the History of the Protectorate of Richard Cromwell and the Restoration of the Stuarts. These two works completed the history begun in 1827. He also wrote during this period of his life the Memoirs on the History of My Own Times; Meditations on the Christian Religion; History of France for my Grandchildren (completed by his daughter, Madame Guizot De Witt), and several other historical and philosophical essays and books.

His most celebrated and best-known works are the History of Representative Government, History of Civilization in Europe, and History of Civilization in France. He was elected in 1832 to the Academy of Moral and Political Science; in 1833, to that of Inscriptions and Belles-Lettres; and in 1836, to the French Academy, the highest literary honor in France. He died at his home, September 13, 1874, at the age of eighty-six.

The character of M. Guizot was such as to place him among the foremost men of the century. He is conspicuous among public men for the purity of his private life and for his simple, honest Christian belief. As a statesman he attained a high rank; he was a fairly consistent and unswerving advocate of constitutional monarchy, but lacked the practical force and knowledge requisite for the highest success in a field where pure theory must often yield to the attainable. His fame will always rest chiefly on his historical writings. His style was clear and attractive; his knowledge of facts wide and accurate; his analysis of historical forces clear and sharp; his generalizations and conclusions remarkably sound and well-founded. His early and constant devotion to the cause of constitutional monarchy colored all his political writing, and accounts in the present course of lectures for many of the positions that can hardly be accepted with the full and unqualified application with which they are stated by the author. Nevertheless, his historical works will always command the careful consideration of the student, and will hold for him a place among the foremost historical writers of modern times.

BIBLIOGRAPHICAL NOTE.

The list of general works given below will be helpful in the further study of matters touched upon in this work. No attempt has been made to include works not readily accessible, and the list is merely suggestive, not exhaustive. Authorities upon special fields and subjects are not included here, but, where needed, are given in the notes.

Adams, G. B. Civilization during the Middle Ages. New York, 1894.

Andrews, E. B. Brief Institutes of General History. Boston, 1887. Contains good bibliographies.

Bryce, James. The Holy Roman Empire. London and New York.

Church, R. W. The Beginnings of the Middle Ages. London, 1882.

Duruy, V. A History of France. Abridged and translated from the French. New York, 1889.

Duruy, V. The History of the Middle Ages, with notes and revisions by George B. Adams. New York, 1891.

Duruy, V. History of Modern Times. Translated from the French. New York, 1894.

Emerton, E. An Introduction to the Study of the Middle Ages (375-814). Boston, 1888.

Emerton, E. Mediæval Europe (814-1300). Boston, 1895.

Fisher, G. P. History of the Christian Church. New York, 1887.

Fisher, G. P. Outlines of Universal History. New York, 1885. Contains good bibliographies.

Gibbon, Edward. The Decline and Fall of the Roman Empire. 5 to 8 volumes. Numerous editions.

Guizot, F. P. G. History of Civilization in France. 4 volumes.

Hallam, Henry. View of the State of Europe during the Middle Ages. 3 volumes. Numerous editions.

Henderson, E. F. Select Historical Documents of the Middle Ages. 1892.

Hodgkin, Thomas. Italy and her Invaders. Oxford, 1880—'85.

Kitchin, G. W. History of France. 3 volumes. Oxford, 1873—'77.

Mathews, Shailer. Select Mediæval Documents illustrating the History of Church and Empire. 1892.

Menzel, W. History of Germany. 3 volumes. London.

Milman, II. II. History of Latin Christianity. 8 volumes.

Möller, W. History of the Christian Church. Translated from the German. 3 volumes. 1892—'94.

Myers, P. V. N. Outlines of Mediæval and Modern History. Boston, 1885.

Ploetz, Carl. Epitome of Ancient, Mediæval, and Modern History. Translated with extensive additions by William H. Tillinghast. Boston, 1883.

Ranke, L. History of the Popes. 3 volumes. London.

De Sismondi, J. C. L. Italian Republics. London, 1835.

Stillé, C. J. Studies in Mediæval History. Philadelphia, 1883.

Translations and Reprints from the Original Sources of European History. Edited by J. H. Robinson. Philadelphia, 1895.

GENERAL HISTORY OF CIVILIZATION IN MODERN EUROPE, FROM THE FALL OF THE ROMAN EMPIRE TO THE FRENCH REVOLUTION.

LECTURE I.: CIVILIZATION IN GENERAL.

Having been called upon to give a course of lectures, and having considered what subject would be most agreeable and convenient to fill up the short space allowed us from now to the close of the year, it has occurred to me that a general sketch of the History of Modern Europe, considered more especially with regard to the progress of civilization—that a general survey of the history of European civilization, of its origin, its progress, its end, its character, would be the most profitable subject upon which I could engage your attention.

I say European civilization, because there is evidently so striking a uniformity in the civilization of the different states of Europe, as fully to warrant this appellation. Civilization has flowed to them all from sources so much alike—it is so connected in them all, notwithstanding the great differences of time, of place, and circumstances, by the same principles, and it so tends in them all to bring about the same results, that no one will doubt the fact of there being a civilization essentially European.

At the same time it must be observed that this civilization cannot be found in—its history cannot be collected from, the history of any single state of Europe. However similar in its general appearance throughout the whole, its variety is not less remarkable, nor has it ever yet developed itself completely in any particular country. Its characteristic features are widely spread, and we shall be obliged to seek, as occasion may require in England, in France, in Germany, in Spain, for the elements of its history.

The situation in which we are placed, as Frenchmen, affords us a great advantage for entering upon the study of European civilization; for, without intending to flatter the country to which I am bound by so many ties, I cannot but regard France as the center, as the focus, of the civilization of Europe. It would be going too far to say that she has always been, upon every occasion, in advance of other nations. Italy, at various epochs, has outstripped her in the arts; England, as regards political institutions, is by far before her; and, perhaps, at certain moments, we may find other nations of Europe superior to her in various particulars: but it must still be allowed, that whenever France has set forward in the career of civilization, she has sprung forth with new vigor, and has soon come up with, or passed by, all her rivals.

Not only is this the case, but those ideas, those institutions which promote civilization, but whose birth must be referred to other countries, have, before they could become general, or produce fruit,—before they could be transplanted to other lands, or benefit the common stock of European civilization, been obliged to undergo in France a new preparation: it is from France, as from a second country more rich and fertile, that they have started forth to make the conquest of Europe. There is not a single great idea, not a single great principle of civilization, which, in order to become universally spread, has not first passed through France.

There is, indeed, in the genius of the French, something of a sociableness, of a sympathy,— something which spreads itself with more facility and energy, than in the genius of any other people; it may be in the language, or the particular turn of mind of the French nation; it may be in their manners, or that their ideas, being more popular, present themselves more clearly to the masses, penetrate among them with greater ease; but, in a word, clearness, sociability, sympathy, are the particular characteristics of France, of its civilization; and these qualities render it eminently qualified to march at the head of European civilization.

In studying, then, the history of this great fact, it is neither an arbitrary choice, nor convention, that leads us to make France the central point from which we shall study it; but it is because we feel that, in so doing, we in a manner place ourselves in the very heart of civilization itself—in the heart of the very fact which we desire to investigate.

I say fact, and I say it advisedly: civilization is just as much a fact as any other—it is a fact which like any other may be studied, described, and have its history recounted.

It has been the custom for some time past, and very properly, to talk of the necessity of confining history to facts; nothing can be more just; but it would be almost absurd to suppose that there are no facts but such as are material and visible: there are moral, hidden facts, which are no less real than battles, wars, and the public acts of government. Besides these individual facts, each of which has its proper name, there are others of a general nature, without a name, of which it is impossible to say that they happened in such a year, or on such a day, and which it is impossible to confine within any precise limits, but which are yet just as much facts as the battles and public acts of which we have spoken.

That very portion, indeed, which we are accustomed to hear called the philosophy of history— which consists in showing the relation of events with each other—the chain which connects them—the causes and effects of events—this is history just as much as the description of battles, and all the other exterior events which it recounts. Facts of this kind are undoubtedly more difficult to unravel; the historian is more liable to deceive himself respecting them; it requires more skill to place them distinctly before the reader; but this difficulty does not alter their nature; they still continue not a whit the less, for all this, to form an essential part of history.

Civilization is just one of this kind of facts; it is so general in its nature that it can scarcely be seized; so complicated that it can scarcely be unravelled; so hidden as scarcely to be discernible. The difficulty of describing it, of recounting its history, is apparent and acknowledged; but its existence, its worthiness to be described and to be recounted, is not less certain and manifest. Then, respecting civilization, what a number of problems remain to be solved! It may be asked, it is even now disputed, whether civilization be a good or an evil? One party decries it as teeming with mischief to man, while another lauds it as the means by which he will attain his highest dignity and excellence.* Again, it is asked whether this fact is universal—whether there is a general civilization of the whole human race—a course for humanity to run—a destiny for it to accomplish; whether nations have not transmitted from age to age something to their successors which is never lost, but which grows and continues as a common stock, and will thus be carried on to the end of all things. For my part, I feel assured that human nature has such a destiny; that a general civilization pervades the human race; that at every epoch it augments; and that there, consequently, is a universal history of civilization to be written. Nor have I any hesitation in asserting that this history is the most noble, the most interesting of any, and that it comprehends every other.

Is it not indeed clear that civilization is the great fact in which all others merge; in which they all end, in which they are all condensed, in which all others find their importance? Take all the facts of which the history of a nation is composed, all the facts which we are accustomed to consider as the elements of its existence—take its institutions, its commerce, its industry, its wars, the various details of its government; and if you would form some idea of them as a whole, if you would see their various bearings on each other, if you would appreciate their value, if you would pass a judgment upon them, what is it you desire to know? Why, what they have done to forward the progress of civilization—what part they have acted in this great drama,—what influence they have exercised in aiding its advance. It is not only by this that we form a general opinion of these facts, but it is by this standard that we try them, that we estimate their true value. These are, as it were, the rivers of whom we ask how much water they have carried to the ocean. Civilization is, as it were, the grand emporium of a people, in which all its wealth—all the elements of its life— all the powers of its existence are stored up. It is so true that we judge of minor facts accordingly as they affect this greater one, that even some which are naturally detested and hated, which prove a heavy calamity to the nation upon which they fall—say, for instance, despotism, anarchy, and so forth,—even these are partly forgiven, their evil nature is partly overlooked, if they have aided in any considerable degree the march of civilization. Wherever the progress of this principle is visible, together with the facts which have urged it forward, we are tempted to forget the price it has cost—we overlook the dearness of the purchase.

Again, there are certain facts which, properly speaking, cannot be called social—individual facts which rather concern the human intellect than public life: such are religious doctrines, philosophical opinions, literature, the sciences and arts. All these seem to offer themselves to individual man for his improvement, instruction, or amusement; and to be directed rather to his intellectual melioration and pleasure, than to his social condition. Yet still, how often do these facts come before us—how often are we compelled to consider them as influencing civilization! In all times, in all countries, it has been the boast of religion, that it has civilized the people among whom it has dwelt. Literature, the arts, and sciences, have put in their claim for a share of this glory; and mankind has been ready to laud and honor them whenever it has felt that this praise was fairly their due. In the same manner, facts the most important—facts of themselves, and independently of their exterior consequences, the most sublime in their nature, have increased in importance, have reached a higher degree of sublimity, by their connection with civilization. Such is the worth of this great principle, that it gives a value to all it touches. Not only so, but there are even cases, in which the facts of which we have spoken, in which philosophy, literature, the sciences, and the arts, are especially judged, and condemned or applauded, according to their influence upon civilization.

Before, however, we proceed to the history of this fact, so important, so extensive, so precious, and which seems, as it were, to embody the entire life of nations, let us consider it for a moment in itself, and endeavor to discover what it really is.

I shall be careful here not to fall into pure philosophy; I shall not lay down a certain rational principle, and then, by deduction, show the nature of civilization as a consequence; there would be too many chances of error in pursuing this method. Still, without this, we shall be able to find a fact to establish and to describe.

For a long time past, and in many countries, the word civilization has been in use; ideas more or less clear, and of wider or more contracted signification, have been attached to it; still it has been constantly employed and generally understood. Now, it is the popular, common signification of this word that we must investigate. In the usual, general acceptation of terms, there will nearly always be found more truth than in the seemingly more precise and rigorous definitions of science. It is common sense which gives to words their popular signification, and common sense is the genius of humanity. The popular signification of a word is formed by degrees and while the facts it represents are themselves present. As often as a fact comes before us which seems to answer to the signification of a known term, this term is naturally applied to it, its signification gradually extending and enlarging itself, so that at last the various facts and ideas which, from the nature of things, ought to be brought together and embodied in this term, will be found collected and embodied in it. When, on the contrary, the signification of a word is determined by science, it is usually done by one or a very few individuals, who, at the time, are under the influence of some particular fact which has taken possession of their imagination. Thus it comes to pass that scientific definitions are, in general, much narrower, and, on that very account, much less correct, than the popular significations given to words. So, in the investigation of the meaning of the word civilization as a fact—by seeking out all the ideas it comprises, according to the common sense of mankind, we shall arrive much nearer to the knowledge of the fact itself, than by attempting to give our own scientific definition of it, though this might at first appear more clear and precise.

I shall commence this investigation by placing before you a series of hypotheses. I shall describe society in various conditions, and shall then ask if the state in which I so describe it is, in the general opinion of mankind, the state of a people advancing in civilization—if it answers to the signification which mankind generally attaches to this word.

First, imagine a people whose outward circumstances are easy and agreeable; few taxes, few hardships; justice is fairly administered; in a word, physical existence, taken altogether, is satisfactorily and happily regulated. But with all this the moral and intellectual energies of this people are studiously kept in a state of torpor and inertness. It can hardly be called oppression; its tendency is not of that character—it is rather compression. We are not without examples of this state of society. There have been a great number of little aristocratic republics, in which the people have been thus treated like so many flocks of sheep, carefully tended, physically happy, but without the least intellectual and moral activity. Is this civilization? Do we recognize here a people in a state of moral and social advancement?

Let us take another hypothesis. Let us imagine a people whose outward circumstances are less favorable and agreeable; still, however, supportable. As a set-off, its intellectual and moral cravings have not here been entirely neglected. A certain range has been allowed them—some few pure and elevated sentiments have been here distributed; religious and moral notions have reached a certain degree of improvement; but the greatest care has been taken to stifle every principle of liberty. The moral and intellectual wants of this people are provided for in the way that, among some nations, the physical wants have been provided for; a certain portion of truth is doled out to each, but no one is permitted to help himself—to seek for truth on his own account. Immobility is the character of its moral life; and to this condition are fallen most of the populations of Asia, in which theocratic government restrains the advance of man: such, for example, is the state of the Hindoos. I again put the same question as before—Is this a people among whom civilization is going on?

I will change entirely the nature of the hypothesis: suppose a people among whom there reigns a very large stretch of personal liberty, but among whom also disorder and inequality almost everywhere abound. The weak are oppressed, afflicted, destroyed; violence is the ruling character of the social condition. Every one knows that such has been the state of Europe. Is this a civilized state? It may without doubt contain germs of civilization which may progressively shoot up; but the actual state of things which prevails in this society is not, we may rest assured, what the common sense of mankind would call civilization.

I pass on to a fourth and last hypothesis. Every individual here enjoys the widest extent of liberty; inequality is rare, or, at least, of a very slight character. Every one does as he likes, and scarcely differs in power from his neighbor. But then here scarcely such a thing is known as a general interest; here exist but few public ideas; hardly any public feeling; but little society: in short, the life and faculties of individuals are put forth and spent in an isolated state, with but little regard to society, and with scarcely a sentiment of its influence. Men here exercise no influence upon one another; they leave no traces of their existence. Generation after generation pass away, leaving society just as they found it. Such is the condition of the various tribes of savages; liberty and equality dwell among them, but no touch of civilization.

I could easily multiply these hypotheses; but I presume that I have gone far enough to show what is the popular and natural signification of the word civilization.

It is evident that none of the states which I have just described will correspond with the common notion of mankind respecting this term. It seems to me that the first idea comprised in the word civilization (and this may be gathered from the various examples which I have placed before you) is the notion of progress, of development. It calls up within us the notion of a people advancing, of a people in a course of improvement and melioration.

Now what is this progress? What is this development? In this is the great difficulty. The etymology of the word seems sufficiently obvious—it points at once to the improvement of civil life. The first notion which strikes us in pronouncing it is the progress of society; the melioration of the social state; the carrying to higher perfection the relations between man and man. It awakens within us at once the notion of an increase of national prosperity, of a greater activity and better organization of the social relations. On one hand there is a manifest increase in the power and well-being of society at large; and on the other a more equitable distribution of this power and this well-being among the individuals of which society is composed.

But the word civilization has a more extensive signification than this, which seems to confine it to the mere outward, physical organization of society. Now, if this were all, the human race would be little better than the inhabitants of an ant-hill or bee-hive; a society in which nothing was sought for beyond order and well-being—in which the highest, the sole aim, would be the production of the means of life, and their equitable distribution.

But our nature at once rejects this definition as too narrow. It tells us that man is formed for a higher destiny than this. That this is not the full development of his character—that civilization comprehends something more extensive, something more complex, something superior to the perfection of social relations, of social power and well-being.

That this is so, we have not merely the evidence of our nature, and that derived from the signification which the common sense of mankind has attached to the word; but we have likewise the evidence of facts.

No one, for example, will deny that there are communities in which the social state of man is better—in which the means of life are better supplied, are more rapidly produced, are better distributed, than in others, which yet will be pronounced by the unanimous voice of mankind to be superior in point of civilization.

Take Rome, for example, in the splendid days of the republic, at the close of the second Punic war; the moment of her greatest virtues, when she was rapidly advancing to the empire of the world—when her social condition was evidently improving. Take Rome again under Augustus, at the commencement of her decline, when, to say the least, the progressive movement of society halted, when bad principles seemed ready to prevail: but is there any person who would not say that Rome was more civilized under Augustus than in the days of Fabricius or Cincinnatus?

Let us look further: let us look at France in the seventeenth and eighteenth centuries. In a merely social point of view, as respects the quantity and the distribution of well-being among individuals, France, in the seventeenth and eighteenth centuries, was decidedly inferior to several of the other states of Europe; to Holland and England in particular. Social activity, in these countries, was greater, increased more rapidly, and distributed its fruits more equitably among individuals. Yet consult the general opinion of mankind, and it will tell you that France in the seventeenth and eighteenth centuries was the most civilized country of Europe. Europe has not hesitated to acknowledge this fact, and evidence of its truth will be found in all the great works of European literature.

It appears evident, then, that all that we understand by this term is not comprised in the simple idea of social well-being and happiness; and, if we look a little deeper, we discover that, besides the progress and melioration of social life, another development is comprised in our notion of civilization: namely, the development of individual life, the development of the human mind and its faculties—the development of man himself.

It is this development which so strikingly manifested itself in France and Rome at these epochs; it is this expansion of human intelligence which gave to them so great a degree of superiority in civilization. In these countries the godlike principle which distinguishes man from the brute exhibited itself with peculiar grandeur and power, and compensated in the eyes of the world for the defects of their social system. These communities had still many social conquests to make; but they had already glorified themselves by the intellectual and moral victories they had achieved. Many of the conveniences of life were here wanting; from a considerable portion of the community were still withheld their natural rights and political privileges: but see the number of illustrious individuals who lived and earned the applause and approbation of their fellow-men. Here, too, literature, science, and art, attained extraordinary perfection, and shone in more splendor than perhaps they had ever done before. Now, wherever this takes place, wherever man sees these glorious idols of his worship displayed in their full luster—wherever he sees this fund of rational and refined enjoyment for the godlike part of his nature called into existence, there he recognizes and adores civilization.*

Two elements, then, seem to be comprised in the great fact which we call civilization;—two circumstances are necessary to its existence—it lives upon two conditions—it reveals itself by two symptoms: the progress of society, the progress of individuals; the melioration of the social system, and the expansion of the mind and faculties of man. Wherever the exterior condition of man becomes enlarged, quickened, and improved; wherever the intellectual nature of man distinguishes itself by its energy, brilliancy, and its grandeur; wherever these two signs concur, and they often do so, notwithstanding the gravest imperfections in the social system, there man proclaims and applauds civilization.

Such, if I mistake not, would be the notion mankind in general would form of civilization, from a simple and rational inquiry into the meaning of the term. This view of it is confirmed by History. If we ask of her what has been the character of every great crisis favorable to civilization, if we examine those great events which all acknowledge to have carried it forward, we shall always find one or other of the two elements which I have just described. They have all been epochs of individual or social improvement; events which have either wrought a change in individual man, in his opinions, his manners; or in his exterior condition, his situation as regards his relations with his fellowmen. Christianity, for example: I allude not merely to the first moment of its appearance, but to the first centuries of its existence—Christianity was in no way addressed to the social condition of man; it distinctly disclaimed all interference with it. It commanded the slave to obey his master. It attacked none of the great evils, none of the gross acts of injustice, by which the social system of that day was disfigured:* yet who but will acknowledge that Christianity has been one of the greatest promoters of civilization? And wherefore? Because it has changed the interior condition of man, his opinions, his sentiments: because it has regenerated his moral, his intellectual character.†

We have seen a crisis of an opposite nature; a crisis affecting not the intellectual, but the outward condition of man, which has changed and regenerated society. This also we may rest assured is a decisive crisis of civilization. If we search history through, we shall everywhere find the same result; we shall meet with no important event, which had a direct influence in the advancement of civilization, which has not exercised it in one of the two ways I have just mentioned.

Having thus, as I hope, given you a clear notion of the two elements of which civilization is composed, let us now see whether one of them alone would be sufficient to constitute it: whether either the development of the social condition, or the development of the individual man taken separately, deserves to be regarded as civilization? or whethare not produced simultaneously, sooner or later, one uniformly produces the other?

There are three ways, as it seems to me, in which we may proceed in deciding this question. First: we may investigate the nature itself of the two elements of civilization, and see whether by that they are strictly and necessarily bound together. Secondly: we may examine historically whether, in fact, they have manifested themselves separately, or whether one has always produced the other. Thirdly: we may consult common sense, i. e., the general opinion of mankind. Let us first address ourselves to the general opinion of mankind—to common sense. When any great change takes place in the state of a country—when any great development of social prosperity is accomplished within it—any revolution or reform in the powers and privileges of society, this new event naturally has its adversaries. It is necessarily contested and opposed. Now what are the objections which the adversaries of such revolutions bring against them?

They assert that this progress of the social condition is attended with no advantage; that it does not improve in a corresponding degree the moral state—the intellectual powers of man; that it is a false, deceitful progress, which proves detrimental to his moral character, to the true interests of his better nature. On the other hand, this attack is repulsed with much force by the friends of the movement. They maintain that the progress of society necessarily leads to the progress of intelligence and morality; that, in proportion as the social life is better regulated, individual life becomes more refined and virtuous. Thus the question rests in abeyance between the opposers and partisans of the change.

But reverse this hypothesis; suppose the moral development in progress. What do the men who labor for it generally hope for?—What, at the origin of societies, have the founders of religion, the sages, poets, and philosophers, who have labored to regulate and refine the manners of mankind, promised themselves? What but the melioration of the social condition: the more equitable distribution of the blessings of life? What, now, let me ask, should be inferred from this dispute and from those hopes and promises? It may, I think, be fairly inferred that it is the spontaneous, intuitive conviction of mankind, that the two elements of civilization—the social and moral development—are intimately connected; that, at the approach of one, man looks for the other. It is to this natural conviction, we appeal when, to second or combat either one or the other of the two elements, we deny or attest its union with the other. We know that if men were persuaded that the melioration of the social condition would operate against the expansion of the intellect, they would almost oppose and cry out against the advancement of society. On the other hand, when we speak to mankind of improving society by improving its individual members, we find them willing to believe us, and to adopt the principle. Hence we may affirm that it is the intuitive belief of man, that these two elements of civilization are intimately connected, and that they reciprocally produce one another.

If we now examine the history of the world we shall have the same result. We shall find that every expansion of human intelligence has proved of advantage to society; and that all the great advances in the social condition have turned to the profit of humanity. One or other of these facts may predominate, may shine forth with greater splendor for a season, and impress upon the movement its own particular character. At times, it may not be till after the lapse of a long interval, after a thousand transformations, a thousand obstacles, that the second shows itself, and comes, as it were, to complete the civilization which the first had begun; but when we look closely we easily recognize the link by which they are connected. The movements of Providence are not restricted to narrow bounds: it is not anxious to deduce to-day the consequence of the premises it laid down yesterday. It may defer this for ages, till the fulness of time shall come. Its logic will not be less conclusive for reasoning slowly. Providence moves through time, as the gods of Homer through space—it makes a step, and ages have rolled away! How long a time, how many circumstances intervened, before the regeneration of the moral powers of man, by Christianity, exercised its great, its legitimate influence upon his social condition? Yet who can doubt or mistake its power?

If we pass from history to the nature itself of the two facts which constitute civilization, we are infallibly led to the same result. We have all experienced this. If a man makes a mental advance, some mental discovery, if he acquires some new idea, or some new faculty, what is the desire that takes possession of him at the very moment he makes it? It is the desire to promulgate his sentiment to the exterior world—to publish and realize his thought. When a man acquires a new truth—when his being in his own eyes has made an advance, has acquired a new gift, immediately there becomes joined to this acquirement the notion of a mission. He feels obliged, impelled, as it were, by a secret interest, to extend, to carry out of himself the change, the melioration which has been accomplished within him. To what, but this, do we owe the exertions of great reformers? The exertions of those great benefactors of the human race, who have changed the face of the world, after having first been changed themselves, have been stimulated and governed by no other impulse than this.

So much for the change which takes place in the intellectual man. Let us now consider him in a social state. A revolution is made in the condition of society. Rights and property are more equitably distributed among individuals; this is as much as to say, the appearance of the world is purer—is more beautiful. The state of things, both as respects governments, and as respects men in their relations with each other, is improved. And can there be a question whether the sight of this goodly spectacle, whether the melioration of this external condition of man, will have a corresponding influence upon his moral, his individual character—upon humanity? Such a doubt would belie all that is said of the authority of example, and of the power of habit, which is founded upon nothing but the conviction that exterior facts and circumstances, if good, reasonable, well-regulated, are followed, sooner or later, more or less completely, by intellectual results of the same nature, of the same beauty: that a world better governed, better regulated, a world in which justice more fully prevails, renders man himself more just. That the intellectual man then is instructed and improved by the superior condition of society, and his social condition, his external well-being, meliorated and refined by increase of intelligence in individuals; that the two elements of civilization are strictly connected; that ages, that obstacles of all kinds, may interpose between them—that it is possible they may undergo a thousand transformations before they meet together; but that sooner or later this union will take place is certain; for it is a law of their nature that they should do so—the great facts of history bear witness that such is really the case—the instinctive belief of man proclaims the same truth.

Thus, though I have not by a great deal advanced all that might be said upon this subject, I trust I have given a tolerably correct and adequate notion, in the foregoing cursory account, of what civilization is, of what are its offices, and what its importance. I might here quit the subject; but I cannot part with it, without placing before you another question, which here naturally presents itself—a question not purely historical, but rather, I will not say hypothetical, but conjectural; a question which we can see here but in part; but which, however, is not less real, but presses itself upon our notice at every turn of thought.

Of the two developments, of which we have just now spoken, and which together constitute civilization,—of the development of society on one part, and of the expansion of human intelligence on the other—which is the end? which are the means? Is it for the improvement of the social condition, for the melioration of his existence upon the earth, that man fully develops himself, his mind, his faculties, his sentiments, his ideas, his whole being? Or is the melioration of the social condition, the progress of society,—is indeed society itself merely the theatre, the occasion, the motive and excitement for the development of the individual? In a word, is society formed for the individual, or the individual for society? Upon the reply to this question depends our knowledge of whether the destiny of man is purely social, whether society exhausts and absorbs the entire man, or whether he bears within him something foreign, something superior to his existence in this world?

One of the greatest philosophers and most distinguished men of the present age, whose words become indelibly engraved upon whatever spot they fall, has resolved this question; he has resolved it, at least, according to his own conviction. The following are his words: "Human societies are born, live, and die, upon the earth; there they accomplish their destinies. But they contain not the whole man. After his engagement to society there still remains in him the more noble part of his nature; those high faculties by which he elevates himself to God, to a future life, and to the unknown blessings of an invisible world. We, individuals, each with a separate and distinct existence, with an identical person, we, truly beings endowed with immortality, we have a higher destiny than that of states."*

I shall add nothing on this subject; it is not my province to handle it; it is enough for me to have placed it before you. It haunts us again at the close of the history of civilization.—Where the history of civilization ends, when there is no more to be said of the present life, man invincibly demands if all is over—if that be the end of all things? This, then, is the last problem, and the grandest, to which the history of civilization can lead us. It is sufficient that I have marked its place, and its sublime character.*

From the foregoing remarks, it becomes evident that the history of civilization may be considered from two different points of view—may be drawn from two different sources. The historian may take up his abode during the time prescribed, say a series of centuries, in the human soul, or with some particular nation. He may study, describe, relate, all the circumstances, all the transformations, all the revolutions, which may have taken place in the intellectual man; and when he had done this he would have a history of the civilization among the people, or during the period which he had chosen. He might proceed differently: instead of entering into the interior of man, he might take his stand in the external world. He might take his station in the midst of the great theatre of life; instead of describing the change of ideas, of the sentiments of the individual being, he might describe his exterior circumstances, the events, the revolutions of his social condition. These two portions, these two histories of civilization, are strictly connected with each other; they are the counterpart, the reflected image of one another. They may, however, be separated.* Perhaps it is necessary, at least in the beginning, in order to be exposed in detail and with clearness, that they should be. For my part I have no intention, upon the present occasion, to enter upon the history of civilization in the human mind; the history of the exterior events of the visible and social world is that to which I shall call your attention. It would give me pleasure to be able to display before you the phenomenon of civilization in the way I understand it, in all its bearings, in its widest extent—to place before you all the vast questions to which it gives rise. But, for the present, I must restrain my wishes; I must confine myself to a narrower field: it is only the history of the social state that I shall attempt to narrate.

My first object will be to seek out the elements of European civilization at the time of its birth, at the fall of the Roman empire—to examine carefully society such as it was in the midst of these famous ruins. I shall endeavor to pick out these elements, and to place them before you, side by side; I shall endeavor to put them in motion, and to follow them in their progress through the fifteen centuries which have rolled away since that epoch.

We shall not, I think, proceed far in this study, without being convinced that civilization is still in its infancy. How distant is the human mind from the perfection to which it may attain—from the perfection for which it was created! How incapable are we of grasping the whole future destiny of man! Let any one even descend into his own mind—let him picture there the highest point of perfection to which man, to which society may attain, that he can conceive, that he can hope;— let him then contrast this picture with the present state of the world, and he will feel assured that society and civilization are still in their childhood: that however great the distance they have advanced, that which they have before them is incomparably, is infinitely greater. This, however, should not lessen the pleasure with which we contemplate our present condition. When you have run over with me the great epochs of civilization during the last fifteen centuries, you will see, up to our time, how painful, how stormy, has been the condition of man; how hard has been his lot, not only outwardly as regards society, but internally, as regards the intellectual man. For fifteen centuries the human mind has suffered as much as the human race. You will see that it is only lately that the human mind, perhaps for the first time, has arrived, imperfect though its condition still be, to a state where some peace, some harmony, some freedom is found. The same holds with regard to society—its immense progress is evident—the condition of man, compared with what it has been, is easy and just. In thinking of our ancestors we may almost apply to ourselves the verses of Lucretius:—

"Suave, mari magno turbantibus æquora ventis, E terra magnum alterius spectare laborem."* Without any great degree of pride we may, as Sthenelus is made to do in Homer, Ἡμεῖς τοι πατέρων μεγ' ἀμείνονες εὐχόμεθ' εἶναι, "Return thanks to God that we are infinitely better than our fathers."

We must, however, take care not to deliver ourselves up too fully to a notion of our happiness and our improved condition. It may lead us into two serious evils, pride and inactivity;—it may give us an overweening confidence in the power and success of the human mind, of its present attainments; and, at the same time, dispose us to apathy, enervated by the agreeableness of our condition. I know not if this strikes you as it does me, but in my judgment we continually oscillate between an inclination to complain without sufficient cause, and to be too easily satisfied. We have an extreme susceptibility of mind, an inordinate craving, an ambition in our thoughts, in our desires, and in the movements of our imagination; yet when we come to practical life—when trouble, when sacrifices, when efforts are required for the attainment of our object, we sink into lassitude and inactivity. We are discouraged almost as easily as we had been excited. Let us not, however, suffer ourselves to be invaded by either of these vices. Let us estimate fairly what our abilities, our knowledge, our power enable us to do lawfully; and let us aim at nothing that we cannot lawfully, justly, prudently—with a proper respect to the great principles upon which our social system, our civilization is based—attain. The age of barbarian Europe, with its brute force, its violence, its lies and deceit,—the habitual practice under which Europe groaned during four or five centuries is passed away for ever, and has given place to a better order of things. We trust that the time now approaches when man's condition shall be progressively improved by the force of reason and truth, when the brute part of nature shall be crushed, that the godlike spirit may unfold. In the mean time let us be cautious that no vague desires, that no extravagant theories, the time for which may not yet be come, carry us beyond the bounds of prudence, or beget in us a discontent with our present state. To us much has been given, of us much will be required. Posterity will demand a strict account of our conduct—the public, the government, all is now open to discussion, to examination. Let us then attach ourselves firmly to the principles of our civilization, to justice, to law, to liberty; and never forget, that, if we have the right to demand that all things shall be laid open before us, and judged by us, we likewise are before the world, who will examine us, and judge us according to our works.

LECTURE II.: OF EUROPEAN CIVILIZATION IN PARTICULAR: ITS DISTINGUISHING CHARACTERISTICS—ITS SUPERIORITY—ITS ELEMENTS.

In the preceding Lecture, I endeavored to give an explanation of civilization in general. Without referring to any civilization in particular, or to circumstances of time and place, I essayed to place it before you in a point of view purely philosophical. I purpose now to enter upon the History of the Civilization of Europe; but before doing so, before going into its proper history, I must make you acquainted with the peculiar character of this civilization—with its distinguishing features, so that you may be able to recognize and distinguish European civilization from every other.

When we look at the civilizations which have preceded that of modern Europe, whether in Asia or elsewhere, including even those of Greece and Rome, it is impossible not to be struck with the unity of character which reigns among them. Each appears as though it had emanated from a single fact, from a single idea. One might almost assert that society was under the influence of one single principle, which universally prevailed and determined the character of its institutions, its manners, its opinions—in a word, all its developments.

In Egypt, for example, it was the theocratic principle that took possession of society, and showed itself in its manners, in its monuments, and in all that has come down to us of Egyptian civilization. In India the same phenomenon occurs—it is still a repetition of the almost exclusively prevailing influence of theocracy.* In other regions a different organization may be observed—perhaps the domination of a conquering caste: and where such is the case, the principle of force takes entire possession of society, imposing upon it its laws and its character. In another place, perhaps, we discover society under the entire influence of the democratic principle; such was the case in the commercial republics which covered the coasts of Asia Minor and Syria—in Ionia and Phœnicia. In a word, whenever we contemplate the civilizations of the ancients, we find them all impressed with one ever-prevailing character of unity, visible in their institutions, their ideas, and manners—one sole, or at least one very preponderating influence, seems to govern and determine all things.

I do not mean to aver that this overpowering influence of one single principle, of one single form, prevailed without any exception in the civilization of those states. If we go back to their earliest history, we shall find that the various powers which dwelt in the bosom of these societies frequently struggled for mastery. Thus among the Egyptians, the Etruscans, even among the Greeks and others, we may observe the warrior caste struggling against that of the priests. In other places we find the spirit of clanship struggling against the spirit of free association, the spirit of aristocracy against popular rights. These struggles, however, mostly took place in periods beyond the reach of history, and no evidence of them is left beyond a vague tradition. Sometimes, indeed, these early struggles broke out afresh at a later period in the history of the nations; but in almost every case they were quickly terminated by the victory of one of the powers which sought to prevail, and which then took sole possession of society. The war always ended by the domination of some special principle, which, if not exclusive, at least greatly preponderated. The co-existence and strife of various principles among these nations were no more than a passing, an accidental circumstance.

From this cause a remarkable unity characterizes most of the civilizations of antiquity, the results of which, however, were very different. In one nation, as in Greece, the unity of the social principle led to a development of wonderful rapidity; no other people ever ran so brilliant a career in so short a time. But Greece had hardly become glorious, before she appeared worn out: her decline, if not quite so rapid as her rise, was strangely sudden. It seems as if the principle which called Greek civilization into life was exhausted. No other came to invigorate it, or supply its place.*

In other states, say, for example, in India and Egypt, where again only one principle of civilization prevailed, the result was different. Society here became stationary; simplicity produced monotony; the country was not destroyed; society continued to exist; but there was no progression; it remained torpid and inactive.

To this same cause must be attributed that character of tyranny which prevailed, under various names, and the most opposite forms, in all the civilizations of antiquity. Society belonged to one exclusive power, which could bear with no other. Every principle of a different tendency was proscribed. The governing principle would nowhere suffer by its side the manifestation and influence of a rival principle.

This character of simplicity, of unity, in their civilization, is equally impressed upon their literature and intellectual productions. Who that has run over the monuments of Hindoo literature lately introduced into Europe, but has seen that they are all struck from the same die? They all seem the result of one same fact; the expression of one same idea. Religious and moral treatises, historical traditions, dramatic poetry, epics, all bear the same physiognomy. The same character of unity and monotony shines out in these works of mind and fancy, as we discover in their life and institutions. Even in Greece, notwithstanding the immense stores of knowledge and intellect which it poured forth, a wonderful unity still prevailed in all relating to literature and the arts. How different from all this is the case as respects the civilization of modern Europe! Take ever so rapid a glance at this, and it strikes you at once as diversified, confused, and stormy. All the principles of social organization are found existing together within it; powers temporal, powers spiritual, the theocratic, monarchic, aristocratic, and democratic elements, all classes of society, all the social situations, are jumbled together, and visible within it; as well as infinite gradations of liberty, of wealth, and of influence. These various powers, too, are found here in a state of continual struggle among themselves, without any one having sufficient force to master the others, and take sole possession of society. Among the ancients, at every great epoch, all communities seem cast in the same mould: it was now pure monarchy, now theocracy or democracy, that became the reigning principle, each in its turn reigning absolutely. But modern Europe contains examples of all these systems, of all the attempts at social organization, pure and mixed monarchies, theocracies, republics more or less aristocratic, all live in common, side by side, at one and the same time; yet, notwithstanding their diversity, they all bear a certain resemblance to each other, a kind of family likeness which it is impossible to mistake, and which shows them to be essentially European.

In the moral character, in the notions and sentiments of Europe, we find the same variety, the same struggle. Theocratic opinions, monarchical opinions, aristocratic opinions, democratic opinions, cross and jostle, struggle, become interwoven, limit, and modify each other. Open the boldest treatises of the middle age: in none of them is an opinion carried to its final consequences. The advocates of absolute power flinch, almost unconsciously, from the results to which their doctrine would carry them. We see that the ideas and influences around them frighten them from pushing it to its uttermost point. Democracy felt the same control. That imperturbable boldness, so striking in ancient civilizations, nowhere found a place in the European system. In sentiments we discover the same contrasts, the same variety; an indomitable taste for independence dwelling by the side of the greatest aptness for submission; a singular fidelity between man and man, and at the same time an imperious desire in each to do his own will, to shake off all restraint, to live alone, without troubling himself with the rest of the world. Minds were as much diversified as society.

The same characteristic is observable in literature. It cannot be denied that in what relates to the form and beauty of art, modern Europe is very inferior to antiquity; but if we look at her literature as regards depth of feeling and ideas, it will be found more powerful and rich. The human mind has been employed upon a greater number of objects, its labors have been more diversified, it has gone to a greater depth. Its imperfection in form is owing to this very cause. The more plenteous and rich the materials, the greater is the difficulty of forcing them into a pure and simple form. That which gives beauty to a composition, that which in works of art we call form, is the clearness, the simplicity, the symbolical unity of the work. With the prodigious diversity of ideas and sentiments which belong to European civilization, the difficulty of attaining this grand and chaste simplicity has been increased.*

In every part, then, we find this character of variety to prevail in modern civilization. It has undoubtedly brought with it this inconvenience, that when we consider separately any particular development of the human mind in literature, in the arts, in any of the ways in which human intelligence may go forward, we shall generally find it inferior to the corresponding development in the civilization of antiquity; but, as a set-off to this, when we regard it as a whole, European civilization appears incomparably more rich and diversified: if each particular fruit has not attained the same perfection, it has ripened an infinitely greater variety. Again, European civilization has now endured fifteen centuries, and in all that time it has been in a state of progression.* It may be true that it has not advanced so rapidly as the Greek; but, catching new impulses at every stop, it is still advancing. An unbounded career is open before it; and from day to day it presses forward to the race with increasing rapidity, because increased freedom attends upon all its movements. While in other civilizations the exclusive domination, or at least the excessive preponderance of a single principle, of a single form, led to tyranny, in modern Europe the diversity of the elements of social order, the incapability of any one to exclude the rest, gave birth to the liberty which now prevails. The inability of the various principles to exterminate one another compelled each to endure the others, made it necessary for them to live in common, for them to enter into a sort of mutual understanding. Each consented to have only that part of civilization which fell to its share. Thus, while everywhere else the predominance of one principle has produced tyranny, the variety of elements of European civilization, and the constant warfare in which they have been engaged, have given birth in Europe to that liberty which we prize so dearly.

It is this which gives to European civilization its real, its immense superiority—it is this which forms its essential, its distinctive character. And if, carrying our views still further, we penetrate beyond the surface into the very nature of things, we shall find that this superiority is legitimate—that it is acknowledged by reason as well as proclaimed by facts. Quitting for a moment European civilization, and taking a glance at the world in general, at the common course of earthly things, what is the character we find it to bear? What do we here perceive? Why just that very same diversity, that very same variety of elements, that very same struggle which is so strikingly evinced in European civilization. It is plain enough that no single principle, no particular organization, no simple idea, no special power has ever been permitted to obtain possession of the world, to mould it into a durable form, and to drive from it every opposing tendency, so as to reign itself supreme. Various powers, principles, and systems here intermingle, modify one another, and struggle incessantly—now subduing, now subdued—never wholly conquered, never conquering. Such is apparently the general state of the world, while diversity of forms, of ideas, of principles, their struggles and their energies, all tend towards a certain unity, a certain ideal, which, though perhaps it may never be attained, mankind is constantly approaching by dint of liberty and labor. Hence European civilization is the reflected image of the world— like the course of earthly things, it is neither narrowly circumscribed, exclusive, nor stationary. For the first time, civilization appears to have divested itself of its special character: its development presents itself for the first time under as diversified, as abundant, as laborious an aspect as the great theatre of the universe itself.

European civilization has, if I may be allowed the expression, at last penetrated into the ways of eternal truth—into the scheme of Providence;—it moves in the ways which God has prescribed. This is the rational principle of its superiority.

Let it not, I beseech you, be forgotten—bear in mind, as we proceed with these lectures, that it is in this diversity of elements, and their constant struggle, that the essential character of our civilization consists. At present I can do no more than assert this; its proof will be found in the facts I shall bring before you. Still I think you will acknowledge it to be a confirmation of this assertion, if I can show you that the causes, and the elements of the character which I have just attributed to it, can be traced to the very cradle of our civilization. If, I say, at the very moment of her birth, at the very hour in which the Roman empire fell, I can show you, in the state of the world, the circumstances which, from the beginning, have concurred to give to European civilization that agitated and diversified, but at the same time prolific character which distinguishes it, I think I shall have a strong claim upon your assent to its truth. In order to accomplish this, I shall begin by investigating the condition of Europe at the fall of the Roman empire, so that we may discover in its institutions, in its opinions, its ideas, its sentiments, what were the elements which the ancient world bequeathed to the modern. And upon these elements you will see strongly impressed the character which I have just described.

It is necessary that we should first see what the Roman empire was, and how it was formed. Rome in its origin was a mere municipality, a corporation. The Roman government was nothing more than an assemblage of institutions suitable to a population enclosed within the walls of a city; that is to say, they were municipal institutions;—this was their distinctive character.

This was not peculiar to Rome. If we look, in this period, at the part of Italy which surrounded Rome, we find nothing but cities. What were then called nations were nothing more than confederations of cities. The Latin nation was a confederation of Latin cities. The Etrurians, the Samnites, the Sabines, the nations of Magna Græcia, were all composed in the same way.

At this time there were no country places, no villages; at least the country was nothing like what it is in the present day. It was cultivated, no doubt, but it was not peopled. The proprietors of lands and of country estates dwelt in cities; they left these occasionally to visit their rural property, where they usually kept a certain number of slaves; but that which we now call the country, that scattered population, sometimes in lone houses, sometimes in hamlets and villages, and which everywhere dots our land with agricultural dwellings, was altogether unknown in ancient Italy.

And what was the case when Rome extended her boundaries? If we follow her history, we shall find that she conquered or founded a host of cities. It was with cities she fought, it was with cities she treated, it was into cities she sent colonies. In short, the history of the conquest of the world by Rome is the history of the conquest and foundation of a vast number of cities. It is true that in the East the extension of the Roman dominion bore somewhat of a different character: the population was not distributed there in the same way as in the western world; it was under a social system, partaking more of the patriarchal form, and was consequently much less concentrated in cities. But, as we have only to do with the population of Europe, I shall not dwell upon what relates to that of the East.

Confining ourselves, then, to the West, we shall find the fact to be such as I have described it. In the Gauls, in Spain, we meet with nothing but cities. At any distance from these, the country consisted of marshes and forests. Examine the character of the monuments left us of ancient

Rome—the old Roman roads. We find great roads extending from city to city; but the thousands of little by-paths, which now intersect every part of the country, were then unknown. Neither do we find any traces of that immense number of lesser objects—of churches, castles, country-seats, and villages, which were spread all over the country during the middle ages. Rome has left no traces of this kind; her only bequest consists of vast monuments impressed with a municipal character, destined for a numerous population, crowded into a single spot. In whatever point of view you consider the Roman world, you meet with this almost exclusive preponderance of cities, and an absence of country populations and dwellings. This municipal character of the Roman world evidently rendered the unity, the social tie of a great state, extremely difficult to establish and maintain.

A municipal corporation like Rome might be able to conquer the world, but it was a much more difficut task to govern it, to mould it into one compact body. Thus, when the work seemed done, when all the West, and a great part of the East, had submitted to the Roman yoke, we find an immense host of cities, of little states formed for separate existence and independence, breaking their chains, escaping on every side. This was one of the causes which made the establishment of the empire necessary; which called for a more concentrated form of government, one better able to hold together elements which had so few points of cohesion. The empire endeavored to unite and to bind together this extensive and scattered society; and to a certain point it succeeded. Between the reigns of Augustus and Diocletian, during the very time that her admirable civil legislation was being carried to perfection, that vast and despotic administration was established, which, spreading over the empire a sort of chain-work of functionaries subordinately arranged, firmly knit together the people and the imperial court, serving at the same time to convey to society the will of the government, and to bring to the government the tribute and obedience of society.*

This system, besides rallying the forces, and holding together the elements, of the Roman world, introduced with wonderful celerity into society a taste for despotism, for central power. It is truly astonishing to see how rapidly this incoherent assemblage of little republics, this association of municipal corporations, sunk into an humble and obedient respect for the sacred name of emperor. The necessity for establishing some tie between all these parts of the Roman world must have been very apparent and powerful, otherwise we can hardly conceive how the spirit of despotism could so easily have made its way into the minds and almost into the affections of the people.

It was with this spirit, with this administrative organization, and with the military system connected with it, that the Roman empire struggled against the dissolution which was working within it, and against the barbarians who attacked it from without. But, though it struggled long, the day at length arrived when all the skill and power of despotism, when all the pliancy of servitude, was insufficient to prolong its fate. In the fourth century, all the ties which had held this immense body together seem to have been loosened or snapped; the barbarians broke in on every side; the provinces no longer resisted, no longer troubled themselves with the general destiny. At this crisis an extraordinary idea entered the minds of one or two of the emperors: they wished to try whether the hope of general liberty, whether a confederation, a system something like what we now call the representative system, would not better defend the Roman empire than the despotic administration which already existed. There is a mandate of Honorius and the younger Theodosius, addressed, in the year 418, to the prefect of Gaul, the object of which was to establish a sort of representative government in the south of Gaul, and by its aid still to preserve the unity of empire.

Rescript of the Emperors Honorius and Theodosius the Younger, addressed, in the year 418, to the Prefect of the Gauls, residing at Arles.

"Honorius and Theodosius, Augusti, to Agricoli, Prefect of the Gauls.

"In consequence of the very salutary representation which your Magnificence has made to us, as well as upon other information obviously advantageous to the republic, we decree, in order that they may have the force of a perpetual law, that the following regulations should be made, and that obedience should be paid to them by the inhabitants of our seven provinces,* and which are such as they themselves should wish for and require. Seeing that from motives, both of public and private utility, responsible persons of special deputies should be sent, not only by each province, but by each city, to your Magnificence, not only to render up accounts, but also to treat of such matters as concern the interest of landed proprietors, we have judged that it would be both convenient and highly advantageous to have annually, at a fixed period, and to date from the present year, an assembly for the inhabitants of the seven provinces held in the Metropolis, that is to say, in the city of Arles. By this institution our desire is to provide both for public and private interests. First, by the union of the most influential inhabitants in the presence of their illustrious Prefect (unless he should be absent from causes affecting public order), and by their deliberations, upon every subject brought before them, the best possible advice will be obtained. Nothing which shall have been treated of and determined upon, after a mature discussion, shall be kept from the knowledge of the rest of the provinces; and such as have not assisted at the assembly shall be bound to follow the same rules of justice and equity. Furthermore, by ordaining that an assembly should be held every year in the city of Constantine,† we believe that we are doing not only what will be advantageous to the public welfare, but what will also multiply its social relations. Indeed, this city is so favorably situated, foreigners resort to it in such large numbers, and it possesses so extensive a commerce, that all the varied productions and manufactures of the rest of the world are to be seen within it. All that the opulent East, the perfumed Arabia, the delicate Assyria, the fertile Africa, the beautiful Spain, and the courageous Gaul, produce worthy of note, abound here in such profusion, that all things admired as magnificent in the different parts of the world seem the productions of its own climate. Further, the union of the Rhone and the Tuscan sea so facilitate intercourse, that the countries which the former traverses, and the latter waters in its winding course, are made almost neighbors. Thus, as the whole earth yields up its most esteemed productions for the service of this city, as the particular commodities of each country are transported to it by land, by sea, by rivers, by ships, by rafts, by wagons, how can our Gaul fail of seeing the great benefit we confer upon it by convoking a public assembly to be held in this city, upon which, by a special gift, as it were, of Divine Providence, has been showered all the enjoyments of life, and all the facilities for commerce?

"The illustrious Prefect Petronius* did, some time ago, with a praiseworthy and enlightened view, ordain that this custom should be observed; but as its practice was interrupted by the troubles of the times and the reign of usurpers, we have resolved to put it again in force, by the prudent exercise of our authority. Thus, then, dear and well-beloved cousin Agricoli, your Magnificence, conforming to our present ordinance and the custom established by your predecessors, will cause the following regulations to be observed in the provinces:—

"It will be necessary to make known unto all persons honored with public functions or proprietors of domains, and to all the judges of provinces, that they must attend in council every year in the city of Arles, between the Ides of August and September, the days of convocation and of session to be fixed at pleasure.

"Novempopulana and the second Aquitaine, being the most distant provinces, shall have the power, according to custom, to send, if their judges should be detained by indispensable duties, deputies in their stead.

"Such persons as neglect to attend at the place appointed, and within the prescribed period, shall pay a fine: viz., judges, five pounds of gold; members of the curiæ and other dignitaries, three pounds.†

"By this measure we conceive we are granting great advantages and favor to the inhabitants of our provinces. We have also the certainty of adding to the welfare of the city of Arles, to the fidelity of which, according to our father and countryman, we owe so much.‡

"Given the 15th of the calends of May; received at Arles the 10th of the calends of June."

Notwithstanding this call, the provinces and cities refused the proffered boon; nobody would name deputies, none would go to Arles. This centralization, this unity, was opposed to the primitive nature of this society. The spirit of locality, and of municipality, everywhere reappeared; the impossibility of reconstructing a general society, of building up the whole into one general state, became evident. The cities, confining themselves to the affairs of their own corporations, shut themselves up within their own walls, and the empire fell, because none would belong to the empire; because citizens wished but to belong to their city. Thus the Roman empire, at its fall, was resolved into the elements of which it had been composed, and the preponderance of municipal rule and government was again everywhere visible. The Roman world had been formed of cities, and to cities again it returned.*

This municipal system was the bequest of the ancient Roman civilization to modern Europe. It had no doubt become feeble, irregular, and very inferior to what it had been at an earlier period; but it was the only living principle, the only one that retained any form, the only one that survived the general destruction of the Roman world.

When I say the only one, I mistake. There was another phenomenon, another idea, which likewise outlived it. I mean the remembrance of the empire, and the title of the emperor,—the idea of imperial majesty, and of absolute power attached to the name of emperor. It must be observed, then, that the two elements which passed from the Roman civilization into ours were, first, the system of municipal corporations, its habits, its regulations, its principle of liberty—a general civil legislation, common to all; secondly, the idea of absolute power;—the principle of order and the principle of servitude.*

Meanwhile, within the very heart of Roman society, there had grown up another society of a very different nature, founded upon different principles, animated by different sentiments, and which has brought into European civilization elements of a widely different character: I speak of the Christian church. I say the Christian church, and not Christianity, between which a broad distinction is to be made. At the end of the fourth century, and the beginning of the fifth, Christianity was no longer a simple belief, it was an institution—it had formed itself into a corporate body. It had its government, a body of priests; a settled ecclesiastical polity for the regulation of their different functions; revenues; independent means of influence. It had the rallying points suitable to a great society, in its provincial, national, and general councils, in which were wont to be debated in common the affairs of society. In a word, the Christian religion, at this epoch, was no longer merely a religion, it was a church.

Had it not been a church, it is hard to say what would have been its fate in the general convulsion which attended the overthrow of the Roman empire. Looking only to worldly means, putting out of the question the aids and superintending power of Divine Providence, and considering only the natural effects of natural causes, it would be difficult to say how Christianity, if it had continued what it was at first, a mere belief, an individual conviction, could have withstood the shock occasioned by the dissolution of the Roman empire and the invasion of the barbarians. At a later period, when it had even become an institution, an established Church, it fell in Asia and the north of Africa, upon an invasion of a like kind—that of the Mohammedans; and circumstances seem to point out that it was still more likely such would have been its fate at the fall of the Roman empire. At this time there existed none of those means by which in the present day moral influences become established or rejected without the aid of institutions; none of those means by which an abstract truth now makes way, gains an authority over mankind, governs their actions, and directs their movements. Nothing of this kind existed in the fourth century; nothing which could give to simple ideas, to personal opinions, so much weight and power. Hence I think it may be assumed, that only a society firmly established, under a powerful government and rules of discipline, could hope to bear up amid such disasters—could hope to weather so violent a storm. I think, then, humanly speaking, that it is not too much to aver, that in the fourth and fifth centuries it was the Christian church that saved Christianity; that it was the Christian church, with its institutions, its magistrates, its authority—the Christian church, which struggled so vigorously to prevent the interior dissolution of the empire, which struggled against the barbarian, and which, in fact, overcame the barbarian,—it was this Church, I say, that became the great connecting link—the principle of civilization between the Roman and the barbarian world. It is the state of the Church, then, rather than religion strictly understood,— rather than that pure and simple faith of the Gospel which all true believers must regard as its highest triumph,—that we must look at in the fifth century, in order to discover what influence Christianity had from this time upon modern civilization, and what are the elements it has introduced into it.

Let us see what at this epoch the Christian church really was.

If we look, still in an entirely worldly point of view—if we look at the changes which Christianity underwent from its first rise to the fifth century—if we examine it (still, I repeat, not in a religious, but solely in a political sense), we shall find that it passed through three essentially different states.

In its infancy, in its very babyhood, Christian society presents itself before us as a simple association of men possessing the same faith and opinions, the same sentiments and feelings. The first Christians met to enjoy together their common emotions, their common religious convictions. At this time we find no settled form of doctrine, no settled rules of discipline, no body of magistrates.

Still, it is perfectly obvious, that no society, however young, however feebly held together, or whatever its nature, can exist without some moral power which animates and guides it; and thus, in the various Christian congregations, there were men who preached, who taught, who morally governed the congregation. Still there was no settled magistrate, no discipline; a simple association of believers in a common faith, with common sentiments and feelings, was the first condition of Christian society.

But the moment this society began to advance, and almost at its birth, for we find traces of them in its earliest documents, there gradually became moulded a form of doctrine, rules of discipline, a body of magistrates: of magistrates called πρεσβύτεροι, or elders who afterwards became priests; of ἐπίσκοποι, inspectors or overseers, who became bishops;* and of διάκονοι, or deacons, whose office was the care of the poor and the distribution of alms.

It is almost impossible to determine the precise functions of these magistrates; the line of demarcation was probably very vague and wavering; yet here was the embryo of institutions.

Still, however, there was one prevailing character in this second epoch: it was that the power, the authority, the preponderating influence, still remained in the hands of the general body of believers. It was they who decided in the election of magistrates, as well as in the adoption of rules of discipline and doctrine. No separation had as yet taken place between the Christian government and the Christian people; neither as yet existed apart from, or independently of, the other, and it was still the great body of Christian believers who exercised the principal influence in the society.

In the third period all this was entirely changed. The clergy were separated from the people, and now formed a distinct body, with its own wealth, its own jurisdiction, its own constitution; in a word, it had its own government, and formed a complete society of itself,—a society, too, provided with all the means of existence, independently of the society to which it applied itself, and over which it extended its influence. This was the third state of the Christian church, and in this state it existed at the opening of the fifth century. The government was not yet completely separated from the people; for no such government as yet existed, and less so in religious matters than in any other; but, as respects the relation between the clergy and Christians in general it was the clergy who governed, and governed almost without control.†

But, besides the influence which the clergy derived from their spiritual functions, they possessed considerable power over society, from their having become chief magistrates in the city corporations. We have already seen, that, strictly speaking, nothing had descended from the Roman empire, except its municipal system. Now it had fallen out that by the vexations of despotism, and the ruin of the cities, the curiales, or officers of the corporations, had sunk into insignificance and inanity; while the bishops and the great body of the clergy, full of vigor and zeal, were naturally prepared to guide and watch over them. It is not fair to accuse the clergy of usurpation in this matter, for it fell out according to the common course of events: the clergy alone possessed moral strength and activity, and the clergy everywhere succeeded to power— such is the common law of the universe.

The change which had taken place in this respect shows itself in every part of the legislation of the Roman emperors at this period. In opening the Theodosian and Justinian codes,* we find innumerable enactments, which place the management of the municipal affairs in the hands of the clergy and bishops. I shall cite a few.

Cod. Just., lib. i, tit. iv, De Episcopali audientia, § 26.—With regard to the yearly affairs of the cities (whether as respects the ordinary city revenues, the funds arising from the city estates, from legacies or particular gifts, or from any other source; whether as respects the management of the public works, of the magazines of provisions, of the aqueducts; of the maintenance of the public baths, the city gates, of the building of walls or towers, the repairing of bridges and roads, or of any lawsuit in which the city may be engaged on account of public or private interests), we ordain as follows:—The right reverend bishop, and three men of good report, from among the chiefs of the city, shall assemble together; every year they shall examine the works done; they shall take care that those who conduct, or have conducted them, measure them correctly, give a true account of them, and cause it to be seen that they have fulfilled their contracts whether in the care of the public monuments, in the moneys expended in provisions and the public baths, of all that is expended for the repairs of the roads, aqueducts, and all other matters.

Ibid., § 30.—With respect to the guardianship of youth, of the first and second age, and of all those to whom the law gives curators, if their fortune is not more than 5,000 aurei, we ordain that the nomination of the president of the province should not be waited for, on account of the great expense it would occasion, especially if the president should not reside in the city in which it becomes necessary to provide for the guardianship. The nomination of the curators or tutors shall, in this case, be made by the magistrate of the city . . . in concert with the right reverend bishop and other persons invested with public authority, if more than one should reside in the city.

Ibid., lib. i, tit. v, De Defensoribus, § 8.—We desire the defenders of cities, well instructed in the holy mysteries of the orthodox faith, should be chosen and instituted into their office by the reverend bishops, the clerks, notables, proprietors, and the curiales. With regard to their installation, it must be committed to the glorious power of the prefects of the prætorium, in order that their authority should have all the stability and weight which the letters of admission granted by his Magnificence are likely to give.

I could cite numerous other laws to the same effect, and in all of them you would see this one fact very strikingly prevail: namely, that between the Roman municipal system, and that of the free cities of the middle ages, there intervened an ecclesiastical municipal system; the preponderance of the clergy in the management of the affairs of the city corporations succeeded to that of the ancient Roman municipal magistrates, and paved the way for the organization of our modern free communities.

It will at once be seen what an amazing accession of power the Christian church gained by these means, not only in its own peculiar circle, by its increased influence on the body of Christians, but also by the part which it took in temporal matters. And it is from this period we should date its powerful co-operation in the advance of modern civilization, and the extensive influence it has had upon its character. Let us briefly run over the advantages which it introduced into it. And, first, it was of immense advantage to European civilization that a moral influence, a moral power—a power resting entirely upon moral convictions, upon moral opinions and sentiments— should have established itself in society, just at this period, when it seemed upon the point of being crushed by the overwhelming physical force which had taken possession of it. Had not the Christian church at this time existed, the whole world must have fallen a prey to mere brute force. The Christian church alone possessed a moral power; it maintained and promulgated the idea of a precept, of a law superior to all human authority; it proclaimed that great truth which forms the only foundation of our hope for humanity: namely, that there exists a law above all human law, which, by whatever name it may be called, whether reason, the law of God, or what not, is, in all times and in all places, the same law under different names.*

Finally, the Church commenced an undertaking of great importance to society—I mean the separation of temporal and spiritual authority. This separation is the only true source of liberty of conscience; it was based upon no other principle than that which serves as the groundwork for the strictest and most extensive liberty of conscience. The separation of temporal and spiritual power rests solely upon the idea that physical, that brute force, has no right or authority over the mind, over convictions, over truth. It flows from the distinction established between the world of thought and the world of action, between our inward and intellectual nature and the outward world around us. So that, however paradoxical it may seem, that very principle of liberty of conscience for which Europe has so long struggled, so much suffered, which has only so lately prevailed, and that, in many instances, against the will of the clergy,—that very principle was acted upon under the name of a separation of the temporal and spiritual power, in the infancy of European civilization. It was, moreover, the Christian church itself, driven to assert it by the circumstances in which it was placed, as a means of defence against barbarism, that introduced and maintained it.

The establishment, then, of a moral influence, the maintenance of this divine law, and the separation of temporal and spiritual power, may be enumerated as the great benefits which the Christian church extended to European society in the fifth century.

Unfortunately, all its influences, even at this period, were not equally beneficial. Already, even before the close of the fifth century, we discover some of those vicious principles which have had so baneful an effect on the advancement of our civilization. There already prevailed in the bosom of the Church a desire to separate the governing and the governed. The attempt was thus early made to render the government entirely independent of the people under its authority—to take possession of their mind and life, without the conviction of their reason or the consent of their will. The Church, moreover, endeavored with all her might to establish the principle of theocracy, to usurp temporal authority, to obtain universal dominion. And when she failed in this, when she found she could not obtain absolute power for herself, she did what was almost as bad: to obtain a share of it, she leagued herself with temporal rulers, and enforced, with all her might, their claim to absolute power at the expense of the liberty of the subject.*

Such, then, I think, were the principal elements of civilization which Europe derived, in the fifth century, from the Church and from the Roman empire. Such was the state of the Roman world when the barbarians came to make it their prey; and we have now only to study the barbarians themselves, in order to be acquainted with the elements which were united and mixed together in the cradle of our civilization.

It must be here understood that we have nothing to do with the history of the barbarians. It is enough for our purpose to know, that with the exception of a few Slavonian tribes, such as the Alans, they were all of the same German origin; and that they were all in pretty nearly the same state of civilization. It is true that some little difference might exist in this respect, accordingly as these nations had more or less intercourse with the Roman world; and there is no doubt but the Goths had made a greater progress, and had become more refined than the Franks; but in a general point of view, and with regard to the matter before us, these little differences are of no consequence whatever.

A general notion of the state of society among the barbarians, such, at least, as will enable us to judge of what they have contributed towards modern civilization, is all that we require. This information, small as it may appear, it is now almost impossible to obtain. Respecting the municipal system of the Romans and the state of the Church we may form a tolerably accurate idea. Their influence has lasted to the present times; we have vestiges of them in many of our institutions, and possess a thousand means of becoming acquainted with them; but the manners and social state of the barbarians have completely perished, and we are driven to conjecture what they were, either from a very few ancient historical remains, or by an effort of the imagination.* There is one sentiment, one in particular, which it is necessary to understand before we can form a true picture of a barbarian; it is the pleasure of personal independence—the pleasure of enjoying, in full force and liberty, all his powers in the various ups and downs of fortune; the foundness for activity without labor; for a life of enterprise and adventure. Such was the prevailing character and disposition of the barbarians; such were the moral wants which put these immense masses of men into motion. It is extremely difficult for us, in the regulated society in which we move, to form anything like a correct idea of this feeling, and of the influence which it exercised upon the rude barbarians of the fourth and fifth centuries. There is, however, a history of the Norman conquest of England, written by M. Thierry, in which the character and disposition of the barbarian are depicted with much life and vigor. In this admirable work, the motives, the inclinations and impulses that stir men into action in a state of life bordering on the savage, have been felt and described in a truly masterly manner. There is nowhere else to be found so correct a likeness of what a barbarian was, or of his course of life. Something of the same kind, but, in my opinion, much inferior, is found in the novels of Mr. Cooper, in which he depicts the manners of the savages of America. In these scenes, in the sentiments and social relations which these savages hold in the midst of their forests, there is unquestionably something which, to a certain point, calls up before us the manners of the ancient Germans. No doubt these pictures are a little imaginative, a little poetical; the worst features in the life and manners of the barbarians are not given in all their naked coarseness. I allude not merely to the evils which these manners forced into the social condition, but to the inward individual condition of the barbarian himself. There is in this passionate desire for personal independence something of a grosser, more material character than we should suppose from the work of M. Thierry—a degree of brutality, of headstrong passion, of apathy, which we do not discover in his details. Still, notwithstanding this alloy of brutal and stupid selfishness, there is, if we look more profoundly into the matter, something of a noble and moral character, in this taste for independence, which seems to derive its power from our moral nature. It is the pleasure of feeling one's self a man; the sentiment of personality; of human spontaneity in its unrestricted development.

It was the rude barbarians of Germany who introduced this sentiment of personal independence, this love of individual liberty, into European civilization; it was unknown among the Romans, it was unknown in the Christian church, it was unknown in nearly all the civilizations of antiquity. The liberty which we meet with in ancient civilizations is political liberty; it is the liberty of the citizen. It was not about his personal liberty that man troubled himself, it was about his liberty as a citizen. He formed part of an association, and to this alone he was devoted. The case was the same in the Christian church. Among its members a devoted attachment to the Christian body, a devotedness to its laws, and an earnest zeal for the extension of its empire, were everywhere conspicuous; the spirit of Christianity wrought a change in the moral character of man, opposed to this principle of independence; for under its influence his mind struggled to extinguish its own liberty, and to deliver itself up entirely to the dictates of his faith. But the feeling of personal independence, a fondness for genuine liberty displaying itself without regard to consequences, and with scarcely any other aim than its own satisfaction—this feeling, I repeat, was unknown to the Romans and to the Christians. We are indebted for it to the barbarians, who introduced it into European civilization, in which, from its first rise, it has played so considerable a part, and has produced such lasting and beneficial results, that it must be regarded as one of its fundamental principles, and could not be passed without notice.*

There is another, a second element of civilization, which we likewise inherit from the barbarians alone: I mean military patronage, the tie which became formed between individuals, between warriors, and which, without destroying the liberty of any, without even destroying in the commencement the equality up to a certain point which existed between them, laid the foundation of a graduated subordination, and was the origin of that aristocratical organization which, at a later period, grew into the feudal system. The germ of this connection was the attachment of man to man; the fidelity which united individuals, without apparent necessity, without any obligation arising from the general principles of society. In none of the ancient republics do you see any example of individuals particularly and freely attached to other individuals. They were all attached to the city. Among the barbarians this tie was formed between man and man; first by the relationship of companion and chief, when they came in bands to overrun Europe; and at a later period, by the relationship of sovereign and vassal. This second principle, which has had so vast an influence in the civilization of modern Europe—this devotedness of man to man—came to us entirely from our German ancestors; it formed part of their social system, and was adopted into ours.*

Let me now ask if I was not fully justified in stating, as I did at the outset, that modern civilization, even in its infancy, was diversified, agitated, and confused? Is it not true that we find at the fall of the Roman empire nearly all the elements which are met within in the progressive career of our civilization? We have found at this epoch three societies all different; first, municipal society, the last remains of the Roman empire; secondly, Christian society; and lastly, barbarian society. We find these societies very differently organized; founded upon principles totally opposite; inspiring men with sentiments altogether different. We find the love of the most absolute independence by the side of the most devoted submission; military patronage by the side of ecclesiastical domination; spiritual power and temporal power everywhere together; the canons of the Church, the learned legislation of the Romans, the almost unwritten customs of the barbarians; everywhere a mixture or rather coexistence of nations, of languages, of social situations, of manners, of ideas, of impressions, the most diversified. These, I think, afford a sufficient proof of the truth of the general character which I have endeavored to picture of our civilization.

There is no denying that we owe to this confusion, this diversity, this tossing and jostling of elements, the slow progress of Europe, the storms by which she has been buffeted, the miseries to which ofttimes she has been a prey. But however dear these have cost us, we must not regard them with unmingled regret. In nations, as well as in individuals, the good fortune to have all the faculties called into action, so as to ensure a full and free development of the various powers both of mind and body, is an advantage not too dearly paid for by the labor and pain with which it is attended. What we might call the hard fortune of European civilization—the trouble, the toil it has undergone—the violence it has suffered in its course—have been of infinitely more service to the progress of humanity than that tranquil, smooth simplicity, in which other civilizations have run their course. I shall now halt. In the rude sketch which I have drawn, I trust you will recognize the general features of the world such as it appeared upon the fall of the Roman empire, as well as the various elements which conspired and mingled together to give birth to European civilization. Henceforward these will move and act under our notice. We shall next put these in motion, and see how they work together. In the next lecture I shall endeavor to show what they became and what they performed in the epoch which is called the Barbarous Period; that is to say, the period during which the chaos of invasion continued.*

LECTURE III.: OF POLITICAL LEGITIMACY—COEXISTENCE OF ALL THE SYSTEMS OF GOVERNMENT IN THE FIFTII CENTURY— ATTEMPTS TO REORGANIZE SOCIETY.

In my last lecture, I brought you to what may be called the porch to the history of modern civilization. I briefly placed before you the primary elements of European civilization, as found when, at the dissolution of the Roman empire, it was yet in its cradle. I endeavored to give you a preliminary sketch of their diversity, their continual struggles with each other, and to show you that no one of them succeeded in obtaining the mastery in our social system; at least such a mastery as would imply the complete subjugation or expulsion of the others. We have seen that these circumstances form the distinguishing character of European civilization. We will to-day begin the history of its childhood in what is commonly called the dark or middle age, the age of barbarism.

It is impossible for us not to be struck, at the first glance at this period, with a fact which seems quite contradictory to the statement we have just made. No sooner do we seek for information respecting the opinions that have been formed relative to the ancient condition of modern Europe, than we find that the various elements of our civilization, that is to say, monarchy, theocracy, aristocracy, and democracy, each would have us believe that, originally, European society belonged to it alone, and that it has only lost the power it then possessed by the usurpation of the other elements. Examine all that has been written, all that has been said on this subject, and you will find that every author who has attempted to build up a system which should represent or explain our origin, has asserted the exclusive predominance of one or other of these elements of European civilization.

First, there is the school of civilians, attached to the feudal system, among whom we may mention Boulainvilliers* as the most celebrated, who boldly asserts, that, at the downfall of the Roman empire, it was the conquering nation, forming afterwards the nobility, who alone possessed authority, or right, or power. Society, it is said, was their domain, of which kings and people have since despoiled them; and hence, the aristocratic organization is affirmed to have been in Europe the primitive and genuine form.

Next to this school we may place the advocates of monarchy, the Abbé Dubos,† for example, who maintains, on the other side, that it was to royalty that European society belonged. According to him, the German kings succeeded to all the rights of the Roman emperors; they were even invited in by the ancient nations, among others by the Gauls and Saxons; they alone possessed legitimate authority, and all the conquests of the aristocracy were only so many encroachments upon the power of the monarchs.

The liberals, republicans, or democrats, whichever you may choose to call them, form a third school. Consult the Abbé de Mably.‡ According to this school, the government by which society was ruled in the fifth century, was composed of free institutions; of assemblies of freemen, of the nation properly so called. Kings and nobles enriched themselves by the spoils of this primitive Liberty; it has fallen under their repeated attacks, but it reigned before them.

Another power, however, claimed the right of governing society, and upon much higher grounds than any of these. Monarchical, aristocratic, and popular pretensions were all of a worldly nature: the Church of Rome founded her pretensions upon her sacred mission and divine right. By her labors, Europe, she said, had attained the blessings of civilization and truth, and to her alone belonged the right to govern it.

Here, then, is a difficulty which meets us at the very outset. We have stated our belief that no one of the elements of European civilization obtained an exclusive mastery over it, in the whole course of its history; that they lived in a constant state of proximity, of amalgamation, of strife, and of compromise; yet here, at our very first step, we are met by the directly opposite opinion, that one or other of these elements, even in the very infancy of civilization, even in the very heart of barbarian Europe, took entire possession of society. And it is not in one country alone, it is in every nation of Europe, that the various principles of our civilization, under forms a little varied, at epochs a little apart, have displayed these irreconcilable pretensions. The historic schools which I have enumerated are met with everywhere.

This fact is important, not in itself, but because it reveals some other facts which make a great figure in our history. By this simultaneous advancement of claims the most opposed to the exclusive possession of power, in the first stage of modern Europe, two important facts are revealed: first, the principle, the idea of political legitimacy; an idea which has played a considerable part in the progress of European civilization. The second is the particular, the true character of the state of barbarian Europe during that period, which now more expressly demands attention.

It is my task, then, to explain these two facts; and to show you how they may be fairly deduced from the early struggle of the pretensions which I have just called to your notice.

Now what do these various elements of our civilization,—what do theocracy, monarchy, aristocracy, and democracy aim at, when they each endeavor to make out that it alone was the first which held possession of European society? Is it any thing beyond the desire of each to establish its sole claim to legitimacy? For what is political legitimacy? Evidently nothing more than a right founded upon antiquity, upon duration, which is obvious from the simple fact, that priority of time is pleaded as the source of right, as proof of legitimate power. But, observe again, this claim is not peculiar to one system, to one element of our civilization, but is made alike by all. The political writers of the Continent have been in the habit, for some time past, of regarding legitimacy as belonging, exclusively, to the monarchical system. This is an error; legitimacy may be found in all the systems. It has already been shown that, of the various elements of our civilization, each wished to appropriate it to itself. But advance a few steps further into the history of Europe, and you will see social forms of government, the most opposed in principles, alike in possession of this legitimacy. The Italian and Swiss aristocracies and democracies, the little republic of San Marino,* as well as the most powerful monarchies, have considered themselves legitimate, and have been acknowledged as such; all founding their claim to this title upon the antiquity of their institutions; upon the historical priority and duration of their particular system of government.

If we leave modern Europe, and turn our attention to other times and to other countries, we shall everywhere find this same notion prevail respecting political legitimacy. It everywhere attaches itself to some portion of government; to some institution; to some form, or to some maxim.

There is no country, no time, in which you may not discover some portion of the social system, some public authority, that has assumed, and been acknowledged to possess, this character of legitimacy, arising from antiquity, prescription, and duration.

Let us for a moment see what this legitimacy is? of what it is composed? what it requires? and how it found its way into European civilization?

You will find that all power—I say all, without distinction—owes its existence in the first place partly to force. I do not say that force alone has been, in all cases, the foundation of power, or that this, without any other title, could in every case have been established by force alone. Other claims undoubtedly are requisite. Certain powers become established in consequence of certain social expediencies, of certain relations with the state of society, with its customs or opinions. But it is impossible to close our eyes to the fact, that violence has sullied the birth of all the authorities in the world, whatever may have been their nature or their form.

This origin, however, no one will acknowledge. All authorities, whatever their nature, disclaim it. None of them will allow themselves to be considered as the offspring of force. Governments are warned by an invincible instinct that force is no title—that might is not right—and that, while they rest upon no other foundation than violence, they are entirely destitute of right. Hence, if we go back to some distant period, in which the various systems, the various powers, are found struggling one against the other, we shall hear them each exclaiming, "I existed before you; my claim is the oldest; my claim rests upon other grounds than force; society belonged to me before this state of violence, before this strife in which you now find me. I was legitimate; I have been opposed, and my rights have been torn from me."

This fact alone proves that the idea of violence is not the foundation of political legitimacy,—

that it rests upon some other basis. This disavowal of violence made by every system, proclaims, as plainly as facts can speak, that there is another legitimacy, the true foundation of all the others, the legitimacy of reason, of justice, of right. It is to this origin that they seek to link themselves. As they feel scandalized at the very idea of being the offspring of force, they pretend to be invested, by virtue of their antiquity, with a different title. The first characteristic, then, of political legitimacy, is to disclaim violence as the source of authority, and to associate it with a moral notion, a moral force—with the notion of justice, of right, of reason. This is the primary element from which the principle of political legitimacy has sprung forth. It has issued from it, aided by time, aided by prescription. Let us see how.

Violence presides at the birth of governments, at the birth of societies; but time rolls on. He changes the works of violence. He corrects them. He corrects them, simply because society endures, and because it is composed of men. Man bears within himself certain notions of order, of justice, of reason, with a certain desire to bring them into play—he wishes to see them predominate in the sphere in which he moves. For this he labors unceasingly; and if the social system in which he lives, continues, his labor is not in vain. Man naturally brings reason, morality, and legitimacy into the world in which he lives.

Independently of the labor of man, by a special law of Providence which it is impossible to mistake, a law analogous to that which rules the material world, there is a certain degree of order, of intelligence, of justice, indispensable to the duration of human society. From the simple fact of its duration we may argue, that a society is not completely irrational, savage, or iniquitous; that it is not altogether destitute of intelligence, truth, and justice, for without these, society cannot hold together. Again, as society develops itself, it becomes stronger, more powerful; if the social system is continually augmented by the increase of individuals who accept and approve its regulations, it is because the action of time gradually introduces into it more right, more intelligence, more justice; it is because a gradual approximation is made in its affairs to the principles of true legitimacy.

Thus forces itself into the world, and from the world into the mind of man, the notion of political legitimacy. Its foundation in the first place, at least to a certain extent, is moral legitimacy—is justice, intelligence, and truth; it next obtains the sanction of time, which gives reason to believe that affairs are conducted by reason, that the true legitimacy has been introduced. At the epoch which we are about to study, you will find violence and fraud hovering over the cradle of monarchy, aristocracy, democracy, and even over the Church itself; you will see this violence and fraud everywhere gradually abated; and justice and truth taking their place in civilization. It is this introduction of justice and truth into our social system, that has nourished and gradually matured political legitimacy; and it is thus that it has taken firm root in modern civilization.*

All those then who have attempted at various times to set up this idea of legitimacy as the foundation of absolute power, have wrested it from its true origin. It has nothing to do with absolute power. It is under the name of justice and righteousness that it has made its way into the world and found footing. Neither is it exclusive. It belongs to no party in particular; it springs up in all systems where truth and justice prevail. Political legitimacy is as much attached to liberty as to power; to the rights of individuals as to the forms under which are exercised the public functions. As we go on we shall find it, as I said before, in systems the most opposed; in the feudal system; in the free cities of Flanders and Germany; in the republics of Italy, as well as in monarchy. It is a quality which appertains to all the divers elements of our civilization, and which it is necessary should be well understood before entering upon its history.

The second fact revealed to us by that simultaneous advancement of claims, of which I spoke at the beginning of this lecture, is the true character of what is called the period of barbarism. Each of the elements of European civilization pretends, that at this epoch Europe belonged to it alone; hence we may conclude that it really belonged to no one of them. When any particular kind of government prevails in the world, there is no difficulty in recognizing it. When we come to the tenth century, we acknowledge, without hesitation, the preponderance of feudalism. At the seventeenth we have no hesitation in asserting, that the monarchical principle prevails. If we turn our eyes to the free communities of Flanders, to the republics of Italy, we confess at once the predominance of democracy. Whenever, indeed, any one principle really bears sway in society, it cannot be mistaken.

The dispute, then, that has arisen among the various systems which hold a part in European civilization, respecting which bore chief sway at its origin, proves that they all existed there together, without any one of them having prevailed so generally as to give to society its form or its name.

This is, indeed, the character of the dark age: it was a chaos of all the elements; the childhood of all the systems; a universal jumble, in which even strife itself was neither permanent nor systematic. By an examination of the social system of this period under its various forms, I could show you that in no part of them is there to be found anything like a general principle, anything like stability. I shall, however, confine myself to two essential particulars—the state of persons, the state of institutions. This will be sufficient to give a general picture of society.

We find at this time four classes of persons: 1. Freemen, that is to say, men who, depending upon no superior, upon no patron, held their property and life in full liberty, without being fettered by any obligation towards another individual. 2. The Luedes, Fideles, Antrustions, etc., who were connected at first by the relationship of companion and chief, and afterwards by that of vassal and lord, towards another individual to whom they owed fealty and service, in consequence of a grant of lands, or some other gifts.* 3. Freedmen. 4. Slaves.

But were these various classes fixed? Were men once placed in a certain rank bound to it? Were the relations, in which the different classes stood towards each other, regular or permanent? Not at all. Freemen were continually changing their condition, and becoming vassals to nobles, in consideration of some gift which these might have to bestow; while others were falling into the class of slaves or serfs. Vassals were continually struggling to shake off the yoke of patronage, to regain their independence, to return to the class of freemen. Every part of society was in motion. There was a continual passing and repassing from one class to the other. No man continued long in the same rank; no rank continued long the same.

Property was in much the same state. I need scarcely tell you, that possessions were distinguished into allodial, or entirely free, and beneficiary or such as were held by tenure, with certain obligations to be discharged towards a superior.* Some writers attempt to trace out a regular and established system with respect to the latter class of proprietors, and lay it down as a rule that benefices were at first bestowed for a determinate number of years; that they were afterwards granted for life; and finally, at a later period, became hereditary. The attempt is vain. Lands were held in all these various ways at the same time, and in the same places. Benefices for a term of years, benefices for life, hereditary benefices, are found in the same period; even the same lands, within a few years, passed through these different states.† There was nothing more settled, nothing more general, in the state of lands than in the state of persons. Everything shows the difficulties of the transition from the wandering life to the settled life; from the simple personal relations which existed among the barbarians as invading migratory hordes, to the mixed relations of persons and property. During this transition all was confused, local, and disordered.

In institutions we observe the same unfixedness, the same chaos. We find here three different systems at once before us:—First, Monarchy; second, Aristocracy, or the proprietorship of men and lands, as lord and vassal; and, third, Free institutions, or assemblies of free men deliberating in common. No one of these systems entirely prevailed. Free institutions existed; but the men who should have formed part of these assemblies seldom troubled themselves to attend them. Baronial jurisdiction was not more regularly exercised. Monarchy, the most simple institution, the most easy to determine, here had no fixed character; at one time it was elective, at another hereditary—here the son succeeded to his father, there the election was confined to a family; in another place it was open to all, purely elective, and the choice fell on a distant relation, or perhaps a stranger. In none of these systems can we discover anything fixed; all the institutions, as well as the social conditions, dwelt together, continually confounded, continually changing. The same unsettledness existed with regard to states; they were created, suppressed, united, and divided; no governments, no frontiers, no nations; a general jumble of situations, principles, events, races, languages; such was barbarian Europe.

Let us now fix the limits of this extraordinary period. Its origin is strongly defined; it began with the fall of the Roman empire. But where did it close? To settle this question, we must find out the cause of this state of society; we must see what were the causes of barbarism.

I think I can point out two:—one material, arising from exterior circumstances, from the course of events; the other, moral, arising from the mind, from the intellects of man.

The material, or outward cause, was the continuance of invasion; for it must not be supposed that the invasions of the barbarian hordes stopped all at once in the fifth century. Do not believe that because the Roman empire was fallen, and kingdoms of barbarians founded upon its ruins, that the movement of nations was over. There are plenty of facts to prove that this was not the case, and that this movement lasted a long time after the destruction of the empire.

If we look to the Franks, or French, we shall find even the first race of kings continually carrying on wars beyond the Rhine. We see Clotaire, Dagobert, making expedition after expedition into Germany, and engaged in a constant struggle with the Thuringians, the Danes, and the Saxons who occupied the right bank of that river. And why was this but because these nations wished to cross the Rhine and get a share in the spoils of the empire? How came it to pass that the Franks, established in Gaul, and principally the Eastern, or Austrasian Franks, much about the same time, threw themselves in such large bodies upon Switzerland, and invaded Italy by crossing the Alps? It was because they were pushed forward by new populations from the northeast. These invasions were not mere pillaging inroads, they were not expeditions undertaken for the purpose of plunder, they were the result of necessity. The people, disturbed in their own settlements, pressed forward to better their fortune and find new abodes elsewhere. A new German nation entered upon the arena, and founded the powerful kingdom of the Lombards in Italy. In Gaul, or France, the Merovingian dynasty gave way to the Carlovingian; a change which is now generally acknowledged to have been, properly speaking, a new irruption of Franks into Gaul—a movement of nations, which substituted the Eastern Franks for the Western. Under the second race of kings, we find Charlemagne playing the same part against the Saxons, which the Merovingian princes played against the Thuringians: he carried on an unceasing war against the nations beyond the Rhine, who were precipitated upon the west by the Wiltzians, the Swabians, the Bohemians, and the various tribes of Slavonians, who trod on the heels of the German race. Throughout the northeast emigrations were going on and changing the face of affairs.

In the south, a movement of the same nature took place. While the German and Slavonian tribes pressed along the Rhine and Danube, the Saracens began to ravage and conquer the various coasts of the Mediterranean.

The invasion of the Saracens, however, had a character peculiarly its own. In them the spirit of conquest was united with the spirit of proselytism; the sword was drawn as well for the promulgation of a faith as the acquisition of territory. There is a vast difference between their invasion and that of the Germans. In the Christian world spiritual force and temporal force were quite distinct. The zeal for the propagation of a faith and the lust of conquest are not inmates of the same bosom.* The Germans, after their conversion, preserved the same manners, the same sentiments, the same tastes, as before; they were still guided by passions and interests of a worldly nature. They had become Christians, but not missionaries. The Saracens, on the contrary, were both conquerors and missionaries. The power of the Koran and of the sword was in the same hands. And it was this peculiarity which, I think, gave to Mohammedan civilization the wretched character which it bears. It was in this union of the temporal and spiritual powers, and the confusion which it created between moral authority and physical force, that that tyranny was born which seems inherent in their civilization. This I believe to be the principal cause of that stationary state into which it has everywhere fallen. This effect, however, did not show itself upon the first rise of Mohammedanism; the union, on the contrary, of military ardor and religious zeal, gave to the Saracen invasion a prodigious power. Its ideas and moral passions had at once a brilliancy and splendor altogether wanting in the Germanic invasions; it displayed itself with more energy and enthusiasm, and had a correspondent effect upon the minds and passions of men.

Such was the situation of Europe from the fifth to the ninth century. Pressed on the south by the Mohammedans, and on the north by the Germans and Slavonians, it could not be otherwise than that the reaction of this double invasion should keep the interior of Europe in a state of continual ferment. Populations were incessantly displaced, crowded one upon another; there was no regularity, nothing permanent or fixed. Some differences undoubtedly prevailed between the various nations. The chaos was more general in Germany than in the other parts of Europe. Here was the focus of movement. France was more agitated than Italy. But nowhere could society become settled and regulated; barbarism everywhere continued, and from the same cause that introduced it.*

Thus much for the material cause depending upon the course of events; let us now look to the moral cause, founded on the intellectual condition of man, which, it must be acknowledged, was not less powerful.

For, certainly, after all is said and done, whatever may be the course of external affairs, it is man himself who makes our world. It is according to the ideas, the sentiments, the moral and intellectual dispositions of man himself, that the world is regulated, and marches onward. It is upon the intellectual state of man that the visible form of society depends.

Now let us consider for a moment what is required to enable men to form themselves into a society somewhat durable, somewhat regular? It is evidently necessary, in the first place, that they should have a certain number of ideas sufficiently enlarged to settle upon the terms by which this society should be formed; to apply themselves to its wants, to its relations. In the second place, it is necessary that these ideas should be common to the greater part of the members of the society; and finally, that they should put some constraint upon their own inclinations and actions.

It is clear that where men possess no ideas extending beyond their own existence, where their intellectual horizon is bounded in self, if they are still delivered up to their own passions, and their own wills,—if they have not among them a certain number of notions and sentiments common to them all, round which they may all rally, it is clear that they cannot form a society: without this each individual will be a principle of agitation and dissolution in the social system of which he forms a part.

Wherever individualism reigns nearly absolute, wherever man considers but himself, wherever his ideas extend not beyond himself, wherever he only yields obedience to his own passions, there society—that is to say, society in any degree extended or permanent—becomes almost impossible. Now this was just the moral state of the conquerors of Europe at the epoch which engages our attention. I remarked, in the last lecture, that we owe to the Germans the powerful sentiment of personal liberty, of human individualism. Now, in a state of extreme rudeness and ignorance, this sentiment is mere selfishness, in all its brutality, with all its unsociability. Such was its character from the fifth to the eighth century, among the Germans. They cared for nothing beyond their own interest, for nothing beyond the gratification of their own passions, their own inclinations; how, then, could they accommodate themselves, in any tolerable degree, to the social condition? The attempt was made to bring them into it; they endeavored of themselves to enter into it; but an act of improvidence, a burst of passion, a lack of intelligence, soon threw them back to their old position. At every instant we see attempts made to form man into a social state, and at every instant we see them overthrown by the failings of man, by the absence of the moral conditions necessary to its existence.*

Such were the two causes which kept our forefathers in a state of barbarism; so long as these continued, so long barbarism endured. Let us see if we can discover when and from what causes it at last ceased.

Europe labored to emerge from this state. It is contrary to the nature of man, even when sunk into it by his own fault, to wish to remain in it. However rude, however ignorant, however selfish, however headstrong, there is yet in him a still small voice, an instinct, which tells him he was made for something better;—that he has another and higher destiny. In the midst of confusion and disorder, he is haunted and tormented by a taste for order and improvement. The claims of justice, of prudence, of development, disturb him, even under the yoke of the most brutish egotism. He feels himself impelled to improve the material world, society, and himself; he labors to do this, without attempting to account to himself for the want which urges him to the task. The barbarians aspired to civilization, while they were yet incapable of it—nay, more—while they even detested it whenever its laws restrained their selfish desires.

There still remained, too, a considerable number of wrecks and fragments of Roman civilization. The name of the empire, the remembrance of that great and glorious society still dwelt in the memory of many, and especially among the senators of cities, bishops, priests, and all those who could trace their origin to the Roman world.

Among the barbarians themselves, or their barbarian ancestors, many had witnessed the greatness of the Roman empire; they had served in its armies; they had conquered it. The image, the name of Roman civilization dazzled them; they felt a desire to imitate it; to bring it back again, to preserve some portion of it. This was another cause which ought to have forced them out of the state of barbarism, which I have described.

A third cause, and one which readily presents itself to every one was the Christian church. The Christian church was a regularly constituted society, having its maxims, its rules, its discipline, together with an ardent desire to extend its influence, to conquer its conquerors. Among the Christians of this period, in the Catholic clergy, there were men of profound and varied learning; men who had thought deeply, who were versed in ethics and politics; who had formed definite opinions and vigorous notions, upon all subjects; who felt a praiseworthy zeal to propagate information, and to advance the cause of learning. No society ever made greater efforts than the Christian church did from the fifth to the tenth century, to influence the world around it, and to assimilate it to itself. When its history shall become the particular object of our examination, we shall more clearly see what it attempted—it attacked, in a manner, barbarism at every point, in order to civilize it and rule over it.

Finally, a fourth cause of the progress of civilization, a cause which it is impossible strictly to appreciate, but which is not therefore the less real, was the appearance of great men. To say why a great man appears on the stage at a certain epoch, or what of his own individual development he imparts to the world at large, is beyond our power; it is the secret of Providence; but the fact is still certain. There are men to whom the spectacle of society, in a state of anarchy or immobility, is revolting and almost unbearable; it occasions them an intellectual shudder, as a thing that should not be; they feel an unconquerable desire to change it; to restore order; to introduce something general, regular, and permanent, into the world which is placed before them. Tremendous power! often tyrannical, committing a thousand iniquities, a thousand errors, for human weakness accompanies it. Glorious and salutary power! nevertheless, for it gives to humanity, and by the hand of man, a new and powerful impulse.

These various causes, these various powers working together, led to several attempts, between the fifth and ninth centuries, to draw European society from the barbarous state into which it had fallen.

The first of these was the compilation of the barbarian laws; an attempt which, though it effected but little, we cannot pass over, because it was made by the barbarians themselves. Between the sixth and eighth centuries, the laws of nearly all the barbarous nations (which, however, were nothing more than the rude customs by which they had been regulated, before their invasion of the Roman empire) were reduced to writing. Of these there are enumerated the codes of the Burgundians, the Salii, and Ripuarian Franks, the Visigoths, the Lombards, the Saxons, the Frisians, the Bavarians, the Germans, and some others. This was evidently a commencement of civilization—an attempt to bring society under the authority of general and fixed principles. Much, however, could not be expected from it. It published the laws of a society which no longer existed; the laws of the social system of the barbarians before their establishment in the Roman territory—before they had changed their wandering life for a settled one; before the nomad warriors became lost in the landed proprietors. It is true, that here and there may be found an article respecting the lands conquered by the barbarians, or respecting their relations with the ancient inhabitants of the country; some few bold attempts were made to regulate the new circumstances in which they were placed. But the far greater part of these laws were taken up with their ancient life, their ancient condition in Germany; were totally inapplicable to the new state of society, and had but a small share in its advancement.

In Italy and the south of Gaul, another attempt of a different character was made about this time. In these places Roman society had not been so completely rooted out as elsewhere; in the cities, especially, there still remained something of order and civil life; and in these civilization seemed to make a stand. If we look, for example, at the kingdom of the Ostrogoths in Italy under Theodoric we shall see, even under the dominion of a barbarous nation and king, the municipal form taking breath, as it were, and exercising a considerable influence upon the general tide of events. Here Roman manners had modified the Gothic, and brought them in a great degree to assume a likeness to their own. The same thing took place in the south of Gaul. At the opening of the sixth century, Alaric, a Visigothic king of Toulouse, caused a collection of the Roman laws

to be made, and published under the name of Breviarum Aniani, a code for his Roman subjects.*
In Spain, a different power, that of the Church, endeavored to restore the work of civilization.
Instead of the ancient German assemblies of warriors, the assembly that had most influence in
Spain was the Council of Toledo; and in this council the bishops bore sway, although it was
attended by the higher order of the laity. Open the laws of the Visigoths, and you will discover
that it is not a code compiled by barbarians, but bears convincing marks of having been drawn up
by the philosophers of the age—by the clergy. It abounds in general views, in theories, and in
theories, indeed, altogether foreign to barbarian manners. Thus, for example, we know that the
legislation of the barbarians was a personal legislation; that is to say, the same law only applied
to one particular race of men. The Romans were judged by the old Roman laws, the Franks were
judged by the Salian or Ripuarian code; in short, each people had its separate laws, though united
under the same government, and dwelling together in the same territory. This is what is called
personal legislation, in contradistinction to real legislation, which is founded upon territory. Now
this is exactly the case with the legislation of the Visigoths; it is not personal, but territorial. All
the inhabitants of Spain, Romans, Visigoths, or what not, were compelled to yield obedience to
one law. Read a little further, and you will meet with still more striking traces of philosophy.
Among the barbarians a fixed price was put upon man, according to his rank in society—the life
of the barbarian, the Roman, the freeman, and vassal, were not valued at the same amount—there
was a graduated scale of prices. But the principle that all men's lives are of equal worth in the
eyes of the law, was established by the code of the Visigoths. The same superiority is observable
in their judicial proceedings:—instead of the ordeal, the oath of compurgators, or trial by battle,
you will find the proofs established by witnesses, and a rational examination made of the fact,
such as might take place in a civilized society. In short, the code of the Visigoths bore
throughout evident marks of learning, system, and polity. In it we trace the hand of the same
clergy that acted in the Council of Toledo, and which exercised so large and beneficial an
influence upon the government of the country.*
In Spain, then, up to the time of the great invasion of the Saracens, it was the hierarchy which
made the greatest efforts to advance civilization.
In France, the attempt was made by another power. It was the work of great men, and above all
of Charlemagne. Examine his reign under its different aspects; and you will see that the darling
object of his life was to civilize the nations he governed. Let us regard him first as a warrior. He
was always in the field; from the south to the northeast, from the Ebro to the Elbe and Weser.
Perhaps you imagine that these expeditions were the effect of choice, and sprung from a pure
love of conquest? No such thing. I will not assert that he pursued any very regular system, or that
there was much diplomacy or strategy in his plans; but what he did sprang from necessity, and a
desire to repress barbarism. From the beginning to the end of his reign he was occupied in
staying the progress of a double invasion—that of the Mohammedans in the south, and that of
the Germanic and Slavonic tribes in the north. This is what gave the reign of Charlemagne its
military cast. I have already said that his expeditions against the Saxons were undertaken for the
same purpose. If we pass on from his wars to his government, we shall find the case much the
same: his leading object was to introduce order and unity in every part of his extensive
dominions. I have not said kingdom or state, because these words are too precise in their
signification, and call up ideas which bear but little relation to the society of which Charlemagne
stood at the head. Thus much, however, seems certain, that when he found himself master of this
vast territory, it mortified and grieved him to see all within it so precarious and unsettled—to see
anarchy and brutality everywhere prevailing,—and it was the first wish of his heart to better this

wretched condition of society. He endeavored to do this at first by his missi regii, whom he sent into every part of his dominions to find out and correct abuses; to amend the maladministration of justice, and to render him an account of all that was wrong; and afterwards by the general assemblies or parliaments as they have been called of the Champ de Mars, which he held more regularly than any of his predecessors. These assemblies he made nearly every considerable person in his dominions to attend. They were not assemblies formed for the preservation of the liberty of the subject, there was nothing in them bearing any likeness to the deliberations of our own days. But Charlemagne found them a means by which he could become well informed of facts and circumstances, and by which he could introduce some regulation, some unity, into the restless and disorganized populations he had to govern.

In whatever point of view, indeed, we regard the reign of Charlemagne, we always find its leading characteristic to be a desire to overcome barbarism, and to advance civilization. We see this conspicuously in his foundation of schools, in his collecting of libraries, in his gathering about him the learned of all countries; in the favor he showed towards the influence of the Church, for everything, in a word, which seemed likely to operate beneficially upon society in general, or the individual man.

An attempt of the same nature was made very soon afterwards in England, by Alfred the Great. These are some of the means which were in operation, from the fifth to the ninth century, in various parts of Europe, which seemed likely to put an end to barbarism.

None of them succeeded. Charlemagne was unable to establish his great empire, and the system of government by which he wished to rule it. The Church succeeded no better in its attempt in Spain to found a system of theocracy. And though in Italy and the south of France, Roman civilization made several attempts to raise its head, it was not till a later period, till towards the end of the tenth century, that it in reality acquired any vigor. Up to this time, every effort to put an end to barbarism failed: they supposed men more advanced than they in reality were. They all desired, under various forms, to establish a society more extensive, or better regulated, than the spirit of the age was prepared for. The attempts, however, were not lost to mankind. At the commencement of the tenth century, there was no longer any visible appearance of the great empire of Charlemagne, nor of the glorious councils of Toledo, but barbarism was drawing nigh its end. Two great results were obtained:

1. The movement of the invading hordes had been stopped both in the north and in the south. Upon the dismemberment of the empire of Charlemagne, the states, which became formed upon the right bank of the Rhine, opposed an effectual barrier to the tribes which advanced from the east. The Danes and Normans are an incontestable proof of this. Up to this time, if we except the Saxon attacks upon England, the invasions of the German tribes by sea had not been very considerable: but in the course of the ninth century they became constant and general. And this happened, because invasions by land had become exceedingly difficult; society had acquired, on this side, frontiers more fixed and secure; and that portion of the wandering nations, which could not be pressed back, were at least turned from their ancient course, and compelled to proceed by sea. Great as undoubtedly was the misery occasioned to the west of Europe by the incursions of these pirates and marauders, they still were much less hurtful than the invasions by land, and disturbed much less generally the newly-forming society. In the south, the case was much the same. The Arabs had settled in Spain, and the struggle between them and the Christians still continued; but this occasioned no new emigration of nations. Bands of Saracens still, from time to time, infested the coasts of the Mediterranean, but the great career of Islamism was arrested.

2. In the interior of Europe we begin at this time to see the wandering life decline; populations

became fixed; estates and landed possessions became settled; the relations between man and man no longer varied from day to day under the influence of force or chance. The interior and moral condition of man himself began to undergo a change; his ideas, his sentiments, began, like his life, to assume a more fixed character. He began to feel an attachment to the place in which he dwelt; to the connections and associations which he there formed; to those domains which he now calculated upon leaving to his children; to that dwelling which hereafter became his castle; to that miserable assemblage of serfs and slaves, which was one day to become a village. Little societies everywhere began to be formed; little states to be cut out according to the measure, if I may so say, of the capacities and prudence of men. There, societies gradually became connected by a tie, the origin of which is to be found in the manners of the German barbarians: the tie of a confederation which would not destroy individual freedom. On one side we find every considerable proprietor settling himself in his domains, surrounded only by his family and retainers; on the other, a certain graduated subordination of services and rights existing among all these military proprietors scattered over the land. Here we have the feudal system oozing at last out of the bosom of barbarism. Of the various elements of our civilizations, it was natural enough that the Germanic element should first prevail. It was already in possession of power; it had conquered Europe: from it European civilization was to receive its first form—its first social organization.*

The character of this form—the character of feudalism, and the influence it has exercised upon European civilization—will be the object of my next lecture; while in the very bosom of this system, in its meridian, we shall, at every step, meet with the other elements of our own social system, monarchy, the Church, and the communities or free cities. We shall feel pre-assured that these were not destined to fall under this feudal form, to which they adapted themselves while struggling against it; and that we may look forward to the hour when victory will declare itself for them in their turn.†

LECTURE IV.: THE FEUDAL SYSTEM.*

I have thus far endeavored to give you a view of the state of Europe upon the fall of the Roman empire; of its state in the first period of modern history—in the period of barbarism. We have seen that at the end of the period, towards the beginning of the tenth century, the first principle, the first system, which took possession of European society, was the feudal system—that out of the very bosom of barbarism sprung feudalism. The investigation of this system will be the subject of the present lecture.

I need scarcely remind you that it is not the history of events, properly so called, that we propose to consider. I shall not here recount the destinies of the feudal system. The subject which engages our attention is the history of civilization; it is that general, hidden fact, which we have to seek for, out of all the exterior facts in which its existence is contained.

Thus the events, the social crises, the various states through which society has passed, will in no way interest us, except so far as they are connected with the growth of civilization; we have only to learn from them how they have retarded or forwarded this great work; what they have given it, and what they have withheld from it. It is only in this point of view that we shall consider the feudal system.

In the first of these lectures we settled what civilization was; we endeavored to discover its elements; we saw that it consisted, on one side, in the development of man himself, of the individual, of humanity; on the other, of his outward or social condition. When then we come to any event, to any system, to any general condition of society, we have this two-fold question to put to it: What has it done for or against the development of man—for or against the development of society? It will, however, be at once seen that, in the investigation we have undertaken, it will be impossible for us not to come in contact with some of the grandest questions in moral philosophy. When we would, for example, know in what an event, a system, has contributed to the progress of man and of society, it is necessary that we should know what is the true development of society and of man; and be enabled to detect those developments which are deceitful, illegitimate,—which pervert instead of meliorate,—which cause them to retrograde instead of to advance. We shall not attempt to elude this task. By so doing we should mutilate and weaken our ideas, as well as the facts themselves. Besides, the present state of the world, the spirit of the age, compels us at once frankly to welcome this inevitable alliance of philosophy and history.

This indeed forms a striking, perhaps the essential, characteristic of the present times. We are now compelled to consider—science and reality—theory and practice—right and fact—and to make them move side by side. Down to the present time these two powers have lived apart. The world has been accustomed to see theory and practice following two different routes, unknown to each other, or at least never meeting. When doctrines, when general ideas, have wished to intermeddle in affairs, to influence the world, it has only been able to effect this under the appearance and by the aid of fanaticism. Up to the present time the government of human societies, the direction of their affairs, have been divided between two sorts of influences; on one side theorists, men who would rule all according to abstract notions—enthusiasts; on the other, men ignorant of all rational principle,—experimentalists, whose only guide is expediency. This state of things is now over. The world will no longer agitate for the sake of some abstract principle, some fanciful theory—some Utopian government which can only exist in the imagination of an enthusiast; nor will it put up with practical abuses and oppressions, however favored by prescription and expediency, where they are opposed to the just principles and the legitimate end of government. To ensure respect, to obtain confidence, governing powers must now unite theory and practice; they must know and acknowledge the influence of both. They must regard as well principles as facts; must respect both truth and necessity—must shun, on one hand, the blind pride of the fanatic theorist, and, on the other, the no less blind pride of the libertine practician. To this better state of things we have been brought by the progress of the human mind and the progress of society. On one side the human mind is so elevated and enlarged that it is able to view at once, as a whole, the subject or fact which comes under its notice, with all the various circumstances and principles which affect it—these it calculates and combines—it so opposes, mixes, and arranges them—that while the everlasting principle is placed boldly and prominently forward so as not to be mistaken, care is taken that it shall not be endangered, that its progress shall not be retarded by a negligent or rash estimate of the circumstances which oppose it. On the other side, social systems are so improved as no longer to shrink from the light of truth; so improved, that facts may be brought to the test of science— practice may be placed by the side of theory, and, notwithstanding its many imperfections, the comparison will excite in us neither discouragement nor disgust.

I shall give way, then, freely to this natural tendency—to this spirit of the age, by passing continually from the investigation of circumstances to the investigation of ideas—from an exposition of facts to the consideration of doctrines. Perhaps there is, in the present disposition of the public, another reason in favor of this method. For some time past there has existed among us a decided taste, a sort of predilection for facts, for looking at things in a practical point of view. We have been so much a prey to the despotism of abstract ideas, of theories,—they have, in some respects, cost us so dear, that we now regard them with a degree of distrust. We like better to refer to facts, to particular circumstances, and to judge and act accordingly. Let us not complain of this. It is a new advance—it is a grand step in knowledge, and towards the empire of truth; provided, however, we do not suffer ourselves to be carried too far by this disposition—provided that we do not forget that truth alone has a right to reign in the world; that facts have no merit but in proportion as they bear its stamp, and assimilate themselves more and more to its image; that all true grandeur proceeds from mind; that all expansion belongs to it. The civilization of France possesses this peculiar character; it has never been wanting in intellectual grandeur. It has always been rich in ideas. The power of mind has been great in French society—greater, perhaps, than anywhere else. It must not lose this happy privilege—it must not fall into that lower, that somewhat material condition which prevails in other societies. Intelligence, theories, must still maintain in France the same rank which they have hitherto occupied.

I shall not then attempt to shun these general and philosophical questions: I will not go out of my way to seek them, but when circumstances bring them naturally before me, I shall attack them without hesitation or embarrassment. This will be the case more than once in considering the feudal system as connected with the history of European civilization.

A great proof that in the tenth century the feudal system was necessary, and the only social system practicable, is the universality of its adoption. Wherever barbarism ceased, feudalism became general. This at first struck men as the triumph of chaos. All unity, all general civilization seemed gone; society on all sides seemed dismembered; a multitude of petty, obscure, isolated, incoherent societies arose. This appeared, to those who lived and saw it, universal anarchy—the dissolution of all things.* Consult the poets and historians of the day: they all believed that the end of the world was at hand. Yet this was, in truth, a new and real social system which was forming: feudal society was so necessary, so inevitable, so altogether the only consequence that could flow from the previous state of things, that all entered into it, all adopted its form. Even elements the most foreign to this system, the Church, the free communities, royalty, all were constrained to accommodate themselves to it. Churches became sovereigns and vassals; cities became lords and vassals; royalty was hidden under the feudal suzerain. All things were given in fief, not only estates, but rights and privileges: the right to cut wood in the forests, the privilege of fishing. The churches gave their surplice-fees in fief: the revenues of baptism—the fees for churching women. In the same manner, too, that all the great elements of society were drawn within the feudal enclosure, so even the smallest portions, the most trifling circumstances of common life, became subject to feudalism.

In observing the feudal system thus taking possession of every part of society, one might be apt, at first, to believe that the essential, vital principle of feudalism everywhere prevailed. This would be a grand mistake. Although they put on the feudal form, yet the institutions, the elements of society which were not analogous to the feudal system, did not lose their nature, the principles by which they were distinguished. The feudal church, for example, never ceased for a moment to be animated and governed at bottom by the principles of theocracy, and she never for a moment relaxed her endeavors to gain for this the predominancy. Now she leagued with royalty, now with the pope, and now with the people, to destroy this system, whose livery, for the time, she was compelled to put on. It was the same with royalty and the free cities: in one the principle of monarchy, in the others the principle of democracy, continued fundamentally to prevail: and, notwithstanding their feudal appearance, these various elements of European society constantly labored to deliver themselves from a form so foreign to their nature, and to put on that which corresponded with their true and vital principle.

Though perfectly satisfied, therefore, of the universality of the feudal form, we must take care not to conclude on that account, that the feudal principle was equally universal. We must be no less cautious not to take our ideas of feudalism indifferently from every object which bears its physiognomy. In order to know and understand this system thoroughly—to unravel and judge of its effects upon modern civilization—we must seek it where the form and spirit dwell together; we must study it in the hierarchy of the laic possessors of fiefs; in the association of the conquerors of the European territory. This was the true residence of the feudal system, and into this we will now endeavor to penetrate.

I said a few words, just now, on the importance of questions of a moral nature; and on the danger and inconvenience of passing them by without proper attention. A matter of a totally opposite character arises here, and demands our consideration; it is one which has been, in general, too much neglected. I allude to the physical condition of society; to the changes which take place in the life and manners of a people in consequence of some. new event, some revolution, some new state into which it may be thrown. These changes have not always been sufficiently attended to. The modification which these great crises in the history of the world have wrought in the material existence of mankind—in the physical conditions of the relations of men to one another—have not been investigated with so much advantage as they might have been. These modifications have more influence upon the general body of society than is imagined. Every one knows how much has been said upon the influence of climate, and of the importance which Montesquieu attached to it. Now if we regard only the direct influence of climate upon man, perhaps it has not been so extensive as is generally supposed; it is, to say the least, vague and difficult to appreciate; but the indirect influence of climate, that, for example, which arises from the circumstance that in a hot country man lives in the open air, while in a cold one he lives shut up in his habitation—that he lives here upon one kind of food, and there upon another; these are facts of extreme importance, inasmuch as a simple change in physical life may have a powerful effect upon the course of civilization. Every great revolution leads to modifications of this nature in the social system, and consequently claims our consideration.

The establishment of the feudal system wrought a change of this kind, which had a powerful and striking influence upon European civilization. It changed the distribution of the population. Hitherto the lords of the territory, the conquering population, had lived united in masses more or less numerous, either settled in cities, or moving about the country in bands; but by the operation of the feudal system these men were brought to live isolated, each in his own dwelling, at long distances apart. You will instantly perceive the influence which this change must have exercised upon the character and progress of civilization. The social preponderance—the government of society, passed at once from cities to the country; the baronial courts of the great landed proprietors took the place of the great national assemblies—the public body was lost in the thousand little sovereignties into which every kingdom was split. This was the first consequence—a consequence purely physical, of the triumph of the feudal system. The more closely we examine this circumstance, the more clearly and forcibly will its effects present themselves to our notice.

Let us now examine this society in itself, and trace out its influence upon the progress of civilization. We will take feudalism, in the first place, in its most simple state, in its primitive fundamental form. We will visit a possessor of a fief in his lonely domain; we will see the course of life which he leads there, and the little society by which he is surrounded.

Having fixed upon an elevated solitary spot, strong by nature, and which he takes care to render secure, the lordly proprietor of the domain builds his castle. Here he settles himself, with his wife and children, and perhaps some few freemen, who, not having obtained fiefs, not having themselves become proprietors, have attached themselves to his fortunes, and continued to live with him and form a part of his household. These are the inhabitants of the interior of the castle. At the foot of the hill on which this castle stands we find huddled together a little population of peasants, of serfs, who cultivate the lands of the possessor of the fief. In the midst of this group of cottages religion soon planted a church and a priest. A priest, in these early days of feudalism, was generally the chaplain of the baron, and the curate of the village; two offices which by and by became separated, and the village had its pastor dwelling by the side of his church.

Such is the first form, the elementary principle, of feudal society. We will now examine this simple form, in order to put to it the twofold question we have to ask of every fact, namely, what it has done towards the progress—first, of man, himself; secondly, of society?

It is with peculiar propriety that we put this twofold question to the little society I have just described, and that we should attach importance to its answers, forasmuch as this society is the type, the faithful picture, of feudal society in the aggregate; the baron, the people of his domain, and the priest, compose, whether upon a large or smaller scale, the feudal system* when separated from monarchy and cities, two distinct and foreign elements.

The first circumstance which strikes us in looking at this little community is the great importance with which the possessor of the fief must have been regarded, not only by himself, but by all around him. A feeling of personal consequence, of individual liberty, was a prevailing feature in the character of the barbarians. The feeling here, however, was of a different nature; it was no longer simply the liberty of the man, of the warrior, it was the importance of the proprietor, of the head of the family, of the master. His situation, with regard to all around him, would naturally beget in him an idea of superiority—a superiority of a peculiar nature, and very different from that we meet with in other systems of civilization. Look, for example, at the Roman patrician, who was placed in one of the highest aristocratic situations of the ancient world. Like the feudal lord, he was head of the family, superior, master; and besides this, he was a religious magistrate, high priest over his household. But mark the difference: his importance as a religious magistrate is derived from without. It is not an importance strictly personal, attached to the individual: he receives it from on high; he is the delegate of divinity, the interpreter of religious faith. The Roman patrician, moreover, was the member of a corporation which lived united in the same place—a member of the senate—again, an importance which he derived from without, from his corporation. The greatness of these ancient aristocrats, associated with a religious and political character, belonged to the situation, to the corporation in general, rather than to the individual. That of the proprietor of a fief belonged to himself alone; he held nothing of any one;* all his rights, all his power, centered in himself. He is no religious magistrate; he forms no part of a senate; it is in the individual, in his own person, that all his importance resides—all that he is, he is of himself, in his own name alone. What a vast influence must a situation like this have exercised over him who enjoyed it! What haughtiness, what pride, must it have engendered! Above him, no superior of whom he was but the representative and interpreter; near him no equals; no general and powerful law to restrain him—no exterior force to control him; his will suffered no check but from the limits of his power, and the presence of danger. Such seems to me the moral effect that would naturally be produced upon the character or disposition of man, by the situation in which he was placed under the feudal system.

I shall proceed to a second consequence equally important, though too little noticed; I mean the peculiar character of the feudal family.

Let us consider for a moment the various family systems. Let us look, in the first place, at the patriarchal family, of which so beautiful a picture is given us in the Bible, and in numerous Oriental treatises. We find it composed of a great number of individuals—it was a tribe. The chief, the patriarch, in this case, lives in common with his children, with his neighbors, with the various generations assembled around him—all his relations or his servants. He not only lives with them, he has the same interests, the same occupations, he leads the same life. This was the situation of Abraham, and of the patriarchs; and is still that of the Bedouin Arabs, who, from generation to generation, continue to follow the same patriarchal mode of life.

Let us look next at the clan—another family system, which now scarcely exists, except in Scotland and Ireland, but through which probably the greater part of the European world has passed. This is no longer the patriarchal family. A great difference is found here between the chief and the rest of the community; he leads not the same life; the greater part are employed in husbandry, and in supplying his wants, while the chief himself lives in idleness or war. Still they all descend from the same stock; they all bear the same name; and their common parentage, their ancient traditions, the same remembrances, and the same associations, create a moral tie, a sort of equality, between all the members of the clan.

These are the two principal forms of family society as represented by history. Does either of them, let me ask you, resemble the feudal family? Certainly not. At the first glance, there may, indeed, seem some similarity between the feudal family and the clan; but the difference is marked and striking. The population which surrounds the possessor of the fief is quite foreign to him; it bears not his name. They are unconnected by relationship, or by any historical or moral tie. The same holds with respect to the patriarchal family. The feudal proprietor neither leads the same life, nor follows the same occupations as those who live around him; he is engaged in arms, or lives in idleness: the others are laborers. The feudal family is not numerous—it forms no tribe—it is confined to a single family properly so called; to the wife and children, who live separated from the rest of the people in the interior of the castle. The peasantry and serfs form no part of it; they are of another origin, and immeasurably beneath it. Five or six individuals, at a vast height above them, and at the same time foreigners, make up the feudal family. Is it not evident that the peculiarity of its situation must have given to this family a peculiar character? Confined, concentrated, called upon continually to defend itself; mistrusting, or at least shutting itself up from the rest of the world, even from its servants, in-door life, domestic manners must naturally have acquired a great preponderance. We cannot keep out of sight, that the grosser passions of the chief, the constantly passing his time in warfare or hunting, opposed a considerable obstacle to the formation of a strictly domestic society. But its progress, though slow, was certain. The chief, however violent and brutal his out-door exercises, must habitually return into the bosom of his family. He there finds his wife and children, and scarcely any but them; they alone are his constant companions; they alone divide his sorrows and soften his joys; they alone are interested in all that concerns him. It could not but happen in such circumstances, that domestic life must have acquired a vast influence; nor is there any lack of proofs that it did so. Was it not in the bosom of the feudal family that the importance of women, that the value of the wife and mother, at last made itself known? In none of the ancient communities, not merely speaking of those in which the spirit of family never existed, but in those in which it existed most powerfully—say, for example, in the patriarchal system—in none of these did women ever attain to anything like the place which they acquire in Europe under the feudal system. It is to the progress, to the preponderance of domestic manners in the feudal halls and castles, that they owe this change, this improvement in their condition. The cause of this has been sought for in the peculiar manners of the ancient Germans; in a national respect which they are said to have borne, in the midst of their forests, to the female sex.* Upon a single phrase of Tacitus, Germanic patriotism has founded a high degree of superiority—of primitive and ineffable purity of manners—in the relations between the two sexes among the Germans. Pure chimeras! Phrases like this of Tacitus—sentiments and customs analogous to those of the Germans of old, are found in the narratives of a host of writers, who have seen, or inquired into, the manners of savage and barbarous tribes. There is nothing primitive, nothing peculiar to a certain race in this matter. It was in the effects of a very decided social situation—it was in the increase and preponderance of domestic manners, that the importance of the female sex in Europe had its rise, and the preponderance of domestic manners in Europe very early became an essential characteristic in the feudal system.

A second circumstance, a fresh proof of the influence of domestic life, forms a striking feature in the picture of a feudal family: I mean the principle of inheritance—the spirit of perpetuity which so strongly predominates in its character. This spirit of inheritance is a natural off-shoot of the spirit of family, but it nowhere took such deep root as in the feudal system, where it was nourished by the nature of the property with which the family was, as it were, incorporated. The fief differed from other possessions in this, that it constantly required a chief, or owner, who could defend it, manage it, discharge the obligations by which it was held, and thus maintain its rank in the general association of the great proprietors of the kingdom. There thus became a kind of identification of the possessor of the fief with the fief itself, and with all its future possessors. This circumstance powerfully tended to strengthen and knit together the ties of family, already so strong by the nature of the feudal system itself.

Quitting the baronial dwelling, let us now descend to the little population that surrounds it. Everything here wears a different aspect. The disposition of man is so kindly and good, that it is almost impossible for a number of individuals to be placed for any length of time in a social situation without giving birth to a certain moral tie between them: sentiments of protection, of benevolence, of affection, spring up naturally. Thus it happened in the feudal system. There can be no doubt, but that after a certain time, kind and friendly feelings would grow up between the feudal lord and his serfs. This, however, took place in spite of their relative situation, and by no means through its influence. Considered in itself, this situation was radically vicious. There was nothing morally common between the holder of the fief and his serfs. They formed part of his estate; they were his property; and under this word property are comprised, not only all the rights which we delegate to the public magistrate to exercise in the name of the state, but likewise all those which we possess over private property: the right of making laws, of levying taxes, of inflicting punishment, as well as that of disposing of them—or selling them. There existed not, in fact, between the lord of the domain and its cultivators, so far as we consider the latter as men, either rights, guarantee, or society.

From this I believe has arisen that almost universal, invincible hatred which country people have at all times borne to the feudal system, to every remnant of it—to its very name. We are not without examples of men having submitted to the heavy yoke of despotism, of their having become accustomed to it, nay more, of their having freely accepted it. Religious despotism, monarchical despotism, have more than once obtained the sanction, almost the love, of the population which they governed. But feudal despotism has always been repulsed, always hateful. It tyrannized over the destinies of men, without ruling in their hearts. Perhaps this may be partly accounted for by the fact, that, in religious and monarchical despotism, authority is always exercised by virtue of some belief or opinion common to both ruler and subjects; he is the representative, the minister, of another power superior to all human powers. He speaks or acts in the name of Divinity or of a common feeling, and not in the name of man himself, of man alone. Feudal despotism differed from this; it was the authority of man over man; the domination of the personal, capricious will of an individual. This perhaps is the only tyranny to which man, much to his honor, never will submit. Wherever in a ruler, or master, he sees but the individual man,—the moment that the authority which presses upon him is no more than an individual, a human will, one like his own, he feels mortified and indignant, and struggles against the yoke which he is compelled to bear. Such was the true, the distinctive character of the feudal power, and such was the origin of the hatred which it has never ceased to inspire.

The religious element which was associated with the feudal power was but little calculated to alleviate its yoke. I do not see how the influence of the priest could be very great in the society which I have just described, or that he could have much success in legitimizing the connection between the enslaved people and the lordly proprietor. The Church has exercised a very powerful influence in the civilization of Europe, but then it has been by proceeding in a general manner—by changing the general dispositions of mankind. When we enter intimately into the little feudal society, properly so called, we find the influence of the priest between the baron and his serfs to have been very slight. It most frequently happened that he was as rude and nearly as much under control as the serf himself; and therefore not very well fitted, either by his position or talents, to enter into a contest with the lordly baron. We must, to be sure, naturally suppose, that, called upon as he was by his office to administer and to keep alive among these poor people the great moral truths of Christianity, he became endeared and useful to them in this respect; he consoled and instructed them; but I believe he had but little power to soften their hard condition.

Having examined the feudal system in its rudest, its simplest form; having placed before you the principal consequences which flowed from it, as respects the possessor of the fief himself, as respects his family, and as respects the population gathered about him; let us now quit this narrow precinct. The population of the fief was not the only one in the land: there were other societies more or less like his own of which he was a member—with which he was connected. What, then, let us ask, was the influence which this general society to which he belonged might be expected to exercise upon civilization?

One short observation before we reply: both the possessor of the fief and the priest, it is true, formed part of a general society; in the distance they had numerous and frequent connections; not so the cultivators—the serfs. Every time that, in speaking of the population of the country at this period, we make use of some general term, which seems to convey the idea of one single and same society—such for example as the word people—we speak without truth. For this population there was no general society—its existence was purely local. Beyond the estate in which they dwelt, the serfs had no relations whatever,—no connection either with persons, things, or government. For them there existed no common destiny, no common country—they formed not a nation. When we speak of the feudal association as a whole, it is only the great proprietors that are alluded to.

Let us now see what the relations of the little feudal society were with the general society to which it held, and what consequences these relations may be expected to have led to in the progress of civilization.

We all know what the ties were which bound together the possessors of fiefs; what conditions were attached to their possessions; what were the obligations of service on one part, and of protection on the other. I shall not enter into a detail of these obligations; it is enough for the present purpose that you have a general idea of them.* This system, however, seemed naturally to pour into the mind of every possessor of a fief a certain number of ideas and moral sentiments—ideas of duty, sentiments of affection. That the principles of fidelity, devotedness, loyalty, became developed, and maintained by the relations in which the possessors of fiefs stood towards one another, is evident. The fact speaks for itself.

The attempt was made to change these obligations, these duties, these sentiments, and so on, into laws and institutions. It is well known that feudalism wished legally to settle what services the possessor of a fief owed to his sovereign; what services he had a right to expect from him in return; in what cases the vassal might be called upon to furnish military or pecuniary aid to his lord; in what way the lord might obtain the services of his vassals, in those affairs, in which they were not bound to yield them by the mere possession of their fiefs. The attempt was made to place all these rights under the protection of institutions founded to ensure their respect. Thus the baronial jurisdictions were erected to administer justice between the possessors of fiefs, upon complaints duly laid before their common suzerain. Thus every baron of any consideration collected his vassals in parliament, to debate in common the affairs which required their consent or concurrence. There was, in short, a combination of political, judicial, and military means, which show the attempt to organize the feudal system—to convert the relations between the possessors of fiefs into laws and institutions. But these laws, these institutions, had no stability— no guarantee.

If it should be asked what is a political guarantee, I am compelled to look back to its fundamental character, and to state that this is the constant existence, in the bosom of society, of a will, of an authority disposed and in a condition to impose a law upon the wills and powers of private individuals—to enforce their obedience to the common rule, to make them respect the general law.

There are only two systems of political guarantees possible; there must be either a will, a particular power, so superior to the others that none of them can resist it, but are obliged to yield to its authority whenever it is interposed; or, on the other, a public will, the result of the concurrence—of the development of the wills of individuals, and which likewise is in a condition, when once it has expressed itself, to make itself obeyed and respected by all.

These are the only two systems of political guarantees possible; the despotism of one alone, or of a body; or free government. If we examine the various systems, we shall find that they may all be brought under one of these two.

Well, neither of these existed, or could exist, under the feudal system.

Without doubt the possessors of fiefs were not all equal among themselves. There were some much more powerful than others; and very many sufficiently powerful to oppress the weaker. But there was none, from the king, the first of the proprietors, downward, who was in a condition to impose law upon all the others; in a condition to make himself obeyed. Call to mind that none of the permanent means of power and influence at this time existed—no standing army—no regular taxes—no fixed tribunals. The social authorities—the institutions, had, in a manner, to be new formed every time they were wanted. A tribunal had to be formed for every trial—an army to be formed for every war—a revenue to be formed every time that money was needed. All was occasional—accidental—special; there was no central, permanent, independent means of government. It is evident that in such a system no individual had the power to enforce his will upon others; to compel all to respect and obey the general law.* On the other hand, resistance was easy, in proportion as repression was difficult. Shut up in his castle, with but a small number of enemies to cope with, and aware that other vassals in a like situation were ready to join and assist him, the possessor of a fief found but little difficulty in defending himself.

It must then, I think, be confessed, that the first system of political guarantees—namely, that which would make all responsible to the strongest—has been shown to be impossible under the feudal system.

The other system—that of free government, of a public power, a public authority—was just as impracticable. The reason is simple enough. When we speak now of a public power, of what we call the rights of sovereignty—that is, the right of making laws, of imposing taxes, of inflicting punishment, we know, we bear in mind, that these rights belong to nobody; that no one has, on his own account, the right to punish others, or to impose any burden or law upon them. These are rights which belong only to the great body of society, which are exercised only in its name; they are emanations from the people, and held in trust for their benefit. Thus it happens that when an individual is brought before an authority invested with these rights, the sentiment that predominates in his mind, though perhaps he himself may be unconscious of it, is, that he is in the presence of a public legitimate authority, invested with the power to command him, an authority which, beforehand, he has tacitly acknowledged. This was by no means the case under the feudal system. The possessor of a fief, within his domain, was invested with all the rights and privileges of sovereignty; he inherited them with the territory; they were a matter of private property. What are now called public rights were then private rights; what are now called public authorities were then private authorities. When the possessor of a fief, after having exercised sovereign power in his own name, as proprietor over all the population which lived around him, attended an assembly, attended a parliament held by his sovereign—a parliament not in general very numerous, and composed of men of the same grade, or nearly so, as himself—he did not carry with him any notion of a public authority. This idea was in direct contradiction to all about him—to all his notions, to all that he had done within his own domains. All he saw in these assemblies were men invested with the same rights as himself, in the same situation as himself, acting as he had done by virtue of their own personal title. Nothing led or compelled him to see or acknowledge in the very highest portion of the government, or in the institutions which we call public, that character of superiority or generality which seems to us bound up with the notion of political power. Hence, if he was dissatisfied with its decision, he refused to concur in it, and perhaps called in force to resist it.

Force, indeed, was the true and usual guarantee of right under the feudal system, if force can be called a guarantee. Every law continually had recourse to force to make itself respected or acknowledged. No institution succeeded in doing this. This was so perfectly felt that institutions were scarcely ever applied to. If the agency of the baronial courts or parliaments of vassals had been of any importance, we should find them more generally employed than from history they appear to have been. Their rarity proves their insignificance.

This is not astonishing. There is another reason for it more profound and decisive than any I have yet adduced.

Of all the systems of government and political guarantee, it may be asserted, without fear of contradiction, that the most difficult to establish and render effectual is the federative system; a system which consists in leaving in each place or province, in every separate society, all that portion of government which can abide there, and in taking from it only so much of it as is indispensable to a general society, in order to carry it to the center of this larger society, and there to embody it under the form of a central government. This federative system, theoretically the most simple, is found in practice the most complex; for in order to reconcile the degree of independence, of local liberty, which is permitted to remain, with the degree of general order, of general submission, which in certain cases it supposes and exacts, evidently requires a very advanced state of civilization—requires, indeed, that the will of man, that individual liberty, should concur in the establishment and maintenance of the system much more than in any other, because it possesses less than any other the means of coercion.

The federative system, then, is one which evidently requires the greatest maturity of reason, of morality, of civilization in the society to which it is applied. Yet we find that this was the kind of government which the feudal system attempted to establish: for feudalism, as a whole, was truly a confederation. It rested upon the same principles, for example, as those on which is based, in the present day, the federative system of the United States of America. It affected to leave in the hands of each great proprietor all that portion of the government, of sovereignty, which could be exercised there, and to carry to the suzerain, or to the general assembly of barons, the least possible portion of power, and only this in cases of absolute necessity. You will easily conceive the impossibility of establishing a system like this in a world of ignorance, of brute passions, or, in a word, where the moral condition of man was so imperfect as under the feudal system. The very nature of such a government was in opposition to the notions, the habits and manners of the very men to whom it was to be applied. How then can we be astonished at the bad success of this attempt at organization?

We have now considered the feudal system, first, in its most simple element, in its fundamental principle; and then in its collective form, as a whole; we have examined it under these two points of view, in order to see what it did and what it might have been expected to do; what has been its influence on the progress of civilization. These investigations, I think, bring us to this twofold conclusion:—

1. Feudalism seems to have exercised a great, and, upon the whole, a salutary influence upon the intellectual development of individuals. It gave birth to elevated ideas and feelings in the mind, to moral wants, to grand developments of character and passion.

2. With regard to society, it was incapable of establishing either legal order or political guarantee. In the wretched state to which society had been reduced by barbarism, in which it was incapable of a more regular or enlarged form, the feudal system seemed indispensable as a step towards reassociation; still this system, in itself radically vicious, could neither regulate nor enlarge society. The only political right which the feudal system was capable of exercising in European society, was the right of resistance: I will not say legal resistance, for there can be no question of legal resistance in a society so little advanced. The progress of society consists pre-eminently in substituting, on one hand, public authority for private will; and, on the other, legal resistance for individual resistance. This is the great end, the chief perfection, of social order; a large field is left to personal liberty, but when personal liberty offends, when it becomes necessary to call it to account, our only appeal is to public reason; public reason is placed in the judge's chair to pass sentence on the charge which is preferred against individual liberty. Such is the system of legal order and of legal resistance. You will easily perceive, that there was nothing bearing any resemblance to this in the feudal system. The right of resistance, which was maintained and practised in this system, was the right of personal resistance; a terrible and antisocial right, inasmuch as its only appeal is to brute force—to war—which is the destruction of society itself; a right, however, which ought never to be entirely erased from the mind of man, because by its abolition he puts on the fetters of servitude. The notion of the right of resistance had been banished from the Roman community, in the general disgrace and infamy into which it had fallen, and it could not be regenerated from its ruins. It could not, in my opinion, have sprung more naturally from the principles of Christian society. It is to the feudal system that we are indebted for its re-introduction among us. The glory of civilization is to render this principle for ever inactive and useless; the glory of the feudal system is its having constantly professed and

defended it.

Such, if I am not widely mistaken, is the result of our investigation of the feudal community, considered in itself, in its general principles, and independently of its historical progress. If we now turn to facts, to history, we shall find it to have fallen out, just as might have been expected, that the feudal system accomplished its task; that its destiny has been conformable to its nature. Events may be adduced in proof of all the conjectures, of all the inductions, which I have drawn from the nature and essential character of this system.

Take a glance, for example, at the general history of feudalism, from the tenth to the thirteenth centuries, and say, is it not impossible to deny that it exercised a vast and salutary influence upon the progress of individual man—upon the development of his sentiments, his disposition, and his ideas? Where can we open the history of this period, without discovering a crowd of noble sentiments, of splendid achievements, of beautiful developments of humanity, evidently generated in the bosom of feudal life. Chivalry, which in reality bears scarcely the least resemblance to feudalism, was nevertheless its offspring. It was feudalism which gave birth to that romantic thirst and fondness for all that is noble, generous, and faithful—for that sentiment of honor, which still raises its voice in favor of the system by which it was nursed.*

But turn to another side. Here we see that the first sparks of European imagination, that the first attempts of poetry, of literature, that the first intellectual gratifications which Europe tasted in emerging from barbarism, sprung up under the protection, under the wings, of feudalism. It was in the baronial hall that they were born, and cherished, and protected. It is to the feudal times that we trace back the earliest literary monuments of England, France, and Germany, the earliest intellectual enjoyments of modern Europe.

As a set-off to this, if we question history respecting the influence of feudalism upon the social system, its reply is, though still in accordance with our conjectures, that the feudal system has everywhere opposed not only the establishment of general order, but at the same time the extension of general liberty. Under whatever point of view we consider the progress of society, the feudal system always appears as an obstacle in its way.* Hence, from the earliest existence of feudalism, the two powers which have been the prime movers in the progress of order and liberty—monarchical power on the one hand, and popular power on the other—that is to say, the king and the people—have both attacked it, and struggled against it continually. What few attempts were made at different periods to regulate it, to impart to it somewhat of a legal, a general character—as was done in England, by William the Conqueror and his sons; in France, by St. Louis; and by several of the German emperors—all these endeavors, all these attempts failed. The very nature itself of feudality is opposed to order and legality. In the last century, some writers of talent attempted to dress out feudalism as a social system; they endeavored to make it appear a legitimate, well-ordered, progressive state of society, and represented it as a golden age. Ask them, however, where it existed: summon them to assign it a locality, and a time, and they will be found wanting. It is a Utopia without date, a drama, for which we find, in the past, neither theatre nor actors. The cause of this error is noways difficult to discover; and it accounts as well for the error of the opposite class, who cannot pronounce the name of feudalism without coupling to it an absolute anathema. Both these parties have looked at it, as the two knights did at the statue of Janus, only on one side. They have not considered the two different points of view from which feudalism may be surveyed. They do not distinguish, on one hand, its influence upon the progress of the individual man, upon his feelings, his faculties, his disposition and passions; nor, on the other, its influence upon the social condition. One party could not imagine that a social system in which were to be found so many noble sentiments, so many virtues, in which were seen sprouting forth the earliest buds of literature and science; in which manners became not only more refined, but attained a certain elevation and grandeur; in such a system they could not imagine that the evil was so great or so fatal as it was made to appear. The other party, seeing but the misery which feudalism inflicted on the great body of the people—the obstacles which it opposed to the establishment of order and liberty—would not believe that it could produce noble characters, great virtues, or any improvement whatsoever. Both these parties have misunderstood the twofold principle of civilization; they have not been aware that it consists of two movements, one of which for a time may advance independently of the other, although after a lapse of centuries, and perhaps a long series of events, they must at last reciprocally recall and bring forward each other.

To conclude, feudalism, in its character and influence, was just what its nature would lead us to expect. Individualism, the energy of personal existence, was the prevailing principle among the vanquishers of the Roman world; and the development of the individual man, of his mind, and faculties, might above all be expected to result from the social system, founded by them and for them. That which man himself carries into a social system, his intellectual moral disposition at the time he enters it, has a powerful influence upon the situation in which he establishes himself—upon all around him. This situation in its turn reacts upon his dispositions, strengthens and improves them. The individual prevailed in German society; and the influence of the feudal system, the offspring of German society, displayed itself in the improvement and advance of the individual. We shall find the same fact to recur in the other elements of our civilization: they all hold faithful to their original principle; they have advanced and pushed the world in that same road by which they first entered. The subject of the next lecture—the history of the Church, and its influence upon European civilization, from the fifth to the twelfth century—will furnish us with a new and striking example of this fact.*

LECTURE V.: THE CHURCH.

Having investigated the nature and influence of the feudal system, I shall take the Christian church, from the fifth to the twelfth century, as the subject of the present lecture. I say the Christian church, because, as I have observed once before, it is not about Christianity itself, Christianity as a religious system, that I shall occupy your attention, but the Church as an ecclesiastical society—the Christian hierarchy.

This society was almost completely organized before the close of the fifth century. Not that it has not undergone many and important changes since that period, but from this time the Church, considered as a corporation, as the government of the Christian world, may be said to have attained a complete and independent existence.*

A single glance will be sufficient to convince us that there existed, in the fifth century, an immense difference between the state of the Church and that of the other elements of European civilization. You will remember that I have pointed out, as primary elements of our civilization, the municipal system, the feudal system, monarchy, and the Church. The municipal system, in the fifth century, was no more than a fragment of the Roman empire, a shadow without life, or definite form. The feudal system was still a chaos. Monarchy existed only in name. All the civil elements of modern society were either in their decline or infancy. The Church alone possessed youth and vigor; she alone possessed at the same time a definite form, with activity and strength; she alone possessed at once movement and order, energy and system, that is to say, the two greatest means of influence. Is it not, let me ask you, by mental vigor, by intellectual movement on one side, and by order and discipline on the other, that all institutions acquire their power and influence over society? The Church, moreover, awakened attention to, and agitated all the great questions which interest man; she busied herself with all the great problems of his nature, with all he had to hope or fear for futurity. Hence her influence upon modern civilization has been so powerful—more powerful, perhaps, than its most violent adversaries, or its most zealous defenders, have supposed. They, eager to advance or abuse her, have only regarded the Church in a contentious point of view; and with that contracted spirit which controversy engenders, how could they do her justice, or grasp the full scope of her sway?

To us, the Church, in the fifth century, appears as an organized and independent society, interposed between the masters of the world, the sovereigns, the possessors of temporal power, and the people, serving as a connecting link between them, and exercising its influence over all. To know and completely understand its agency, then, we must consider it from three different points of view: we must consider it first in itself—we must see what it really was, what was its internal constitution, what the principles which there bore sway, what its nature. We must next consider it in its relations with temporal rulers—kings, lords, and others; and, finally, in its relations with the people. And when by this threefold investigation we have formed a complete picture of the Church, of its principles, its situation, and the influence which it exercised, we will verify this picture by history; we will see whether facts, whether what we properly call events, from the fifth to the twelfth century, agree with the conclusions which our threefold examination of the Church, of its own nature, of its relations with the masters of the world, and with the people, had previously led us to come to respecting it.

Let us first consider the Church in itself, its internal condition, its own nature.

The first, and perhaps the most important fact that demands our attention here, is its existence; the existence of a government of religion, of a priesthood, of an ecclesiastical corporation.

In the opinion of many enlightened persons, the very notion of a religious corporation, of a priesthood, of a government of religion, is absurd. They believe that a religion, whose object is the establishment of a clerical body, of a priesthood legally constituted, in short, of a government of religion, must exercise, upon the whole, an influence more dangerous than useful. In their opinion religion is a matter purely individual betwixt man and God; and that whenever religion loses this character, whenever an exterior authority interferes between the individual and the object of his religious belief, that is, between him and God, religion is corrupted, and society in danger.

It will not do to pass by this question without taking a deeper view of it. In order to know what has been the influence of the Christian church, we must know what ought to be, from the nature of the institution itself, the influence of a church, the influence of a priesthood. To judge of this influence we must inquire more especially whether religion is, in fact, purely individual; whether it excites and gives birth to nothing beyond this intimate relation between each individual and God; or whether it does not, in fact, necessarily become a source of new relations between man and man, and so necessarily lead to the formation of a religious society, and from that to a government of this society.

If we reduce religion to what is properly called religious feeling—to that feeling which, though very real, is somewhat vague, somewhat uncertain in its object, and which we can scarcely characterize but by naming it—to that feeling which addresses itself at one time to exterior nature, at another to the inmost recesses of the soul; to-day to the imagination, to-morrow to the mysteries of the future; which wanders everywhere, and settles nowhere; which, in a word, exhausts both the world of matter and of fancy in search of a resting-place, and yet finds none— if we reduce religion to this feeling; then, it would seem, it may remain purely individual. Such a feeling may give rise to a passing association; it may, it will indeed, find a pleasure in sympathy; it will feed upon it, it will be strengthened by it; but its fluctuating and doubtful character will prevent its becoming the principle of permanent and extensive association; will prevent it from accommodating itself to any system of precepts, of discipline, of forms; will prevent it, in a word, from giving birth to a society, to a religious government.

But either I have strangely deceived myself, or this religious feeling does not comprehend the whole religious nature of man. Religion, in my opinion, is quite another thing, and infinitely more comprehensive than this.

Joined to the destinies and nature of man, there are a number of problems whose solution we cannot work out in the present life; these, though connected with an order of things strange and foreign to the world around us, and apparently beyond the reach of human faculties, do not the less invincibly torment the soul of man, part of whose nature it seems to be, anxiously to desire and struggle for the clearing up of the mystery in which they are involved. The solution of these problems,—the creeds and dogmas which contain it, or at least are supposed to contain it—such is the first object, the first source, of religion.

Another road brings us to the same point. To those among us who have made some progress in the study of moral philosophy, it is now, I presume, become sufficiently evident, that morality may exist independently of religious ideas; that the distinction between moral good and moral evil, the obligation to avoid evil and to cleave to that which is good, are laws as much acknowledged by man, in his proper nature, as the laws of logic; and which spring as much from a principle within him, as in his actual life they find their application. But granting these truths to be proved, yielding up to morality its independence, a question naturally arises in the human mind: whence cometh morality, whither doth it lead? This obligation to do good, which exists of itself, is it a fact standing by itself, without author, without aim? Doth it not conceal, or rather doth it not reveal to man, an origin, a destiny, reaching beyond this world? By this question, which rises spontaneously and inevitably, morality, in its turn, leads man to the porch of religion, and opens to him a sphere from which he has not borrowed it.

Thus on one side the problems of our nature, on the other, the necessity of seeking a sanction, an origin, an aim, for morality, open to us fruitful and certain sources of religion. Thus it presents itself before us under many other aspects besides that of a simple feeling such as I have described. It presents itself as an assemblage:

First, of doctrines called into existence by the problems which man finds in himself.

Secondly, of precepts which correspond with these doctrines, and give to natural morality a signification and sanction.

Thirdly, and lastly, of promises which address themselves to the hopes of humanity respecting futurity.

This is truly what constitutes religion. This is really what it is at bottom, and not a mere form of sensibility, a sally of the imagination, a species of poetry.

Religion thus brought back to its true element, to its essence, no longer appears as an affair purely individual, but as a powerful and fruitful principle of association. Would you regard it as a system of opinions, of dogmas? The answer is, truth belongs to no one; it is universal, absolute; all men are prone to seek it, to profess it in common. Would you rest upon the precepts which are associated with the doctrines? The reply is, law obligatory upon one is obligatory upon all—man is bound to promulgate it, to bring all under its authority. It is the same with respect to the promises which religion makes as the rewards of obedience to its faith and its precepts; it is necessary they should be spread, and that these fruits of religion should be offered to all. From the essential elements of religion then is seen to spring up a religious society; and it springs from them so infallibly, that the word which expresses the social feeling with the greatest energy, which expresses our invincible desire to propagate ideas, to extend society, is proselytism—a term particularly applied to religious creeds, to which it seems almost exclusively consecrated. A religious society once formed, when a certain number of men are joined together by the same religious opinions and belief, yield obedience to the same law of religious precepts, and are inspired with the same religious hopes, needs a government. No society can exist a week, no, not even an hour, without a government. At the very instant in which a society is formed, by the very act of its formation it calls forth a government, which proclaims the common truth that holds them together, which promulgates and maintains the precepts that this truth may be expected to bring forth. That a religious society, like all others requires a controlling power, a government, is implied in the very fact that a society exists.

And not only is a government necessary, but it naturally arises of itself. I cannot spare much time to show how governments rise and become established in society in general. I shall only remark that, when matters are left to take their natural course, when no exterior force is applied to drive them from their usual route, power will fall into the hands of the most capable, of the most worthy, into the hands of those who will lead society on its way. Are there thoughts of a military expedition? the bravest will have the command. Is society anxious about some discovery, some learned enterprise? the most skilful will be sought for. The same will take place in all other matters. Let but the common order of things be observed, let the natural inequality of men freely display itself, and each will find the station that he is best fitted to fill. So as regards religion, men will be found no more equal in talents, in abilities, and in power, than they are in other matters: this man has a more striking method than others in proclaiming the doctrines of religion and making converts; another has more power in enforcing religious precepts; a third may excel in exciting religious hopes and emotions, and keeping the soul in a devout and holy frame. The same inequality of faculties and of influence, which gives rise to power in civil society, will be found to exist in religious society. Missionaries, like generals, go forth to conquer. So that while, on the one hand, religious government naturally flows from the nature of religious society, it as naturally develops itself, on the other, by the simple effect of human faculties, and their unequal distribution.

Thus the moment that religion takes possession of a man, a religious society begins to be formed; and the moment this religious society appears it gives birth to a government.

A grave objection, however, here presents itself: in this case there is nothing to command, nothing to impose; no kind of force can here be legitimate. There is no place for government, because here the most perfect liberty ought to prevail.

Be it so. But is it not forming a gross and degrading idea of government to suppose that it resides only, to suppose that it resides chiefly, in the force which it exercises to make itself obeyed, in its coercive element?

Let us quit religion for a moment, and turn to civil governments. Trace with me, I beseech you, the simple march of circumstances. Society exists. Something is to be done, no matter what, in its name and for its interests; a law has to be executed, some measure to be adopted, a judgment to be pronounced. Now, certainly, there is a proper method of supplying these social wants; there is a proper law to make, a proper measure to adopt, a proper judgment to pronounce. Whatever may be the matter in hand, whatever may be the interest in question, there is, upon every occasion, a truth which must be discovered, and which ought to decide the matter, and govern the conduct to be adopted.

The first business of government is to seek this truth, is to discover what is just, reasonable, and suitable to society. When this is found, it is proclaimed: the next business is to introduce it to the public mind; to get it approved by the men upon whom it is to act; to persuade them that it is reasonable. In all this is there anything coercive? Not at all. Suppose now that the truth which ought to decide upon the affair, no matter what; suppose, I say, that the truth being found and proclaimed, all understandings should be at once convinced; all wills at once determined; that all should acknowledge that the government was right, and obey it spontaneously. There is nothing yet of compulsion, no occasion for the employment of force. Does it follow then that a government does not exist? Is there nothing of government in all this? To be sure there is a government, and it has accomplished its task. Compulsion appears not till the resistance of individuals calls for it—till the idea, the decision which authority has adopted, fails to obtain the approbation or the voluntary submission of all. Then government employs force to make itself obeyed. This is a necessary consequence of human imperfection; an imperfection which resides as well in power as in society. There is no way of entirely avoiding this; civil governments will always be obliged to have recourse, to a certain degree, to compulsion. Still it is evident they are not made up of compulsion, because, whenever they can, they are glad to do without it, to the great blessing of all; and their highest point of perfection is to be able to discard it, and to trust to means purely moral, to their influence upon the understanding: so that, in proportion as government can dispense with compulsion and force, the more faithful it is to its true nature, and the better it fulfils the purpose for which it is sent. This is not to shrink, this is not to give way, as people commonly cry out; it is merely acting in a different manner, in a manner much more general and powerful. Those governments which employ the most compulsion perform much less than those which scarcely ever have recourse to it. Government, by addressing itself to the understanding, by engaging the free-will of its subjects, by acting by means purely intellectual, instead of contracting, expands and elevates itself; it is then that it accomplishes most, and attains to the grandest objects. On the contrary, it is when government is obliged to be constantly employing its physical arm that it becomes weak and restrained—that it does little, and does that little badly.

The essence of government then by no means resides in compulsion, in the exercise of brute force; it consists more especially of a system of means and powers, conceived for the purpose of discovering upon all occasions what is best to be done; for the purpose of discovering the truth which by right ought to govern society, for the purpose of persuading all men to acknowledge this truth, to adopt and respect it willingly and freely. Thus I think I have shown that the necessity for, and the existence of a government, are very conceivable, even though there should be no room for compulsion, even though it should be absolutely forbidden.

This is exactly the case in the government of religious society. There is no doubt but compulsion is here strictly forbidden; there can be no doubt, as its only territory is the conscience of man, but that every species of force must be illegal, whatever may be the end designed. But government does not exist the less on this account. It still has to perform all the duties which we have just now enumerated. It is incumbent upon it to seek out the religious doctrines which resolve the problems of human destiny; or, if a general system of faith beforehand exists, in which these problems are already resolved, it will be its duty to discover and set forth its consequences in each particular case. It will be its duty to promulgate and maintain the precepts which correspond to its doctrines. It will be its duty to preach them, to teach them, and, if society wanders from them, to bring it back again to the right path. No compulsion; but the investigation, the preaching, the teaching of religious truths; the administering to religious wants; admonishing;

censuring; this is the task which religious government has to perform. Suppress all force and coercion as much as you desire, still you will see all the essential questions connected with the organization of a government present themselves before you, and demand a solution. The question, for example, whether a body of religious magistrates is necessary, or whether it is possible to trust to the religious inspiration of individuals? This question, which is a subject of debate between most religious societies and that of the Quakers, will always exist, it must always remain a matter of discussion. Again, granting a body of religious magistrates to be necessary, the question arises whether a system of equality is to be preferred, or an hierarchal constitution—a graduated series of powers? This question will not cease because you take from the ecclesiastical magistrates, whatever they may be, all means of compulsion. Instead then of dissolving religious society in order to have the right to destroy religious government, it must be acknowledged that religious society forms itself naturally, that religious government flows no less naturally from religious society, and that the problem to be solved is on what conditions this government ought to exist, on what it is based, what are its principles, what the conditions of its legitimacy? This is the investigation which the existence of religious government, as of all others, compels us to undertake.

The conditions of legitimacy are the same in the government of a religious society as in all others. They may be reduced to two: the first is, that authority should be placed and constantly remain, as effectually at least as the imperfection of all human affairs will permit, in the hands of the best, the most capable; so that the legitimate superiority, which lies scattered in various parts of society, may be thereby drawn out, collected, and delegated to discover the social law—to exercise its authority. The second is, that the authority thus legitimately constituted should respect the legitimate liberties of those over whom it is called to govern. A good system for the formation and organization of authority, a good system of securities for liberty, are the two conditions in which the goodness of government in general resides, whether civil or religious. And it is by this standard that all governments should be judged.

Instead, then, of reproaching the Church, the government of the Christian world, with its existence, let us examine how it was constituted, and see whether its principles correspond with the two essential conditions of all good government.

Let us examine the Church in this twofold point of view.

In the first place, with regard to the formation and transmission of authority in the Church, there is a word, which has often been made use of, which I wish to get rid of altogether. I mean the word caste. This word has been too frequently applied to the Christian clergy, but its application to that body is both improper and unjust. The idea of hereditary right is inherent to the idea of caste. In every part of the world, in every country in which the system of caste has prevailed—in Egypt, in India—from the earliest time to the present day—you will find that castes have been everywhere essentially hereditary: they are, in fact, the transmission of the same rank and condition, of the same power, from father to son. Now where there is no inheritance there is no caste, but a corporation. The esprit de corps, or that certain degree of love and interest which every individual of an order feels towards it as a whole, as well as towards all its members, has its inconveniences, but differs very essentially from the spirit of caste. The celibacy of the clergy of itself renders the application of this term to the Christian church altogether improper.

The important consequences of this distinction cannot have escaped you. To the system of castes, to the circumstance of inheritance, certain peculiar privileges are necessarily attached; the very definition of caste implies this. Where the same functions, the same powers become hereditary in the same families, it is evident that they possess peculiar privileges, which none can acquire independently of birth. This is indeed exactly what has taken place wherever the religious government has fallen into the hands of a caste; it has become a matter of privilege; all were shut out from it but those who belonged to the families of the caste. Now nothing like this is found in the Christian church. Not only is the Church entirely free from this fault, but she has constantly maintained the principle, that all men, whatever their origin, are equally privileged to enter her ranks, to fill her highest offices, to enjoy her proudest dignities. The ecclesiastical career, particularly from the fifth to the twelfth century, was open to all. The Church was recruited from all ranks of society, from the lower as well as the higher, indeed, most frequently from the lower. When all around her fell under the tyranny of privilege, she alone maintained the principle of equality, of competition and emulation; she alone called the superior of all classes to the possession of power. This is the first great consequence which naturally flowed from the fact that the Church was a corporation and not a caste.

I will show you a second. It is the inherent nature of all castes to possess a degree of immobility. This assertion requires no proof. Turn over the pages of history, and you will find that wherever the tyranny of castes has predominated, society, whether religious or political, has universally become sluggish and torpid. A dread of improvement was certainly introduced at a certain epoch, and up to a certain point, into the Christian church. But whatever regret this may cost us, it cannot be said that this feeling ever generally prevailed. It cannot be said that the Christian church ever remained inactive and stationary. For a long course of centuries she was always in motion; at one time pushed forward by her opponents without, at others driven on by an inward impulse—by the desire of reform, or of interior development. The Church, indeed, taken as a whole, has been constantly changing—constantly advancing—her history is diversified and progressive. Can it be doubted that she was indebted for this to the admission of all classes to the priestly offices, to the continual filling up of her ranks, upon a principle of equality, by which a stream of young and vigorous blood was ever flowing into her veins, keeping her unceasingly active and stirring, and defending her from the reproach of apathy and immobility which might otherwise have triumphed over her?

But how did the Church, in admitting all classes to power, satisfy herself that they had the right to be so admitted? How did she discover and proceed in taking from the bosom of society, the legitimate superiorities who should have a share in her government? In the Church two principles were in full vigor: first, the election of the inferior by the superior, which, in fact, was nothing more than choice or nomination; secondly, the election of the superior by the subordinates, or election properly so called, and such as we conceive to be election in the present day.

The ordination of priests, for example, the power of raising a man to the priestly office, rested solely with the superior. He alone made choice of the candidate for holy orders. The case was the same in the collation to certain ecclesiastical benefices,* such as those attached to feudal grants, and some others; it was the superior whether king, pope, or lord, who nominated to the benefice. In other cases the true principle of election prevailed. The bishops had been, for a long time, and were still, often, in the period under consideration, elected by the inferior clergy; even the people sometimes took part in them. In monasteries the abbot was elected by the monks. At Rome, the pope was elected by the college of cardinals; and, at an earlier date, even all the Roman clergy had a voice in his election. You may here clearly observe, then, the two principles, the choice of the inferior by the superior, and the election of the superior by the subordinates; which were admitted and acted upon in the Church, particularly at the period which now engages our attention. It was by one of these two means that men were appointed to the various offices in the Church, or obtained any portion of ecclesiastical authority.

These two principles were not only in operation at the same time, but being altogether opposite in their nature, a constant struggle prevailed between them. After a strife for centuries, after many vicissitudes, the nomination of the inferior by the superior gained the day in the Christian church. Yet, from the fifth to the twelfth century, the opposite principle, the election of the superior by the subordinates, continued generally to prevail.

We must not be astonished at the co-existence of these two opposite principles. If we look at society in general, at the common course of affairs, at the manner in which authority is there transmitted, we shall find that this transmission is sometimes effected by one of these modes, and sometimes the other. The Church did not invent them, she found them in the providential government of human things, and borrowed them from it. There is somewhat of truth, of utility, in both. Their combination would often prove the best mode of discovering legitimate power. It is a great misfortune, in my opinion, that only one of them, the choice of the inferior by the superior, should have been victorious in the Church. The second, however, was never entirely banished, but under various names, with more or less success, has reappeared in every epoch, with at least sufficient force to protest against, and interrupt, prescription.*

The Christian church, at the period of which we are speaking, derived an immense force from its respect for equality and the various kinds of legitimate superiority. It was the most popular society of the time—the most accessible; it alone opened its arms to all the talents, to all the ambitiously noble of our race. To this, above all, it owed its greatness, at least certainly much more than to its riches, and the illegitimate means which it but too often employed.

With regard to the second condition of a good government, namely, a respect for liberty, that of the Church leaves much to be desired.

Two bad principles here met together. One avowed, forming part and parcel, as it were, of the doctrines of the Church; the other, in no way a legitimate consequence of her doctrines, was introduced into her bosom by human weakness.

The first was a denial of the rights of individual reason—the claim of transmitting points of faith from the highest authority, downwards, throughout the whole religious body, without allowing to any one the right of examining them for himself.* But it was more easy to lay this down as a principle than to carry it out in practice; and the reason is obvious, for a conviction cannot enter into the human mind unless the human mind first opens the door to it; it cannot enter by force. In whatever way it may present itself, whatever name it may invoke, reason looks to it, and if it forces an entrance, it is because reason is satisfied. Thus individual reason has always continued to exist, and under whatever name it may have been disguised, has always considered and reflected upon the ideas which have been attempted to be forced upon it. Still, however, it must be admitted but as too true, that reason often becomes impaired; that she loses her power, becomes mutilated and contracted—that she may be brought not only to make a sorry use of her faculties, but to make a more limited use of them than she ought to do. Such indeed was the effect of the bad principle which crept into the Church, but with regard to the practical and complete operation of this principle, it never came into full force—it was impossible it ever should.

The second vicious principle was the right of compulsion assumed by the Romish church; a right, however, contrary to the very nature and spirit of religious society, to the origin of the Church itself, and to its primitive maxims. A right, too, disputed by some of the most illustrious fathers of the Church—by St. Ambrose, St. Hilary, St. Martin—but which, nevertheless, prevailed and became an important feature in its history. The right it assumed of forcing belief, if these two words can stand together, or of punishing faith physically, of persecuting heresy, that is to say, a contempt for the legitimate liberty of human thought, was an error which found its way into the Romish church before the beginning of the fifth century, and has in the end cost her very dear.*

If then we consider the state of the Church with regard to the liberty of its members, we must confess that its principles in this respect were less legitimate, less salutary, than those which presided at the rise and formation of ecclesiastical power. It must not, however, be supposed, that a bad principle radically vitiates an institution; nor even that it does it all the mischief of which it is pregnant. Nothing tortures history more than logic. No sooner does the human mind seize upon an idea, than it draws from it all its possible consequences; makes it produce, in imagination, all that it would in reality be capable of producing, and then pictures it in history with all the extravagant additions which itself has conjured up. This, however, is nothing like the truth. Events are not so prompt in their consequences, as the human mind in its deductions. There is in all things a mixture of good and evil, so profound, so inseparable, that, in whatever part you penetrate, if even you descend to the lowest elements of society, or into the soul itself, you will there find these two principles dwelling together, developing themselves side by side, perpetually struggling and quarrelling with each other, but neither of them ever obtaining a complete victory, or absolutely destroying its fellow. Human nature never reaches to the extreme either of good or evil. It passes, without ceasing, from one to the other; it recovers itself at the moment when it seems lost for ever. It slips and loses ground at the moment when it seems to have assumed the firmest position.

We again discover here that character of discordance, of diversity, of strife, to which I formerly called your attention, as the fundamental character of European civilization. Besides this, there is another general fact which characterizes the government of the Church, which we must not pass over without notice. In the present day, when the idea of government presents itself to our mind, we know, of whatever kind it may be, that it will scarcely pretend to any authority beyond the outward actions of men, beyond the civil relations between man and man. Governments do not profess to carry their rule further than this. With regard to human thought, to the human conscience, to the intellectual powers of man; with regard to individual opinions, to private morals,—with these they do not interfere: this would be to invade the domain of liberty.

The Christian church did, and was bent upon doing, exactly the contrary. What she undertook to govern was the human thought, human liberty, private morals, individual opinions. She did not draw up a code like ours, which took account only of those crimes that are at the same time offensive to morals and dangerous to society, punishing them only when, and because, they bore this twofold character; but prepared a catalogue of all those actions, criminal more particularly in a moral point of view, and punished them all under the name of sins. Her aim was their entire suppression. In a word, the government of the Church did not, like our modern governments, direct her attention to the outward man, or to the purely civil relations of men among themselves; she addressed herself to the inward man, to the thought, to the conscience; in fact, to that which of all things is most hidden and secure, most free, and which spurns the least restraint. The Church, then, by the very nature of its undertaking, combined with the nature of some of the principles upon which its government was founded, stood in great peril of falling into tyranny; of an illegitimate employment of force. In the mean time, this force was encountered by a resistance within the Church itself, which it could never overcome. Human thought and liberty, however fettered, however confined for room and space in which to exercise their faculties, oppose with so much energy every attempt to enslave them, that their reaction makes even despotism itself to yield, and give up something every moment. This took place in the very bosom of the Christian church. We have seen heresy proscribed—the right of free inquiry condemned; a contempt shown for individual reason, the principle of the imperative transmission of doctrines by human authority established. And yet where can we find a society in which individual reason more boldly developed itself than in the Church? What are sects and heresies, if not the fruit of individual opinions? These sects, these heresies, all these oppositions which arose in the Christian church, are the most decisive proof of the life and moral activity which reigned within her: a life stormy, painful, sown with perils, with errors and crimes—yet splendid and mighty, and which has given place to the noblest developments of intelligence and mind.* But leaving the opposition, and looking to the ecclesiastical government itself—how does the case stand here? You will find it constituted, you will find it acting, in a manner quite opposite to what you would expect from some of its principles. It denies the right of inquiry, it wishes to deprive individual reason of its liberty; yet it appeals to reason incessantly; practical liberty actually predominates in its affairs. What are its institutions, its means of action? Provincial councils, national councils, general councils;† a perpetual correspondence, a perpetual publication of letters, of admonitions, of writings. No government ever went so far in discussions and open deliberations. One might fancy one's self in the midst of the philosophical schools of Greece. But it was not here a mere discussion, it was not a simple search after truth that here occupied the attention; it was questions of authority, of measures to be taken, of decrees to be drawn up, in short, the business of a government. Such indeed was the energy of intellectual life in the bosom of this government, that it became its predominant, universal character; to this all others gave way; and that which shone forth from all its parts, was the exercise of reason and liberty.*

I am far, notwithstanding all this, from believing that the vicious principles, which I have endeavored to explain, and which, in my opinion, existed in the Christian church, existed there without producing any effect. In the period now under review, they already bore very bitter fruits; at a later period they bore others still more bitter; still they did not produce all the evils which might have been expected, they did not choke the good which sprang up in the same soil. Such was the Church considered in itself, in its interior, in its own nature.

Let us now consider it in its relations with sovereigns, with the holders of temporal authority. This is the second point of view in which I have promised to consider it.

When at the fall of the western empire, when, instead of the ancient Roman government, under which the Church had been born, under which she had grown up, with which she had common habits and old connections, she found herself surrounded by barbarian kings, by barbarian chieftains, wandering from place to place, or shut up in their castles, with whom she had nothing in common, between whom and her there was as yet no tie—neither traditions, nor creeds, nor feelings; her danger appeared great, and her fears were equally so.

One only idea became predominant in the Church; it was to take possessions of these new-comers—to convert them. The relations of the Church with the barbarians had, at first, scarcely any other aim.*

To gain these barbarians, the most effective means seemed to be to dazzle their senses and work upon their imagination. Thus it came to pass that the number, pomp, and variety of religious ceremonies were at this epoch wonderfully increased. The ancient chronicles particularly show, that it was principally in this way that the Church worked upon the barbarians. She converted them by grand spectacles.†

But even when they had become settled and converted, even after the growth of some common ties between them, the danger of the Church was not over. The brutality, the unthinking, the unreflecting character of the barbarians were so great, that the new faith, the new feelings with which they had been inspired, exercised but a very slight empire over them. When every part of society fell a prey to violence, the Church could scarcely hope altogether to escape. To save herself she announced a principle, which had already been set up, though but very vaguely, under the empire; the separation of spiritual and temporal power, and their mutual independence. It was by the aid of this principle that the Church dwelt freely by the side of the barbarians; she maintained that force had no authority over religious belief, hopes, or promises, and that the spiritual and temporal worlds are completely distinct.

You cannot fail to see at once the beneficial consequences which have resulted from this principle. Independently of the temporary service it was of to the Church, it has had the inestimable effect of founding in justice the separation of the two authorities, of preventing one from controlling the other. In addition to this, the Church, by asserting the independence of the intellectual world, in its collective form, prepared the independence of the intellectual world in individuals—the independence of thought. The Church declared that the system of religious belief could not be brought under the yoke of force, and each individual has been led to hold the same language for himself. The principle of free inquiry, the liberty of individual thought, is exactly the same as that of the independence of the spiritual authority in general, with regard to temporal power.

The desire for liberty, unfortunately, is but a step from the desire for power. The Church soon passed from one to the other. When she had established her independence, it was in accordance with the natural course of ambition that she should attempt to raise her spiritual authority above temporal authority. We must not, however, suppose that this claim had no other origin than the weaknesses of humanity; some of these are very profound, and it is of importance that they should be known.

When liberty prevails in the intellectual world, when the thoughts and consciences of men are not enthralled by a power which calls in question their right of deliberating, of deciding, and employs its authority against them; when there is no visible constituted spiritual government laying claim to the right of dictating opinions; in such circumstances, the idea of the domination of the spiritual order over the temporal could scarcely spring up. Such is very nearly the present state of the world. But when there exists, as there did in the tenth century, a government of the spiritual order; when the human thought and conscience are subject to certain laws, to certain institutions, to certain authorities, which have arrogated to themselves the right to govern, to constrain them; in short, when spiritual authority is established, when it has effectively taken possession, in the name of right and power, of the human reason and conscience, it is natural that it should go on to assume a domination over the temporal order; that it should argue: "What! have I a right, have I an authority over that which is most elevated, most independent in man— over his thoughts, over his interior will, over his conscience; and have I not a right over his exterior, his temporal and material interests? Am I the interpreter of divine justice and truth, and yet not able to regulate the affairs of this world according to justice and truth?"*

The force of this reasoning shows that the spiritual order had a natural tendency to encroach on the temporal. This tendency was increased by the fact, that the spiritual order, at this time, comprised all the intelligence of the age, every possible development of the human mind. There was but one science, theology; but one spiritual order, the theological: all the other sciences, rhetoric, arithmetic, and even music, centered in theology.

The spiritual power, finding itself thus in possession of all the intelligence of the age, at the head of all intellectual activity, was naturally enough led to arrogate to itself the general government of the world.

A second cause, which very much favored its views, was the dreadful state of the temporal order, the violence and iniquity which prevailed in all temporal governments.

For some centuries past men might speak, with a degree of confidence, of temporal power; but temporal power, at the epoch of which we are speaking, was mere brutal force, a system of rapine and violence. The Church, however imperfect might be her notions of morality and justice, was infinitely superior to a temporal government such as this; and the cry of the people continually urged her to take its place.

When a pope or bishop proclaimed that a sovereign had lost his rights, that his subjects were released from their oath of fidelity, this interference, though undoubtedly liable to the greatest abuses, was often, in the particular case to which it was directed, just and salutary. It generally holds, indeed, that where liberty is wanting, religion, in a great measure, supplies its place. In the tenth century, the oppressed nations were not in a state to protect themselves, to defend their rights against civil violence—religion, in the name of Heaven, placed itself between them. This is one of the causes which most contributed to the success of the usurpations of the Church. There is a third cause, which, in my opinion, has not been sufficiently noticed. This is the manifold character and situation of the leaders of the Church; the variety of aspects under which they appeared in society. On one side they were prelates, members of the ecclesiastical order, a portion of the spiritual power, and as such independent: on the other, they were vassals, and by this title formed one of the links of civil feudalism. But this was not all: besides being vassals, they were also subjects. Something similar to the ancient relations in which the bishops and clergy had stood towards the Roman emperors now existed between the clergy and the barbarian sovereigns. A series of causes, which it would be tedious to detail, had brought the bishops to look upon the barbarian kings, to a certain degree, as the successors of the Roman emperors, and to attribute to them the same rights. The heads of the clergy then had a threefold character: first, they were ecclesiastics, and as such held to the performance of certain duties; secondly, they were feudal vassals, with the rights and obligations of such; thirdly, they were mere subjects, and as such bound to render obedience to an absolute sovereign. Observe the necessary consequence of this. The temporal sovereigns, no whit less covetous, no whit less ambitious than the bishops, frequently made use of their temporal power, as superiors or sovereigns, to attack the independence of the Church, to usurp the right of collating to benefices, of nominating to bishoprics, and so on. On the other side, the bishops often sheltered themselves under their spiritual independence to refuse the performance of their obligations as vassals and subjects; so that on both sides there was an inevitable tendency to trespass on the rights of the other; on the side of the sovereigns, to destroy spiritual independence; on the side of the heads of the Church, to make their spiritual independence the means of universal dominion.

This result showed itself sufficiently plain in events well known to you all; in the quarrel respecting investitures;* in the struggle between the Holy See and the empire. The threefold character of the heads of the Church, and the difficulty of preventing them from trespassing on one another, was the real cause of the uncertainty and strife of all its pretensions.

Finally, the Church had a third connection with the sovereigns, and it was to her the most disastrous and fatal. She laid claim to the right of coercion, to the right of restraining and punishing heresy. But she had no means by which to do this; she had no physical force at her disposal: when she had condemned the heretic, she was without the power to carry her sentence into execution. What was the consequence? She called to her aid the secular arm; she had to borrow the power of the civil authority as the means of compulsion. To what a wretched shift was she thus driven by the adoption of the wicked and detestable principles of coercion and persecution!

I must stop here. There is not sufficient time for us to finish our investigation of the Church. We have still to consider its relation with the people, the principles which prevailed in its intercourse with them, and what consequences resulted from its bearing upon civilization in general. I shall afterwards endeavor to confirm by history, by facts, by what befell the Church from the fifth to the twelfth century, the inductions which we have drawn from the nature of her institutions and principles.*

LECTURE VI.: THE CHURCH.

In the present lecture we shall conclude our inquiries respecting the state of the Church. In the last, I stated that I should place it before you in three principal points of view: first, in itself—in its interior constitution and nature, as a distinct and independent society; secondly, in its relations with sovereigns, with temporal power; thirdly, in its relations with the people. Having then been able to accomplish no more than the first two parts of my task, it remains for me to-day to place before you the Church in its relations with the people. I shall endeavor, after I have done this, to sum up this threefold examination, and to give a general judgment respecting the influence of the Church from the fifth to the twelfth century; finally, I shall close this part of my subject by verifying my statements by an appeal to facts, by an examination of the history of the Church during this period.

You will easily understand that, in speaking of the relations of the Church with the people, I shall be obliged to confine myself to very general views. It is impossible that I should enter into a detail of the practices of the Church, or recount the daily intercourse of the clergy with their charge. It is the prevailing principles, and the great effects of the system and conduct of the Church towards the body of Christians, that I shall endeavor to bring before you.

A striking feature, and, I am bound to say, a radical vice in the relations of the Church with the people, was the separation of the governors and the governed which left the governed without any influence upon their government, which established the independence of the clergy with respect to the general body of Christians.

It would seem as if this evil was called forth by the state of man and society, for it was introduced into the Christian Church at a very early period. The separation of the clergy and the people was not altogether perfected at the time of which we are speaking; there were certain occasions—the election of bishops, for example—upon which the people, at least sometimes, took part in church government. This interference, however, became weaker and weaker, as well as more rare; even in the second century it had begun rapidly and visibly to decline. Indeed, the tendency of the Church to detach itself from the rest of society, the establishment of the independence of the clergy, forms, to a great extent, the history of the Church from its very cradle.

It is impossible to disguise the fact, that from this circumstance sprang the greater number of abuses, which, from this period, cost the Church so dear; as well as many others which entered into her system in after-times. We must not, however, impute all its faults to this principle, nor must we regard this tendency to isolation as peculiar to the Christian clergy. There is in the very nature of religious society a powerful inclination to elevate the governors above the governed; to regard them as something distinct, something divine. This is the effect of the mission with which they are charged; of the character in which they appear before the people. This effect, however, is more hurtful in a religious society than in any other. For with what do they pretend to interfere? With the reason and conscience and future destiny of man: that is to say, with that which is the closest locked up; with that which is most strictly individual, with that which is most free. We can imagine how, up to a certain point, a man, whatever ill may result from it, may give up the direction of his temporal affairs to an outward authority. We can conceive a notion of that philosopher who, when one told him that his house was on fire, said, "Go and tell my wife; I never meddle with household affairs." But when our conscience, our thoughts, our intellectual existence are at stake—to give up the government of one's self, to deliver over one's very soul to the authority of a stranger, is, indeed, a moral suicide: is, indeed, a thousand times worse than bodily servitude—than to become a mere appurtenance of the soil.

Such, nevertheless, was the evil, which without ever, as I shall presently show, completely prevailing, invaded more and more the Christian church in its relations with the people. We have already seen, that even in the bosom of the Church itself, the lower orders of the clergy had no guarantee for their liberty; it was much worse, out of the Church, for the laity. Among churchmen there was at least discussion, deliberation, the display of individual faculties; the struggle, itself, supplied in some measure the place of liberty. There was nothing, however, like this between the clergy and the people. The laity had no further share in the government of the Church than as simple lookers-on. Thus we see quickly shoot up and thrive, the idea that theology, that religious questions and affairs, were the privileged territory of the clergy; that the clergy alone had the right, not only to decide upon all matters respecting it, but likewise that they alone had the right to study it, and that the laity ought not to intermeddle with it. At the period of which we are now speaking, this theory had fully established its authority, and it has required ages, and revolutions full of terror, to overcome it; to restore to the public the right of debating religious questions, and inquiring into their truths.

In principle, then, as well as in fact, the legal separation of the clergy and the laity was nearly completed before the twelfth century.

It must not, however, be understood, that the Christian world had no influence upon its government during this period. Of legal interference it was destitute, but not of influence. It is, indeed, almost impossible that such should be the case under any kind of government, and more particularly so of one founded upon the common opinions and belief of the governing and governed. For, wherever this community of ideas springs up and expands, wherever the same intellectual movement prevails with government and the people, there necessarily becomes formed between them a tie, which no vice in their organization can ever altogether break. To make you clearly understand what I mean, I will give you an example, familiar to us all, taken from the political world. At no period in the history of France had the French nation less power of a legal nature, I mean by way of institutions, of interfering in the government, than in the seventeenth and eighteenth centuries, during the reigns of Louis XIV and XV. All the direct and official means by which the people could exercise any authority had been cut off and suppressed. Yet there cannot be a doubt but that the public, the country, exercised, at this time, more influence upon the government than at any other, more, for example, than when the states-general had been frequently convoked; than when the parliaments* intermeddled to a considerable extent in politics, than when the people had a much greater legal participation in the government.

It must have been observed by all that there exists a power which no law can comprise or suppress, and which, in times of need, goes even further than institutions. Call it the spirit of the age, public intelligence, opinion, or what you will, you cannot doubt its existence. In France, during the seventeenth and eighteenth centuries, this public opinion was more powerful than at any other epoch; and, though it was deprived of the legal means of acting upon the government, yet it acted indirectly, by the force of ideas common to the governing and the governed, by the absolute necessity under which the governing found themselves of attending to the opinions of the governed. What took place in the Church from the fifth to the twelfth century was very similar to this. The body of the Christian world, it is true, had no legal means of expressing its desires; but there was a great advancement of mind in religious matters: this movement bore along clergy and laity together, and in this way the people acted upon the Church.

It is of the greatest importance that these indirect influences should be kept in view in the study of history. They are much more efficacious, and often more salutary, than we take them to be. It is very natural that men should wish their influence to be prompt and apparent; that they should covet the credit of promoting success, of establishing power, of procuring triumph. But this is not always either possible or useful. There are times and situations when the indirect, unperceived influence is more beneficial, more practicable. Let me borrow another illustration from politics. We know that the English parliament more than once, and particularly in 1641, demanded, as many other popular assemblies have done in such cases, the power to nominate the ministers and great officers of the crown. The immense direct force which by this means it would exercise upon the government was regarded as a precious guarantee. But how has it turned out? Why, in the few cases in which it has been permitted to possess this power, the result has been always unfavorable. The choice has been badly concerted; affairs badly conducted. But what is the case in the present day? Is it not the influence of the two houses of parliament which determines the choice of ministers, and the nomination to all the great offices of state? And, though this influence be indirect and general, it is found to work better than the direct interference of parliament, which has always terminated badly.

There is one reason why this should be so, which I must beg leave to lay before you, at the expense of a few minutes of your time. The direct action upon government supposes those to whom it is confided possessed of superior talents—of superior information, understanding, and prudence. As they go to the object at once, and per saltem as it were, they must be sure not to miss their mark. Indirect influences, on the contrary, pursuing a tortuous course—only arriving at their object through numerous difficulties—become rectified and adapted to their end by the very obstacles they have to encounter. Before they can succeed, they must undergo discussion, be combated and controlled; their triumph is slow, conditional, and partial. It is on this account that where society is not sufficiently advanced to make it prudent to place immediate power in the hands of the people, these indirect influences, though often insufficient, are nevertheless to be preferred. It was by such that the Christian world acted upon its government;—acted, I must allow, very inadequately—by far too little; but still it is something that it acted at all.

There was another thing which strengthened the tie between the clergy and laity. This was the dispersion of the clergy into every part of the social system. In almost all other cases, where a church has been formed independent of the people whom it governed, the body of priests has been composed of men in nearly the same condition of life. I do not mean that the inequalities of rank were not sufficiently great among them, but that the power was lodged in the hands of colleges of priests living in common, and governing the people submitted to their laws from the innermost recess of some sacred temple. The organization of the Christian church was widely different. From the thatched cottage of the husbandman—from the miserable hut of the serf at the foot of the feudal chateau to the palace of the monarch—there was everywhere a clergyman. This diversity in the situation of the Christian priesthood, their participation in all the varied fortunes of humanity—of common life—was a great bond of union between the laity and clergy; a bond which has been wanting in most other hierarchies invested with power. Besides this, the bishops, the heads of the Christian clergy, were, as we have seen, mixed up with the feudal system: they were, at the same time, members of the civil and of the ecclesiastical governments. This naturally led to similarity of feeling, of interests, of habits, and of manners, in the clergy and laity. There has been a good deal said, and with reason, of military bishops, of priests who led secular lives; but we may be assured that this evil, however great, was not so hurtful as the system which kept priests for ever locked up in a temple, altogether separated from common life. Bishops who took a share in the cares, and, up to a certain point, in the disorders of civil life, were of more use in society than those who were altogether strangers to the people, to their wants, their affairs, and their manners. In our system there has been, in this respect, a similarity of fortune, of condition, which, if it have not altogether corrected, has, at least, softened the evil which the separation of the governing and governed must in all cases prove.

Now, having pointed out this separation, having endeavored to determine its extent, let us see how the Christian church governed—let us see in what way it acted upon the people under its authority.

What did it do, on one hand, for the development of man, for the intellectual progress of the individual?

What did it do, on the other, for the melioration of the social system?

With regard to individual development, I fear the Church, at this epoch, gave herself but little trouble about it. She endeavored to soften the rugged manners of the great, and to render them more kind and just in their conduct towards the weak. She endeavored to inculcate a life of morality among the poor, and to inspire them with higher sentiments and hopes than the lot in which they were cast would give rise to. I do not believe, however, that for individual man—for the drawing forth or advancement of his capacities—the Church did much, especially for the laity, during this period. What she did in this way was confined to the bosom of her own society. For the development of the clergy, for the instruction of the priesthood, she was anxiously alive: to promote this she had her schools, her colleges, and all other institutions which the deplorable state of society would permit. These schools and colleges, it is true, were all theological, and destined for the education of the clergy alone;* and though, from the intimacy between the civil and religious orders, they could not but have some influence upon the rest of the world, it was very slow and indirect. It cannot, indeed, be denied but the Church, too, necessarily excited and kept alive a general activity of mind, by the career which she opened to all those whom she judged worthy to enlist into her ranks, but beyond this she did little for the intellectual improvement of the laity.

For the melioration of the social state her labors were greater and more efficacious.

She combated with much perseverance and pertinacity the great vices of the social condition, particularly slavery. It has been frequently asserted that the abolition of slavery in the modern world must be altogether carried to the credit of Christianity. I believe this is going too far: slavery subsisted for a long time in the bosom of Christian society without much notice being taken of it—without any great outcry against it. To effect its abolition required the co-operation of several causes—a great development of new ideas, of new principles of civilization. It cannot, however, be denied that the Church employed its influence to restrain it; the clergy in general, and especially several popes, enforced the manumission of their slaves as a duty incumbent upon laymen, and loudly inveighed against the scandal of keeping Christians in bondage. Again, the greater part of the forms by which slaves were set free, at various epochs, are founded upon religious motives. It is under the impression of some religious feeling—the hopes of the future, the equality of all Christian men, and so on—that the freedom of the slave is granted.* These, it must be confessed, are rather convincing proofs of the influence of the Church, and of her desire for the abolition of this evil of evils, this iniquity of iniquities!

The Church labored no less worthily for the improvement of civil and criminal legislation. We know how absurd and wretched this was, notwithstanding some few principles of liberty in it; we have read of the irrational and superstitious proofs to which the barbarians occasionally had recourse—their trial by battle, their ordeals, their oaths of compurgation—as the only means by which they could discover the truth. To replace these by more rational and legitimate proceedings, the Church earnestly labored, and labored not in vain.* I have already spoken of the striking difference between the laws of the Visigoths, mostly promulgated by the councils of Toledo, and the codes of the barbarians. It is impossible to compare them without at once admitting the immense superiority of the notions of the Church in matters of jurisprudence, justice, and legislation—in all relating to the discovery of truth, and a knowledge of human nature. It must certainly be admitted that the greater part of these notions were borrowed from Roman legislation; but it is not less certain that they would have perished if the Church had not preserved and defended them—if she had not labored to spread them abroad.† If the question, for example, is respecting the employment of oaths, open the laws of the Visigoths, and see with what prudence it controls their use:—

"Let the judge, in order to come at the truth, first interrogate the witnesses, then examine the papers, and not allow of oaths too easily. The investigation of truth and justice demands, that the documents on both sides should be carefully examined, and that the necessity of the oath, suspended over the head of both parties, should only come unexpectedly. Let the oath only be adopted in causes in which the judge shall be able to discover no written documents, no proof, nor guide to the truth."

In criminal matters, the punishment is proportioned to the offence, according to tolerably correct notions of philosophy, morals, and justice; the efforts of an enlightened legislator struggling against the violence and caprice of barbarian manners. The chapter De cæde et morte hominum gives us a very favorable example of this, when compared with the corresponding laws of the other nations. Among the latter, it is the damage alone which seems to constitute the crime; and the punishment is sought for in the pecuniary reparation which is made in compounding for it; but in the code of the Visigoths the crime is traced to its true and moral principle—the intention of the perpetrator. Various shades of guilt—involuntary homicide, accidental homicide, justifiable homicide, unpremeditated homicide, and wilful murder—are distinguished and defined nearly as accurately as in our modern codes; the punishments likewise varying, so as to make a fair approximation to justice. The legislator, indeed, carried the principle of justice still further. He endeavored, if not to abolish, at least to lessen, that difference of legal value, which the other barbarian laws put upon the life of man. The only distinction here made was between the freeman and the slave. With regard to the freeman, the punishment did not vary either according to the perpetrator, or according to the rank of the slain, but only according to the moral guilt of the murderer. With regard to slaves, not daring entirely to deprive masters of the right of life and death, he at least endeavored to restrain it and destroy its brutal character by subjecting it to an open and regular procedure.

The law itself is worthy of citation:

"If no one who is culpable, or the accomplice in a crime, ought to go unpunished, how much more reasonable is it that those should be restrained who commit homicide maliciously, or from a slight cause! Thus, as masters in their pride often put their slaves to death without any cause, it is proper to extirpate altogether this license, and to decree that the present law shall be for ever binding upon all. No master or mistress shall have power to put to death any of their slaves, male or female, or any of their dependants, without public judgment. If any slave, or other servant, commits a crime which renders him subject to capital punishment, his master or his accuser shall immediately give information to the judge, or count, or duke, of the place in which the crime has been perpetrated. After the matter has been tried, if the crime is proved, let the criminal receive, either by the judge or by his own master, the sentence of death which he has merited; in such manner, however, that if the judge desires not to put the accused to death, he must draw up against him in writing, a capital sentence, and then it will remain with his master to kill him or grant him his life. But when, indeed, a slave, by a fatal audacity, in resisting his master, shall strike, or attempt to strike him with his arm, with a stone, or by any other means; and the master, in defending himself, kills the slave in his anger, the master shall in nowise be liable to the punishment of homicide. But it will be necessary to prove the fact; and that by the testimony or oath of the slaves, male or female, who witnessed it, and also by the oath of the person himself who committed the deed. Whosoever from pure malice shall himself kill a slave, or employ another to do so, without his having been publicly tried, shall be considered infamous, shall be declared incapable of giving evidence, shall be banished for life, and his property be given to his nearest heirs.—(For. Jud., lib. vi, tit. v, 1, 12.)

There is another circumstance connected with the institutions of the Church, which has not, in general, been so much noticed as it deserves. I allude to its penitential system, which is the more interesting in the present day, because, so far as the principles and applications of moral law are concerned, it is almost completely in unison with the notions of modern philosophy. If we look closely into the nature of the punishments inflicted by the Church at public penance, which was its principal mode of punishing, we shall find that their object was, above all other things, to excite repentance in the soul of the guilty; in that of the lookers on, the moral terror of example. But there is another idea which mixes itself up with this—the idea of expiation. I know not, generally speaking, whether it be possible to separate the idea of punishment from that of expiation; and whether there be not in all punishment, independently of the desire to awaken the guilty to repentance, and to deter those from vice who might be under temptation, a secret and imperious desire to expiate the wrong committed. Putting this question, however, aside, it is sufficiently evident that repentance and example were the objects proposed by the Church in every part of its system of penance.* And is not the attainment of these very objects the end of every truly philosophical legislation? Is it not for the sake of these very principles that the most enlightened lawyers have clamored for a reform in the penal legislation of Europe? Open their books—those of Jeremy Bentham for example*—and you will be astonished at the numerous resemblances which you will everywhere find between their plans of punishment and those adopted by the Church. We may be quite sure that they have not borrowed them from her; and the Church could scarcely foresee that her example would one day be quoted in support of the system of philosophers not very remarkable for their devotion.

Finally, she endeavored by every means in her power to suppress the frequent recourse which at this period was had to violence and the continual wars to which society was so prone. It is well known what the truce of God was, as well as a number of other similar measures by which the Church hoped to prevent the employment of physical force, and to introduce into the social system more order and gentleness. The facts under this head are so well known, that I shall not go into any detail concerning them.†

Having now run over the principal points to which I wished to draw attention respecting the relations of the Church to the people; having now considered it under the three aspects, which I proposed to do, we know it within and without; in its interior constitution, and in its twofold relations with society. It remains for us to deduce from what we have learned by way of inference, by way of conjecture, its general influence upon European civilization. This is already partly done. The simple recital of the predominant facts and principles of the Church, both reveals and explains its influence: the results have in a manner been brought before us with the causes. If, however, we endeavor to sum them up, we shall be led, I think, to two general conclusions.

The first is, that the Church has exercised a vast and important influence upon the moral and intellectual order of Europe; upon the notions, sentiments, and manners of society. This fact is evident; the intellectual and moral progress of Europe has been essentially theological. Look at its history from the fifth to the sixteenth century, and you will find throughout that theology has possessed and directed the human mind; every idea is impressed with theology; every question that has been started, whether philosophical, political, or historical, has been considered from a religious point of view. So powerful, indeed, has been the authority of the Church in matters of intellect, that even the mathematical and physical sciences have been obliged to submit to its doctrines. The spirit of theology has been as it were the blood which has circulated in the veins of the European world down to the time of Bacon and Descartes. Bacon in England, and Descartes in France, were the first who carried the human mind out of the pale of theology. We shall find the same fact hold if we travel through the regions of literature: the habits, the sentiments, the language of theology there show themselves at every step.

This influence, taken altogether, has been salutary. It not only kept up and ministered to the intellectual movement in Europe, but the system of doctrines and precepts, by whose authority it stamped its impress upon that movement, was incalculably superior to any which the ancient world had known.*

The influence of the Church, moreover, has given to the development of the human mind, in our modern world, an extent and variety which it never possessed elsewhere. In the East, intelligence was altogether religious: among the Greeks, it was almost exclusively human: in the former human culture—humanity, properly so called, its nature and destiny—actually disappeared; with the latter it was man alone, his passions, his feelings, his present interests, which occupied the field. In our world the spirit of religion mixes itself with all but excludes nothing. Human feelings, human interests, occupy a considerable space in every branch of our literature; yet the religious character of man, that portion of his being which connects him with another world, appears at every turn in them all. Could modern intelligence assume a visible shape, we should recognize at once, in its mixed character, the finger of man and the finger of God. Thus the two great sources of human development, humanity and religion, have been open at the same time and have flowed in plenteous streams. Notwithstanding all the evil, all the abuses, which may have crept into the Church—notwithstanding all the acts of tyranny of which she has been guilty, we must still acknowledge her influence upon the progress and culture of the human intellect to have been beneficial; that she has assisted in its development rather than its compression, in its extension rather than its confinement.†

The case is widely different when we look at the Church in a political point of view. By softening the rugged manners and sentiments of the people; by raising her voice against a great number of practical barbarisms, and doing what she could to expel them, there is no doubt but the Church largely contributed to the melioration of the social condition; but with regard to politics, properly so called, with regard to all that concerns the relations between the governing and the governed—between power and liberty—I cannot conceal my opinion, that its influence has been baneful. In this respect the Church has always shown herself as the interpreter and defender of two systems, equally vicious, that is, of theocracy, and of the imperial tyranny of the Roman empire—that is to say, of despotism, both religious and civil. Examine all its institutions, all its laws; peruse its canons, look at its procedure, and you will everywhere find the maxims either of theocracy or of the empire. In her weakness, the Church sheltered herself under the absolute power of the Roman emperors; in her strength she laid claim to it herself, under the name of spiritual power. We must not here confine ourselves to a few particular facts. The Church has often, no doubt, set up and defended the rights of the people against the bad government of their rulers; often, indeed, has she approved and excited insurrection; often too has she maintained the rights and interests of the people in the face of their sovereigns. But when the question of political securities arose between power and liberty; when any step was taken to establish a system of permanent institutions, which might effectually protect liberty from the invasions of power in general; the Church always ranged herself on the side of despotism.

This should not astonish us, neither should we be too ready to attribute it to any particular failing in the clergy, or to any particular vice in the Church. There is a more profound and powerful cause. What is the object of religion? of any religion, true or false? It is to govern the human passions, the human will. All religion is a restraint, an authority, a government. It comes in the name of a divine law, to subdue, to mortify human nature. It is then to human liberty that it directly opposes itself. It is human liberty that resists it, and that it wishes to overcome. This is the grand object of religion, its mission, its hope.

But while it is with human liberty that all religions have to contend, while they aspire to reform the will of man, they have no means by which they can act upon him—they have no moral power over him, but through his own will, his liberty. When they make use of external means, when they resort to force, to seduction, in short, to any means opposed to the free consent of man, when they treat him as we treat water, wind, or any power entirely physical, they fail in their object; they do not attain their end, they do not reach, they cannot govern the will. Before religions can really accomplish their task, it is necessary that they should be accepted by the free-will of man: it is necessary that man should submit, but it must be willingly and freely, and that he still preserves his liberty in the midst of this submission. This is the double problem which religions are called upon to solve.

They have too often mistaken their object. They have regarded liberty as an obstacle, and not as a means; they have forgotten the nature of the power to which they address themselves, and have conducted themselves towards the human soul as they would towards a material force. It is this error that has led them to range themselves on the side of power, on the side of despotism, against human liberty; regarding it as an adversary, they have endeavored to subjugate rather than to protect it. Had religions but fairly considered their means of operation, had they not suffered themselves to be drawn away by a natural but deceitful bias, they would have seen that liberty is a condition, without which man cannot be morally governed; that religion neither has nor ought to have any means of influence not strictly moral: they would have respected the will of man in their attempt to govern it. They have too often forgotten this, and the issue has been that religious power and liberty have suffered together.

I will not push further this investigation of the general consequences that have followed the influence of the Church upon European civilization. I have summed them up in this double result,—a great and salutary influence upon its moral and intellectual condition; an influence rather hurtful than beneficial to its political condition. We have now to try our assertions by facts, to verify by history what we have as yet only deduced from the nature and situation of ecclesiastical society. Let us now see what was the fate of the Christian church from the fifth to the twelfth century, and whether the principles which I have laid down, the results which I have endeavored to draw from them, have really been such as I have represented them.

Let me caution you, however, against supposing that these principles, these results, appeared all at once, and as clearly as they are here set forth by me. We are apt to fall into the great and common error, in looking at the past through centuries of distance, of forgetting moral chronology; we are apt to forget (extraordinary forgetfulness!) that history is essentially successive. Take the life of any man, of Oliver Cromwell, of Cardinal Richelieu, of Gustavus Adolphus. He enters upon his career; he pushes forward in life, and rises; great circumstances act upon him; he acts upon great circumstances. He arrives at the end of all things—and then it is we know him. But it is in his whole character; it is as a complete, a finished piece; such, in a manner, as he is turned out, after long labor, from the workshop of Providence. Now at the outset he was not what he thus became; he was not completed—not finished at any single moment of his life; he was formed progressively. Men are formed morally in the same way as they are physically. They change every day. Their existence is constantly undergoing some modification. The Cromwell of 1650 was not the Cromwell of 1640. It is true, there is always a large stock of individuality; the same man still holds on; but how many ideas, how many sentiments, how many inclinations have changed in him! What a number of things he has lost and acquired! Thus, at whatever moment of his life we may look at a man, he is never such as we see him when his course is finished.

It is here, nevertheless, that a great number of historians have fallen into error. When they have acquired a complete idea of a man, have settled his character, they see him in this same character throughout his whole career. With them, it is the same Cromwell who enters parliament in 1628, and who dies in the palace of Whitehall thirty years afterwards. Just such mistakes as these we are apt to fall into with regard to institutions and general influences. I caution you against them. I have laid down in their complete form, as a whole, the principles of the Church, and the consequences which may be deduced from them. Be assured, however, that historically this picture is not true. All it represents has taken place disjointedly, successively; has been scattered here and there over space and time. Expect not to find, in the recital of events, a similar completeness or whole, the same prompt and systematic connection. One principle will be visible here, another there; all will be incomplete, unequal, dispersed; we must come to modern times, to the end of its career, before we can view it as a whole.

I shall now lay before you the various states through which the Church passed from the fifth to the twelfth century. We may not find, perhaps, the complete demonstration of the statements which I have made, but we shall see enough, I apprehend, to convince us that they are founded in truth.

The first state in which we see the Church in the fifth century, is as the Church imperial—the Church of the Roman empire. Just at the time the empire fell, the Church believed she had attained the summit of her hopes: after a long struggle, she had completely vanquished paganism. Gratian, the last emperor who assumed the pagan dignity of sovereign pontiff, died at the close of the fourth century. The Church believed herself equally victorious in her struggle against heretics, particularly against Arianism, the principal heresy of the time. Theodosius, at the end of the fourth century, put them down by his imperial edicts; and had the double merit of subduing the Arian heresy and abolishing the worship of idols throughout the Roman world. The Church, then, was in possession of the government, and had obtained the victory over her two greatest enemies. It was at this moment that the Roman empire failed her, and she stood in the presence of new pagans, of new heretics—in the presence of the barbarians, the Goths, Vandals, Burgundians and Franks.* The fall was immense. You may easily imagine that an affectionate attachment for the empire was for a long time preserved in the Romish church. Hence we see her cherish so fondly all that was left of it—municipal government and absolute power. Hence, when she had succeeded in converting the barbarians, she endeavored to re-establish the empire; she called upon the barbarian kings, she conjured them to become Roman emperors, to assume the privilege of Roman emperors; to enter into the same relations with the Church which had existed between her and the Roman empire. This was the great object for which the bishops of the fifth and sixth centuries labored.* Such was the general state of the Church.

The attempt could not succeed—it was impossible to make a Roman empire, to mould a Roman society out of barbarians. Like the civil world, the Church herself sunk into barbarism. This was her second state. Comparing the writings of the monkish ecclesiastical chroniclers of the eighth century with those of the preceding six, the difference is immense. All remains of Roman civilization had disappeared, even its very language—all became buried in complete barbarism. On one side the rude barbarians, entering into the Church, became bishops and priests; on the other, the bishops, adopting the barbarian life, became, without quitting their bishoprics, chiefs of bands of marauders, and wandered over the country, pillaging and destroying like so many companies of Clovis. Gregory of Tours† gives an account of several bishops who thus passed their lives, and among others Salone and Sagittarius.

Two important facts took place while the Church continued in this state of barbarism. The first was the separation of the spiritual and temporal powers. Nothing could be more natural than the birth of this principle at this epoch. The Church would have restored the absolute power of the Roman empire that she might partake of it, but she could not; she therefore sought her safety in independence. It became necessary that she should be able in all parts to defend herself by her own power; for she was threatened in every quarter. Every bishop, every priest, saw the rude chiefs in their neighborhood interfering in the affairs of the Church, that they might obtain a part of her wealth, her territory, her power; and no other means of defence seemed left but to say, "The spiritual order is completely separated from the temporal; you have no right to interfere with it." This principle became, at every point of attack, the defensive armor of the Church against barbarism.

A second important fact which took place at this same period, was the establishment of the monastic orders in the West. It was at the commencement of the sixth century that St. Benedict published the rules of his order for the use of the monks of the West, then few in number, but who from this time prodigiously increased. The monks at this epoch did not yet belong to the clerical body, but were still regarded as a part of the laity. Priests and even bishops were sometimes chosen from among them; but it was not till the close of the fifth and beginning of the sixth century that monks in general were considered as belonging to the clergy, properly so called. Priests and bishops now entered the cloister, thinking by so doing they advanced a step in their religious life, and increased the sanctity of their office. The monastic life thus all at once became exceedingly popular throughout Europe. The monks had a greater power over the imagination of the barbarians than the secular clergy. The simple bishop and priest had in some measure lost their hold upon the minds of barbarians, who were accustomed to see them every day; to maltreat, perhaps to pillage them. It was a more important matter to attack a monastery, a body of holy men congregated in a holy place. Monasteries, therefore, became during this barbarous period an asylum for the Church, as the Church was for the laity. Pious men here took refuge, as others in the East had done before in the Thebaid, in order to escape the worldly life and corruption of Constantinople.*

These, then, are the two most important facts in the history of the Church, during the period of barbarism. First, the separation of the spiritual and temporal powers; and, secondly, the introduction and establishment of the monastic orders in the West.

Towards the end of this period of barbarism, a fresh attempt was made to raise up a new Roman empire—I allude to the attempt of Charlemagne. The Church and the civil sovereign again contracted a close alliance. The Holy See was full of docility while this lasted, and greatly increased its power. The attempt, however, again failed. The empire of Charlemagne was broken up; but the advantages which the See of Rome derived from his alliance were great and permanent. The popes henceforward were decidedly the chiefs of the Christian world.

Upon the death of Charlemagne, another period of unsettledness and confusion followed. The Church, together with civil society, again fell into a chaos; again with civil society she arose, and with it entered into the frame of the feudal system. This was the third state of the Church. The dissolution of the empire formed by Charlemagne, was followed by nearly the same results in the Church as in civil life; all unity disappeared, all became local, partial, and individual. Now began a struggle, in the situation of the clergy, such as had scarcely ever before been seen: it was the struggle of the feelings and interest of the possessor of the fief, with the feelings and interest of the priest. The chiefs of the clergy were placed in this double situation; the spirit of the priest and of the temporal baron struggled within them for mastery. The ecclesiastical spirit naturally became weakened and divided by this process—it was no longer so powerful, so universal. Individual interest began to prevail. A taste for independence, the habits of the feudal life, loosened the ties of the hierarchy. In this state of things, the Church made an attempt within its own bosom to correct the effects of the general break-up. It endeavored in several parts of its empire, by means of federation, by common assemblies and deliberations, to organize national Churches. It is during this period, during the sway of the feudal system, that we meet with the greatest number of councils, convocations, and ecclesiastical assemblies, as well provincial as national. In France especially, this endeavor at unity appeared to be followed up with much spirit. Hincmar, archbishop of Rheims, may be considered as the representative of this idea. He labored incessantly to organize the French Church; he sought out and employed every means of correspondence and union which he thought likely to introduce into the feudal church a little more unity. We find him on one side maintaining the independence of the Church with respect to temporal power, on the other its independence with respect to the Roman See; it was he who, learning that the pope wished to come to France, and threatened to excommunicate the bishops, said, Si excommunicaturus venerit, excommunicatus abibit,—If he shall come to excommunicate, he will go away excommunicated.

But the attempt thus to organize a feudal church succeeded no better than the attempt to re-establish the imperial one. There were no means of reproducing any degree of unity among its members; it tended more and more towards dissolution. Each bishop, each prelate, each abbot, isolated himself more and more in his diocese or monastery. Abuses and disorders increased from the same cause. At no time was the crime of simony carried to a greater extent, at no time were ecclesiastical benefices disposed of in a more arbitrary manner, never were the morals of the clergy more loose and disorderly.

Both the people and the better portion of the clergy were greatly scandalized at this sad state of things; and a desire for reform in the Church soon began to show itself—a desire to find some authority round which it might rally its better principles, and which might impose some wholesome restraints on the others. Several bishops, Claude of Turin, Agobard of Lyons, and others, in their respective dioceses attempted this, but in vain; they were not in a condition to accomplish so vast a work. In the whole Church there was only one power that could succeed in this, and that was the Roman See; nor was that power slow in assuming the position which it wished to attain. In the course of the eleventh century, the Church entered upon its fourth state—that of a theocracy supported by monastic institutions.

The person who raised the Holy See to this power, so far as it can be considered the work of an individual, was Gregory VII.*

It has been the custom to represent this great pontiff as an enemy to all improvement, as opposed to intellectual development, to the progress of society; as a man whose desire was to keep the world stationary or retrograding. Nothing is farther from the truth. Gregory, like Charlemagne and Peter the Great, was a reformer of the despotic school. The part he played in the Church was very similar to that which Charlemagne and Peter the Great, the one in France and the other in Russia, played among the laity. He wished to reform the Church first, and next civil society by the Church. He wished to introduce into the world more morality, more justice, more order and regularity; he wished to do all this through the Holy See, and to turn all to its profit.

While Gregory was endeavoring to bring the civil world into subjection to the Church, and the Church to the See of Rome—not, as I have said before, to keep it stationary, or make it retrograde, but with a view to its reform and improvement—an attempt of the same nature, a similar movement, was made within the solitary enclosures of the monasteries. The want of order, of discipline, and of a stricter morality, was severely felt and cried out for with a zeal that would not be said nay. About this time Robert De Molême established his severe rule at Cîteaux; about the same time flourished St. Norbert, and the reform of the canons, the reform of Cluny,* and, at last, the great reform of St. Bernard. A general fermentation reigned within the monasteries: the old monks did not like this; in defending themselves, they called these reforms an attack upon their liberty; pleaded the necessity of conforming to the manners of the times, that it was impossible to return to the discipline of the primitive Church, and treated all these reformers as madmen, as enthusiasts, as tyrants. Dip into the history of Normandy, by Ordericus Vitalius, and you will meet with these complaints at almost every page.

All this seemed greatly in favor of the Church, of its unity, and of its power. While, however, the popes of Rome sought to usurp the government of the world, while the monasteries enforced a better code of morals and a severer form of discipline, a few mighty, though solitary individuals protested in favor of human reason, and asserted its claim to be heard, its right to be consulted, in the formation of man's opinions. The greater part of these philosophers forbore to attack commonly received opinions—I mean religious creeds; all they claimed for reason was the right to be heard—all they declared was, that she had the right to try these truths by her own tests, and that it was not enough that they should be merely affirmed by authority. John Erigena, or John Scotus, as he is more frequently called, Roscelin, Abelard, and others, became the noble interpreters of individual reason, when it now began to claim its lawful inheritance. It was the teaching and writings of these giants of their days that first put in motion that desire for intellectual liberty, which kept pace with the reform of Gregory VII and St. Bernard. If we examine the general character of this movement of mind, we shall find that it sought not a change of opinion, that it did not array itself against the received system of faith; but that it simply advocated the right of reason to work for itself—in short, the right of free inquiry.

The scholars of Abelard, as he himself tells us, in his Introduction to Theology, requested him to give them "some philosophical arguments, such as were fit to satisfy their minds; begged that he would instruct them, not merely to repeat what he taught them, but to understand it; for no one can believe that which he does not comprehend, and it is absurd to set out to preach to others concerning things which neither those who teach nor those who learn can understand. What other end can the study of philosophy have, if not to lead us to a knowledge of God, to which all studies should be subordinate? For what purpose is the reading of profane authors, and of books which treat of worldly affairs, permitted to believers, if not to enable them to understand the truths of the Holy Scriptures, and to give them the abilities necessary to defend them? It is above all things desirable for this purpose, that we should strengthen one another with all the powers of reason; so that in questions so difficult and complicated as those which form the object of Christian faith, you may be able to hinder the subtilties of its enemies from too easily corrupting its purity."

The importance of this first attempt after liberty, or this rebirth of the spirit of free inquiry, was not long in making itself felt. Though busied with its own reform, the Church soon took the alarm, and at once declared war against these new reformers, whose methods gave it more reason to fear than their doctrines. This clamor of human reason was the grand circumstance which burst forth at the close of the eleventh and beginning of the twelfth centuries, just at the time when the Church was establishing its theocratic and monastic form. At this epoch, a serious struggle for the first time broke out between the clergy and the advocates of free inquiry. The quarrels of Abelard and St. Bernard, the councils of Soissons and Sens, at which Abelard was condemned, were nothing more than the expression of this fact, which holds so important a place in the history of modern civilization.* It was the principal occurrence which affected the Church in the twelfth century; the point at which we will, for the present, take leave of it.

But at this same instant another power was put in motion, which, though altogether of a different character, was perhaps one of the most interesting and important in the progress of society during the middle ages—I mean the institution of free cities and boroughs; or what is called the enfranchisement of the commons. How strange is the inconsistency of grossness and ignorance! If it had been told to these early citizens who vindicated their liberties with such enthusiasm, that there were certain men who cried out for the rights of human reason, the right of free inquiry, men whom the Church regarded as heretics, they would have stoned or burned them on the spot. Abelard and his friends more than once ran the risk of suffering this kind of martyrdom. On the other hand, these same philosophers, who were so bold in their demands for the privileges of reason, spoke of the enfranchisement of the commons as an abominable revolution, calculated to destroy civil society. Between the movement of philosophy and the movement of the commons—between political liberty and the liberty of the human mind—a war seemed to be declared; and it has required ages to reconcile these two powers, and to make them understand that their interests are the same. In the twelfth century they had nothing in common, as we shall more fully see in the next lecture, which will be devoted to the formation of free cities and municipal corporations.

LECTURE VII.: RISE OF FREE CITIES.

We have already, in our previous lectures, brought down the history of the two first great elements of modern civilization, the feudal system and the Church, to the twelfth century. The third of these fundamental elements—that of the commons, or free corporate cities—will form the subject of the present, and I propose to limit it to the same period as that occupied by the other two.

It is necessary, however, that I should notice, on entering upon this subject, a difference which exists between corporate cities and the feudal system and the Church. The two latter, although they increased in influence, and were subject to many changes, yet show themselves as completed, as having put on a definite form, between the fifth and the twelfth centuries—we see their rise, growth, and maturity. Not so the free cities. It is not till towards the close of this period—till the eleventh and twelfth centuries—that corporate cities make any figure in history. Not that I mean to assert that their previous history does not merit attention; not that there are not evident traces of their existence before this period; all I would observe is, that they did not, previously to the eleventh century, perform any important part in the great drama of the world, as connected with modern civilization. Again, with regard to the feudal system and the Church; we have seen them, between the fifth century and the twelfth, act with power upon the social system; we have seen the effects they produced; by regarding them as two great principles, we have arrived, by way of induction, by way of conjecture, at certain results which we have verified by referring to facts themselves. This, however, we cannot do with regard to corporations. We only see these in their childhood. I can scarcely go further to-day than inquire into their causes, their origin; and the few observations I shall make respecting their effects—respecting the influence of corporate cities upon modern civilization, will be rather a foretelling of what afterwards came to pass, than a recounting of what actually took place. I cannot, at this period, call in the testimony of known and contemporary events, because it was not till between the twelfth and fifteenth centuries that corporations attained any degree of perfection and influence, that these institutions bore any fruit, and that we can verify our assertions by history. I mention this difference of situation, in order to forewarn you of that which you may find incomplete and premature in the sketch I am about to give you.

Let us suppose that in the year 1789, at the commencement of the terrible regeneration of France, a burgess of the twelfth century had risen from his grave, and made his appearance among us, and some one had put into his hands (for we will suppose he could read) one of those spirit-stirring pamphlets which caused so much excitement, for instance, that of M. Sieyes, What is the Third Estate? ("Qu'est-ce que le tiers état?") If, in looking at this, he had met the following passage, which forms the basis of the pamphlet:—"The third estate is the French nation without the nobility and clergy:" what, let me ask, would be the impression such a sentence would make on this burgess's mind? Is it probable that he would understand it? No: he would not be able to comprehend the meaning of the words, "the French nation," because they remind him of no facts or circumstances with which he would be acquainted, but represent a state of things to the existence of which he is an entire stranger; but if he did understand the phrase, and had a clear apprehension that the absolute sovereignty was lodged in the third estate, it is beyond a question that he would characterize such a proposition as almost absurd and impious, so utterly at variance would it be with his feelings and his ideas of things—so contradictory to the experience and observation of his whole life.

If we now suppose the astonished burgess to be introduced into any one of the free cities of France which had existed in his time—say Rheims, or Beauvais, or Laon, or Noyon—we shall see him still more astonished and puzzled: he enters the town, he sees no towers, ramparts, militia, or any other kind of defence; everything exposed, everything an easy spoil to the first depredator, the town ready to fall into the hands of the first assailant. The burgess is alarmed at the insecurity of this free city, which he finds in so defenceless and unprotected a condition. He then proceeds into the heart of the town; he inquires how things are going on, what is the nature of its government, and the character of its inhabitants. He learns that there is an authority not resident within its walls, which imposes whatever taxes it pleases to levy upon them without their consent; which requires them to keep up a militia, and to serve in the army without their inclination being consulted. They talk to him about the magistrates, about the mayor and aldermen, and he is obliged to hear that the burgesses have nothing to do with their nomination. He learns that the munieipal government is not conducted by the burgesses, but that a servant of the king, a steward living at a distance, has the sole management of their affairs.* In addition to this, he is informed that they are prohibited from assembling to take into consideration matters immediately concerning themselves, that the church bells have ceased to announce public meetings for such purposes. The burgess of the twelfth century is struck dumb with confusion—a moment since he was amazed at the greatness, the importance, the vast superiority which the "Third Estate" so vauntingly arrogated to itself; but now, upon examination, he finds them deprived of all civic rights, and in a state of thraldom and degradation far more intolerable than he had ever before witnessed. He passes suddenly from one extreme to the other, from the spectacle of a corporation exercising sovereign power to a corporation without any power at all: how is it possible that he should understand this, or be able to reconcile it? his head must be turned, and his faculties lost in wonder and confusion.

Now, let us burgesses of the nineteenth century imagine, in our turn, that we are transported back into the twelfth. A twofold appearance, but exactly reversed, presents itself to us in a precisely similar manner. If we regard the affairs of the public in general—the state, the government, the country, the nation at large, we shall neither see nor hear anything of burgesses; they were mere ciphers—of no importance or consideration whatever. Not only so, but if we would know in what estimation they held themselves as a body, what weight, what influence they attached to themselves with respect to their relations towards the government of France as a nation, we shall receive a reply to our inquiry in language expressive of deep humility and timidity; while we shall find their masters, the lords, from whom they subsequently wrested their franchises, treating them, at least as far as words go, with a pride and scorn truly amazing; yet these indignities do not appear, in the slightest degree, to provoke or astonish their submissive vassals. But let us enter one of these free cities, and see what is going on within it. Here things take quite another turn: we find ourselves in a fortified town, defended by armed burgesses. These burgesses fix their own taxes, elect their own magistrates, have their own courts of judicature, their own public assemblies for deliberating upon public measures, from which none are excluded. They make war on their own account, even against their suzerain, and maintain their own militia. In short, they govern themselves, they are sovereigns.

Here we have a similar contrast to that which made France, of the eighteenth century, so perplexing to the burgess of the twelfth; the parts only are changed. In the present day the burgesses, in a national point of view, are everything—municipalities nothing; formerly municipalities were everything, while the burgesses, as respects the nation, were nothing. From this it will appear evident that many things, many extraordinary events, and even many revolutions, must have happened between the twelfth and the eighteenth centuries, in order to bring about so great a change as that which has taken place in the social condition of this class of society. But however vast this change, there can be no doubt but that the commons, the third estate of 1789, politically speaking, are the descendants, the heirs of the free towns of the twelfth century. And the present haughty, ambitious French nation, which aspires so high, which proclaims so pompously its sovereignty, and pretends not only to have regenerated and to govern itself, but to regenerate and rule the whole world, is indisputably descended from those very free burghers who revolted in the twelfth century—with great spirit and courage it must be allowed, but with no nobler object than that of escaping to some remote corner of the land from the vexatious tyranny of a few nobles.

It would be in vain to expect that the condition of the free towns in the twelfth century will reveal the causes of a metamorphosis such as this, which resulted from a series of events that took place between the twelfth and eighteenth centuries. It is in these events that we shall discover the causes of this change as we go on. Nevertheless, the origin of the "Third Estate" has played a striking part in its history; and though we may not be able therein to trace out the whole secret of its destiny, we shall, at least, there meet with the seeds of it; that which it was at first, again occurs in that which it has become, and this to a much greater extent than might be presumed from appearances. A sketch, however imperfect, of the state of the free cities in the twelfth century, will, I think, convince you of this fact.

In order to understand the condition of the free cities at that time properly, it is necessary to consider them from two points of view. There are two great questions to be determined: first, that of the enfranchisement of the commons, or cities—that is to say, how this revolution was brought about, what were its causes, what alteration it effected in the condition of the burgesses, what in that of society in general, and in that of all the other orders of the state. The second question relates to the government of the free cities, the internal condition of the enfranchised towns, with reference to the burgesses residing within them, the principles, forms, and customs that prevailed among them.

From these two sources—namely, the change introduced into the social position of the burgesses, on the one hand, and from the internal government, from their municipal economy, on the other, has flowed all their influence upon modern civilization. All the circumstances that can be traced to their influence, may be referred to one of those two causes. As soon, then, as we thoroughly understand, and can satisfactorily account for, the enfranchisement of the free cities on the one hand, and the formation of their government on the other, we shall be in possession of the two keys to their history. In conclusion, I shall say a few words on the great diversity of conditions in the free cities of Europe. The facts which I am about to lay before you are not to be applied indiscriminately to all the free cities of the twelfth century—to those of Italy, Spain, England, and France alike; many of the facts were undoubtedly common to them all, but the points of difference are great and important. I shall point them out to your notice as I proceed. We shall meet with them again at a more advanced stage of our civilization, and can then examine them more closely.

In acquainting ourselves with the history of the enfranchisement of the free towns, we must remember what was the state of those towns between the fifth and eleventh centuries—from the fall of the Roman empire to the time when municipal revolution commenced. Here, I repeat, the differences are striking: the condition of the towns varied amazingly in the different countries of Europe; still there are some facts which may be regarded as nearly common to them all, and it is to these that I shall confine my observations. When I have gone through these, I shall say a few words more particularly respecting the free towns of France, and especially those of the north, beyond the Rhone and the Loire; these will form prominent figures in the sketch I am about to make.

After the fall of the Roman empire, between the fifth and tenth centuries, the towns were in a state neither of servitude nor of freedom. We here again run the same risk of error in the employment of words, that I spoke to you of in a previous lecture in describing the character of men and events. When a society and its language have lasted a considerable time, its words acquire a complete, a determinate, a precise, a sort of legal official signification. Time has introduced into the signification of every term a multitude of ideas, which are awakened within us every time we hear it pronounced, but which, as they do not all bear the same date, are not all suitable at the same time. The terms servitude and freedom, for example, call to our minds ideas far more precise and definite than are warranted by the facts of the eighth, ninth, or tenth centuries. If we say that the towns in the eighth century were in a state of freedom, we say by far too much; we attach now to the word freedom a signification which does not represent the fact of the eighth century. We shall fall into the same error, if we say that the towns were in a state of servitude; for this term implies a state of things very different from the circumstances of the municipal towns of those days. I say again, then, that the towns were in a state neither of freedom nor of servitude; they suffered all the evils to which weakness is liable; they were a prey to the continual depredations, rapacity, and violence of the strong; yet, notwithstanding these horrid disorders, and their impoverished and diminishing population, the towns had, and still maintained, a certain degree of importance; in most of them there was a clergyman, a bishop who exercised great authority, who possessed great influence over the people, and served as a tie between them and their conquerors, thus maintaining the city in a sort of independence, by throwing over it the protecting shield of religion. Besides this, there were still left in the towns some valuable fragments of Roman institutions. We are indebted to the careful researches of MM. de Savigny and Hullmann, Mademoiselle de Lézardière,* and others, for having furnished us with many circumstances of this nature. We hear often, at this period, of the convocation of the senate, of the curiœ,* of public assemblies, of municipal magistrates. Matters of police, wills, donations, and a multitude of civil transactions, were concluded in the curiœ by the magistrates, in the same way that they had previously been done under the Roman municipal government. These remains of urban activity and freedom were gradually disappearing, it is true, from day to day. Barbarism and disorder, evils always increasing, accelerated depopulation. The establishment of the lords of the country in the rural districts, and the rising preponderance of agricultural life, became added causes of the decline of the cities. The bishops themselves, after they had incorporated themselves into the feudal frame, attached much less importance to their municipal life. Finally, upon the triumph of the feudal system, the towns, without falling into the slavery of the agriculturists, were entirely subjected to the control of a lord, were included in some fief, and lost by this title, somewhat of the independence which still remained to them, and which, indeed, they had continued to possess, even in the most barbarous times—even in the first centuries of invasion. So that from the fifth century up to the time of the complete organization of the feudal system, the state of the towns was continually getting worse.†

When once, however, the feudal system was fairly established, when every man had taken his place, and become fixed as it were to the soil, when the wandering life had entirely ceased, the towns again assumed some importance—a new activity began to display itself within them. This is not surprising. Human activity, as we all know, is like the fertility of the soil,—when the disturbing process is over, it reappears and makes all to grow and blossom; wherever there appears the least glimmering of peace and order the hopes of man are excited, and with his hopes his industry. This is what took place in the cities. No sooner was society a little settled under the feudal system, than the proprietors of fiefs began to feel new wants, and to acquire a certain degree of taste for improvement and melioration; this gave rise to some little commerce and industry in the towns of their domains; wealth and population increased within them,—slowly indeed, but still they increased. Among other circumstances which aided in bringing this about, there is one which, in my opinion, has not been sufficiently noticed,—I mean the asylum, the protection which the churches afforded to fugitives. Before the free towns were constituted, before they were in a condition by their power, their fortifications, to offer an asylum to the desolate population of the country, when there was no place of safety for them but the Church, this circumstance alone was sufficient to draw into the cities many unfortunate persons and fugitives. These sought refuge either in the Church itself or within its precincts; it was not merely the lower orders, such as serfs, villeins, and so on, that sought this protection, but frequently men of considerable rank and wealth, who might chance to be proscribed. The chronicles of the times are full of examples of this kind. We find men lately powerful, who upon being attacked by some more powerful neighbor, or by the king himself, abandon their dwellings, carrying away all the property they can secure, enter into some city, and placing themselves under the protection of a church, become citizens. Refugees of this sort had, in my opinion, a considerable influence upon the progress of the cities; they introduced into them, besides their wealth, elements of a population superior to the great mass of their inhabitants. We know, moreover, that when once an assemblage somewhat considerable is formed in any place, other persons naturally flock to it, perhaps from finding it a place of greater security, or perhaps from that sociable disposition of our nature which never abandons us.*

By the concurrence of all these causes, the cities regained a small portion of power as soon as the feudal system was not restored to an equal extent.* The roving, wandering life had, it is true, in a great measure ceased, but to the conquerors, to the new proprietors of the soil, this roving life was one great means of gratifying their passions. When they desired to pillage, they made an excursion, they went afar to seek a better fortune, another domain. When they became more settled, when they considered it necessary to renounce their predatory expeditions, the same passions, the same gross desires, still remained in full force. But the weight of these now fell upon those whom they found ready at hand, upon the powerful of the world, upon the cities. Instead of going afar to pillage, they pillaged what was near. The exactions of the proprietors of fiefs upon the burgesses were redoubled at the end of the tenth century. Whenever the lord of the domain, by which a city was girt, felt a desire to increase his wealth, he gratified his avarice at the expense of the citizens. It was more particularly at this period that the citizens complained of the total want of commercial security. Merchants, on returning from their trading rounds, could not, with safety, return to their city. Every avenue was taken possession of by the lord of the domain and his vassals. The moment in which industry commenced its career, was precisely that in which security was most wanting. Nothing is more galling to an active spirit, than to be deprived of the long-anticipated pleasure of enjoying the fruits of his industry. When robbed of this, he is far more irritated and vexed than when made to suffer in a state that has become fixed and monotonous, than when that which is torn from him is not the fruit of his own activity, has not excited in him all the joys of hope. There is in the progressive movement, which elevates a man or a people towards a new fortune, a spirit of resistance against iniquity and violence much more energetic than in any other situation.

Such, then, was the state of cities during the course of the tenth century. They possessed more strength, more importance, more wealth, more interests to defend. At the same time, it became more necessary than ever to defend them, for these interests, their wealth and their strength, became objects of desire to the nobles.* With the means of resistance, the danger and difficulty increased also. Besides, the feudal system gave to all connected with it a perpetual example of resistance; the idea of an organized energetic government, capable of keeping society in order and regularity by its intervention, had never presented itself to the spirits of that period. On the contrary, there was a perpetual recurrence of individual will, refusing to submit to authority. Such was the conduct of the major part of the holders of fiefs towards their suzerains, of the small proprietors of land to the greater; so that at the very time when the cities were oppressed and tormented, at the moment when they had new and greater interests to sustain, they had before their eyes a continual lesson of insurrection. The feudal system rendered this service to mankind—it constantly exhibited individual will, displaying itself in all its power and energy. The lesson was applied; in spite of their weakness, in spite of the prodigious inequality which existed between them and the great proprietors, their lords, the cities everywhere broke out into rebellion against them.

It is difficult to fix a precise date to this great event—this general insurrection of the cities. The commencement of their enfranchisement is usually placed at the beginning of the eleventh century. But in all great events, how many unknown and disastrous efforts must have been made, before the successful one! Providence, upon all occasions, in order to accomplish its designs, is prodigal of courage, virtues, sacrifices—finally, of man; and it is only after a vast number of unknown attempts apparently lost, after a host of noble hearts have fallen into despair— convinced that their cause was lost—that it triumphs. Such, no doubt, was the case in the struggle of the free cities. Doubtless in the eighth, ninth, and tenth centuries there were many attempts at resistance, many efforts made for freedom:—many attempts to escape from bondage, which not only were unsuccessful, but the remembrance of which, from their ill success, has remained without glory. Still we may rest assured that these attempts had a vast influence upon succeeding events: they kept alive and maintained the spirit of liberty—they prepared the great insurrection of the eleventh century.

I say insurrection, and I say it advisedly. The enfranchisement of the towns or communities in the eleventh century was the fruit of a real insurrection, of a real war—a war declared by the population of the cities against their lords. The first fact which we always meet with in annals of this nature, is the rising of the burgesses, who seize whatever arms they can lay their hands on;— it is the expulsion of the people of the lord, who come for the purpose of levying contributions, some extortion; it is an enterprise against the neighboring castle;—such is always the character of the war.* If the insurrection fails, what does the conqueror instantly do? He orders the destruction of the fortifications erected by the citizens, not only around their city, but also around each dwelling. We see that at the very moment of confederation, after having promised to act in common, after having taken, in common, the corporation oath, the first act of each citizen was to put his own house in a state of resistance. Some towns, the names of which are now almost forgotten, the little community of Vézelay, in Nevers, for example—sustained against their lord a long and obstinate struggle. At length victory declared for the Abbot of Vézelay; upon the spot he ordered the demolition of the fortifications of the houses of the citizens; and the names of many of the heroes, whose fortified houses were then destroyed, are still preserved.

Let us enter the interior of these habitations of our ancestors; let us examine the form of their construction, and the mode of life which this reveals: all is devoted to war, every thing is impressed with its character.

The construction of the house of a citizen of the twelfth century, so far, at least, as we can now obtain an idea of it, was something of this kind: it consisted usually of three stories, one room in each; that on the ground floor served as a general eating room for the family; the first story was much elevated for the sake of security, and this is the most remarkable circumstance in the construction. The room in this story was the habitation of the master of the house and his wife. The house was, in general, flanked with an angular tower, usually square: another symptom of war; another means of defence. The second story consisted again of a single room; its use is not known, but it probably served for the children and domestics. Above this in most houses, was a small platform, evidently intended as an observatory or watch-tower. Every feature of the building bore the appearance of war. This was the decided characteristic, the true name of the movement, which wrought out the freedom of the cities.

After a war has continued a certain time, whoever may be the belligerent parties, it naturally leads to a peace. The treaties of peace between the cities and their adversaries were so many charters. These charters of the cities were so many positive treaties of peace between the burgesses and their lords.*

The insurrection was general. When I say general, I do not mean that there was any concerted plan, that there was any coalition between all the burgesses of a country; nothing like it took place. But the situation of all the towns being nearly the same, they all were liable to the same danger; a prey to the same disasters. Having acquired similar means of resistance and defence, they made use of those means at nearly the same time. It may be possible, also, that the force of example did something; that the success of one or two communities was contagious. Sometimes the charters appear to have been drawn up from the same model; for instance, that of Noyon served as a pattern for those of Beauvais, St. Quentin,† and others; I doubt, however, whether example had so great an influence as is generally conjectured. Communication between different provinces was difficult and of rare occurrence; the intelligence conveyed and received by hearsay and general report was vague and uncertain; and there is much reason for believing that the insurrection was rather the result of a similarity of situation and of a general spontaneous movement. When I say general, I wish to be understood simply as saying that insurrections took place everywhere; they did not, I repeat, spring from any unanimous concerted movement: all was particular, local; each community rebelled on its own account, against its own lord, unconnected with any other place.

The vicissitudes of the struggle were great. Not only did success change from one side to the other, but even after peace was in appearance concluded, after the charter had been solemnly sworn to by both parties, they violated and eluded its articles in all sorts of ways. Kings acted a prominent part in the alternations of these struggles. I shall speak of these more in detail when I come to royalty itself. Too much has probably been said of the effects of royal influence upon the struggles of the people for freedom. These effects have been often contested, sometimes exaggerated, and in my opinion, sometimes greatly underrated. I shall here confine myself to the assertion that royalty was often called upon to interfere in these contests, sometimes by the cities, sometimes by their lords; and that it played very different parts; acting now upon one principle, and soon after upon another; that it was ever changing its intentions, its designs, and its conduct;* but that, taking it altogether, it did much, and produced a greater portion of good than of evil.

In spite of all these vicissitudes, notwithstanding the perpetual violation of charters in the twelfth century—the freedom of the cities was consummated. Europe, and particularly France, which, during a whole century, had abounded in insurrections, now abounded in charters;* cities rejoiced in them with more or less security, but still they rejoiced; the event succeeded, and the right was acknowledged.

Let us now endeavor to ascertain the more immediate results of this great fact, and what changes it produced in the situation of the burgesses as regarded society.

And, at first, as regards the relations of the burgesses with the general government of the country, or with what we now call the state, it effected nothing; they took no part in this more than before; all remained local, enclosed within the limits of the fief.

One circumstance, however, renders this assertion not strictly true: a connection now began to be formed between the cities and the king. At one time the people called upon the king for support and protection, or solicited him to guaranty the charter which had been promised or sworn to. At another the barons invoked the judicial interference of the king between them and the burgesses. At the request of one or other of the two parties, from a multitude of various causes royalty was called upon to interfere in the quarrel, whence resulted a frequent and close connection between the citizens and the king. In consequence of this connection the cities became a part of the state, they began to have relations with the general government.

Although all still remained local, yet a new general class of society became formed by the enfranchisement of the commons. No coalition of the burgesses of different cities had taken place; as yet they had as a class no public or general existence. But the country was covered with men engaged in similar pursuits, possessing the same views and interests, the same manners and customs; between whom there could not fail to be gradually formed a certain tie, from which originated the general class of burgesses. This formation of a great social class was the necessary result of the local enfranchisement of the burgesses.* It must not, however, be supposed that the class of which we are speaking was then what it has since become. Not only is its situation greatly changed, but its elements are totally different. In the twelfth century, this class was almost entirely composed of merchants or small traders, and little landed or house proprietors who had taken up their residence in the city. Three centuries afterwards there were added to this class lawyers, physicians, men of letters, and the local magistrates. The class of burgesses was formed gradually and of very different elements: history gives us no accurate account of its progress, nor of its diversity. When the body of citizens is spoken of, it is erroneously conjectured to have been, at all times, composed of the same elements. Absurd supposition! It is, perhaps, in the diversity of its composition at different periods of history that we should seek to discover the secret of its destiny; so long as it was destitute of magistrates and of men of letters, so long it remained totally unlike what it became in the sixteenth century; as regards the state, it neither possessed the same character nor the same importance. In order to form a just idea of the changes in the rank and influence of this portion of society, we must take a view of the new professions, the new moral situations, of the new intellectual state which gradually arose within it. In the twelfth century, I must repeat, the body of citizens consisted only of small merchants or traders, who, after having finished their purchases and sales, retired to their houses in the city or town; and of little proprietors of houses or lands who had there taken up their residence. Such was the European burgher class in its primary elements.

The third great result of the enfranchisement of the cities was the struggle of classes; a struggle which constitutes the very fact of modern history, and of which it is full.

Modern Europe, indeed, is born of this struggle between the different classes of society. I have already shown that in other places this struggle has been productive of very different consequences; in Asia, for example, one particular class has completely triumphed, and the system of castes has succeeded to that of classes, and society has there fallen into a state of immobility. Nothing of this kind, thank God! has taken place in Europe. One of the classes has not conquered, has not brought the others into subjection; no class has been able to overcome, to subjugate the others; the struggle, instead of rendering society stationary, has been a principal cause of its progress; the relations of the different classes with one another; the necessity of combating and of yielding by turns; the variety of interests, passions, and excitements; the desire to conquer without the power to do so: from all this has probably sprung the most energetic, the most productive principle of development in European civilization. This struggle of the classes has been constant; enmity has grown up between them; the infinite diversity of situation, of interests, and of manners, has produced a strong moral hostility; yet they have progressively approached, assimilated, and understood each other; every country of Europe has seen the rise and development within it of a certain public spirit, a certain community of interests, of ideas, of sentiments, which have triumphed over this diversity and war. In France, for example, in the seventeenth and eighteenth centuries, the moral and social separation of classes was still very profound, yet there can be no doubt but that their fusion, even then, was far advanced; that even then there was a real French nation, not consisting of any class exclusively, but of a commixture of the whole; all animated with the same feeling, actuated by one common social principle, firmly knit together by the bond of nationality. Thus, from the bosom of variety, enmity, and discord, has issued that national unity, now become so conspicuous in modern Europe; that nationality whose tendency is to develop and purify itself more and more, and every day to increase its splendor.

Such are the great, the important, the conspicuous social effects of the revolution which now occupies our attention. Let us now endeavor to show what were its moral effects; what changes it produced in the minds of the citizens themselves, what they became in consequence, and what they should morally become, in their new situation.

When we take into our consideration the connection of the citizens with the state in general, with the government of the state, and with the interests of the country, as that connection existed not only in the twelfth century, but also in after ages, there is one circumstance which must strike us most forcibly: I mean the extraordinary mental timidity of the citizens; their humility; the excessive modesty of their pretensions to a right of interference in the government of their country; and the little matter that, in this respect, contented them. Nothing was to be seen in them which discovered that genuine political feeling that aspires to the possession of influence, and to the power of reforming and governing; nothing attests in them either energy of mind, or loftiness of ambition; one feels ready to exclaim, "Poor, prudent, simple-hearted citizens!"

There are not, probably, more than two sources whence, in the political world, can flow loftiness of ambition and energy of mind. There must be either the feeling of possessing a great importance, a great power over the destiny of others, and this over a large sphere; or there must be in one's self a powerful feeling of personal independence, the assurance of one's own liberty, the consciousness of having a destiny with which no will can intermeddle beyond that in one's own bosom. To one or other of these two conditions seem to be attached energy of mind, the loftiness of ambition, the desire to act in a large sphere, and to obtain corresponding results. Neither of these conditions is to be found in the situation of the burgesses of the middle ages. These were, as we have just seen, only important to themselves; except within the walls of their own city, their influence amounted to but little; as regarded the state, to almost nothing. Nor could they be possessed of any great feeling of personal independence; that they had conquered, that they had obtained a charter did but little in the way of promoting this noble sentiment. The burgess of a city, comparing himself with the little baron who dwelt near him, and who had just been vanquished by him, would still be sensible of his own extreme inferiority; he was ignorant of that proud sentiment of independence which animated the proprietor of a fief; the share of freedom which he possessed was not derived from himself alone, but from his association with others—from the difficult and precarious succor which they afforded. Hence that retiring disposition, that timidity of mind, that trembling shyness, that humility of speech (though perhaps coupled with firmness of purpose), which is so deeply stamped on the character of the burgesses, not only of the twelfth century, but even of their most remote descendants. They had no taste for great enterprises; if chance pushed them into such, they became vexed and embarrassed; any responsibility was a burden to them; they felt themselves out of their sphere, and endeavored to return into it; they treated upon easy terms. Thus, in running over the history of Europe, and especially of France, we find that municipal communities have been esteemed, consulted, perhaps respected, but rarely feared; they seldom impressed their adversaries with the notion that they were a great and formidable power, a power truly political. There is nothing to be astonished at in the weakness of the modern burgess; the great cause of it may be traced to his origin, in those circumstances of his enfranchisement which I have just placed before you. The loftiness of ambition, independent of social conditions, the breadth and boldness of political views, the desire to be employed in public affairs, the full consciousness of the greatness of man, considered as such, and of the power that belongs to him, if he be capable of exercising it; these sentiments, these dispositions, are of entirely modern growth in Europe, the offspring of modern civilization, and of that glorious and powerful generality which characterizes it, and which will never fail to secure to the public an influence, a weight in the government of the country, that were constantly wanting, and deservedly wanting, to the burgesses our ancestors.

As a set-off to this, in the contests which they had to sustain respecting their local interests—in this narrow field, they acquired and displayed a degree of energy, devotedness, perseverance, and patience, which has never been surpassed. The difficulty of the enterprise was so great, they had to struggle against such perils, that a display of courage almost beyond example became necessary. Our notions of the burgess of the twelfth and thirteenth centuries, and of his life, are very erroneous. The picture which Sir Walter Scott has drawn in Quentin Durward of the burgomaster of Liege, fat, inactive, without experience, without daring, and caring for nothing but passing his life in ease and enjoyment, is only fitted for the stage; the real burgess of that day had a coat of mail continually on his back, a pike constantly in his hand; his life was nearly as stormy, as warlike, as rigid as that of the nobles with whom he contended. It was in these every-day perils, in combating the varied dangers of practical life, that he acquired that bold and masculine character, that determined exertion, which have become more rare in the softer activity of modern times.

None, however, of these social and moral effects of the enfranchisement of corporations became fully developed in the twelfth century; it is only in the course of the two following centuries that they showed themselves so as to be clearly discerned. It is nevertheless certain that the seeds of these effects existed in the primary situation of the commons, in the mode of their enfranchisement, and in the position which the burgesses from that time took in society; I think, therefore, that I have done right in bringing these circumstances before you to-day.

Let us now penetrate into the interior of one of those corporate cities of the twelfth century, that we may see how it was governed, that we may now see what principles and what facts prevailed in the relations of the burgesses with one another. It must be remembered, that in speaking of the municipal system bequeathed by the Roman empire to the modern world, I took occasion to say,* that the Roman world was a great coalition of municipalities, which had previously been as sovereign and independent as Rome itself. Each of these cities had formerly been in the same condition as Rome, a little free republic, making peace and war, and governing itself by its own will. As fast as these became incorporated into the Roman world, those rights which constitute sovereignty—the right of war and peace, of legislation, taxation, etc.—were transferred from each city to the central government at Rome. There remained then but one municipal sovereignty. Rome reigned over a vast number of municipalities, which had nothing left beyond a civic existence. The municipal system became essentially changed: it was no longer a political government, but simply a mode of administration. This was the grand revolution which was consummated under the Roman empire. The municipal system became a mode of administration; it was reduced to the government of local affairs, to the civic interests of the city. This is the state in which the Roman empire, at its fall, left the cities and their institutions. During the chaos of barbarism, notions and facts of all sorts became embroiled and confused; the various attributes of sovereignty and administration were confounded. Distinctions of this nature were no longer regarded. Affairs were suffered to run on in the course dictated by necessity. The municipalities became sovereigns or administrators in the various places, as need might require. Where cities rebelled, they reassumed the sovereignty, for the sake of security, not out of respect for any political theory, nor from any feeling of their dignity, but that they might have the means of contending with the nobles, whose yoke they had thrown off; that they might take upon themselves the right to call out the militia, to tax themselves to support the war, to name their own chiefs and magistrates; in a word, to govern themselves. The internal government of the city was their means of defence, of security. Thus, sovereignty again returned to the municipal system, which had been deprived of it by the conquests of Rome. City corporations again became sovereigns. This is the political characteristic of their enfranchisement.

I do not, however, mean to assert, that this sovereignty was complete. Some trace of an exterior sovereignty always may be found; sometimes it was the baron who retained the right to send a magistrate into the city, with whom the municipal magistrates acted as assessors; perhaps he had the right to collect certain revenues; in some cases a fixed tribute was assured to him. Sometimes the exterior sovereignty of the community was in the hands of the king.

The cities themselves, in their turn, entered into the feudal system; they had vassals, and became suzerains; and by this title possessed that portion of sovereignty which was inherent in the suzerainty. A great confusion arose between the rights which they held from their feudal position, and those which they had acquired by their insurrection; and by this double title they held the sovereignty.

Let us see, as far as the very scanty sources left us will allow, how the internal government of the cities, at least in the more early times, was managed. The entire body of the inhabitants formed the communal assembly: all those who had taken the communal oath—and all who dwelt within the walls were obliged to do so—were summoned, by the tolling of the bell, to the general assembly. In this were named the magistrates. The number chosen, and the power and proceedings of the magistrates, differed very considerably. After choosing the magistrates, the assemblies dissolved; and the magistrates governed almost alone, sufficiently arbitrarily, being under no further responsibility than the new elections, or, perhaps, popular outbreaks, which were, at this time, the great guarantee for good government.*

You will observe that the internal organization of the municipal towns is reduced to two very simple elements, the general assembly of the inhabitants, and a government invested with almost arbitrary power, under the responsibility of insurrections,—general outbreaks. It was impossible, especially while such manners prevailed, to establish anything like a regular government, with proper guarantees of order and duration. The greater part of the population of these cities were ignorant, brutal, and savage to a degree which rendered them exceedingly difficult to govern. At the end of a very short period, there was but little more security within these communities than there had been, previously, in the relations of the burgesses with the baron. There soon, however, became formed a burgess aristocracy. The causes of this are easily understood. The notions of that day, coupled with certain social relations, led to the establishment of trading companies legally constituted.* A system of privileges became introduced into the interior of the cities, and, in the end, a great inequality. There soon grew up in all of them a certain number of considerable, opulent burgesses, and a population, more or less numerous, of workmen, who, notwithstanding their inferiority, had no small influence in the affairs of the community. The free cities thus became divided into an upper class of burgesses, and a population subject to all the errors, all the vices of a mob. The superior citizens thus found themselves pressed between two great difficulties: first, the arduous one of governing this inferior turbulent population; and secondly, that of withstanding the continual attempts of the ancient master of the borough, who sought to regain his former power. Such was the situation of their affairs, not only in France, but in Europe, down to the sixteenth century. This, perhaps, is the cause which prevented these communities from taking, in several countries of Europe, and especially in France, that high political station which seemed properly to belong to them. Two spirits were unceasingly at work within them: among the inferior population, a blind, licentious, furious spirit of democracy; among the superior burgesses, a spirit of timidity, of caution, and an excessive desire to accommodate all differences, whether with the king, or with its ancient proprietors, so as to preserve peace and order in the bosom of the community. Neither of these spirits could raise the cities to a high rank in the state.

All these effects did not become apparent in the twelfth century; still we may foresee them, even in the character of the insurrection, in the manner in which it broke out, in the state of the different elements of the city population.

Such, if I mistake not, are the principal characteristics, the general results, both of the enfranchisement of the cities and of their internal government. I have already premised, that these facts were not so uniform, not so universal, as I have represented them. There are great diversities in the history of the European free cities. In the south of France and in Italy, for example, the Roman municipal system prevailed; the population was not nearly so divided, so unequal, as in the north. Here, also, the municipal organization was much better; perhaps the effect of Roman traditions, perhaps of the better state of the population. In the north, it was the feudal system that prevailed in the city arrangements. Here all seemed subordinate to the struggle against the barons. The cities of the south paid much more regard to their internal constitution, to the work of melioration and progress. We see, from the beginning, that they will become free republics. The career of those of the north, above all those of France, showed itself, from the first, more rude, more incomplete, destined to less perfect, less beautiful developments. If we run over those of Germany, Spain, and England, we shall find among them many other differences. I cannot particularize them, but shall notice some of them, as we advance in the history of civilization. All things at their origin are nearly confounded in one and the same physiognomy; it is only in their after-growth that their variety shows itself. Then begins a new development which urges forward societies towards that free and lofty unity, the glorious object of the efforts and wishes of mankind.*

LECTURE VIII.: GENERAL STATE OF EUROPE FROM THE TWELFTH TO THE FOURTEENTH CENTURY—THE CRUSADES.*

I have not yet laid before you the whole plan of my course. I began by pointing out its object, and I then went straight forward, without taking any comprehensive view of European civilization, and without indicating at once its starting-point, its path, and its goal,—its beginning, middle, and end. We have now, however, arrived at a period when this comprehensive view, this general outline, of the world through which we travel, becomes necessary. The times which have hitherto been the subject of our study, are explained in some measure by themselves, or by clear and immediate results. The times into which we are about to enter can neither be understood nor excite any strong interest, unless we connect them with their most indirect and remote consequences. In an inquiry of such vast extent, a time arrives when we can no longer submit to go forward with a dark and unknown path before us; when we desire to know not only whence we have come and where we are, but whither we are going. This is now the case with us. The period which we approach cannot be understood, or its importance appreciated, unless by means of the relations which connect it with modern times. Its true spirit has been revealed only by the lapse of many subsequent ages.

We are in possession of almost all the essential elements of European civilization. I say almost all, because I have not yet said anything on the subject of monarchy. The crisis which decidedly developed the monarchical principle, hardly took place before the twelfth or even the thirteenth century. It was then only that the institution of monarchy was really established, and began to occupy a definite place in modern society. It is on this account that I have not sooner entered on the subject. With this exception we possess, I repeat, all the great elements of European society. You have seen the origin of the feudal aristocracy, the Church, and the municipalities; you have observed the institutions which would naturally correspond with these facts; and not only the institutions, but the principles and ideas which those facts naturally give rise to. Thus, with reference to feudalism, you have watched the origin of modern domestic life; you have comprehended, in all its energy, the feeling of personal independence, and the place which it must have occupied in our civilization. With reference to the Church, you have observed the appearance of the purely religious form of society, its relations with civil society, the principle of theocracy, the separation between the spiritual and temporal powers, the first blows of persecution, the first cries of liberty of conscience. The infant municipalities have given you a view of a social union founded on principles quite different from those of feudalism; the diversity of the classes of society, their contests with each other, the first and strongly marked features of the manners of the modern inhabitants of towns; timidity of judgment combined with energy of soul, proneness to be excited by demagogues joined to a spirit of obedience to legal authority; all the elements, in short, which have concurred in the formation of European society have already come under your observation.

Let us now transport ourselves into the heart of modern Europe; I do not mean Europe of the present day, after the prodigious metamorphoses we have witnessed, but of the seventeenth and eighteenth centuries. What an immense difference! I have already insisted on this difference with reference to communities; I have endeavored to show you how little resemblance there is between the burgesses of the eighteenth century and those of the twelfth. Make the same experiment on feudalism and the Church, and you will be struck with a similar metamorphosis. There was no more resemblance between the nobility of the court of Louis XV and the feudal aristocracy, or between the Church in the days of Cardinal de Bernis and those of the Abbé Suger, than there is between the burgesses of the eighteenth century and the same class in the twelfth. Between these two periods, though society had already acquired all its elements, it underwent a total transformation.

I am now desirous to trace clearly the general and essential character of this transformation. From the fifth century, society contained all that I have already found and described as belonging to it,—kings, a lay aristocracy, a clergy, burghers, husbandmen, civil and religious authorities; the germs, in short, of every thing necessary to form a nation and a government; and yet there was no government, no nation. In all the period that has occupied our attention, there was no such thing as a people, properly so called, or a government, in the modern acceptation of the word. We have fallen in with a number of particular forces, special facts, and local institutions; but nothing general, nothing public, nothing political, nothing, in short, like real nationality. Let us, on the other hand, survey Europe in the seventeenth and eighteenth centuries: we everywhere see two great objects make their appearance on the stage of the world,—the government and the people. The influence of a general power over an entire country, and the influence of the country in the power which governs it, are the materials of history; the relations between these great forces, their alliances or their contests, are the subjects of its narration. The nobility, the clergy, the citizens, all these different classes and particular powers are thrown into the background, and effaced, as it were, by these two great objects, the people and its government.

This, if I am not deceived, is the essential feature which distinguishes modern Europe from the Europe of the early ages; and this was the change which was accomplished between the thirteenth and the sixteenth century.

It is, then, in the period from the thirteenth to the sixteenth century, into which we are about to enter, that we must endeavor to find the cause of this change. It is the distinctive character of this period, that it was employed in changing Europe from its primitive to its modern state; and hence arise its importance and historical interest. If we did not consider it under this point of view, if we did not endeavor to discover the events which arose out of this period, not only we should never be able to comprehend it, but we should soon become weary of the inquiry.

Viewed in itself and apart from its results, it is a period without character, a period in which confusion went on increasing without apparent causes, a period of movement without direction, of agitation without result; a period when monarchy, nobility, clergy, citizens, all the elements of social order, seemed to turn round in the same circle, incapable alike of progression and of rest. Experiments of all kinds were made and failed; endeavors were made to establish governments and lay the foundations of public liberty; reforms in religion were even attempted; but nothing was accomplished or came to any result. If ever the human race seemed destined to be always agitated, and yet always stationary, condemned to unceasing and yet barren labors, it was from the thirteenth to the fifteenth century that this was the complexion of its condition and history.

I am acquainted only with one work in which this appearance of the period in question is faithfully described; I allude to M. de Barante's History of the Dukes of Burgundy.* I do not speak of the fidelity of his pictures of manners and narratives of adventures, but of that general fidelity which renders the work an exact image, a true mirror of the whole period, of which it at the same time displays both the agitation and the monotony.

Considered, on the contrary, in relation to what has succeeded it, as the transition from Europe in its primitive, to Europe in its modern state, this period assumes a more distinct and animated aspect; we discover in it a unity of design, a movement in one direction, a progression; and its unity and interest are found to reside in the slow and hidden labor accomplished in the course of its duration.

The history of European civilization, then, may be thrown into three great periods: first, a period which I shall call that of origin, or formation; during which the different elements of society disengage themselves from chaos, assume an existence, and show themselves in their native forms, with the principles by which they are animated; this period lasted almost to the twelfth century. The second period is a period of experiments, attempts, groping; the different elements of society approach and enter into combination, feeling each other, as it were, but without producing anything general, regular, or durable; this state of things, to say the truth, did not terminate till the sixteenth century. Then comes the third period, or the period of development, in which human society in Europe takes a definite form, follows a determinate direction, proceeds rapidly and with a general movement, towards a clear and precise object; this is the period which began in the sixteenth century, and is now pursuing its course.*

Such appears, on a general view, to be the aspect of European civilization. We are now about to enter into the second of the above periods; and we have to inquire what were the great and critical events which occurred during its course, and were the determining causes of the social transformation that was its result.

The first great event which presents itself to our view, and which opened, so to speak, the period we are speaking of, was the crusades. They began at the end of the eleventh century, and lasted during the twelfth and thirteenth. It was indeed a great event; for, since its occurrence, it has never ceased to occupy the attention of philosophical historians, who have shown themselves aware of its influence in changing the conditions of nations, and of the necessity of its study in order to comprehend the general course of facts.

The first character of the crusades is their universality; all Europe concurred in them; they were the first European event. Before the crusades, Europe had never been moved by the same sentiment, or acted in a common cause; till then, in fact, Europe did not exist. The crusades made manifest the existence of Christian Europe. The French formed the main body of the first army of crusaders; but there were also Germans, Italians, Spaniards, and English. But look at the second and third crusades, and we find all the nations of Christendom engaged in them. The world had never before witnessed a similar combination.

But this is not all. In the same manner as the crusades were a European event, so, in each separate nation, they were a national event. In every nation, all classes of society were animated with the same impression, yielded to the same idea, and abandoned themselves to the same impulse. Kings, nobles, priests, burghers, country people, all took the same interest and the same share in the crusades. The moral unity of nations was thus made manifest; a fact as new as the unity of Europe.

When such events take place in what may be called the youth of nations; in periods when they act spontaneously, freely, without premeditation or political design, we recognize what history calls heroic events, the heroic ages of nations. The crusades were the heroic event of modern Europe; a movement at the same time individual and general; national, and yet not under political direction.

That this was really their primitive character is proved by every fact, and every document. Who were the first crusaders? Bands of people who set out under the conduct of Peter the Hermit, without preparations, guides, or leaders, followed rather than led by a few obscure knights, traversed Germany and the Greek empire, and were dispersed, or perished, in Asia Minor.

The higher class, the feudal nobility, next put themselves in motion for the crusade. Under the command of Godfrey of Bouillon, the nobles and their men departed full of ardor. When they had traversed Asia Minor, the leaders of the crusaders were seized with a fit of lukewarmness and fatigue. They became indifferent about continuing their course; they were inclined rather to look to their own interest, to make conquests and possess them. The mass of the army, however, rose up, and insisted on marching to Jerusalem, the deliverance of the holy city being the object of the crusade. It was not to gain principalities for Raymond of Toulouse, or for Bohemond, or any other leader, that the crusaders had taken arms. The popular, national, European impulse overcame all the intentions of individuals; and the leaders had not sufficient ascendancy over the masses to make them yield to their personal interests.

The sovereigns, who had been strangers to the first crusade, were now drawn into the general movement as the people had been. The great crusades of the twelfth century were commanded by kings.

I now go at once to the end of the thirteenth century. A great deal was still said in Europe about crusades, and they were even preached with ardor. The popes excited the sovereigns and the people; councils were held to recommend the conquest of the holy land; but no expeditions of any importance were now undertaken for this purpose, and it was regarded with general indifference. Something had entered into the spirit of European society which put an end to the crusades. Some private expeditions still took place; some nobles and some bands of troops still continued to depart for Jerusalem; but the general movement was evidently arrested. Neither the necessity, however, nor the facility of continuing it, seemed to have ceased. The Moslems triumphed more and more in Asia. The Christian kingdom founded at Jerusalem had fallen into their hands. It still appeared necessary to regain it; and the means of success were greater than at the commencement of the crusades. A great number of Christians were established and still powerful in Asia Minor, Syria, and Palestine. The proper means of transport, and of carrying on the war, were better known. Still, nothing could revive the spirit of the crusades. It is evident that the two great forces of society—the sovereigns on the one hand, and the people on the other—no longer desired their continuance.

It has been often said that Europe was weary of these constant inroads upon Asia. We must come to an understanding as to the meaning of the word weariness, frequently used on such occasions. It is exceedingly inexact. It is not true that generations of mankind can be weary of what has not been done by themselves; that they can be wearied by the fatigues of their fathers. Weariness is personal; it cannot be transmitted like an inheritance. The people of the thirteenth century were not weary of the crusades of the twelfth; they were influenced by a different cause. A great change had taken place in opinions, sentiments, and social relations. There were no longer the same wants, or the same desires: the people no longer believed, or wished to believe, in the same things. It is by these moral or political changes, and not by weariness, that the differences in the conduct of successive generations can be explained. The pretended weariness ascribed to them is a metaphor wholly destitute of truth.

Two great causes, the one moral, the other social, impelled Europe into the crusades. The moral cause, as you are aware, was the impulse of religious feeling and belief. From the end of the seventh century, Christianity maintained a constant struggle against Mohammedanism. It had overcome Mohammedanism in Europe, after having been threatened with great danger from it;* and had succeeded in confining it to Spain. Even from thence the expulsion of Mohammedanism was constantly attempted. The crusades have been represented as a sort of accident, an unforeseen event, sprung from the recitals of pilgrims returned from Jerusalem, and the preaching of Peter the Hermit.† They were nothing of the kind. The crusades were the continuation, the height of the great struggle which had subsisted for four centuries between Christianity and Mohammedanism. The theatre of this contest had hitherto been in Europe; it was now transported into Asia. If I had attached any value to those comparisons, those parallels, into which historical facts are sometimes made willing or unwillingly to enter, I might show you Christianity running exactly the same course, and undergoing the same destiny in Asia, as Mohammedanism in Europe. Mohammedanism established itself in Spain, where it conquered, founded a kingdom and various principalities. The Christians did the same thing in Asia. They were there in regard to the Mohammedans, in the same situation as the Mohammedans in Spain with regard to the Christians. The kingdom of Jerusalem corresponds with the kingdom of Granada: but these similitudes, after all, are of little importance. The great fact was the struggle between the two religious and social systems: the crusades were its principal crisis. This is their historical character; the chain which connects them with the general course of events.

Another cause, the social state of Europe in the eleventh century, equally contributed to the breaking out of the crusades. I have been careful to explain why, from the fifth to the eleventh century, there was no such thing as generality in Europe; I have endeavored to show how every thing had assumed a local character; how states, existing institutions, and opinions, were confined within very narrow bounds: it was then that the feudal system prevailed. After the lapse of some time, such a narrow horizon was no longer sufficient; human thought and activity aspired to pass beyond the narrow sphere in which they were confined. The people no longer led their former wandering life, but had not lost the taste for its movement and its adventures; they threw themselves into the crusades as into a new state of existence, in which they were more at large, and enjoyed more variety; which reminded them of the freedom of former barbarism, while it opened boundless prospects for the future.

These were, in my opinion, the two determining causes of the crusades in the twelfth century.* At the end of the thirteenth, neither of these causes continued to exist. Mankind and society were so greatly changed, that neither the moral nor the social incitements which had impelled Europe upon Asia were felt any longer. I do not know whether many of you have read the original historians of the crusades, or have ever thought of comparing the contemporary chroniclers of the first crusades with those of the end of the twelfth and thirteenth centuries; for example, Albert d'Aix, Robert the Monk, and Raynard d'Argile, who were engaged in the first crusade, with William of Tyre and James de Vitry.* When we compare these two classes of writers, it is impossible not to be struck with the distance between them. The first are animated chroniclers, whose imagination is excited, and who relate the events of the crusade with passion: but they are narrowminded in the extreme, without an idea beyond the little sphere in which they lived; ignorant of every science, full of prejudices, incapable of forming an opinion on what was passing around them, or the events which were the subject of their narratives. But open, on the other hand, the history of the crusades by William of Tyre, and you will be surprised to find almost a modern historian; a cultivated, enlarged, and liberal mind, great political intelligence, general views and opinions upon causes and effects. James de Vitry is an example of another species of cultivation; he is a man of learning, who does not confine himself to what immediately concerns the crusades, but describes the state of manners, the geography, the religion, and natural history of the country to which his history relates. There is, in short, an immense distance between the historians feature of the penitential system of the Church. The crusades were vast pilgrimages, the undertaking of which would count for the future salvation of the crusaders. See Adams, of the first and of the last crusades; a distance which manifests an actual revolution in the state of the human mind.

This revolution is most conspicuous in the manner in which these two classes of writers speak of the Mohammedans. To the first chroniclers,—and consequently to the first crusaders, of whose sentiments the first chroniclers are merely the organs,—the Mohammedans are only an object of hatred; it is clear that those who speak of them do not know them, form no judgment respecting them, nor consider them except from the point of view of the religious hostility which exists between them. No vestige of social relation is discoverable between them and the Mohammedans: they detest them, and fight with them; and nothing more. William of Tyre, James de Vitry, Bernard le Trésorier, speak of the Mussulmans quite differently. We see that, even while fighting with them, they no longer regard them as monsters; that they have entered to a certain extent into their ideas, that they have lived with them, and that certain social relations, and even a sort of sympathy, have arisen between them. William of Tyre pronounces a glowing eulogium on Noureddin and Bernard le Trésorier on Saladin. They sometimes even go the length of placing the manners and conduct of the Mussulmans in opposition to those of the Christians;

they adopt the manners and sentiments of the Mussulmans in order to satirize the Christians, in the same manner as Tacitus delineated the manners of the Germans in contrast with those of Rome. You see, then, what an immense change must have taken place between these two periods, when you find in the latter, in regard to the very enemies of the Christians, the very people against whom the crusades were directed, an impartiality of judgment which would have filled the first crusaders with surprise and horror.

The principal effect, then, of the crusades was a great step towards the emancipation of the mind, a great progress towards enlarged and liberal ideas. Though begun under the name and influence of religious belief, the crusades deprived religious ideas, I shall not say of their legitimate share of influence, but of their exclusive and despotic possession of the human mind. This result, though undoubtedly unforeseen, arose from various causes. The first was evidently the novelty, extent, and variety of the scene which displayed itself to the crusaders; what generally happens to travellers happened to them. It is mere common-place to say, that travelling gives freedom to the mind; that the habit of observing different nations, different manners, and different opinions, enlarges the ideas, and disengages the judgment from old prejudices. The same thing happened to those nations of travellers who have been called the crusaders; their minds were opened and raised by having seen a multitude of different things, by having become acquainted with other manners than their own. They found themselves also placed in connection with two states of civilization, not only different from their own, but more advanced—the Greek state of society on the one hand, and the Mussulman on the other. There is no doubt that the society of the Greeks, though enervated, perverted, and decaying, gave the crusaders the impression of something more advanced, polished, and enlightened than their own. The society of the Mussulmans presented them a scene of the same kind. It is curious to observe in the chronicles the impression made by the crusaders on the Mussulmans, who regarded them at first as the most brutal, ferocious, and stupid barbarians they had ever seen. The crusaders, on their part, were struck with the riches and elegance of manners which they observed among the Mussulmans. These first impressions were succeeded by frequent relations between the Mussulmans and Christians. These became more extensive and important than is commonly believed. Not only had the Christians of the East habitual relations with the Mussulmans, but the people of the East and the West became acquainted with, visited, and mingled with each other. It is but lately that one of those learned men who do honor to France in the eyes of Europe, M. Abel Rémusat, has discovered the relations which subsisted between the Mongol emperors and the Christian kings. Mongol ambassadors were sent to the kings of the Franks, and to St. Louis among others, in order to persuade them to enter into alliance, and to resume the crusades for the common interest of the Mongols and the Christians against the Turks. And not only were diplomatic and official relations thus established between the sovereigns, but there was much and various intercourse between the nations of the East and West. I shall quote the words of M. Abel Rémusat:*—

You see, then, what a vast and unexplored world was laid open to the view of European intelligence by the consequences of the crusades. It cannot be doubted that the impulse which led to them was one of the most powerful causes of the development and freedom of mind which arose out of that great event.

There is another circumstance which is worthy of notice. Down to the time of the crusades, the court of Rome, the center of the Church, had been very little in communication with the laity, unless through the medium of ecclesiastics; either legates sent by the court of Rome, or the whole body of the bishops and clergy. There were always some laymen in direct relation with Rome; but upon the whole, it was by means of churchmen that Rome had any communication with the people of different countries. During the crusades, on the contrary, Rome became a halting-place for a great portion of the crusaders, either in going or returning. A multitude of laymen were spectators of its policy and its manners, and were able to discover the share which personal interest had in religious disputes. There is no doubt that this newly-acquired knowledge inspired many minds with a boldness hitherto unknown.

When we consider the state of the general mind at the termination of the crusades, especially in regard to ecclesiastical matters, we cannot fail to be struck with a singular fact: religious notions underwent no change, and were not replaced by contrary or even different opinions. Thought, notwithstanding, had become more free; religious creeds were not the only subject on which the human mind exercised its faculties; without abandoning them, it began occasionally to wander from them, and to take other directions. Thus, at the end of the thirteenth century, the moral cause which had led to the crusades, or which, at least, had been their most energetic principle, had disappeared; the moral state of Europe had undergone an essential modification.

The social state of society had undergone an analogous change. Many inquiries have been made as to the influence of the crusades in this respect; it has been shown in what manner they had reduced a great number of feudal proprietors to the necessity of selling their fiefs to the kings, or to sell their privileges to the communities, in order to raise money for the crusades. It has been shown that, in consequence of their absence, many of the nobles lost a great portion of their power. Without entering into the details of this question, we may collect into a few general facts the influence of the crusades on the social state of Europe.

They greatly diminished the number of petty fiefs, petty domains, and petty proprietors; they concentrated property and power in a smaller number of hands. It is from the time of the crusades that we may observe the formation and growth of great fiefs—the existence of feudal power on a large scale.*

I have often regretted that there was not a map of France divided into fiefs, as we have a map of France divided into departments, arrondissements, cantons and communes, in which all the fiefs were marked, with their boundaries, relations with each other, and successive changes. If we could have compared, by the help of such maps, the state of France before and after the crusades, we should have seen how many small fiefs had disappeared, and to what extent the greater ones had increased. This was one of the most important results of the crusades.

Even in those cases where small proprietors preserved their fiefs, they did not live upon them in such an isolated state as formerly. The possessors of great fiefs became so many centers around which the smaller ones were gathered, and near which they came to live. During the crusades, small proprietors found it necessary to place themselves in the train of some rich and powerful chief, from whom they received assistance and support. They lived with him, shared his fortune, and passed through the same adventures that he did. When the crusaders returned home, this social spirit, this habit of living in intercourse with superiors continued to subsist, and had its influence on the manners of the age. As we see that the great fiefs were increased after the crusades, so we see, also, that the proprietors of these fiefs held, within their castles, a much more considerable court than before, and were surrounded by a greater number of gentlemen, who preserved their little domains, but no longer kept within them.

The extension of the great fiefs, and the creation of a number of central points in society, in place of the general dispersion which previously existed, were the two principal effects of the crusades, considered with respect to their influence upon feudalism.

As to the inhabitants of the towns, a result of the same nature may easily be perceived. The crusades created great civic communities. Petty commerce and petty industry were not sufficient to give rise to communities such as the great cities of Italy and Flanders. It was commerce on a great scale—maritime commerce, and, especially, the commerce of the East and West, which gave them birth; now it was the crusades which gave to maritime commerce the greatest impulse it had yet received.*

On the whole, when we survey the state of society at the end of the crusades, we find that the movement tending to dissolution and dispersion, the movement of universal localization (if I may be allowed such an expression), had ceased, and had been succeeded by a movement in the contrary direction, a movement of centralization. All things tended to mutual approximation; small things were absorbed in great ones, or gathered round them. Such was the direction then taken by the progress of society.

You now understand why, at the end of the thirteenth and in the fourteenth century, neither nations nor sovereigns wished to have any more crusades. They neither needed nor desired them; they had been thrown into them by the impulses of religious spirit, and the exclusive dominion of religious ideas; but this dominion had now lost its energy. They had also sought in the crusades a new way of life, of a less confined and more varied description; but they began to find this in Europe itself, in the progress of the social relations. It was at this time that kings began to see the road to political aggrandizement. Why go to Asia in search of kingdoms, when there were kingdoms to conquer at their very doors? Philip Augustus embarked in the crusade very unwillingly; and what could be more natural? His desire was to make himself King of France. It was the same thing with the people. The road to wealth was open to them; and they gave up adventures for industry. Adventures were replaced, for sovereigns, by political projects; for the people, by industry on a large scale. One class only of society still had a taste for adventure; that portion of the feudal nobility, who, not being in a condition to think of political aggrandizement, and not being disposed to industry, retained their former situation and manners. This class, accordingly, continued to embark in crusades, and endeavored to renew them.

Such, in my opinion, are the real effects of the crusades;* on the one hand the extension of ideas and the emancipation of thought; on the other, a general enlargement of the social sphere, and the opening of a wider field for every sort of activity: they produced, at the same time, more individual freedom and more political unity. They tended to the independence of man and the centralization of society. Many inquiries have been made respecting the means of civilization which were directly imported from the East. It has been said that the largest part of the great discoveries which, in the course of the fourteenth and fifteenth centuries, contributed to the progress of European civilization—such as the compass, printing, and gunpowder—were known in the East, and that the crusaders brought them into Europe. This is true to a certain extent; though some of these assertions may be disputed. But what cannot be disputed is this influence, this general effect of the crusades upon the human mind on the one hand, and the state of society on the other. They drew society out of a very narrow road, to throw it into new and infinitely broader paths; they began that transformation of the various elements of European society into governments and nations, which is the characteristic of modern civilization. The same period witnessed the development of one of those institutions which has most powerfully contributed to this great result—monarchy; the history of which, from the birth of the modern states of Europe to the thirteenth century, will form the subject of our next lecture.*

LECTURE IX.: OF MONARCHY.

I endeavored, at our last meeting, to determine the essential and distinctive character of modern society as compared with the primitive state of society in Europe; and I believed I had found it in this fact, that all the elements of the social state, at first numerous and various, were reduced to two—the government on one hand, and the people on the other. Instead of finding, in the capacity of ruling forces and chief agents in history, the clergy, kings, burghers, husbandmen, and serfs, we now find in modern Europe, only two great objects which occupy the historical stage—the government and the nation.

If such is the fact to which European civilization has led, such, also, is the result to which our researches should conduct us. We must see the birth, the growth, the progressive establishment of this great result. We have entered upon the period to which we can trace its origin: it was, as you have seen, between the twelfth and the sixteenth centuries that those slow and hidden operations took place which brought society into this new form, this definite state. We have also considered the first great event which, in my opinion, evidently had a powerful effect in impelling Europe into this road; I mean the crusades.

About the same period, and almost at the very time when the crusades broke out, that institution began to increase, which has perhaps chiefly contributed to the formation of modern society, and to the fusion of all the social elements into two forces, the government and the people. This institution is monarchy.

It is evident that monarchy has played a vast part in the history of European civilization. Of this we may convince ourselves by a single glance. We see the development of monarchy proceed, for a considerable time, at the same rate as that of society itself: they had a common progression. And not only had they a common progression, but with every step that society made towards its definitive and modern character, monarchy seemed to increase and prosper; so that, when the work was consummated—when there remained, in the great states of Europe, little or no important and decisive influence but that of the government and the public—it was monarchy that became the government.

It was not only in France, where the fact is evident, that this happened, but in most of the countries of Europe. A little sooner or later, and under forms somewhat different, the history of society in England, Spain, and Germany, offers us the same result. In England, for example, it was under the Tudors that the old particular and local elements of English society were dissolved and mingled, and gave way to the system of public authorities;* this, also, was the period when monarchy had the greatest influence. It was the same thing in Germany, Spain, and all the great European states.

If we leave Europe, and cast our eyes over the rest of the world, we shall be struck with an analogous fact. Everywhere we shall find monarchy holding a great place, and appearing as the most general and permanent, perhaps, of all institutions; as that which is the most difficult to exclude where it does not exist, and, where it does exist, the most difficult to extirpate. From time immemorial it has had possession of Asia. On the discovery of America, all the great states of that continent were found, with different combinations, under monarchical governments. When we penetrate into the interior of Africa, wherever we meet with nations of any extent, this is the government which prevails. And not only has monarchy penetrated everywhere, but it has accommodated itself to the most various situations, to civilization and barbarism: to the most peaceful manners, as in China, and to those in which a warlike spirit predominates. It has established itself not only in the midst of the system of castes, in countries whose social economy exhibits the most rigorous distinction of ranks, but also in the midst of a system of equality, in countries where society is most remote from every kind of legal and permanent classification. In some places despotic and oppressive; in others favorable to the progress of civilization and even of liberty; it is like a head that may be placed on many different bodies, a fruit that may grow from many different buds.

In this fact we might discover many important and curious consequences. I shall take only two; the first is, that such a result cannot possibly be the offspring of mere chance, of force or usurpation only; that there must necessarily be, between the nature of monarchy considered as an institution, and the nature either of man as an individual or of human society, a strong and intimate analogy. Force, no doubt, has had its share, in both the origin and progress of the institution; but when we meet with a result like this, when we see a great event develop itself or recur during a long series of ages, and in the midst of many different situations, we should never ascribe it to force. Force performs a great and daily part in human affairs; but it is not the principle which governs their movements: there is always, superior to force, and the part which it performs, a moral cause which governs the general course of events. Force, in the history of society, resembles the body in the history of man. The body assuredly holds a great place in the life of man, but is not the principle of life. Life circulates in it, but does not emanate from it. Such is also the case in human societies; whatever part force may play in them, it does not govern them, or exercise a supreme control over their destinies; this is the province of reason, of the moral influences which are hidden under the accidents of force, and regulate the course of society. We may unhesitatingly declare that it was to a cause of this nature, and not to mere force, that monarchy was indebted for its success.

A second fact of almost equal importance is the flexibility of monarchy, and its faculty of modifying itself and adapting itself to a variety of different circumstances. Observe the contrast which it presents; its form reveals unity, permanence, simplicity. It does not exhibit that variety of combinations which are found in other institutions; yet it accommodates itself to the most dissimilar states of society. It becomes evident then that it is susceptible of great diversity, and capable of being attached to many different elements and principles, both in man as an individual and in society.

It is because we have not considered monarchy in all its extent; because we have not, on the one hand, discovered the principle which forms its essence and subsists under every circumstance to which it may be applied; and because, on the other hand, we have not taken into account all the variations to which it accommodates itself, and all the principles with which it can enter into alliance;—it is, I say, because we have not considered monarchy in this twofold, this enlarged point of view, that we have not thoroughly understood the part it has performed in the history of the world, and have often been mistaken as to its nature and effects.

This is the task which I should wish to undertake with you, so as to obtain a complete and precise view of the effects of this institution in modern Europe, whether they have flowed from its intrinsic principle, or from the modifications which it has undergone.

There is no doubt that the strength of monarchy, that moral power which is its true principle, does not reside in the personal will of the man who for the time happens to be king; there is no doubt that the people in accepting it as an institution, that philosophers in maintaining it as a system, have not meant to accept the empire of the will of an individual—a will essentially arbitrary, capricious, and ignorant.

Monarchy is something quite different from the will of an individual, though it presents itself under that form. It is the personification of legitimate sovereignty—of the collective will and aggregate wisdom of a people—of that will which is essentially reasonable, enlightened, just, impartial,—which knows naught of individual wills, but by the title of legitimate monarchy, earned by these conditions, has the right to govern them. Such is the meaning of monarchy as understood by the people, and such is the motive of their adhesion to it.

Is it true that there is a legitimate sovereignty, a will which has a right to govern mankind? They certainly believe that there is; for they endeavor, have always endeavored, and cannot avoid endeavoring, to place themselves under its empire. Conceive, I shall not say a people, but the smallest community of men; conceive it in subjection to a sovereign who is such only de facto, to a power which has no other right but that of force, which does not govern by the title of reason and justice; human nature instantly revolts against a sovereignty such as this. Human nature, therefore, must believe in legitimate sovereignty. It is this sovereignty alone, the sovereignty de jure, which man seeks for, and which alone he consents to obey. What is history but a demonstration of this universal fact? What are most of the struggles which harass the lives of nations but so many determined impulses towards this legitimate sovereignty, in order to place themselves under its empire? And it is not only the people, but the philosophers, who firmly believe in its existence and incessantly seek it. What are all the systems of political philosophy but attempts to discern the legitimate sovereignty? What is the object of their investigations but to discover who has the right to govern society? Take theocracy, monarchy, aristocracy, democracy; they all boast of having discovered the seat of legitimate sovereignty; they all promise to place society under the authority of its rightful master. This, I repeat, is the object of all the labor of philosophers, as well as of all the efforts of nations.

How can philosophers and nations do otherwise than believe in this legitimate sovereignty? How can they do otherwise than strive incessantly to discover it? Let us suppose the simplest case; for instance, some act to be performed, either affecting society in general, or some portion of its members, or even a single individual; it is evident that in such a case there must be some rule of action, some legitimate will to be followed and applied. Whether we enter into the most minute details of social life, or participate in its most momentous concerns, we shall always meet with a truth to be discovered, a law of reason to be applied to the realities of human affairs. It is this law which constitutes that legitimate sovereignty towards which both philosophers and nations have never ceased, and can never cease, to aspire.

But how far can legitimate sovereignty be represented, generally and permanently, by an earthly power, by a human will? Is there anything necessarily false and dangerous in such an assumption? What are we to think in particular of the personification of legitimate sovereignty under the image of royalty? On what conditions, and within what limits, is this personification admissible? These are great questions, which it is not my business now to discuss, but which I cannot avoid noticing, and on which I shall say a few words in passing.

I affirm, and the plainest common sense must admit, that legitimate sovereignty, in its complete and permanent form, cannot belong to any one; and that every attribution of legitimate sovereignty to any human power whatever is radically false and dangerous. Hence arises the necessity of the limitation of every power, whatever may be its name or form; hence arises the radical illegitimacy of every sort of absolute power, whatever may be its origin, whether conquest, inheritance, or election. We may differ as to the best means of finding the legitimate sovereignty; they vary according to the diversities of place and time; but there is no place or time at which any power can legitimately be the independent possessor of this sovereignty.

This principle being laid down, it is equally certain that monarchy, under whatever system we consider it, presents itself as the personification of the legitimate sovereignty. Listen to the supporters of theocracy; they will tell you that kings are the image of God upon earth, which means nothing more than that they are the personification of supreme justice, truth, and goodness. Turn to the jurists; they will tell you that the king is the living law; which means, again, that the king is the personification of the legitimate sovereignty, of that law of justice which is entitled to govern society. Interrogate monarchy itself in its pure and unmixed form; it will tell you that it is the personification of the state, of the commonwealth. In whatever combination, in whatever situation, monarchy is considered, you will find that it is always held out as representing this legitimate sovereignty, this power, which alone is capable of lawfully governing society.

We need not be surprised at this. What are the characteristics of this legitimate sovereignty, and which are derived from its very nature? In the first place, it is single; since there is but one truth, one justice, so there can be but one legitimate sovereignty. It is, moreover, permanent, and always the same, for truth is unchangeable. It stands on a high vantage-ground, beyond the reach of the vicissitudes and chances of this world, with which it is only connected in the character, as it were, of a spectator and a judge. Well, then, these being the rational and natural characteristics of the legitimate sovereignty, it is monarchy which exhibits them under the most palpable form, and seems to be their most faithful image. Consult the work in which M. Benjamin Constant* has so ingeniously represented monarchy, as a neutral and moderating power, raised far above the struggles and casualties of society, and never interfering but in great and critical conjunctures. Is not this, so to speak, the attitude of the legitimate sovereignty, in the government of human affairs? There must be something in this idea peculiarly calculated to strike the mind, for it has passed, with singular rapidity, from books into the actual conduct of affairs. A sovereign has made it, in the constitution of Brazil, the very basis of his throne. In that constitution, monarchy is represented as a moderating power, elevated above the active powers of the state, like their spectator and their judge.†

Under whatever point of view you consider monarchy, when you compare it with the legitimate sovereignty, you will find a great outward resemblance between them—a resemblance with which the human mind must necessarily have been struck. Whenever the reflection or the imagination of men has especially turned towards the contemplation or study of legitimate sovereignty, and of its essential qualities, it has inclined towards monarchy.* Thus in the times when religious ideas preponderated, the habitual contemplation of the nature of God impelled mankind towards the monarchical system. In the same manner, when the influence of jurists prevailed in society, the habit of studying, under the name of law, the nature of the legitimate sovereignty, was favorable to the dogma of its personification in the institution of monarchy. The attentive application of the human mind to the contemplation of the nature and qualities of the legitimate sovereignty, when there were no other causes to destroy its effect, has always given strength and consideration to monarchy, as being its image.

There are, too, certain junctures, which are particularly favorable to this personification; such, for example, as when individual forces display themselves in the world with all their uncertainties; all their waywardness; when selfishness predominates in individuals, either through ignorance and brutality, or through corruption. At such times, society, distracted by the conflict of individual wills, and unable to attain, by their free concurrence, to a general will, which might hold them in subjection, feels an ardent desire for a sovereign power, to which all individuals must submit; and, as soon as any institution presents itself which bears any of the characteristics of legitimate sovereignty, society rallies round it with eagerness; as people, under proscription, take refuge in the sanctuary of a church. This is what has taken place in the wild and disorderly youth of nations, such as those we have passed through. Monarchy is wonderfully suited to those times of strong and fruitful anarchy, if I may so speak, in which society is striving to form and regulate itself, but is unable to do so by the free concurrence of individual wills. There are other times when monarchy, though from a contrary cause, has the same merit. Why did the Roman world, so near dissolution at the end of the republic, still subsist for more than fifteen centuries, under the name of an empire, which, after all, was nothing but a lingering decay, a protracted death-struggle? Monarchy, alone, could produce such an effect; monarchy, alone, could maintain a state of society which the spirit of selfishness incessantly tended to destroy. The imperial power contended for fifteen centuries against the ruin of the Roman world. It thus appears that there are times when monarchy, alone, can retard the dissolution, and times when it, alone, can accelerate the formation of society. And it is, in both cases, because it represents, more clearly than any other form of government can do, the legitimate sovereignty, that it exercises this power over the course of events.

Under whatever point of view you consider this institution, and at whatever period you take it, you will find, therefore, that its essential character, its moral principle, its true meaning, the cause of its strength, is, its being the image, the personification, the presumed interpreter, of that single, superior, and essentially legitimate will, which alone has a right to govern society.

Let us now consider monarchy under the second point of view, that is to say, in its flexibility, the variety of parts it has performed and of effects it has produced. Let us endeavor to account for this character, and ascertain its causes.

Here we have an advantage; we can at once return to history, and to the history of our own country. By a concurrence of singular circumstances, monarchy in modern Europe has put on every character which it has ever exhibited in the history of the world. European monarchy has been, in some sort, the result of all the possible kinds of monarchy. In running over its history, from the fifth to the twelfth century, you will see the variety of aspects under which it appears, and the extent to which we everywhere find that variety, complication, and contention, which characterize the whole course of European civilization.

In the fifth century, at the time of the great invasion of the Germans, two monarchies were in existence—the barbarian monarchy of Clovis,* and the imperial monarchy of Constantine. They were very different from each other in principles and effects.

The barbarian monarchy was essentially elective. The German kings were elected, though their election did not take place in the form to which we are accustomed to attach that idea. They were military chiefs, whose power was freely accepted by a great number of their companions, by whom they were obeyed as being the bravest and most competent to rule. Election was the true source of this barbarian monarchy, its primitive and essential character.

It is true that this character, in the fifth century, was already somewhat modified, and that different elements were introduced into monarchy. Different tribes had possessed their chiefs for a certain space of time; families had arisen, more considerable and wealthier than the rest. This produced the beginning of hereditary succession; the chief being almost always chosen from these families.† This was the first principle of a different nature which became associated with the leading principle of election.

Another element had already entered into the institution of barbarian monarchy—I mean the element of religion. We find among some of the barbarian tribes—the Goths, for example—the conviction that the families of their kings were descended from the families of their gods or of their deified heroes, such as Odin. This, too, was the case with Homer's monarchs who were the issue of gods or demi-gods, and, by this title, objects of religious veneration, notwithstanding the limited extent of their power.

Such was the barbarian monarchy of the fifth century, whose primitive principle still predominated, though it had itself grown diversified and wavering.

I now take the monarchy of the Roman empire, the principle of which was totally different. It was the personification of the state, the heir of the sovereignty and majesty of the Roman people. Consider the monarchy of Augustus or Tiberius: the emperor was the representative of the senate, of the assemblies of the people, of the whole republic.*

Was not this evident from the modest language of the first emperors—of such of them, at least, as were men of sense and understood their situation? They felt that they stood in the presence of the people, who themselves had lately possessed the sovereign power, which they had abdicated in their favor; and addressed the people as their representatives and ministers. But in reality they exercised all the power of the people, and that, too, in its most exaggerated and fearful form. Such a transformation it is easy for us to comprehend; we have witnessed it ourselves; we have seen the sovereignty transferred from the people to the person of a single individual; this was the history of Napoleon. He also was a personification of the sovereignty of the people; and constantly expressed himself to that effect. "Who has been elected," he said, "like me, by eighteen millions of men? who is, like me, the representative of the people?" and when, upon his coins, we read on one side République Française, and on the other Napoléon Empereur, what is this but an example of the fact which I am describing, of the people having become the monarch? Such was the fundamental character of the imperial monarchy; it preserved this character during the three first centuries of the empire; and it was, indeed, only under Diocletian that it assumed its complete and definitive form.* It was then, however, on the eve of undergoing a great change; a new kind of monarchy was about to appear. During three centuries Christianity had been endeavoring to introduce into the empire the element of religion. It was under Constantine that Christianity succeeded, not in making religion the prevailing element, but in giving it a prominent part to perform. Monarchy here presents itself under a different aspect; it is not of earthly origin: the prince is not the representative of the sovereignty of the public; he is the image, the representative, the delegate of God. Power descends to him from on high while, in the imperial monarchy, power had ascended from below. These were totally different situations, with totally different results. The rights of freedom and political securities are difficult to combine with the principle of religious monarchy; but the principle itself is high, moral, and salutary. I shall show you the idea which was formed of the prince, in the seventh century, under the system of religious monarchy. I take it from the canons of the Council of Toledo.

"The king is called rex because he governs with justice. If he acts justly (recte) he has a legitimate title to the name of king; if he acts unjustly, he loses all claim to it. Our fathers, therefore, said with reason, rex ejus eris si recta facis: si autem non facis, non eris. The two principal virtues of a king are justice and truth (the science of truth, reason).

"The depository of the royal power, no less than the whole body of the people, is bound to respect the laws. While we obey the will of heaven, we make for ourselves, as well as our subjects, wise laws, obedience to which is obligatory on ourselves and our successors, as well as upon all the population of our kingdom. * * *

"God, the creator of all things, in constructing the human body, has raised the head aloft, and has willed that from it should proceed the nerves of all the members, and he has placed in the head the torches of the eyes, in order to throw light upon every dangerous object. In like manner he has established the power of intelligence, giving it the charge of governing all the members, and of prudently regulating their action. * * * * * *

"It is necessary then to regulate, first of all, those things which relate to princes, to provide for their safety, and protect their life, and then those things which concern the people, in such a manner, that in properly securing the safety of kings, that of the people may be, at the same time, and so much the more effectually, secured."*

But, in the system of religious monarchy, there is almost always another element introduced besides monarchy itself. A new power takes its place by its side; a power nearer to God, the source whence monarchy emanates, than monarchy itself. This is the clergy, the ecclesiastical power which interposes between God and kings, and between kings and people, in such sort, that monarchy, though the image of the Divinity, runs the hazard of falling to the rank of an instrument in the hands of the human interpreters of the Divine will. This is a new cause of diversity in the destinies and effects of the institution.

The different kinds of monarchy, then, which, in the fifth century, made their appearance on the ruins of the Roman empire, were, the barbarian monarchy, the imperial monarchy, and religious monarchy in its infancy. Their fortunes were as different as their principles.

In France, under the first race,* barbarian monarchy prevailed. There were, indeed, some attempts on the part of the clergy to impress upon it the imperial or religious character; but the system of election, in the royal family, with some mixture of inheritance and of religious notions, remained predominant.

In Italy, among the Ostrogoths, the imperial monarchy overcame the barbarous customs. Theodoric considered himself as successor of the emperors. It is sufficient to read Cassiodorus† to perceive that this was the character of his government.

In Spain, monarchy appeared more religious than elsewhere. As the councils of Toledo,‡ though I shall not call them absolute, were the influencing power, the religious character predominated, if not in the government, properly so called, of the Visigothic kings, at least in the laws which the clergy suggested to them, and the language they made them speak.

In England, among the Saxons, manners remained almost wholly barbarous. The kingdoms of the heptarchy were little else than the territories of different bands, every one having its chief. Military election appears more evidently among them than anywhere else. The Anglo-Saxon monarchy is the most faithful type of the barbarian monarchy.

Thus, from the fifth to the seventh century, at the same time that all these three sorts of monarchy manifested themselves in general facts, one or other of them prevailed, according to circumstances, in the different states of Europe.

Such was the prevailing confusion at this period, that nothing of a general or permanent nature could be established; and, from vicissitude to vicissitude, we arrive at the eighth century without finding that monarchy has anywhere assumed a definitive character.

Towards the middle of the eighth century, and with the triumph of the second race of the Frank kings, events assume a more general character, and become clearer; as they were transacted on a larger scale, they can be better understood and have more evident results. The different kinds of monarchy were shortly destined to succeed and combine with one another in a very striking manner.

At the time when the Carlovingians replaced the Merovingians, we perceive a return of the barbarian monarchy. Election reappeared; Pippin got himself elected at Soissons.* When the first Carlovingians gave kingdoms to their sons, they took care that they should be acknowledged by the chief men of the states assigned to them. When they divided a kingdom, they desired that the partition should be sanctioned in the national assemblies. In short, the elective principle, under the form of popular acceptance, again assumed a certain reality. You remember that this change of dynasty was like a new inroad of the Germans into the west of Europe, and brought back some shadow of their ancient institutions and manners.

At the same time, we see the religious principle more clearly introducing itself into monarchy, and performing a part of greater importance. Pippin was acknowledged and consecrated by the pope. He felt that he stood in need of the sanction of religion; it was already become a great power, and he sought its assistance. Charlemagne adopted the same policy; and religious monarchy thus developed itself. Still, however, under Charlemagne, religion was not the prevailing character of his government; the imperial system of monarchy was that which he wished to revive. Although he allied himself closely with the clergy, he made use of them, and was not their instrument. The idea of a great state, of a great political combination,—the resurrection, in short, of the Roman empire, was the favorite day-dream of Charlemagne.

He died, and was succeeded by Louis the Pious. Everybody knows the character to which the royal power was then, for a short time, reduced. The king fell into the hands of the clergy, who censured, deposed, re-instated, and governed him; a monarchy subordinate to religious authority seemed on the point of being established.

Thus, from the middle of the eighth to the middle of the ninth century, the diversity of the three kinds of monarchy became manifested by events important, closely connected, and clear. After the death of Louis the Pious, during the state of disorder into which Europe fell, the three kinds of monarchy almost equally disappeared; everything became confounded. At the end of a certain time, when the feudal system had prevailed, a fourth kind of monarchy presented itself, differing from all those which had been hitherto observed: this was feudal monarchy. It is confused in its nature, and cannot easily be defined. It has been said that the king, in the feudal system of government, was the suzerain over suzerains, the lord over lords; that he was connected by firm links, from degree to degree, with the whole frame of society; and that, in calling around him his own vassals, then the vassals of his vassals, and so on in gradation, he exercised his authority over the whole mass of the people, and showed himself to be really a king. I do not deny that this is the theory of feudal monarchy: but it is a mere theory, which has never governed facts. This pretended influence of the king by means of a hierarchical organization, these links which are supposed to have united monarchy to the whole body of feudal society, are the dreams of speculative philosophers. In fact, the greatest part of the feudal chieftains at that period were completely independent of the monarchy; many of them hardly knew it even by name, and had few or no relations with it: every kind of sovereignty was local and independent. The name of king, borne by one of these feudal chiefs, expresses not so much a fact as a remembrance. Such is the state in which monarchy presents itself in the course of the tenth and eleventh centuries.

In the twelfth, at the accession of Louis the Fat, things began to change their aspect.* The king was more frequently spoken of; his influence penetrated into places which it had not previously reached; he assumed a more active part in society. If we inquire into this title, we recognize none of those titles of which monarchy had previously been accustomed to avail itself. It was not by inheritance from the emperors, or by the title of imperial monarchy, that this institution aggrandized itself, and assumed more consistency. Neither was it in virtue of election, or as being an emanation from divine power: every appearance of election had vanished; the principle of inheritance definitively prevailed; and notwithstanding the sanction given by religion to the accession of kings, the minds of men did not appear to be at all occupied with the religious character of the monarchy of Louis the Fat. A new element, a character hitherto unknown, was introduced into monarchy; a new species of monarchy began to exist.

Society, I need hardly repeat, was at this period in very great disorder, and subject to constant scenes of violence. Society, in itself, was destitute of means to struggle against this situation, and to recover some degree of order and unity. The feudal institutions,—those parliaments of barons, those seignorial courts,—all those forms under which, in modern times, feudalism has been represented as a systematic and orderly state of government,—all these things were unreal and powerless; there was nothing in them which could afford the means of establishing any degree of order or justice; so that, in the midst of social anarchy, no one knew to whom recourse could be had, in order to redress a great injustice, remedy a great evil, to constitute something like a state. The name of king remained, and was borne by some chief whose authority was acknowledged by a few others. The different titles, however, under which the royal power had been formerly exercised, though they had no great influence, yet were far from being forgotten, and were recalled on various occasions. It happened that, in order to re-establish some degree of order in a place near the king's residence, or to terminate some difference which had lasted a long time, recourse was had to him; he was called upon to intervene in affairs which were not directly his own; and he intervened as a protector of public order, as arbitrator, as redresser of wrongs. The moral authority which continued to be attached to his name gained for him, by little and little, this great accession of power.

Such was the character which monarchy began to assume under Louis the Fat, and under the administration of Suger.* Now, for the first time, seems to have entered the minds of men the idea, though very incomplete, confused, and feeble, of a public power, unconnected with the local powers which had possession of society, called upon to render justice to those who could not obtain it by ordinary means, and capable of producing, or at least commanding, order;—the idea of a great magistracy, whose essential character was to maintain or re-establish the peace of society, to protect the weak, and to decide differences which could not be otherwise settled. Such was the entirely new character, in which, reckoning from the twelfth century, monarchy appeared in Europe, and especially in France. It was neither as barbarian monarchy, as religious monarchy, nor as imperial monarchy, that the royal power was exercised; this kind of monarchy possessed only a limited, incomplete, and fortuitous power;—a power which I cannot more precisely describe than by saying that it was, in some sort, that of the chief conservator of the public peace. This is the true origin of modern monarchy; this is its vital principle, if I may so speak; it is this which has been developed in the course of its career, and, I have no hesitation in saying, has ensured its success. At different periods of history we observe the reappearance of the various characters of monarchy; we see the different kinds of monarchy which I have described, endeavoring, by turns, to recover the preponderance. Thus, the clergy have always preached religious monarchy; the civilians have labored to revive the principle of imperial monarchy; the nobility would sometimes have wished to renew elective monarchy, or maintain feudal monarchy. And not only have the clergy, the civilians, and the nobility, attempted each to give their own principle a predominance in the monarchy, but monarchy itself has made them all contribute towards the aggrandizement of its own power. Kings have represented themselves sometimes as the delegates of God, sometimes as the heirs of the emperors, or as the first noblemen of the land, according to the occasion or public wish of the moment; they have illegitimately availed themselves of these various titles, but none of them has been the real title of modern monarchy, or the source of its preponderating influence. It is, I repeat, as depositary and protector of public order, of general justice, and of the common interest,—it is under the aspect of a chief magistracy,* the center and bond of society, that modern monarchy has presented itself to the people, and, in obtaining their adhesion, has made their strength its own. You will see, as we proceed, this characteristic of the monarchy of modern Europe, which began, I repeat, in the twelfth century, under the reign of Louis the Fat, confirm and develop itself, and become at length, if I may so speak, the political physiognomy of the institution. It is by this that monarchy has contributed to the great result which now characterizes European society, the

reduction of all the social elements to two—the government and the nation.†
Thus it appears, that, at the breaking out of the crusades, Europe entered upon the path which
was to conduct her to her present state: you have just seen monarchy assume the important part
which it was destined to perform in this great transformation. We shall consider, at our next
meeting, the different attempts at political organization, made from the twelfth to the sixteenth
century, in order to maintain, by regulating it, the order of things that was about to perish. We
shall consider the efforts of feudalism, of the Church, and even of the free cities, to constitute
society according to its ancient principles, and under its primitive forms, and thus to defend
themselves against the general change which was preparing.

LECTURE X.: UNSUCCESSFUL ATTEMPTS AT THE UNIFICATION OF SOCIETY.

At the commencement of this lecture I wish, at once, to determine its object with precision. It
will be recollected, that one of the first facts that struck us, was the diversity, the separation, the
independence, of the elements of ancient European society.* The feudal nobility, the clergy, and
the commons, had each a position, laws, and manners, entirely different; they formed so many
distinct socities whose mode of government was independent of each other. They were in some
measure connected, and in contact, but no real union existed between them; to speak correctly,
they did not form a nation—a state.
The fusion of these distinct portions of society into one is, at length, accomplished; this is
precisely the distinctive organization, the essential characteristic of modern society. The ancient
social elements are now reduced to two—the government and the people; that is to say, diversity
ceased and similitude introduced union. Before, however, this result took place, and even with a
view to its prevention, many attempts were made to bring all these separate portions of society
together, without destroying their diversity and independence. No positive attack was made on
the peculiar position and privileges or on the distinctive nature of any portion, and yet there was
an attempt made to form them into one state, one national body, to bring them all under one and
the same government.
All these attempts failed. The result which I have noticed above, the union of modern society,
attests their want of success. Even in those parts of Europe where some traces of the ancient
diversity of the social elements are still to be met with—in Germany, for instance, where a real
feudal nobility and a distinct body of burghers still exist; in England, where we see an
established Church enjoying its own revenues and its own peculiar jurisdiction—it is clear that
this pretended distinct existence is a shadow, a falsehood; that these special societies are
confounded in general society, absorbed in the state, governed by the public authorities,
controlled by the same system of polity, carried away by the same current of ideas, the same
manners. Again I assert, that even where the form still exists, the separation and independence of
the ancient social elements have no longer any reality.
At the same time, these attempts at rendering the ancient and social elements co-ordinate,
without changing their nature, at forming them into national unity without annihilating their
variety, are entitled to an important place in the history of Europe. The period which now
engages our attention—that period which separates ancient from modern Europe, and in which
was accomplished the metamorphosis of European society—is almost entirely filled with them.
Not only do they form a principal part of the history of this period, but they had a considerable
influence on after events, on the manner in which was effected the reduction of the various social
elements to two—the government and the people. It is clearly, then, of great importance, that we

should become well acquainted with all those endeavors at political organization which were made from the twelfth to the sixteenth century, for the purpose of creating nations and governments, without destroying the diversity of secondary societies placed by the side of each other. These attempts form the subject of the present lecture—a laborious and even painful task. All these attempts at political organization did not, certainly, originate from a good motive; too many of them arose from selfishness and tyranny. Yet some of them were pure and disinterested; some of them had, truly, for their object the moral and social welfare of mankind. Society at this time, was in such a state of incoherence, of violence and iniquity, as could not but be extremely offensive to men of enlarged views—to men who possessed elevated sentiments, and who labored incessantly to discover the means of improving it. Yet even the best of these noble attempts miscarried; and is not the waste of so much courage—of so many sacrifices and endeavors—of so much virtue, a melancholy spectacle? And what is still more painful, a still more poignant sorrow, not only did these attempts at social melioration fail, but an enormous mass of error and of evil was mingled with them. Notwithstanding good intention, the majority of them were absurd, and show a profound ignorance of reason, of justice, of the rights of humanity, and of the conditions of the social state; so that not only were they unsuccessful, but it was right that they should be so. We have here a spectacle, not only of the hard lot of humanity, but also of its weakness. We may here see how the smallest portion of truth suffices so to engage the whole attention of men of superior intellect, that they forget every thing else, and become blind to all that is not comprised within the narrow horizon of their ideas. We may here see how the existence of ever so small a particle of justice in a cause is sufficient to make them lose sight of all the injustice which it contains and permits. This display of the vices and follies of man is, in my opinion, still more melancholy to contemplate than the misery of his condition; his faults affect me more than his sufferings. The attempts already alluded to will bring man before us in both these situations; still we must not shun the painful retrospect; it behooves us not to flinch from doing justice to those men, to those ages that have so often erred, so miserably failed, and yet have displayed such noble virtues, made such powerful efforts, merited so much glory.

The attempts at political organization which were formed from the twelfth to the sixteenth centuries were of two kinds; one having for its object the predominance of one of the social elements—sometimes the clergy, sometimes the feudal nobility, sometimes the free cities—and making all the others subordinate to it, and in this way seeking to introduce unity; the other proposing to cause all the different societies to agree and to act together, leaving to each portion its liberty, and ensuring to each its due share of influence.

The attempts of the former kind are much more open to suspicion of self-interest and tyranny than the latter; in fact, they were not spotless; from their very nature they were essentially tyrannical in their mode of execution; yet some of them might have been, and indeed were, conceived with a pure motive, and with a view to the welfare and advancement of mankind.

The first attempt which presents itself, is the attempt at theocratical organization; that is to say, the design of bringing all the other societies into a state of submission to the principles and sway of ecclesiastical society.

I must here refer to what I have already said relative to the history of the Church.* I have endeavored to show what were the principles it developed—what was the legitimate part of each—how these principles arose from the natural course of events—the good and the evil produced by them. I have characterized the different stages through which the Church passed from the eighth to the twelfth century. I have pointed out the state of the imperial Church, of the barbarian Church, of the feudal Church, and lastly, of the theocratic Church. I take it for granted that all this is present in your recollection, and I shall now endeavor to show you what the clergy did in order to obtain the government of Europe, and why they failed in obtaining it.

The attempt at theocratic organization appeared at an early period, both in the acts of the court of Rome, and in those of the clergy in general; it naturally proceeded from the political and moral superiority of the Church; but, from the commencement, such obstacles were thrown in its way, that, even in its greatest vigor, it never had the power to overcome them.

The first obstacle was the nature itself of Christianity. Very different, in this respect, from the greater part of religious creeds, Christianity established itself by persuasion alone, by simple moral efforts; even at its birth it was not armed with power; in its earliest years it conquered by words alone, and its only conquest was the souls of men. Even after its triumph, even when the Church was in possession of great wealth and consideration, the direct government of society was not placed in its hands. Its origin, purely moral, springing from mental influence alone, was implanted in its constitution. It possessed a vast influence, but it had no power. It gradually insinuated itself into the municipal magistracies;* it acted powerfully upon the emperors and upon all their agents; but the positive administration of public affairs—the government, properly so called—was not possessed by the Church. Now, a system of government, a theocracy, as well as any other, cannot be established in an indirect manner, by mere influence alone; it must possess the judicial and ministerial offices, the command of the forces, be in receipt of the imposts, have the disposal of the revenues, in a word, it must govern—take possession of society. Force of persuasion may do much, it may obtain great influence over a people, and even over governments its sway may be very powerful; but it cannot govern, it cannot found a system, it cannot take possession of the future. Such has been, even from its origin, the situation of the Christian church; it has always sided with government,* but never superseded it, and taken its place; a great obstacle, which the attempt at theocratic organization was never able to surmount.

The attempt to establish a theocracy very soon met with a second obstacle. When the Roman empire was destroyed, and the barbarian states were established on its ruins, the Christian church was found among the conquered. It was necessary for it to escape from this situation; to begin by converting the conquerors, and thus to raise itself to their rank. This accomplished, when the Church aspired to dominion, it had to encounter the pride and the resistance of the feudal nobility. Europe is greatly indebted to the laic members of the feudal system in the eleventh century: the people were almost completely subjugated by the Church; sovereigns could scarcely protect themselves from its domination; the feudal nobility alone would never submit to its yoke, would never give way to the power of the clergy. We have only to recall to our recollection the general appearance of the middle ages, in order to be struck with the singular mixture of loftiness and submission, of blind faith and liberty of mind, in the connection of the lay nobility with the priests. We there find some of the remnants of their primitive situation. It may be remembered how I endeavored to describe the origin of the feudal system, its first elements, and the manner in which feudal society first formed itself around the habitation of the possessor of the fief. I remarked how in that society the priest was below the lord of the fief. Yes, and there always remained, in the hearts of the feudal nobility, a remembrance of this situation; they always considered themselves as not only independent of the Church, but as its superior,—as alone called upon to possess, and in reality to govern, the country; they were willing always to live on good terms with the clergy, at the same time insisting that each should perform his own part, the one not infringing upon the duties of the other. During many centuries it was the lay aristocracy who maintained the independence of society with regard to the Church; they boldly defended it when the sovereigns and the people were subdued. They were the first to oppose, and probably contributed more than any other power to the failure of the attempt at a theocratic organization of society.

A third obstacle stood much in the way of this attempt, an obstacle which has been but little noticed, and the effect of which has often been misunderstood.

In all parts of the world where a clergy made itself master of society, and forced it to submit to a theocratic organization, the government always fell into the hands of a married clergy, of a body of priests who were enabled to recruit their ranks from their own society. Examine history; look at Asia and Egypt; every powerful theocracy you will find to have been the work of a priesthood, of a society complete within itself, and which had no occasion to borrow of any other.

But the celibacy of the clergy placed the Christian priesthood in a very different situation; it was obliged to have recourse incessantly to lay society in order to continue its existence; it was compelled to seek at a distance, among all stations, all social professions, for the means of its duration. In vain, attachment to their order induced them to labor assiduously for the purpose of assimilating these discordant elements; some of the original qualities of these new-comers ever remained; citizens or gentlemen, they always retained some vestige of their former disposition, of their early habits. Doubtless the Catholic clergy, by being placed in a lonely situation by celibacy, by being cut off, as it were, from the common life of men, became more isolated, and separate from society; but then it was forced continually to have recourse to this same lay society, to recruit, to renew itself from it, and consequently to participate in the moral revolutions which it underwent; and I have no hesitation in stating it as my opinion, that this necessity, which was always arising, did much more to prevent the success of the attempt at theocratic organization, than the esprit de corps, strongly supported as it was by celibacy, did to forward it. The clergy, indeed, found within its own body the most powerful opponents of this attempt.

Much has been said of the unity of the Church, and it is true that it has constantly endeavored to obtain this unity, and in some particulars has had the good fortune to succeed. But we must not suffer ourselves to be imposed upon by high-sounding words, nor by partial facts. What society has offered to our view a greater number of civil dissensions, has been subject to more dismemberments than the clergy? What nation has suffered more from divisions, from agitations, from disputes than the ecclesiastical nation? The national churches of the majority of European states have been almost incessantly at variance with the Roman Court;* the Councils have been at war with the popes; heresies have been innumerable and ever springing up anew; schism always breaking out; nowhere was ever witnessed such a diversity of opinions, so much rancor in dispute, such minute parcelling out of power. The internal state of the Church, the disputations which have taken place, the revolutions by which it has been agitated, have been perhaps the greatest of all obstacles to the triumph of that theocratical organization which the Church endeavored to impose upon society.

All these obstacles were visibly in action even so early as the fifth century, even at the commencement of the great attempt of which we are now speaking. They did not, however, prevent the continuance of its exertions, nor retard its progress during several centuries. The period of its greatest glory, its crisis, as it may be termed, was the reign of Gregory the Seventh, at the end of the eleventh century. We have already seen that the predominant wish of Gregory was to render the world subservient to the clergy, the clergy to the pope, and to form Europe into one immense and regular theocracy.* In the scheme by which this was to be effected, this great man appears, so far as one can judge of events which took place so long ago, to have committed two great faults—one as a theorist, the other as a revolutionist. The first consisted in the pompous proclamation of his plan;† in his giving a systematical detail of his principles relative to the nature and the rights of spiritual power, of drawing from them beforehand, like a severe logician, their remotest, their ultimate consequences. He thus threatened and even attacked all the lay sovereignties of Europe, without having secured the means of success: not considering that success in human affairs is not to be obtained by such absolute proceedings, or by a mere appeal to a philosophic argument. Gregory the Seventh also fell into the common error of all revolutionists—that of attempting more than they can perform, and of not fixing the measure and limits of their enterprises within the bounds of possibility. In order to hasten the predominance of his opinions, he entered into a contest against the empire, against all sovereigns, even against the great body of the clergy itself. He never temporized—he consulted no particular interests, but openly proclaimed his determination to reign over all kingdoms as well as over all intellects; and thus raised up against him, not only all temporal powers, who discovered the pressing danger of their situation, but also all those who advocated the right of free inquiry, a party which now began to show itself, and dreaded and exclaimed against all tyranny over the human mind. It seemed indeed probable, on the whole, that Gregory the Seventh injured rather than advanced the cause which he wished to serve.*

This cause, however, still continued to prosper throughout the whole of the twelfth and down to the middle of the thirteenth century. This was the epoch of the greatest power and splendor of the Church. I do not think it can be said that during this period she made much progress; to the end of the reign of Innocent III she rather displayed her glory and power than increased them. But at this very moment of her apparently greatest success, a popular reaction seemed to declare war against her in almost every part of Europe. In the south of France broke out the heresy of the Albigenses, which carried away a numerous and powerful society. Almost at the same time similar notions and desires appeared in the north, in Flanders. Wickliffe, only a little later, attacked in England, with great talent, the power of the Church, and founded a sect which was not destined to perish. Sovereigns soon began to follow the bent of their nations. It was only at the beginning of the thirteenth century, that the emperors of the house of Hohenstaufen, who deservedly rank among the most able and powerful sovereigns of Europe, were overcome in their struggle with the Holy See;† yet before the end of the same century, Saint Louis, the most pious of monarchs, proclaimed the independence of temporal power, and published the first Pragmatic Sanction,* which has served as the basis of all the following.† At the opening of the fourteenth century began the quarrel between Philip the Fair with Boniface VIII: Edward I of England was not more obedient to the court of Rome.‡ At this epoch it is evident, that the attempt at theocratic organization had failed; the Church henceforward acted only upon the defensive; she no longer attempted to force her system upon Europe; but only considered how she might keep what she possessed. It is from the end of the thirteenth century that the emancipation of the laic society of Europe truly dates; it was then that the Church gave up her pretensions to its possession.

A long time before this she had renounced this pretension in the very sphere in which it appeared most likely for her to be successful. Long before in Italy itself, even around the very throne of the Church, theocracy had completely failed, and given way to a system its very opposite in character: to that attempt at democratic organization, of which the Italian republics are the type, and which displayed so brilliant a career in Europe from the eleventh to the sixteenth century.

It will be remembered, that, when speaking of the free cities, of their history, and of the manner of their formation, I observed that their growth had been more precocious and vigorous in Italy than in any other country; they were here more numerous, as well as more wealthy, than in Gaul, England, or Spain; the Roman municipal system had been preserved with more life and regularity. Besides this, the provinces of Italy were less fitted to become the habitation of its new masters than the rest of Europe. The lands had been cleared, drained, and cultivated; it was not covered with forests, and the barbarians could not here devote their lives to the chase, or find occupations similar to what had amused them in Germany. A part of this country, moreover, did not belong to them. The south of Italy, the Campagna di Roma, and Ravenna, were still dependent on the Greek emperors. Favored by distance from the seat of government, and by the vicissitudes of war, the republican system soon took root, and grew very fast in this portion of the country. Italy, too, besides having never been entirely subdued by the barbarians, was favored by the circumstance, that the conquerors who overran it did not remain its tranquil and lasting possessors. The Ostrogoths were destroyed and driven off by Belisarius and Narses; the kingdom of the Lombards was not permanent.* The Franks overthrew it under Pippin and Charlemagne, who, without exterminating the Lombard population, found it their interest to ally themselves with the ancient Italian inhabitants, in order to contend against the Lombards with more success. The barbarians, then, never became in Italy, as in the other parts of Europe, the exclusive and quiet masters of the territory and people. And thus it happened that the feudal system never made much progress beyond the Alps, where it was but weakly established, and its members few and scattered. Neither did the great territorial proprietors ever gain that preponderance here, which they did in Gaul and other countries, but it continued to rest with the towns. When this result clearly showed itself, a great number of the possessors of fiefs, moved by choice or necessity, left their country dwellings and took up their abode within the walls of some city. The barbarian nobles made themselves burgesses. It is easy to imagine what strength and superiority the towns of Italy acquired, compared with the other communities of Europe, by this single circumstance. What we have chiefly dwelt upon, as most observable in the character of town populations, is their timidity and weakness. The burgesses appear like so many courageous freedmen, struggling with toil and care against a master always at their gates. The fate of the Italian towns was widely different; the conquering and conquered populations here mixed together within the same walls; the towns had not the trouble to defend themselves against a neighboring master; their inhabitants were citizens, who, at least for the most part, had always been free; who defended their independence and their rights against distant foreign sovereigns; at one time against the kings of the Franks, and, at a later period, against the emperors of Germany.* This will in some measure account for the immense and precocious superiority of the Italian cities: while in other countries we see poor insignificant communities arise after great trouble and exertion; we here see shoot up, almost at once, republics—states.

Thus becomes explained, why the attempt at republican organization was so successful in this part of Europe. It repressed, almost in its childhood, the feudal system, and became the prevailing form in society. Still it was but little adapted to spread or endure; it contained but few germs of melioration, a necessary condition for the extension and duration of any form of government.

In looking at the history of the Italian republics, from the eleventh to the fifteenth century, we are struck with two facts, seemingly contradictory, yet still indisputable. We see passing before us a wonderful display of courage, of activity, and of genius; an amazing prosperity is the result: we see a movement and a liberty unknown to the rest of Europe. But if we ask what was the real state of the inhabitants, how they passed their lives, what was their real share of happiness, the scene changes; there is, perhaps, no history more sad and gloomy: no period, perhaps, during which the lot of man appears to have been more agitated, subject to more deplorable chances, and which abounds more in dissensions, crimes, and misfortunes. Another fact strikes us at the same moment; in the political life of the greater part of these republics, liberty was continuously diminishing. The want of security was so great, that the people were unavoidably driven to take shelter in a system less stormy, though less popular, than that in which the state existed. Look at the history of Florence, Venice, Genoa, Milan, or Pisa; in all of them we find the course of events, instead of aiding the progress of liberty, instead of enlarging the circle of institutions, tending to repress it; tending to concentrate power in the hands of a smaller number of individuals. In a word, we find in these republics, otherwise so energetic, so brilliant, and so rich, two things wanting—security of life, the first requisite in the social state, and the progress of institutions.*

From these causes sprung a new evil, which prevented the attempt at republican organization from extending itself. It was from without—it was from foreign sovereigns, that the greatest danger was threatened to Italy. Still this danger never succeeded in reconciling these republics, in making them all act in concert; they were never ready to resist in common the common enemy. This has led many Italians, the most enlightened, the best of patriots, to deplore, in the present day, the republican system of Italy in the middle ages, as the true cause which hindered it from becoming a nation; it was parcelled out, they say, into a multitude of little states, not sufficiently master of their passions to confederate, to constitute themselves into one united body. They regret that their country has not, like the rest of Europe, been subject to a despotic centralization which would have formed it into a nation, and rendered it independent of the foreigner.*

It appears, then, that republican organization, even under the most favorable circumstances, did not contain, at this period, any more than it has done since, the principle of progress, duration, and extension.† We may compare, up to a certain point, the organization of Italy, in the middle ages, to that of ancient Greece. Greece, like Italy, was a country covered with little republics, always rivals, sometimes enemies, and sometimes rallying together for a common object. In this comparison the advantage is altogether on the side of Greece. There is no doubt, notwithstanding the frequent iniquities that history makes known, but that there was much more order, security, and justice in the interior of Athens, Lacedemon, and Thebes, than in the Italian republics. See, however, notwithstanding this, how short was the political career of Greece, and what a principle of weakness is contained in this parcelling out of territory and power. No sooner did Greece come in contact with the great neighboring states, with Macedon and Rome, than she fell. These little republics, so glorious and still so flourishing, could not coalesce for defense. How much more likely was a similar result in Italy, where society and human reason had made no such strides as in Greece, and consequently possessed much less power.

If the attempt at republican organization had so little chance of stability in Italy where it had triumphed, where the feudal system had been overcome, it may easily be supposed that it was much less likely to succeed in the other parts of Europe.

I shall take a rapid survey of its fortunes.

There was one portion of Europe which bore a great resemblance to Italy; the south of France, and the adjoining provinces of Spain, Catalonia, Navarre, and Biscay. In these districts the cities had made nearly the same progress, and had risen to considerable importance and wealth. Many little feudal nobles had here allied themselves with the citizens; a part of the clergy had likewise embraced their cause; in a word, the country in these respects was another Italy. So also, in the course of the eleventh and beginning of the twelfth century, the towns of Provence, of Languedoc, and Aquitaine, made a political effort and formed themselves into free republics, as had been done by the towns on the other side of the Alps. But the south of France was connected with a very powerful branch of the feudal system, that of the north. The heresy of the Albigenses appeared. A war broke out between feudal France and municipal France. The history of the crusade against the Albigenses, commanded by Simon de Montfort, is well known: it was the struggle of the feudalism of the North against the attempt at democratic organization of the South.* Notwithstanding the efforts of Southern patriotism, the North gained the day; political unity was wanting in the South, and civilization was not yet sufficiently advanced there to enable men to bring it about. This attempt at republican organization was put down, and the crusade re-established the feudal system in the south of France.

A republican attempt succeeded better a little later, among the Swiss mountains. Here, the theatre was very narrow, the struggle was only against a foreign monarch, who, although much more powerful than the Swiss, was not one of the most formidable sovereigns of Europe.† The contest was carried on with a great display of courage. The Swiss feudal nobility allied themselves, for the most part, with the cities—a powerful help, which also raised the character of the revolution it sustained, and stamped it with a more aristocratical and stationary character than it seemingly ought to have borne.

I cross to the north of France to the free towns of Flanders, to those on the banks of the Rhine, and belonging to the Hanseatic League. Here the democratic organization completely triumphed in the internal government of the cities; but from its origin, it is evident, that it was not destined to take entire possession of society. The free towns of the North were surrounded, pressed on every side by feudalism, by barons, and sovereigns, to such an extent that they were constantly obliged to stand upon the defensive. It is scarcely necessary to say, that they did not trouble themselves to make conquests; they defended themselves sometimes well and sometimes badly. They preserved their privileges, but they remained confined to the inside of their walls. Within these, democratic organization was shut up and arrested; if we walk abroad over the face of the country, we find no semblance of it.

Such, then, was the state of the republican attempt: triumphant in Italy, but with little hope of duration and progress; vanquished in the south of Gaul; victorious upon a small scale in the mountains of Switzerland; while in the North, in the free communities of Flanders, the Rhine, and Hanseatic League, it was condemned not to appear outside their walls. Still, even in this state, evidently inferior to the other elements of society, it inspired the feudal nobility with prodigious terror. The barons became jealous of the wealth of the cities, they feared their power; the spirit of democracy stole into the country; insurrections of the peasantry became more frequent and obstinate. In nearly every part of Europe a coalition was formed among the nobles against the free cities. The parties were not equal; the cities were isolated; there was no correspondence or intelligence between them; all was local. It may be true that there existed, between the burgesses of different countries, a certain degree of sympathy; the success or reverses of the towns of Flanders, in their struggles with the dukes of Burgundy, excited a lively sensation in the French cities; but this was very fleeting, and led to no result; no tie, no true union became established between them; the free communities lent no assistance to one another. The position of feudalism was much superior; yet divided, and without any plan of its own, it was never able to destroy them. After the struggle had lasted a considerable time, when the conviction became settled that a complete victory was impossible, concession became necessary; these petty burgher republics were acknowledged, negotiated with and admitted as members of the state. A new plan was now begun, a new attempt was made at political organization. The object of this was to conciliate, to reconcile, the various elements of society—the feudal nobility, the free cities, the clergy, and monarchs—to make them live and act together, in spite of their rooted hostility. It is to this attempt at mixed organization that I have still to ask your attention.

I presume there is no one who is not acquainted with the nature of the States-General of France, the Cortes of Spain and Portugal, the Parliament of England, and the States of Germany. The elements of these various assemblies were much the same; that is to say, the feudal nobility, the clergy, and the cities or commons, there met together and labored to unite themselves into one sole society, into one same state, under one same law, one same authority. Whatever their various names, this was the tendency, the design of all.

Let us take, as the type of this attempt, the fact which most interests us, as well as being best known to us—the States-General of France. I say this fact is best known, while I am still sure that the term States-General awakens in none of you more than a vague and incomplete idea. Who can say what there was in it of stability, of regularity; the number of its members, the subjects of their deliberations, the times at which they were convoked, or the length of their sessions? Of all this we know nothing, and it is impossible to obtain from history any clear, general, satisfactory information respecting it. The best accounts we can gather from the history of France, as regards the character of these assemblies, would almost lead us to consider them as pure accidents, as the last political resort both of people and kings; the last resort of kings, when they had no money and knew not how to free themselves from embarrassment; the last resort of the people, when some evil became so great that they knew not what remedy to apply to it. The nobles formed part of the States-General; so did the clergy; but they came to them with little interest, for they knew well that it was not in these assemblies that they possessed the greatest influence, that it was not there that they took a true part in the government. The burgesses themselves were not eager to attend them; it was not a right which they were anxious to exercise, but rather a necessity to which they submitted. Again, what was the character of the political proceedings of these assemblies? At one time we find them perfectly insignificant, at others terrible. If the king was the stronger, their humility and docility were extreme; if the situation of the monarch was unfortunate, if he really needed the assistance of the States, they then became factious, either the instrument of some aristocratic intrigue, or of some ambitious demagogues. Their works died almost always with them; they promised much, they attempted much,—and did nothing. No great measure which has truly had any influence upon society in France, no important reform either in the general legislation or administration, ever emanated from the States-General. It must not, however, be supposed that they have been altogether useless, or without effect; they had a moral effect, of which in general we take too little account; they served from time to time as a protestation against political servitude, a forcible proclamation of certain guardian principles,—such, for example, as that a nation has the right to vote its own taxes, to take part in its own affairs, to impose a responsibility upon the agents of power. That these maxims have never perished in France, is mainly owing to the States-General; and it is no slight service rendered to a country, to maintain among its virtues, to keep alive in its thoughts, the remembrance and claims of liberty. The States-General has done us this service, but it never became a means of government; it never entered upon political organization; it never attained the object for which it was formed, that is to say, the fusion into one only body of the various societies which divided the country.*

The Cortes of Portugal and Spain offered the same general result, though in a thousand circumstances they differ. The importance of the Cortes varied according to the kingdoms, and times at which they were held; they were most powerful and most frequently convoked in Aragon and Biscay, during the disputes for the successions to the crown, and the struggles against the Moors. To some of the Cortes—for example, that of Castile, 1370 and 1373—neither the nobles nor the clergy were called. There were a thousand accidents which it would be necessary to notice, if we had time to look closely into events; but in the general sketch to which

I am obliged to confine myself it will be enough to state that the Cortes, like the States-general of France, have been an accident in history, and never a system—never a political organization, or regular means of government.*

The lot of England has been different. I shall not, however, enter into any detail upon this subject at present, as it is my intention to devote a future lecture to the special consideration of the political life of England. All I shall now do is to say a few words upon the causes which gave it a direction totally different from that of the continental states.

And, first, there were no great vassals, no subjects sufficiently powerful to enter single-handed into a contest with the crown. The great barons were obliged, at a very early period, to coalesce, in order to make a common resistance. Thus the principle of association, and proceedings truly political, were forced upon the high aristocracy. Besides this, English feudalism—the little holders of fiefs—were brought by a train of circumstances, which I cannot here recount, to unite themselves with the burgher class, to sit with them in the House of Commons; and by this, the Commons obtained in England a power much superior to those on the Continent, a power really capable of influencing the government of the country. In the fourteenth century, the character of the English Parliament was already formed: the House of Lords was the great council of the king, a council effectively associated in the exercise of authority. The House of Commons, composed of deputies from the possessors of little fiefs, and from the cities, took, as yet, scarcely any part in the government, properly so called; but it asserted and established rights, it defended with great spirit private and local interests. Parliament, considered as a whole, did not yet govern; but already it was a regular institution, a means of government adopted in principle, and often indispensable in fact. Thus the attempt to bring together the various elements of society, and to form them into one body politic, one true state or commonwealth, did succeed in England while it failed in every part of the Continent.

I shall offer but one remark upon Germany, and that only in order to indicate the prevailing character of its history. The attempts made here at political organization, to melt into one body the various elements of society, were spiritless and coldly followed up. These social elements had remained here more distinct, more independent than in the rest of Europe. Were any proof of this wanting, it might be found in its later usages. Germany is the only country of Europe (I say nothing of Poland and the Slavonian nations, which entered so very late into the European system of civilization) in which feudal election has for a long time taken part in the election of royalty; it is likewise the only country of Europe in which ecclesiastical sovereigns were continued; the only one in which were preserved free cities with a true political existence and sovereignty. It is clear, therefore, that the attempt to fuse the elements of primitive European society into one social body, must have been much less active and effective in Germany than in any other nation.

I have now run over all the great attempts at political organization which were made in Europe, down to the end of the fourteenth or beginning of the fifteenth century. All these failed. I have endeavored to point out, in going along, the causes of these failures; to speak truly, they may all be summed up in one: society was not yet sufficiently advanced to adapt itself to unity; all was yet too local, too special, too narrow; too many differences prevailed both in things and in minds. There were no general interests, no general opinions capable of guiding, of bearing sway over particular interests and particular opinions. The most enlightened minds, the boldest thinkers, had as yet no just idea of administration or justice truly public. It was evidently necessary that a very active, powerful civilization should first mix, assimilate, grind together, as it were, all these incoherent elements; it was necessary that there should first be a strong centralization of interests, laws, manners, ideas; it was necessary, in a word, that there should be created a public authority and a public opinion. We are now drawing near to the period in which this great work was at last consummated. Its first symptoms—the state of manners, mind, and opinions, during the fifteenth century, their tendency towards the formation of a central government and a public opinion—will be the subject of the following lecture.

LECTURE XI.: THE RISE OF CENTRALIZED GOVERNMENT.*

We have now reached the threshold of modern history, in the proper sense of the term. We now approach that state of society which may be considered as our own, and the institutions, the opinions, and the manners which were those of France forty years ago, are those of Europe still, and, notwithstanding the changes produced by our revolution, continue to exercise a powerful influence upon us. It is in the sixteenth century, as I have already told you, that modern society really commences.

Before entering into a consideration of this period, let us review the ground over which we have already passed. We have discovered among the ruins of the Roman empire, all the essential elements of modern Europe; we have seen them separate themselves and expand, each on its own account, and independently of the others. We have observed, during the first historical period, the constant tendency of these elements to separation, and to a local and special existence. But scarcely has this object appeared to be attained; scarcely have feudalism, municipal communities, and the clergy, each taken their distinct place and form, when we have seen them tend to approximate, unite, and form themselves into a general social system, into a national body, a national government. To arrive at this result, the various countries of Europe had recourse to all the different systems which existed among them: they endeavored to lay the foundations of social union, and of political and moral obligations, on the principles of theocracy, of aristocracy, of democracy, and of monarchy. Hitherto all these attempts have failed. No particular system has been able to take possession of society, and to secure it, by its sway, a destiny truly public. We have traced the cause of this failure to the absence of general interests and general ideas; we have found that everything, as yet, was too special, too individual, too local; that a long and powerful process of centralization was necessary, in order that society might become at once extensive, solid, and regular, the object which it necessarily seeks to attain. Such was the state in which we left Europe at the close of the fourteenth century. Europe, however, was then very far from understanding her own state, such as I have now endeavored to explain it to you. She did not know distinctly what she required, or what she was in search of. Yet she set about endeavoring to supply her wants as if she knew perfectly what they were. When the fourteenth century had expired, after the failure of every attempt at political organization, Europe entered naturally, and as if by instinct, into the path of centralization. It is the characteristic of the fifteenth century that it constantly tended to this result, that it endeavored to create general interests and general ideas, to raise the minds of men to more enlarged views, and to create, in short, what had not, till then, existed on a great scale—nations and governments. The actual accomplishment of this change belongs to the sixteenth and seventeenth centuries, though it was in the fifteenth that it was prepared. It is this preparation, this silent and hidden process of centralization, both in the social relations and in the opinions of men—a process accomplished, without premeditation or design, by the natural course of events—that we have now to make the subject of our inquiry.

It is thus that man advances in the execution of a plan which he has not conceived, and of which he is not even aware. He is the free and intelligent artificer of a work which is not his own. He does not perceive or comprehend it, till it manifests itself by external appearances and real results; and even then he comprehends it very incompletely. It is through his instrumentality, however, and by the development of his intelligence and freedom, that it is accomplished. Conceive a great machine, the design of which is centered in a single mind, though its various parts are intrusted to different workmen, separated from, and strangers to each other. No one of them understands the work as a whole, nor the general result which he concurs in producing; but every one executes, with intelligence and freedom, by rational and voluntary acts, the particular task assigned to him. It is thus, that by the hand of man, the designs of Providence are wrought out in the government of the world. It is thus that the two great facts which are apparent in the history of civilization come to coexist; on the one hand, those portions of it which may be considered as fated, or which happen without the control of human knowledge or will; on the other hand, the part played in it by the freedom and intelligence of man, and what he contributes to it by means of his own judgment and will.

In order that we may clearly understand the fifteenth century; in order that we may give a distinct account of this prelude, if we may use the expression, to the state of society in modern times, we will separate the facts which bear upon the subject into different classes. We will first examine the political facts—the changes which have tended to the formation either of nations or of governments. Thence we will proceed to the moral facts: we will consider the changes which took place in ideas and in manners; and we shall then see what general opinions began, from that period, to be in a state of preparation.

In regard to political facts, in order to proceed with quickness and simplicity, I shall survey all the great countries of Europe, and place before you the influence which the fifteenth century had upon them—how it found them, how it left them.

I shall begin with France. The last half of the fourteenth, and the first half of the fifteenth century, were, as you all know, a time of great national wars against the English. This was the period of the struggle for the independence of the French territory and the French name against foreign domination.* It is sufficient to open the book of history, to see with what ardor, notwithstanding a multitude of treasons and dissensions, all classes of society in France joined in this struggle, and what patriotism animated the feudal nobility, the burghers, and even the peasantry. If we had nothing but the story of Joan of Arc to show the popular spirit of the time, it alone would suffice for that purpose. Joan of Arc sprang from among the people; it was by the sentiments, the religious belief, the passions of the people, that she was inspired and supported. She was looked upon with mistrust, with ridicule, with enmity even, by the nobles of the court and the leaders of the army; but she had always the soldiers and the people on her side. It was the peasants of Lorraine who sent her to succor the citizens of Orleans. No event could show in a stronger light the popular character of that war, and the feeling with which the whole country engaged in it.

Thus the nationality of France began to be formed. Down to the reign of the house of Valois, the feudal character prevailed in France; a French nation, a French spirit, French patriotism, as yet had no existence. With the princes of the house of Valois begins the history of France, properly so called.* It was in the course of their wars, amid the various turns of their fortune, that, for the first time, the nobility, the citizens, the peasants, were united by a moral tie, by the tie of a comman name, a common honor, and by one burning desire to overcome the foreign invader. We must not, however, at this time, expect to find among them any real political spirit, any great design of unity in government and institutions, according to the conceptions of the present day. The unity of France, at that period, dwelt in her name, in her national honor, in the existence of a national monarchy, no matter of what character, provided that no foreigner had anything to do with it. It was in this way that the struggle against the English contributed strongly to form the French nation, and to impel it towards unity.

At the same time that France was thus forming herself in a moral point of view, she was also extending herself physically, as it may be called, by enlarging, fixing, and consolidating her territory. This was the period of the incorporation of most of the provinces which now constitute France. Under Charles VII [1422—1461] after the expulsion of the English, almost all the provinces which they had occupied—Normandy, Angoumois, Touraine, Poitou, Saintonge, etc., became definitively French. Under Louis XI [1461—1483], ten provinces, three of which have been since lost and regained, were also united to France—Roussillon and Cerdagne, Burgundy, Franche-Comté, Picardy, Artois, Provence, Maine, Anjou, and Perche. Under Charles VIII and Louis XII [1483—1515] the successive marriages of Anne with these two kings gave France Brittany. Thus, at the same period, and during the course of the same events, France, morally as well as physically, acquired at once strength and unity.

Let us turn from the nation to the government, and we shall see the accomplishment of events of the same nature; we shall advance towards the same result. The French government had never been more destitute of unity, of cohesion, and of strength, than under the reign of Charles VI [1380—1422], and during the first part of the reign of Charles VII.* At the end of this reign [1461], the appearance of everything was changed. There were evident marks of a power which was confirming, extending, organizing itself. All the great resources of government, taxation, military force, and administration of justice, were created on a great scale, and almost simultaneously. This was the period of the formation of a standing army and permanent militia— the compagnies-d'ordonnance, consisting of cavalry, and the free archers, the infantry. By these companies, Charles VII re-established a degree of order in the provinces, which had been desolated by the license and exactions of the soldiery, even after the war had ceased. All contemporary historians expatiate on the wonderful effects of the compagnies-d'ordonnance. It was at this period that the taille, one of the principal revenues of the crown, was made perpetual; a serious inroad on the liberty of the people, but which contributed powerfully to the regularity and strength of the government.* At the same time the great instrument of power, the administration of justice, was extended and organized; parliaments were multiplied, five new parliaments having been instituted in a short space of time:—under Louis XI, the parliaments of Grenoble (in 1451), of Bordeaux (in 1462), and of Dijon (in 1477); under Louis XII, the parliaments of Rouen (in 1499), and of Aix (in 1501).† The parliament of Paris also acquired, about the same time, much additional importance and stability, both in regard to the administration of justice, and the superintendence of the police within its jurisdiction.

Thus, in relation to the military force, the power of taxation, and the administration of justice, that is to say, in regard to those things which form its essence, government acquired in France, in the fifteenth century, a character of unity, regularity, and permanence, previously unknown; and the feudal powers were finally superseded by the power of the state.

At the same time, too, was accomplished a change of very different character; a change not so visible, and which has not so much attracted the notice of historians, but still more important, perhaps, than those which have been mentioned:—the change effected by Louis XI in the mode of governing.

A great deal has been said about the struggle of Louis XI [1461—1483] against the grandees of the kingdom, of their depression, and of his partiality for the citizens and the inferior classes. There is truth in all this, though it has been much exaggerated, and though the conduct of Louis

XI towards the different classes of society more frequently disturbed than benefited the state. But he did something of deeper import. Before his time the government had been carried on almost entirely by force, and by mere physical means. Persuasion, address, care in working upon men's minds, and in bringing them over to the views of the government—in a word, what is properly called policy—a policy, indeed, of falsehood and deceit, but also of management and prudence—had hitherto been little attended to. Louis XI substituted intellectual for material means, cunning for force, Italian for feudal policy. Take the two men whose rivalry engrosses this period of our history, Charles the Bold* and Louis XI: Charles is the representative of the old mode of governing; he has recourse to no other means than violence; he constantly appeals to arms; he is unable to act with patience, or to address himself to the dispositions and tempers of men in order to make them the instruments of his designs. Louis XI, on the contrary, takes pleasure in avoiding the use of force, and in gaining an ascendancy over men, by conversation with individuals, and by skilfully bringing into play their interests and peculiarities of character. It was not the public institutions or the external system of government that he changed; it was the secret proceedings, the tactics, of power. It was reserved for modern times to attempt a still greater revolution; to endeavor to introduce into the means, as well as the objects, of public policy, justice in place of self-interest, publicity instead of cunning. Still, however, a great step was gained by renouncing the continued use of force, by calling in the aid of intellectual superiority, by governing through the understandings of men, and not by overturning everything that stood in the way of the exercise of power. This is the great change which, among all his errors and crimes, in spite of the perversity of his nature, and solely by the strength of his powerful intellect, Louis XI has the merit of having begun.†

From France I turn to Spain; and there I find movements of the same nature. It was also in the fifteenth century that Spain was consolidated into one kingdom. At this time an end was put to the long struggle between the Christians and Moors, by the conquest of Grenada. Then, too, the Spanish territory became centralized: by the marriage of Ferdinand the Catholic, and Isabella, the two principal kingdoms, Castile and Aragon, were united under the same dominion. In the same manner as in France, the monarchy was extended and confirmed. It was supported by severer institutions, which bore more gloomy names. Instead of parliaments, it was the Inquisition* that had its origin in Spain. It contained the germ of what it afterwards became; but at first it was of a political rather than a religious nature, and was destined to maintain civil order rather than defend religious faith. The analogy between the countries extends beyond their institutions; it is observable even in the persons of the sovereigns. With less subtlety of intellect, and a less active and intriguing spirit, Ferdinand the Catholic, in his character and government, strongly resembles Louis XI. I pay no regard to arbitrary comparisons or fanciful parallels; but here the analogy is strong and observable in general facts as well as in minute details.

A similar analogy may be discovered in Germany. It was in the middle of the fifteenth century, in 1438, that the house of Austria came to the empire;* and that the imperial power acquired a permanence which it had never before possessed. From that time election was merely a sanction given to hereditary right. At the end of the fifteenth century, Maximilian I definitively established the preponderance of his house and the regular exercise of the central authority; Charles VII was the first in France who, for the preservation of order, created a permanent militia; Maximilian, too, was the first in his hereditary dominions, who accomplished the same end by the same means. Louis XI had established in France, the post-office for the conveyance of letters; Maximilian I introduced it into Germany. In the progress of civilization the same steps were everywhere taken, in a similar way, for the advantage of central government.

The history of England in the fifteenth century consists of two great events—the war with France abroad, and the contest of the two Roses at home.† These two wars, though different in their nature, were attended with similar results. The contest with France was maintained by the English people with a degree of ardor which went entirely to the profit of royalty. The people, already remarkable for the prudence and determination with which they defended their resources and treasures, surrendered them at that period to their monarchs, without foresight or measure. It was in the reign of Henry V that a considerable tax, consisting of custom-house duties, was granted to the king for his lifetime, almost at the beginning of his reign. The foreign war was scarcely ended, when the civil war, which had already broken out, was carried on; the houses of York and Lancaster disputed the throne. When at length these sanguinary struggles were brought to an end, the English nobility were ruined, diminished in number, and no longer able to preserve the power which they had previously exercised. The coalition of the great barons was no longer able to govern the throne. The Tudors ascended it; and with Henry VII, in 1485, begins the era of political centralization, the triumph of royalty.

Monarchy did not establish itself in Italy, at least under that name; but this made little difference as to the result. It was in the fifteenth century that the fall of the Italian republics took place. Even where the name was retained, the power became concentrated in the hands of one, or of a few families. The spirit of republicanism was extinguished. In the north of Italy, almost all the Lombard republics merged in the Duchy of Milan. In 1434, Florence fell under the dominion of the Medicis. In 1464, Genoa became subject to Milan. The greater part of the republics, great and small, yielded to the power of sovereign houses; and soon afterwards began the pretensions of foreign sovereigns to the dominion of the north and south of Italy; to the Milanese and kingdom of Naples.

Indeed, to whatever country of Europe we cast our eyes, whatever portion of its history we consider, whether it relates to the nations themselves or their governments, to their territories or their institutions, we everywhere see the old elements, the old forms of society, disappearing. Those liberties which were founded on tradition were lost; new powers arose, more regular and concentrated than those which previously existed. There is something deeply melancholy in this view of the fall of the ancient liberties of Europe. Even in its own time it inspired feelings of the utmost bitterness. In France, in Germany, and above all, in Italy, the patriots of the fifteenth century resisted with ardor, and lamented with despair, that revolution which everywhere produced the rise of what they were entitled to call despotism. We must admire their courage and feel for their sorrow; but at the same time we must be aware that this revolution was not only inevitable, but useful. The primitive system of Europe—the old feudal and municipal liberties— had failed in the organization of a general society. Security and progress are essential to social existence. Every system which does not provide for present order, and progressive advancement for the future, is vicious, and speedily abandoned. And this was the fate of the old political forms of society, of the ancient liberties of Europe in the fifteenth century. They could not give to society either security or progress. These objects naturally became sought for elsewhere; to obtain them, recourse was had to other principles and other means; and this is the import of all the facts to which I have just called your attention.

To this same period may be assigned another circumstance which has had a great influence on the political history of Europe. It was in the fifteenth century that the relations of governments with each other began to be frequent, regular, and permanent. Now, for the first time, became formed those great combinations by means of alliance, for peaceful as well as warlike objects, which, at a later period, gave rise to the system of the balance of power. European diplomacy originated in the fifteenth century. In fact you may see, towards its close, the principal powers of the continent of Europe, the Popes, the Dukes of Milan, the Venetians, the German Emperors, and the Kings of France and Spain, entering into a closer correspondence with each other than had hitherto existed; negotiating, combining, and balancing their various interests. Thus at the very time when Charles VIII set on foot his expedition to conquer the kingdom of Naples,* a great league was formed against him, between Spain, the Pope, and the Venetians. The league of Cambray was formed some years later (in 1508), against the Venetians. The holy league directed against Louis XII succeeded, in 1511, to the league of Cambray. All these combinations had their rise in Italian policy; in the desire of different sovereigns to possess its territory; and in the fear lest any of them, by obtaining an exclusive possession, should acquire an excessive preponderance. This new order of things was very favorable to the career of monarchy. On the one hand, it belongs to the very nature of the external relations of states that they can be conducted only by a single person, or by a very small number, and that they require a certain degree of secrecy: on the other hand, the people were so little enlightened that the consequences of a combination of this kind quite escaped them. As it had no direct bearing on their individual or domestic life, they troubled themselves little about it; and, as usual, left such transactions to the discretion of the central government. Thus diplomacy, in its very birth, fell into the hands of kings; and the opinion, that it belongs to them exclusively; that the nation, even when free, and possessed of the right of voting its own taxes, and interfering in the management of its domestic affairs, has no right to intermeddle in foreign matters;—this opinion, I say, became established in all parts of Europe, as a settled principle, a maxim of common law.* Look into the history of England in the sixteenth and seventeenth centuries, and you will observe the great influence of that opinion, and the obstacles it presented to the liberties of England in the reigns of Elizabeth, James I, and Charles I. It is always under the sanction of the principle, that peace and war, commercial relations, and all foreign affairs, belong to the royal prerogative, that absolute power defends itself against the rights of the country. The people are remarkably timid in disputing this portion of the prerogative; and their timidity has cost them the dearer, for this reason, that, from the commencement of the period into which we are now entering (that is to say, the sixteenth century), the history of Europe is essentially diplomatic. For nearly three centuries, foreign relations form the most important part of history. The domestic affairs of countries began to be regularly conducted; the internal government, on the Continent at least, no longer produced any violent convulsions, and no longer kept the public mind in a state of agitation and excitement. Foreign relations, wars, treaties, alliances, alone occupy the attention and fill the page of history; so that we find the destinies of nations abandoned in a great measure to the royal prerogative, to the central power of the state.

It could scarcely have happened otherwise. Civilization must have made great progress, intelligence and political habits must be widely diffused, before the public can interfere with advantage in matters of this kind. From the sixteenth to the eighteenth century, the people were far from being sufficiently advanced to do so. Observe what occurred in England, under James I, at the beginning of the seventeenth century. His son-in-law, the Elector Palatine, who had been elected king of Bohemia, had lost his crown, and had even been stripped of his hereditary dominions, the Palatinate. Protestantism everywhere espoused his cause; and, on this ground, England took a warm interest in it. There was a great manifestation of public opinion in order to force James to take the part of his son-in-law, and obtained for him the restoration of the Palatinate. Parliament insisted violently for war, promising ample means to carry it on. James was indifferent on the subject; he made several attempts to negotiate, and sent some troops to

Germany; he then told parliament that he required £900,000 sterling, to carry on the war with any chance of success. It is not said, and indeed it does not appear, that his estimate was exaggerated. But parliament shrunk back with astonishment and terror at the sound of such a sum, and could hardly be prevailed upon to vote £70,000 sterling, to reinstate a prince, and reconquer a country three hundred leagues distant from England.* Such were the ignorance and political incapacity of the public in affairs of this nature; they acted without any knowledge of facts, or any consideration of consequences. How then could they be capable of interfering in a regular and effectual manner? This is the cause which principally contributed to make foreign relations fall into the hands of the central power; no other was in a condition to conduct them, I shall not say for the public benefit, which was very far from being always consulted, but with anything like consistency and good sense.

It may be seen, then, that in whatever point of view we regard the political history of Europe at this period—whether we look upon the internal condition of different nations, or upon their relation with each other—whether we consider the means of warfare, the administration of justice, or the levying of taxes, we find them pervaded by the same character; we see everywhere the same tendency to centralization, to unity, to the formation and preponderance of general interests and public powers. This was the hidden working of the fifteenth century, which, at the period we are speaking of, had not yet produced any very apparent result, or any actual revolution in society, but was preparing all those consequences which afterwards took place.

I shall now bring before you a class of facts of a different nature; moral facts, such as stand in relation to the development of the human mind and the formation of general ideas. In these again we shall discover the same phenomena, and arrive at the same result.

I shall begin with an order of facts which has often engaged our attention, and under the most various forms, has always held an important place in the history of Europe—the facts relative to the Church. Down to the fifteenth century, the only general ideas which had a powerful influence on the masses were those connected with religion. The Church alone was invested with the power of regulating, promulgating, and prescribing them. Attempts, it is true, at independence, and even at separation, were frequently made; and the Church had much to do to overcome them. Down to this period, however, she had been successful. Creeds rejected by the Church had never taken any general or permanent hold on the minds of the people; even the Albigenses had been repressed. Dissension and strife were incessant in the Church, but without any decisive and striking result. The fifteenth century opened with the appearance of a different state of things. New ideas, and a public and avowed desire of change and reformation, began to agitate the Church herself. The end of the fourteenth and beginning of the fifteenth century were marked by the great schism of the West, resulting from the removal of the papal chair to Avignon, and the creation of two popes, one at Avignon, and the other at Rome. The contest between these two papacies is what is called the great schism of the West.* It began in 1378. In 1409, the Council of Pisa endeavored to put an end to it by deposing the two rival popes and electing another. But instead of ending the schism, this step only rendered it more violent.

There were now three popes instead of two; and disorders and abuses went on increasing. In 1414, the Council of Constance assembled, convoked by desire of the Emperor Sigismund. This council set about a matter of far more importance than the nomination of a new pope; it undertook the reformation of the Church. It began by proclaiming the indissolubility of the universal council, and its superiority over the papal power. It endeavored to establish these principles in the Church, and to reform the abuses which had crept into it, particularly the exactions by which the court of Rome obtained money. To accomplish this object the council appointed what we should call a commission of inquiry, in other words, a Reform College, composed of deputies to the council, chosen in the different Christian nations. This college was directed to inquire into the abuses which polluted the Church, and into the means of remedying them, and to make a report to the council, in order that it might deliberate on the proceedings to be adopted. But while the council was thus engaged, the question was started, whether it could proceed to the reform of abuses without the visible concurrence of the head of the Church, without the sanction of the pope. It was carried in the negative through the influence of the Roman party supported by some well-meaning but timid individuals. The council elected a new pope, Martin V, in 1417. The pope was instructed to present, on his part, a plan for the reform of the Church. This plan was rejected, and the council separated. In 1431, a new council assembled at Basel with the same design. It resumed and continued the reforming labors of the Council of Constance, but with no better success. Schism broke out in this assembly as it had done in Christendom. The pope removed the council to Ferrara, and afterwards to Florence. A portion of the prelates refused to obey the pope, and remained at Basel, and, as there had formerly been two popes, so now there were two councils. That of Basel continued its projects of reform; named as its pope, Felix V; some time afterward removed to Lausanne; and dissolved itself in 1449, without having effected anything.

In this manner papacy gained the day, remained in possession of the field of battle, and of the government of the Church. The council could not accomplish that which it had set about; but it did something else which it had not thought of, and which survived its dissolution. Just at the time the Council of Basel failed in its attempts at reform, sovereigns were adopting the ideas which it had proclaimed, and some of the institutions which it had suggested. In France, and with the decrees of the Council of Basel, Charles VII formed the Pragmatic Sanction,* which he proclaimed at Bourges in 1438; it authorized the election of bishops, the suppression of annates (or first-fruits), and the reform of the principal abuses introduced into the Church. The pragmatic sanction was declared in France to be a law of the state. In Germany, the Diet of Mayence adopted it in 1439, and also made it a law of the German empire. What spiritual power had tried without success, temporal power seemed determined to accomplish.

But the projects of the reformers met with a new reverse of fortune. As the council had failed, so did the pragmatic sanction. It perished very soon in Germany. It was abandoned by the Diet in 1448, in virtue of a negotiation with Nicholas V. In 1516, Francis I abandoned it also, substituting for it his concordat with Leo X.* The reform attempted by princes did not succeed better than that set on foot by the clergy. But we must not conclude that it was entirely thrown away. In like manner as the council had done things which survived it, so the pragmatic sanction had effects which survived it also, and will be found to make an important figure in modern history. The principles of the Council of Basel were strong and fruitful. Men of superior minds, and of energetic characters, had adopted and maintained them. John of Paris, D'Ailly, Gerson, and many distinguished men of the fifteenth century, had devoted themselves to their defence. It was in vain that the council was dissolved; it was in vain that the pragmatic sanction was abandoned; their general doctrines respecting the government of the Church, and the reforms which were necessary, took root in France. They were spread abroad, found their way into parliaments, took a strong hold of the public mind, and gave birth first to the Jansenists, and then to the Gallicans.† This entire series of maxims and efforts tending to the reform of the Church, which began with the Council of Constance, and terminated in the four propositions of Bossuet, emanated from the same source, and was directed to the same object.‡ It is the same fact which has undergone successive transformations. Notwithstanding the failure of the legal attempts at reform made in the fifteenth century, they indirectly had an immense influence upon the progress of civilization; and must not be left out of its history.

The councils were right in trying for a legal reform, for it was the only way to prevent a revolution. Nearly at the time when the Council of Pisa was endeavoring to put an end to the great western schism, and the Council of Constance to reform the Church, the first attempts at popular religious reform broke out in Bohemia. The preaching of John Huss,* and his progress as a reformer, commenced in 1404, when he began to teach at Prague. Here, then, we have two reforms going on side by side; the one in the very bosom of the Church,—attempted by the ecclesiastical aristocracy itself,—cautious, embarrassed, and timid; the other originating without the Church, and directed against it,—violent, passionate, and impetuous. A contest began between these two powers, these two parties. The council enticed John Huss and Jerome of Prague to Constance, and condemned them to the flames as heretics and revolutionists. These events are perfectly intelligible to us now. We can very well understand this simultaneous existence of separate reforms, one undertaken by governments, the other by the people, hostile to each other, yet springing from the same cause, and tending to the same object, and, though opposed to each other, finally concurring in the same result. This is what happened in the fifteenth century. The popular reform of John Huss was stifled for the moment; the war of the Hussites broke out three or four years after the death of their master; it was long and violent, but at last the empire was successful in subduing it. The failure of the councils in the work of reform, their not being able to attain the object they were aiming at, only kept the public mind in a state of fermentation. The spirit of reform still existed; it waited but for an opportunity again to break out, and this it found at the beginning of the sixteenth century. Had the reform undertaken by the councils been brought to any good issue, perhaps the popular reform would have been prevented. But it was impossible that one or the other of them should not succeed, for their coincidence shows their necessity.

Such, then, is the state, in respect to religious creeds, in which Europe was left by the fifteenth century: an aristocratic reform attempted without success, with a popular suppressed reform begun, but still ready to break out anew.

It was not solely to religious creeds that the human mind was directed, and about which it busied itself at this period. It was in the course of the fourteenth century, as you all know, that Greek and Roman antiquity was (if I may use the expression) restored to Europe. You know with what ardor Dante, Petrarch, Boccaccio, and all their contemporaries, sought for Greek and Latin manuscripts, published them, and spread them abroad; and what general joy was produced by the smallest discovery in this branch of learning. It was in the midst of this excitement that the classical school took its rise; a school which has performed a much more important part in the development of the human mind than has generally been ascribed to it. But we must be cautious of attaching to this term, classical school, the meaning given to it at present. It had to do, in those days, with matters very different from literary systems and disputes. The classical school of that period inspired its disciples with admiration, not only for the writings of Virgil and Homer, but for the entire frame of ancient society, for its institutions, its opinions, its philosophy, as well as its literature. Antiquity, it must be allowed, whether as regards politics, philosophy, or literature, was greatly superior to the Europe of the fourteenth and fifteenth centuries. It is not surprising, therefore, that it should have exercised so great an influence; that lofty, vigorous, elegant, and fastidious minds should have been disgusted with the coarse manners, the confused ideas, the barbarous modes of their own time, and should have devoted themselves with enthusiasm, and almost with veneration, to the study of a state of society, at once more regular and more perfect than their own. Thus was formed that school of bold thinkers which appeared at the commencement of the fifteenth century, and in which prelates, jurists, and men of learning were united by common sentiments and common pursuits.*

In the midst of this movement happened the taking of Constantinople by the Turks, 1453, the fall of the Eastern empire, and the influx of the fugitive Greeks into Italy. These brought with them a greater knowledge of antiquity, numerous manuscripts, and a thousand new means of studying the civilization of the ancients. You may easily imagine how this must have redoubled the admiration and ardor of the classic school. This was the most brilliant period of the Church, especially in Italy, not in respect of political power, but of wealth and luxury. The Church gave herself up to all the pleasures of an indolent, elegant, licentious civilization; to a taste for letters, the arts, and social and physical enjoyments. Look at the way in which the men who played the greatest political and literary parts at that period passed their lives—Cardinal Bembo,* for example—and you will be surprised by the mixture which it exhibits of luxurious effeminacy and intellectual culture, of enervated manners and mental vigor. In surveying this period, indeed, when we look at the state of opinions and of social relations, we might imagine ourselves living among the French of the eighteenth century. There was the same desire for the progress of intelligence, and for the acquirement of new ideas; the same taste for an agreeable and easy life, the same luxury, the same licentiousness; there was the same want of political energy and of moral principles, combined with singular sincerity and activity of mind. The literati of the fifteenth century stood in the same relation to the prelates of the Church as the men of letters and philosophers of the eighteenth did to the nobility. They had the same opinions and manners, lived agreeably together, and gave themselves no uneasiness about the storms that were brewing round them. The prelates of the fifteenth century, and Cardinal Bembo among the rest, no more foresaw Luther and Calvin, than the courtiers of Louis XIV foresaw the French revolution. The analogy between the two cases is striking and instructive.

We observe, then, three great facts in the moral order of society at this period—on one hand, an ecclesiastical reform attempted by the Church itself; on another a popular, religious reform; and lastly, an intellectual revolution, which formed a school of free-thinkers; and all these transformations were prepared in the midst of the greatest political change that has ever taken place in Europe, in the midst of the process of the centralization of nations and governments. But this is not all. The period in question was also one of the most remarkable for the display of physical activity among men. It was a period of voyages, travels, enterprises, discoveries, and inventions of every kind. It was the time of the great Portuguese expedition along the coast of Africa; of the discovery of the new passage to India by the Cape of Good Hope, by Vasco de Gama; of the discovery of America, by Christopher Columbus; of the wonderful extension of European commerce. A thousand new inventions started up; others already known, but confined within a narrow sphere, became popular and in general use. Gunpowder changed the system of war; the compass changed the system of navigation. Painting in oil was invented, and filled Europe with masterpieces of art. Engraving on copper, invented in 1406, multiplied and diffused them. Paper made of linen became common. Finally, between 1436 and 1452, was invented printing,—printing, the theme of so many declamations and common-places, but to whose merits and effect no common-places or declamations will ever be able to do justice.

From all this, some idea may be formed of the greatness and activity of the fifteenth century; a greatness which, at the time, was not very apparent; an activity of which the results did not immediately take place. Violent reforms seemed to fail; governments acquired stability. It might have been supposed that society was now about to enjoy the benefits of better order, and more rapid progress. The mighty revolutions of the sixteenth century were at hand; the fifteenth century prepared them.—They shall be the subject of the following lecture.

LECTURE XII.: THE REFORMATION.

I have often referred to and lamented the disorder, the chaotic situation of European society; I have complained of the difficulty of comprehending and describing a state of society so loose, so scattered, and incoherent; and I have kept you waiting with impatience for the period of general interests, order, and social union. This period we have now reached; but, in treating of it, we encounter a difficulty of another kind. Hitherto, we have found it difficult to connect historical facts one with another, to class them together, to seize their common features, to discover their points of resemblance. The case is different in modern Europe; all the elements, all the incidents of social life modify, act and react upon each other; the mutual relations of men are much more numerous and complicated; so also are their relations with the government and the state, the relations of states with each other, and all the ideas and operations of the human mind. In the periods through which we have already traveled, we have found a great number of facts which were insulated, foreign to each other, and without any reciprocal influence. From this time, however, we find nothing insulated; all things press upon one another, and become modified and changed by their mutual contact and friction. What, let me ask, can be more difficult than to seize the real point of unity in the midst of such diversity, to determine the direction of such a widely spread and complicated movement, to sum up this prodigious number of various and closely connected elements, to point out at last the general and leading fact which is the sum of a long series of facts; which characterizes an era, and is the true expression of its influence, and of the part it has performed in the history of civilization? You will be able to measure at a glance the extent of this difficulty, in the great event which is now to engage our attention.

In the twelfth century we met with an event which was religious in its origin if not in its nature; I mean the crusades. Notwithstanding the greatness of this event, its long duration, and the variety of incidents which it brought about, it was easy enough for us to discover its general character, and to determine its influence with some degree of precision.

We have now to consider the religious revolution of the sixteenth century, which is commonly called the Reformation. Let me be permitted to say in passing, that I shall use this word reformation as a simple ordinary term, synonymous with religious revolution, and without attaching it to any opinion. You must, I am sure, foresee at once, how difficult it is to discover the real character of this great crisis, and to explain in a general manner what has been its nature and its effects.

The period of our inquiry must extend from the beginning of the sixteenth to the middle of the seventeenth century; for this period embraces, so to speak, the life of this event from its birth to its termination. All historical events have in some sort a determinate career. Their consequences are prolonged to infinity; they are connected with all the past and all the future; but it is not the less true, on this account, that they have a definite and limited existence; that they have their origin and their increase, occupy with their development a certain portion of time, and then diminish and disappear from the scene, to make way for some new event which runs a similar course.

The precise date which may be assigned to the Reformation is not of much importance. We may take the year 1520, when Luther publicly burnt at Wittenberg the bull of Leo X, containing his condemnation, and thus formally separated himself from the Romish church.* The interval between this period and the middle of the seventeenth century, the year 1648, when the treaty of

Westphalia was concluded, comprehends the life of the Reformation. That this is the case, may be thus proved. The first and greatest effect of the religious revolution was to create in Europe two classes of states, the Catholic and the Protestant, to set them against each other and force them into hostilities. With many vicissitudes, the struggle between these two parties lasted from the beginning of the sixteenth century to the middle of the seventeenth. It was by the treaty of Westphalia, in 1648, that the Catholic and Protestant states reciprocally acknowledged each other, and engaged to live in amity and peace, without regard to difference of religion. After this, from 1648, difference of religion ceased to be the leading principle of the classification of states, of their external policy, their relations and alliances. Down to that time, notwithstanding great variations, Europe was essentially divided into a Catholic league and a Protestant league. After the treaty of Westphalia this distinction disappeared; and alliances or divisions among states took place from considerations altogether foreign to religious belief. At this point, therefore, the preponderance, or, in other words, the career of the Reformation came to an end, although its consequences, instead of decreasing, continued to develop themselves.

Let us now take a rapid survey of this career, and merely mentioning names and events, point out its course. You will see from this simple indication, from this dry and incomplete outline, what must be the difficulty of summing up a series of such various and complicated facts into one general fact; of determining what is the true character of the religious revolution of the sixteenth century, and of assigning to it its true part in the history of civilization.

The moment in which the Reformation broke out is remarkable for its political importance. It was in the midst of the great struggle between Francis I and Charles V—between France and Spain; a struggle at first for the possession of Italy, but afterwards for the German empire, and finally for preponderance in Europe. It was the moment in which the house of Austria elevated itself and became predominant in Europe. It was also the moment in which England, through Henry VIII, interfered in continental politics, more regularly, permanently, and extensively than she had ever done before.

If we follow the course of the sixteenth century in France, we shall find it entirely occupied by the great religious wars between Protestants and Catholics; wars which became the means and the occasion of a new attempt of the great nobles to repossess themselves of the power which they had lost, and to obtain an ascendancy over the sovereign. This was the political meaning of the religious wars of France, of the League,* of the struggle between the houses of Guise and Valois,—a struggle which was put an end to by the accession of Henry IV.

In Spain, the revolution of the United Provinces broke out about the middle of the reign of Philip II. The Inquisition on one hand, and civil and religious liberty on the other, made these provinces the theatre of war under the names of the Duke of Alva and the Prince of Orange. Perseverance and prudence secured the triumph of liberty in Holland, but it perished in Spain, where absolute power, ecclesiastical and civil, reigned without control.

In England, the circumstances to be noted are, the reigns of Mary and Elizabeth; the struggle of Elizabeth, as head of the Protestant interests, against Philip II; the accession of James Stuart to the throne of England; and the rise of the great dispute between the monarchy and the people.* About the same time we note the creation of new powers in the north. Sweden was raised into existence by Gustavus Vasa, in 1523. Prussia was created by the secularization of the Teutonic order. The northern powers assumed a place in the politics of Europe which they had not occupied before, and the importance of which soon afterwards showed itself in the Thirty Years' War.

I now come back to France, to note the reign of Louis XIII; the change in the internal administration of this country effected by Cardinal Richelieu; the relations of France with Germany, and the support which she afforded to the Protestant party.† In Germany, during the latter part of the sixteenth century, there was the war with the Turks; in the beginning of the seventeenth, the Thirty Years' War, the greatest of modern events in eastern Europe; Gustavus Adolphus, Wallenstein, Tilly, the Duke of Brunswick, the Duke of Weimar, are the greatest names of which Germany at this time could boast.

At the same period, in France, took place the accession of Louis XIV and the commencement of the Fronde;‡ in England broke out the great revolution, or, as it is sometimes improperly called, the Great Rebellion, which dethroned Charles I.

In this survey, I have only glanced at the most prominent events of history, events which everybody has heard of; you see their number, their variety, their importance. If we seek for events of another kind, events less conspicuous and less distinguished by great names, we shall find them not less abundant during this period; a period remarkable for the great changes which took place in the political institutions of almost every country; the period in which pure monarchy prevailed in most of the great states, while in Holland there arose the most powerful republic in Europe; and in England constitutional monarchy achieved, or nearly achieved, a final triumph. Then, in the Church, it was during this period that the old monastic orders lost almost all their political power, and were replaced by a new order of a different character, and whose importance, erroneously perhaps, is considered much superior to that of its precursors,—I mean the Jesuits. At the same period the Council of Trent obliterated all that remained of the influence of the Councils of Constance and Basel, and secured the definitive ascendency of the Court of Rome in ecclesiastical affairs.* Leaving the Church, and taking a passing glance at the philosophy of the age, at the unfettered career of the human mind, we observe two men, Bacon and Descartes, the authors of the greatest philosophical revolution which the modern world has undergone, the chiefs of the two schools which contended for supremacy. It was in this period too that Italian literature shone forth in its fullest splendor, while that of France and England was still in its infancy. Lastly, it was in this period that the colonial system of Europe had its origin; that great colonies were founded; and that commercial activity and enterprise were carried to an extent never before known.

Thus, under whatever point of view we consider this era, we find its political, ecclesiastical, philosophical, and literary events, more numerous, varied, and important, than in any of the preceding ages. The activity of the human mind displayed itself in every way; in the relations of men with each other—in their relations with the governing powers—in the relations of states, and in the intellectual labors of individuals. In short, it was the age of great men and of great things. Yet, among the great events of this period, the religious revolution which now engages our attention was the greatest. It was the leading fact of the period; the fact which gives it its name, and determines its character.* Among the many powerful causes which have produced so many powerful effects, the Reformation was the most powerful; it was that to which all the others contributed; that which has modified, or been modified by, all the rest. The task which we have now to perform, then, is to review, with precision, this event; to examine this cause, which, in a period of the greatest causes, produced the greatest effects—this event, which, in this period of great events, prevailed over all the rest.

You must, at once, perceive how difficult it is to link together facts so diversified, so immense, and so closely connected, into one great historical unity. It must, however, be done; when events are once consummated, when they have become matter of history, the most important business is then to be attempted; that which man most seeks for are general facts—the linking together of causes and effects. This is what I may call the immortal portion of history, which all generations must study, in order to understand the past as well as the present time. This desire after generalization, of obtaining rational results, is the most powerful and noblest of all our intellectual desires; but we must beware of being satisfied with hasty and incomplete generalizations. No pleasure is more seducing than that of indulging ourselves in determining on the spot, and at first sight, the general character and permanent results of an era or an event. The human intellect, like the human will, is eager to be in action, impatient of obstacles, and desirous of coming to conclusions. It willingly forgets such facts as impede and constrain its operations; but while it forgets, it cannot destroy them; they still live to convict it of error at some after period. There is only one way of escaping this danger; it is by a resolute and dogged study of facts, till their meaning is exhausted, before attempting to generalize, or coming to conclusions respecting their effects. Facts are, for the intellect, what the rules of morals are for the will. The mind must be thoroughly acquainted with facts, and must know their weight; and it is only when she has fulfilled this duty—when she has completely traversed, in every direction, the ground of investigation and inquiry—that she is permitted to spread her wings and take her flight towards that higher region, whence she may survey all things in their general bearings and results. If she endeavor to ascend prematurely, without having first acquired a thorough knowledge of the territory which she desires to contemplate from above, she incurs the most imminent risk of error and downfall. As, in a calculation of figures, an error at the outset leads to others, ad infinitum, so, in history, if we do not, in the first instance, take every fact into account—if we allow ourselves to indulge in a spirit of precipitate generalization—it is impossible to tell how far we may be led astray from the truth.

In these observations, I am, in some measure, putting you on your guard against myself. In this course I have been able to do little more than make some attempts at generalization, and take some general views of facts which we had not studied closely and together. Having now arrived at a period where this task is much more difficult, and the chances of error greater than before, I think it necessary to make you aware of the danger, and warn you against my own speculations. Having done so, I shall now continue them, and treat the Reformation in the same way that I have other events. I shall endeavor to discover its leading fact, to describe its general character, and to show the part which this great event has performed in the process of European civilization.

You remember the situation in which we left Europe, at the end of the fifteenth century.* We saw, in the course of it, two great attempts at religious revolution or reform; an attempt at legal reform by the councils, and an attempt at revolutionary reform, in Bohemia, by the Hussites; we saw both these stifled and rendered abortive; and yet we concluded that the event was one which could not be staved off, but that it must necessarily reappear in one shape or another; and that what the fifteenth century attempted would be inevitably accomplished by the sixteenth.† I shall not enter into any details respecting the religious revolution of the sixteenth century, which I consider as being generally known.‡ I shall confine myself solely to the consideration of its general influence on the destinies of mankind.

In the inquiries which have been made into the causes which produced this great event, the enemies of the Reformation have imputed it to accidents and mischances, in the course of civilization; for instance, to the sale of indulgences* having been intrusted to the Dominicans, which the jealousy of the Augustines. Luther was an Augustine; and this, therefore, was the moving power which put the Reformation in action. Others have ascribed it to the ambition of sovereigns—to their rivalry with the ecclesiastical power, and to the avidity of the lay nobility, who wished to take possession of the property of the Church. In this manner the Reformation has been accounted for, by looking at the evil side of human nature and human affairs; by having recourse to the private interests and selfish passions of individuals.

On the other hand, the friends and partisans of the Reformation have endeavored to account for it by the pure desire of effectually reforming the existing abuses of the Church. They have represented it as a redress of religious grievances, as an enterprise conceived and executed with the sole design of reconstituting the Church in its primitive purity. Neither of these explanations appears to me well founded. There is more truth in the latter than in the former; at least, the cause assigned is greater, and in better proportion to the extent and importance of the event; but, still, I do not consider it as correct. In my opinion, the Reformation neither was an accident, the result of some casual circumstance, or some personal interest, nor arose from unmingled views of religious improvement, the fruit of Utopian humanity and truth. It had a more powerful cause than all these; a general cause, to which all the others were subordinate. It was a vast effort made by the human mind to achieve its freedom; it was a new born desire which it felt to think and judge, freely and independently, of facts and opinions which, till then, Europe received, or was considered bound to receive, from the hands of authority. It was a great endeavor to emancipate human reason; and to call things by their right names, it was an insurrection of the human mind against the absolute power of spiritual order. Such, in my opinion, was the true character and leading principle of the Reformation.

When we consider, on one hand, the state of the human mind, at this time, and, on the other, the state of the spiritual power of the Church, which had the government of the human mind, a double fact presents itself to our notice.

In looking at the human mind, we observe much greater activity, and a much greater desire to develop its powers, than it had ever felt before. This new activity was the result of various causes which had been accumulating for ages. For example, there were ages in which heresies sprang up, subsisted for a time, and then gave way to others; there were other ages in which philosophical opinions ran just the same course as heresies. The labors of the human mind, whether in the sphere of religion or of philosophy, had been accumulating from the eleventh to the sixteenth century; and the time was now come when they must necessarily have a result. Besides this, the means of instruction created or favored in the bosom of the Church itself, had brought forth fruit. Schools* had been instituted; these schools had produced men of considerable knowledge, and their number had daily increased. These men began to wish to think for themselves, for they felt themselves stronger than they had ever been before. At last came that restoration of the human mind to a pristine youth and vigor, which the revival of the learning and arts of antiquity brought about, the progress and effects of which I have already described. These various causes combined, gave, at the beginning of the sixteenth century, a new and powerful impulse to the human mind, an imperious desire to go forward.

The situation of the spiritual power, which then had the government of the human mind, was totally different; it, on the contrary, had fallen into a state of imbecility, and remained stationary. The political influence of the Church and Court of Rome was much diminished. European society had passed from the dominion of Rome to that of temporal governments. Yet in spite of all this, the spiritual power still preserved its pretensions, splendor, and outward importance. The same thing happened to it which has so often happened to long established governments. Most of the complaints made against it were now almost groundless. It is not true, that in the sixteenth century, the Court of Rome was very tyrannical; it is not true, that its abuses were more numerous and crying than they had been at former periods. Never, perhaps, on the contrary, had the government of the Church been more indulgent, more tolerant, more disposed to let things take their course, provided it was not itself implicated, provided that the rights it had hitherto enjoyed were acknowledged even though left unexercised, and that it was assured of its usual existence, and received its usual tributes. It would willingly have left the human mind to itself, if the human mind had been as tolerant towards its offences. But it usually happens, that just when governments have begun to lose their influence and power, just when they are comparatively harmless, that they are most exposed to attack; it is then that, like the sick lion, they may be attacked with impunity, though the attempt would have been desperate when they were in the plenitude of their power.

It is evident, therefore, simply from the consideration of the state of the human mind at this period, and of the power which then governed it, that the Reformation must have been, I repeat it, a sudden effort made by the human mind to achieve its liberty, a great insurrection of human intelligence. This, doubtless, was the leading cause of the Reformation, the cause which soared above all the rest; a cause superior to every interest either of sovereigns or of nations, superior to the need of reform properly so called, or of the redress of the grievances which were complained of at this period.

Let us suppose, that after the first years of the Reformation had passed away, when it had made all its demands, and insisted on all its grievances,—let us suppose, I say, that the spiritual power had conceded everything, and said, "Well, be it so; I will make every reform you desire; I will return to a more legal, more truly religious order of affairs. I will suppress arbitrary exactions and tributes; even in matters of belief I will modify my doctrines, and return to the primitive standard of Christian faith. But, having thus redressed all your grievances, I must preserve my station, and retain, as formerly, the government of the human mind, with all the powers and all the rights which I have hitherto enjoyed."—Can we believe that the religious revolution would have been satisfied with these concessions, and would have stopped short in its course? I cannot think so; I firmly believe that it would have continued its career, and that after having obtained reform, it would have demanded liberty. The crisis of the sixteenth century was not merely of a reforming character; it was essentially revolutionary. It cannot be deprived of this character, with all the good and evil that belongs to it; its nature may be traced in its effects.

Let us take a glance at the destinies of the Reformation; let us see, more particularly, what it has produced in the different countries in which it developed itself. It can hardly escape observation that it exhibited itself in very different situations, and with very different chances of success; if then we find that, notwithstanding this diversity of situations and chances, it has always pursued a certain object, obtained a certain result, and preserved a certain character, it must be evident that this character, which has surmounted all the diversities of situation, all the inequalities of chance, must be the fundamental character of the event; and that this result must be the essential object of its pursuit.

Well then, wherever the religious revolution of the sixteenth century prevailed, if it did not accomplish a complete emancipation of the human mind, it procured it a new and great increase of liberty. It doubtless left the mind subject to all the chances of liberty or thraldom which might arise from political institutions; but it abolished or disarmed the spiritual power, the systematic and formidable government of the mind. This was the result obtained by the Reformation, notwithstanding the infinite diversity of circumstances under which it took place. In Germany there was no political liberty; the Reformation did not introduce it; it rather strengthened than enfeebled the power of princes; it was rather opposed to the free institutions of the middle ages than favorable to their progress. Still, in spite of this, it excited and maintained in Germany a greater freedom of thought, probably, than in any other country. In Denmark, too, a country in which absolute power predominated in the municipal institutions, as well as the general institutions of the state, thought was emancipated through the influence of the Reformation, and freely exercised on every subject. In Holland, under a republic; in England, under a constitutional monarchy, and in spite of a religious tyranny which was long very severe, the emancipation of the human mind was accomplished by the same influence. And lastly, in France, which seemed from its situation the least likely of any to be affected by this religious revolution, even in this country, where it was actually overcome, it became a principle of mental independence, of intellectual freedom. Till the year 1685, that is, till the revocation of the Edict of Nantes,* the Reformation enjoyed a legal existence in France. During this long space of time, the reformers wrote, disputed, and provoked their adversaries to write and dispute with them. This single fact, this war of tracts and disputations between the old and new opinions, diffused in France a greater degree of real and active liberty than is commonly believed; a liberty which redounded to the advantage of science and morality, to the honor of the French clergy, and to the benefit of the mind in general. Look at the conferences of Bossuet with Claude,† and at all the religious controversy of that period, and ask yourselves if Louis XIV would have permitted a similar degree of freedom on any other subject. It was between the reformers and the opposite party that the greatest freedom of opinion existed in the seventeenth century. Religious questions were treated in a bolder and freer spirit of speculation than political, even by Fenelon himself in his Telemachus. This state of things lasted till the revocation of the edict of Nantes. Now, from the year 1685 to the explosion of the human mind in the eighteenth century, there was not an interval of forty years; and the influence of the religious revolution in favor of intellectual liberty had scarcely ceased when the influence of the revolution in philosophy began to operate.

You see, then, that wherever the Reformation penetrated, wherever it acted an important part, whether conqueror or conquered, its general, leading, and constant result was an immense progress in mental activity and freedom; an immense step towards the emancipation of the human mind.

Again, not only was this the result of the Reformation, but it was content with this result. Wherever this was obtained, no other was sought for; so entirely was it the very foundation of the event, its primitive and fundamental character! Thus, in Germany, far from demanding political liberty, the Reformation accepted, I shall not say servitude, but the absence of liberty. In England, it consented to the hierarchical constitution of the clergy, and to the existence of a Church, as full of abuses as ever the Romish church had been, and much more servile. Why did the Reformation, so ardent and rigid in certain respects, exhibit, in these instances, so much facility and suppleness? Because it had obtained the general result to which it tended, the abolition of the spiritual power, and the emancipation of the human mind. I repeat it; wherever the Reformation attained this object, it accommodated itself to every form of government, and to every situation.

Let us now test this fact by the opposite mode of proof; let us see what happened in those countries into which the Reformation did not penetrate, or in which it was early suppressed. We learn from history that, in those countries, the human mind was not emancipated; witness two great countries, Spain and Italy. While, in those parts of Europe into which the Reformation very largely entered, the human mind, during the last three centuries, has acquired an activity and freedom previously unknown;—in those other parts, into which it was never allowed to make its way, the mind, during the same period, has become languid and inert: so that opposite sets of facts, which happened at the same time, concur in establishing the same result.*

The impulse which was given to human thought, and the abolition of absolute power in the spiritual order, constituted, then, the essential character of the Reformation, the most general result of its influence, the ruling fact in its destiny.

I use the word fact, and I do so designedly. The emancipation of the human mind, in the course of the Reformation, was a fact rather than a principle, a result rather than an intention.† The Reformation, I believe, has in this respect, performed more than it undertook,—more, probably, than it desired. Contrary to what has happened in many other revolutions, the effects of which have not come up to their design, the consequences of the Reformation have gone beyond the object it had in view; it is greater, considered as an event, than as a system; it never completely foresaw all that it effected, nor, if it had, would it have completely avowed it.

What are the reproaches constantly applied to the Reformation by its enemies? Which of its results are thrown in its face, as it were, as unanswerable?

The two principal reproaches are, first, the multiplicity of sects, the excessive license of thought, the destruction of all spiritual authority, and the entire dissolution of religious society; secondly, tyranny and persecution. "You provoke licentiousness," it has been said to the Reformers,—"you produced it; and, after having been the cause of it, you wish to restrain and repress it. And how do you repress it? By the most harsh and violent means. You take upon yourselves, too, to punish heresy, and that by virtue of an illegitimate authority."

If we take a review of all the principal charges which have been made against the Reformation, we shall find, if we set aside all questions purely doctrinal, that the above are the two fundamental reproaches to which they may all be reduced.

These charges gave great embarrassment to the reform party. When they were taxed with the multiplicity of their sects, instead of advocating the freedom of religious opinion, and maintaining the right of every sect to entire toleration, they denounced sectarianism, lamented it, and endeavored to find excuses for its existence. Were they accused of persecution? They were troubled to defend themselves; they used the plea of necessity; they had, they said, the right to repress and punish error, because they were in possession of the truth. Their articles of belief, and their institutions, they contended, were the only legitimate ones; and if the Church of Rome had not the right to punish the reformed party, it was because she was in the wrong and they in the right.

And when the charge of persecution was applied to the ruling party in the Reformation, not by its enemies, but by its own offspring; when the sects denounced by that party said, "We are doing just what you did; we separate ourselves from you, just as you separated yourselves from the Church of Rome," this ruling party were still more at a loss to find an answer, and frequently the only answer they had to give was an increase of severity.

The truth is, that while laboring for the destruction of absolute power in the spiritual order, the religious revolution of the sixteenth century was not aware of the true principles of intellectual liberty. It emancipated the human mind, and yet pretended still to govern it by laws. In point of fact it produced the prevalence of free inquiry; in point of principle it believed that it was substituting a legitimate for an illegitimate power. It had not looked up to the primary motive, nor down to the ultimate consequences of its own work. It thus fell into a double error. On the one side it did not know or respect all the rights of human thought; at the very moment that it was demanding these rights for itself, it was violating them towards others.* On the other side, it was unable to estimate the rights of authority in matters of reason. I do not speak of that coercive authority which ought to have no rights at all in such matters, but of that kind of authority which is purely moral,* and acts solely by its influence upon the mind. In most reformed countries something is wanting to complete the proper organization of intellectual society, and to the regular action of old and general opinions. What is due to and required by traditional belief, has not been reconciled with what is due to and required by freedom of thinking; and the cause of this undoubtedly is, that the Reformation did not fully comprehend and accept its own principles and effects.

Hence, too, the Reformation acquired an appearance of inconsistency and narrowness of mind, which has often given an advantage to its enemies. The latter knew very well what they were about, and what they wanted; they cited the principles of their conduct without scruple, and avowed all its consequences. There never was a government more consistent and systematic than that of the Church of Rome. In point of fact, the Court of Rome made more compromises and concessions than the Reformation; in point of principle, it adhered much more closely to its system, and maintained a more consistent line of conduct. Great strength is gained by a thorough knowledge of the nature of one's own views and actions, by a complete and rational adoption of a certain principle and design: and a striking example of this is to be found in the course of the religious revolution of the sixteenth century. Everybody knows that the principal power instituted to contend against the Reformation was the order of the Jesuits.* Look for a moment at their history; they failed everywhere; wherever they interfered, to any extent, they brought misfortune upon the cause in which they meddled. In England they ruined kings; in Spain, whole masses of the people. The general course of events, the development of modern civilization, the freedom of the human mind, all these forces with which the Jesuits were called upon to contend, rose up against them and overcame them. And not only did they fail, but you must remember what sort of means they were constrained to employ. There was nothing great or splendid in what they did; they produced no striking events, they did not put in motion powerful masses of men. They proceeded by dark and hidden courses; courses by no means calculated to strike the imagination, or to conciliate that public interest which always attaches itself to great things, whatever may be their principle and object. The party opposed to them, on the contrary, not only overcame, but overcame signally; did great things and by great means; overspread Europe with great men; changed, in open day, the condition and form of states. Every thing, in short, was against the Jesuits, both fortune and appearances; reason, which desires success,—and imagination, which requires éclat,—were alike disappointed by their fate. Still, however, they were undoubtedly possessed of grandeur; great ideas are attached to their name, their influence, and their history. The reason is, that they knew what they did, and what they wished to accomplish; that they were fully and clearly aware of the principles upon which they acted, and of the object which they had in view. They possessed grandeur of thought and of will; and it was this that saved them from the ridicule which attends constant reverses, and the use of paltry means. Wherever, on the contrary, the event has been greater than the design, wherever there is an appearance of ignorance of the first principles and ultimate results of an action, there has always remained a degree of incompleteness, inconsistency, and narrowness of view, which has placed the very victors in a state of rational or philosophical inferiority, the influence of which has sometimes been apparent in the course of events. This, I think, in the struggle between the old and the new order of things, in matters of religion, was the weak side of the Reformation, which often embarrassed its situation, and prevented it from defending itself so well as it had a right to do.

I might consider the religious revolution of the sixteenth century under many other aspects. I have said nothing, and have nothing to say, respecting it as a matter of doctrine—respecting its effects on religion, properly so called, or respecting the relations of the human soul with God and an eternal futurity; but I might exhibit it in its various relations with social order, everywhere producing results of immense importance. For example, it introduced religion into the midst of the laity, into the world, so to speak, of believers. Till then, religion had been the exclusive domain of the ecclesiastical order. The clergy distributed the proceeds, but reserved to themselves the disposal of the capital, and almost the exclusive right even to speak of it. The Reformation again threw matters of religious belief into general circulation, and again opened to believers the field of faith into which they had not been permitted to enter. It had, at the same time, a further result; it banished, or nearly so, religion from polities, and restored the independence of the temporal power. At the same moment that religion returned into the possession of believers, it quitted the government of society. In the reformed countries, in spite of the diversities of ecclesiastical constitutions, even in England, whose constitution is most nearly akin to the old order of things, the spiritual power has no longer any serious pretensions to the government of the temporal power.*

I might enumerate many other consequences of the Reformation, but I must limit myself to the above general views; and I am satisfied with having placed before you its principal feature—the emancipation of the human mind, and the abolition of absolute power in the spiritual order; an abolition which, though, undoubtedly, not complete, is yet the greatest step which, down to our own times, has ever been made towards the attainment of that object.

Before concluding, I pray you to remark, what a striking resemblance of destiny there is to be found, in the history of modern Europe, between civil and religious society, in the revolutions they have had to undergo.

Christian society, as we have seen when I spoke of the Church, was, at first, a state of society perfectly free, formed entirely in the name of a common belief, without institutions or government, properly so called; regulated, solely, by moral and variable powers, according to the exigencies of the moment. Civil society began, in like manner, in Europe, partly, at least, by bands of barbarians; it was a state of society perfectly free, in which every one remained, because he wished to do so, without laws or powers created by institutions. In emerging from that state which was inconsistent with any great social development, religious society placed itself under a government essentially aristocratic; its governors were the clergy, the bishops, the councils, the ecclesiastical aristocracy. A fact of the same kind took place in civil society when it emerged from barbarism; it was, in like manner, the aristocracy, the feudalism of the laity, which laid hold of the power of government. Religious society quitted the aristocratic form of government to assume that of pure monarchy; this was the rationale of the triumph of the Court of Rome over the Councils and the ecclesiastical aristocracy of Europe. The same revolution was accomplished in civil society; it was, in like manner, by the destruction of the aristocratic power, that monarchy prevailed, and took possession of the European world. In the sixteenth century, in the heart of religious society, an insurrection broke out against the system of pure ecclesiastical monarchy, against absolute power in the spiritual order. This revolution produced, sanctioned, and established freedom of inquiry in Europe. In our own time we have witnessed a similar event in civil society.* Absolute temporal power, in like manner, was attacked and overcome. You see, then, that the two orders of society have undergone the same vicissitudes and revolutions; only religious society has always been the foremost in this career.

We are now in possession of one of the great facts in the history of modern society—freedom of inquiry, the liberty of the human mind. We see, at the same time, the almost universal prevalence of political centralization. In my next lecture I shall consider the revolution in England; the event in which freedom of inquiry and a pure monarchy, both results of the progress of civilization, came, for the first time, into collision.†

LECTURE XIII.: THE ENGLISH REVOLUTION.

We have seen, that during the course of the sixteenth century, all the elements, all the facts, of ancient European society had merged in two essential facts, the right of free examination, and centralization of power; one prevailing in religious society, the other in civil society. The emancipation of the human mind and absolute monarchy triumphed at the same moment over Europe in general.

It could hardly be conceived that a struggle between these two facts—the characters of which appear so contradictory—would not, at some time, break out; for while one was the defeat of absolute power in the spiritual order, the other was the triumph of absolute power in the temporal order; one forced on the decline of the ancient ecclesiastical monarchy, the other was the consummation of the ruin of the ancient feudal and municipal liberty. Their simultaneous appearance was owing, as I have already observed, to the circumstance that the revolutions of the religious society followed more rapidly than those of the civil; one had arrived at the point in which the freedom of individual thought was secured, while the other still lingered on the spot where the concentration of all the powers in one general power took place. The coincidence of these two facts, so far from being the consequence of their similitude, did not even prevent their contradiction. They were both advances in the march of civilization, but they were advances connected with different situations; advances of a different moral date, if I may be allowed the expression, although coincident in time. From their position it seemed inevitable that they must clash and combat before a reconciliation could be effected between them.

The first shock between them took place in England. The struggle of the right of free inquiry, the fruit of the Reformation, against the entire suppression of political liberty, the object aimed at by pure monarchy—the attempt to abolish absolute power in the temporal order, as had already been done in the spiritual order—this is the true sense of the English revolution; this is the part it took in the work of civilization.

But how, it may be asked, came it to pass, that this struggle took place in England sooner than anywhere else? How happened it that the revolutions of a political character coincided here with those of a moral character sooner than they did on the Continent?

In England, the royal power had undergone the same vicissitudes as it had on the Continent. Under the Tudors it had reached a degree of concentration and vigor which it had never attained to before. I do not mean to say that the practical despotism of the Tudors was more violent and vexatious than that of their predecessors; there were quite as many, perhaps more, tyrannical proceedings, vexations, and acts of injustice, under the Plantagenets, as under the Tudors. Perhaps, too, at this very period the government of pure monarchy was more severe and arbitrary on the Continent than in England. The new fact under the Tudors was, that absolute power became systematic; royalty laid claim to a primitive, independent sovereignty; it maintained a tone which it had never held before. The theoretic claims of Henry VIII, Elizabeth, James I, and Charles I, are very different from those of Edward I and III, although, in point of fact, the power of the two latter monarchs was nowise less arbitrary or extensive.* I repeat, then, it was the principle, the rational system of monarchy, which changed in England, in the sixteenth century, rather than its practical power; royalty now declared itself absolute and superior to all laws, even to those which it declared itself willing to respect.

There is another point to be considered; the religious revolution had not been accomplished in England in the same way as on the Continent; it was here the work of the monarchs themselves.

It must not be supposed that the seeds had not been sown, or that even attempts had not been made at a popular reform, which would probably have soon broken out. But Henry VIII took the lead; power became revolutionary; and hence it happened, at least in its origin, that, as a redress of ecclesiastical abuses, as an emancipation of the human mind, the reform in England was much less complete than upon the Continent. It was made, as might naturally be expected, in accordance with the interests of its authors. The king and the episcopacy, which was here continued, divided between themselves the riches and the power, of which they despoiled their predecessors, the popes. The effect of this was soon felt. The Reformation, people cried out, had been closed, while the greater part of the abuses which had induced them to desire it, were still continued.

The Reformation reappeared under a more popular form; it made the same demands of the bishops that had already been made of the Holy See; it accused them of being so many popes. As often as the general fate of the religious revolution was compromised; whenever a struggle against the ancient Church took place, the various portions of the Reformation party rallied together, and made common cause against the common enemy: but this danger over, the struggle again broke out among themselves; the popular reform again attacked the aristocratic and royal reform, denounced its abuses, complained of its tyranny, called upon it to make good its promises, and not itself usurp the power which it had just dethroned.

At about the same time a movement for liberty took place in civil society; a desire before unknown, or at least but weakly expressed, was now felt for political freedom. In the course of the sixteenth century, the commercial prosperity of England had increased with amazing rapidity, while during the same time, much territorial wealth, much baronial property had changed hands. The numerous divisions of landed property, which took place during the sixteenth century, in consequence of the ruin of the feudal nobility, and from various other causes which I cannot now stop to enumerate,* form a fact which has not been sufficiently noticed. A variety of documents prove how greatly the number of landed properties increased; the estates going generally into the hands of the gentry, composed of the lesser nobility, and persons who had acquired property by trade. The high nobility, the House of Lords, did not, at the beginning of the seventeenth century, nearly equal, in riches, the House of Commons. There had taken place, then, at the same time in England, a great increase in wealth among the industrial classes, and a great change in landed property. While these two facts were being accomplished, there happened a third, a new march of mind.

The reign of Queen Elizabeth must be regarded as a period of great literary and philosophical activity in England, a period remarkable for bold and pregnant thought; the Puritans followed, without hesitation, all the consequences of a narrow, but powerful creed; other intellects, with less morality, but more freedom and boldness, alike regardless of principle or system, seized with avidity upon every idea, which seemed to promise some gratification to their curiosity, some food for their mental ardor. And it may be regarded as a maxim, that wherever the progress of intelligence is a true pleasure, a desire for liberty is soon felt, nor is it long in passing from the public mind to the state.

A feeling of the same kind, a sort of creeping desire for political liberty, almost manifested itself in some of the countries on the Continent in which the Reformation had made some way; but these countries, being without the means of success, made no progress; they knew not how to make their desire felt; they could find no support for it either in institutions, or in the habits and usages of the people; hence this desire remained vague, uncertain, and sought in vain for the means of satisfying its cravings. In England the case was widely different: the spirit of political liberty which showed itself here in the sixteenth century, as a sort of appendix to the Reformation, found both a firm support and the means of speaking and acting in the ancient institutions of the country, and indeed in the whole framework of English society.

There is hardly anyone who does not know the origin of the free institutions of England. How, in 1215, a coalition of the great barons wrested Magna Charta from John; but it is not quite so generally known, that this charter was renewed and confirmed, from time to time, by almost every king. It was confirmed upwards of thirty times between the thirteenth and sixteenth centuries, besides which new statutes were passed to confirm and extend its enactments. Thus it lived, as it were, without gap or interval. In the mean time the House of Commons had been formed, and taken its place among the sovereign institutions of the country.* Under the Plantagenets it had taken deep root and become firmly established; not that at this time it played any great part or had even much influence in the government; it scarcely indeed interfered in this except when called upon to do so by the king, and then only with hesitation and regret; afraid rather of bringing itself into trouble and danger, than jealous of augmenting its power and authority. But the case was different when it was called upon to defend private rights, the house or property of the citizens, or in short the rights and privileges of individuals; this duty the House of Commons performed with wonderful energy and perseverance, putting forward and establishing all those principles which have become the basis of the English constitution. Under the Tudors the House of Commons, or rather the Parliament altogether, put on a new character. It no longer defended individual liberty so well as under the Plantagenets. Arbitrary detentions, and violations of private rights, which became much more frequent, were often passed in silence. But, as a counterbalance for this, the Parliament interfered to a much greater extent than formerly in the general affairs of government. Henry VIII, in order to change the religion of the country, and to regulate the succession, required some public support, some public instrument, and he had recourse to Parliament, and especially to the House of Commons, for this purpose.† This, which under the Plantagenets had only been a means of resistance, a guarantee of private rights, became now, under the Tudors, an instrument of government, of general policy; so that at the end of the sixteenth century, notwithstanding it had been the tool, and submitted to the will of nearly all sorts of tyrannies, its importance had greatly increased; the foundation of its power was laid, the foundation of that power upon which truly rests representative government.

In taking a view, then, of the free institutions of England at the end of the sixteenth century, we find them to consist: first, of maxims—of principles of liberty, which had been constantly acknowledged in written documents, and of which the legislation and country had never lost sight; secondly, of precedents, of examples of liberty; these, it is true, were mixed with a great number of precedents and examples of an opposite nature; still they were quite sufficient to maintain, to give a legal character to the claims of the friends of liberty, and to support them in their struggle against arbitrary and tyrannical government; thirdly, particular and local institutions, pregnant with the seeds of liberty, the jury, the right of holding public meetings, of bearing arms, to which must be added the independence of municipal administration and jurisdiction; fourthly and finally, the parliament and its authority became more necessary now than ever to the monarchs, as these having dilapidated the greater part of their independent revenues, crown domains, feudal rights, etc., could not support even the expenses of their households, without having recourse to a vote of parliament.

The political state of England then was very different from that of the Continent; notwithstanding the tyranny of the Tudors, notwithstanding the systematic triumph of absolute monarchy, there still remained here a firm support for the new spirit of liberty, a sure means by which it could act.

At this epoch, two national wants were felt in England: on one hand, a want of religious liberty and of a continuation of the reformation already begun; on the other, a want of political liberty, which seemed arrested by the absolute monarchy now establishing its power. These two parties formed an alliance; the party which wished to carry forward religious reform, invoked, political liberty to the aid of its faith and conscience against the bishops and the crown. The friends of political liberty, in like manner, sought the aid of the friends of popular religious reform. The two parties joined their forces to struggle against absolute power, both spiritual and political, now concentrated in the hands of the king. Such is the origin and signification of the English revolution.

It appears, then, to have been essentially devoted to the defence or achievement of liberty. For the religious party it was a means, for the political party it was an end; but the object of both was still liberty, and they were determined to pursue it in common. Properly speaking, there had been no true quarrel between the episcopal and Puritan party; the struggle was not about doctrines, about matters of faith, properly so called. I do not mean that these were not very positive, very important, and differences of great consequence between them; but this was not the main affair. What the Puritan party wished to obtain from the episcopal was practical liberty; this was the object for which it struggled. It must, however, be admitted that there did exist at the same time, a religious party which had a system to found; a set of doctrines, a form of discipline, an ecclesiastic constitution, which it wished to establish—I mean the Presbyterians; but though it did its best, it had not the power to obtain its object. Acting upon the defensive, oppressed by the bishops, unable to take a step without the sanction of the political reformers, its necessary allies and chieftains, liberty naturally became its predominant interest; this was the general interest, the common desire of all the parties which concurred in the movement, however different in other respects might be their views. Taking these matters then altogether, we must come to the conclusion, that the English revolution was essentially political; it was accomplished in the midst of a religious people and a religious age; religious ideas and passions often became its instruments; but its primary intention and its definite object were decidedly political, a tendency to liberty, the destruction of all absolute power.

I shall now briefly run over the various phases of this revolution, and analyze it into the great parties that succeeded one another in its course. I shall afterwards connect it with the general career of European civilization; I shall show its place and influence therein; and you will be satisfied, from the detail of facts as well as from its first aspect, that it was truly the first collision of free inquiry and pure monarchy, the first onset that took place in the struggle between these two great and opposite powers.

Three principal parties appeared upon the stage at this important crisis; three revolutions seem to have been contained within it, and to have successively appeared upon the scene. In each party, in each revolution, two parties moved together in alliance, a political party and a religious party; the former took the lead, the second followed, but one could not go without the other, so that a double character seems to be imprinted upon it in all its changes.

The first party which appeared in the field,* and under whose banners at the beginning marched all the others, was the high, pure-monarchy party, advocating legal reform. When the revolution began, when the Long Parliament assembled in 1640, it was generally said, and sincerely believed by many, that a legal, a constitutional reform would suffice; that the ancient laws and practices of the country were sufficient to correct every abuse, to establish a system of government which would fully meet the wishes of the public.

This party highly blamed and earnestly desired to put a stop to illegal imposts, to arbitrary imprisonments—to all acts, indeed, contrary to the known law and usages of the country. But under these ideas, there lay hid, as it were, a belief in the divine right of the king, and in his absolute power. A secret instinct seemed to warn it that there was something false and dangerous in this notion; and on this account it appeared always desirous to avoid the subject. Forced, however, at last to speak out, it acknowledged the divine right of kings, and admitted that they possessed a power superior to all human origin, to all human control; and as such they defended it in time of need. Still, however, they believed that this sovereignty, though absolute in principle, was bound to exercise its authority according to certain rules and forms; that it could not go beyond certain limits; and that these rules, these forms, and these limits were sufficiently established and guaranteed in Magna Charta, in the confirmatory statutes, in the ancient laws and usages of the country. Such was the political creed of this party. In religious matters, it believed that the episcopacy had greatly encroached; that the bishops possessed far too much political power; that their jurisdiction was far too extensive, that it required to be restrained, and its proceedings jealously watched. Still it held firmly to episcopacy, not merely as an ecclesiastical institution, not merely as a form of church government, but as a necessary support of the royal prerogative, and as a means of defending and maintaining the supremacy of the king in matters of religion. The absolute power of the king over the body politic, exercised according to the forms and within the limits legally acknowledged; the supremacy of the king as head of the Church, applied and sustained by the episcopacy, was the twofold system of the legal reform party. We may enumerate as its chiefs, Lord Clarendon,* Colepepper, Capel, and, though a more ardent friend of public liberty, Lord Falkland; and into their ranks were enlisted nearly all the nobility and gentry not servilely devoted to the court.

Behind this party advanced a second, which I shall call the political-revolutionary party; it differed from the foregoing, inasmuch as it did not believe the ancient guarantees, the ancient legal barriers sufficient to secure the rights and liberties of the people. It saw that a great change, a genuine revolution was wanting, not only in the forms, but in the spirit and essence of the government; that it was necessary to deprive the king and his council of the unlimited power which they possessed, and to place the preponderance in the House of Commons; so that the government should, in fact, be in the hands of this assembly and its leaders. This party made no such open and systematic profession of its principles and intentions as I have done; but this was the real character of its opinions, and of its political tendencies. Instead of acknowledging the absolute sovereignty of the king, it contended for the sovereignty of the House of Commons as the representatives of the people. Under this principle was hid that of the sovereignty of the people; a notion which the party was as far from considering in its full extent, as it was from desiring the consequences to which it might ultimately lead, but which they nevertheless admitted when it presented itself to them in the form of the sovereignty of the House of Commons.

The religious party most closely allied to this political-revolutionary one was that of the Presbyterians. This sect wished to bring about much the same revolution in the Church as their allies were endeavoring to effect in the state. They desired to erect a system of church government emanating from the people, and composed of a series of assemblies dovetailed, as it were, into each other; and thus to give to their national assembly the same authority in ecclesiastical matters that their allies wished to give in political to the House of Commons: only that the revolution contemplated by the Presbyterians was more complete and daring than the other, forasmuch as it aimed at changing the form as well as the principles of the government of the Church; while the views of the political party went no farther than to place the influence, the preponderance, in the body of the people, without meditating any great alteration in the form of their institutions.

Hence the leaders of this political party were not all favorable to the Presbyterian organization of the Church. Hampden and Holles, as well as some others, it appears, would have given the preference to a moderate episcopacy, confined strictly to ecclesiastical functions, with a greater extent of liberty of conscience. They were obliged, however, to give way, as they could do nothing without the assistance of their fanatical allies.

The third party, going much beyond these two, declared that a change was required not only in the form, but also in the foundation of the government; that its constitution was radically vicious and bad. This party paid no respect to the past life of England; it renounced her institutions, it swept away all national remembrances, it threw down the whole fabric of English government, that it might build up another founded on pure theory, or at least one that existed only in its own fancy. It aimed not merely at a revolution in the government, but at a complete revolution of the whole social system. The party of which I have just spoken, the political-revolutionary party, proposed to make a great change in the relations in which the parliament stood with the crown; it wished to extend the power of the two houses, particularly of the commons, by giving to it the nomination of the great officers of state, and the supreme direction of affairs in general; but its notions of reform scarcely went beyond this. It had no idea, for example, of changing the electoral system, the judicial system, the administrative and municipal systems of the country. The republican party contemplated all these changes, dwelt upon their necessity, wished, in a word, to reform not only the public administration, but the relations of society, and the distribution of private rights.

Like the two preceding, this party was composed of a religious sect, and a political sect. Its political portion were the genuine republicans, the theorists, Ludlow, Harrington, Milton, and others. To these may be added the republicans of circumstance, of interest, such as the principal officers of the army, Ireton, Cromwell, Lambert, and others, who were more or less sincere at the beginning of their career, but were soon controlled and guided by personal motives and the force of circumstances. Under the banners of this party marched the religious republicans, all those religious sects which would acknowledge no power as legitimate but that of Jesus Christ, and who, awaiting his second coming, desired only the government of his elect. Finally, in the train of this party followed a mixed assemblage of subordinate free-thinkers, fanatics, and levellers, some hoping for license, some for an equal distribution of property, and others for universal suffrage.*

In 1653, after twelve years of struggle, all these parties had successively appeared and failed; they appear at least to have thought so, and the public was sure of it. The legal reform party quickly disappeared; it saw the old constitution and laws insulted, trampled under foot, and innovations forcing their way on every side. The political-revolutionary party saw the destruction of parliamentary forms in the new use which it was proposed to make of them—it had seen the House of Commons reduced, by the successive expulsions of royalists and Presbyterians, to a few members, despised, detested by the public, and incapable of governing. The republican party appeared to have succeeded better; it seemed to be left master of the field and of power;* the House of Commons consisted of but fifty or sixty members, all republicans. They might fancy themselves, and call themselves, the rulers of the country; but the country rejected their government; they were nowhere obeyed; they had no power either over the army or the nation. No social bond, no social security was now left; justice was no longer administered, or if it was, it was controlled by passion, chance, or party. Not only was there no security in the relations of private life, but the highways were covered with robbers and companies of brigands. Anarchy in every part of the civil, as well as of the moral world, prevailed; and neither the House of Commons, nor the republican Council of State, had the power to restrain it.

Thus, the three great parties which had brought about the revolution, and which in their turn had been called upon to conduct it—had been called upon to govern the country according to their principles and their will—had all signally failed. They could do nothing—they could settle nothing. "Now it was," says Bossuet, "that a man was found who left nothing to fortune, which he could gain by counsel and foresight;" a remark which has no foundation whatever in truth, and which every part of history contradicts. No man ever left more to fortune than Cromwell. No one ever risked more—no one ever pushed forward more rashly, without design, without an aim, yet determined to go as far as fate would carry him. Unbounded ambition, and admirable tact for drawing from every day, from every circumstance, some new progress—the art of profiting by fortune without seeming ever to possess the desire to constrain it, formed the character of Cromwell. In one particular his career was singular, and differs from that of every individual with whom we are apt to compare him: he adapted himself to all the various changes, numerous as they were, as well as to the state of things they led to, of the revolution. He appears a prominent character in every scene, from the rise of the curtain to the close of the play. He was now the instigator of the insurrection—now the abettor of anarchy—now the most fiery of the revolutionists—now the restorer of order and social reorganization; thus playing himself all the principal parts which, in the common run of revolutions, are usually distributed among the greatest actors. He was not a Mirabeau, for he failed in eloquence, and, though very active, he made no great figure in the first years of the Long Parliament. But he was successively Danton and Bonaparte.* Cromwell did more than any one to overthrow authority; he raised it up again, because there was no other than he that could take it and manage it. The country required a ruler; all others failed, and he succeeded. This was his title. Once master of the government, Cromwell, whose boundless ambition had exerted itself so vigorously, who had so constantly pushed fortune before him, and seemed determined never to stop in his career, displayed a good sense, a prudence, a knowledge of how much was possible, which overruled his most violent passions. There can be no doubt of his extreme fondness for absolute power, nor of his desire to place the crown upon his own head and keep it in his family.* He saw the peril of this latter design and renounced it; and though, in fact, he did exercise absolute authority, he saw very well that the spirit of the times would not bear it; that the revolution which he had helped to bring about, which he had followed through all its phases, had been directed against despotism, and that the uncontrollable will of England was to be governed by a parliament and parliamentary forms. He endeavored, therefore, despot as he was, by taste and by deeds, to govern by a parliament. For this purpose he had recourse to all the various parties; he tried to form a parliament from the religious enthusiasts, from the republicans, from the Presbyterians, and from the officers of the army. He tried every means to obtain a parliament able and willing to take part with him in the government; but he tried in vain; every party, the moment it was seated in St. Stephen's, endeavored to wrest from him the authority which he exercised, and to rule in its turn. I do not mean to deny that his personal interest, the gratification of his darling ambition was his first care; but it is no less certain that if he had abdicated his authority one day, he would have been obliged to resume it the next. Puritans or royalists, republicans or officers, there was no one but Cromwell who was in a state at this time to govern with anything like order or justice. The experiment had been made. It seemed absurd to think of leaving to parliaments, that is to say, to the faction sitting in parliament, a government which it could not maintain. Such was the extraordinary situation of Cromwell: he governed by a system which he knew very well was foreign and hateful to the country, he exercised an authority which was acknowledged necessary by all, but which was acceptable to none. No party looked upon his domination as a definitive government. Royalists, Presbyterians, republicans, even the army itself, which appears to have been the party most devoted to Cromwell, all looked upon his rule as transitory. He had no hold upon the affections of the people; he was never more than a makeshift, a last resort, a temporary necessity. The Protector, the absolute master of England, was obliged all his life to have recourse to force to preserve his power; no party could govern so well as he, but no party liked to see the government in his hands; he was repeatedly attacked by them all at once.*

Upon Cromwell's death, there was no party in a situation to seize upon the government except the republicans; they did seize upon it, but with no better success than before. This happened from no lack of confidence, at least, in the enthusiasts of the party. A spirited and talented tract, published at this juncture by Milton, is entitled A Ready and Easy Way to establish a free Commonwealth. You may judge of the blindness of these men, who soon fell into a state which showed that it was quite as impossible for them to carry on the government now as it had been before. Monk undertook the direction of that event which all England now seemed anxious for. The Restoration was accomplished.

The restoration of the Stuarts was an event generally pleasing to the nation. It brought back a government which still dwelt in its memory, which was founded upon its ancient traditions, while, at the same time, it had some of the advantages of a new government, in that it had not recently been tried, in that its faults and its power had not lately been felt. The ancient monarchy was the only system of government which had not been decried, within the last twenty years, for its abuses and want of capacity in the administration of the affairs of the kingdom. From these two causes the restoration was extremely popular; it was unopposed by any but the dregs of the most violent factions, while the public rallied round it with great sincerity. All parties in the country seemed now to believe that this offered the only chance left of a stable and legal government, and this was what, above all things, the nation now desired. This also was what the restoration seemed especially to promise; it took much pains to present itself under the aspect of legal government.*

The first royalist party, indeed, to whom, upon the return of Charles the Second, the management of affairs was intrusted, was the legal party, represented by its able leader, the Lord Chancellor Clarendon. From 1660 to 1667, Clarendon was prime minister,† and had the chief direction of affairs; he and his friends brought back with them their ancient principles of government, the absolute sovereignty of the king, kept within legal bounds, limited by the House of Commons as regards taxation, by the public tribunals, in matters of private right, or relating to individual liberty,—possessing, nevertheless, in point of government, properly so called, an almost complete independence, and the most decided preponderance, to the exclusion or even in opposition to the votes of the majorities of the two houses, but particularly to that of the House of Commons. In other matters there was not much to complain of: a tolerable degree of respect was paid to legal order; there was a tolerable degree of solicitude for the national interests; a sufficiently noble sentiment of national dignity was preserved, and a color of morality that was grave and honorable. Such was the character of Clarendon's administration, during the seven years the government was committed to his charge.

But the fundamental principles upon which this administration was based—the absolute sovereignty of the king, and a government beyond the preponderating control of parliament— were now become old and powerless. Notwithstanding the temporary reaction which took place at the first burst of the restoration, twenty years of parliamentary rule against royalty had destroyed them for ever. A new party soon showed itself among the royalists; libertines, profligates, wretches, who, imbued with the free opinions of the times, and seeing that power was with the commons,—caring themselves but little about legal order, or the absolute power of the king,—were only anxious for success, and to discover the means of influence and power in whatever quarter they were likely to be found. These formed a party, and allying themselves with the national, discontented party, and Clarendon was discarded.*

A new system of government now took place under that portion of the royalists I have just described; profligates and libertines formed the administration of the Cabal, and several others which followed it. What was their character? Without inquietude respecting principles, laws, or rights, or care for justice or truth; they sought the means of success upon every occasion, whatever these means might be; if success depended on the influence of the commons, the commons were everything; if it was necessary to cajole the commons, the commons were cajoled without scruple, even though they had to apologize to them the next day. At one moment they attempted corruption, at another they flattered the national wishes; no regard was shown for the general interests of the country, for its dignity or its honor; in a word, it was a government profoundly selfish and immoral, totally unacquainted with all theory, principle, or public object; but, withal, in the practical management of affairs, showing considerable intelligence and liberality. Such was the character of the Cabal ministry,* of Earl Danby's, and of the English government from 1667 to 1679. Yet notwithstanding its immorality, notwithstanding its disdain of all principle, and of the true interests of the country, this government was not so unpopular, not so odious to the nation as that of Clarendon; and this simply because it adapted itself better to the times, better understood the sentiments of the people, even while it derided them. It was neither foreign nor antiquated, like that of Clarendon; and though infinitely more dangerous to the country, the people accommodated themselves better to it.

But this corruption, this servility, this contempt of public rights and public honor, were at last carried to such a pitch as to be no longer supportable. A general outcry was raised against this government of profligates. A patriotic party, supported by the nation, became gradually formed in the House of Commons, and the king was obliged to take the leaders of it into his council. Lord Essex, the son of him who had commanded the first parliamentary armies in the civil war, Lord Russell, and Lord Shaftesbury, who, without any of the virtues of the other two, was much their superior in political abilities, were now called to the management of affairs. The national party, to whom the direction of the government was now committed, proved itself unequal to the task: it could not gain possession of the moral force of the country: it could neither manage the interests, the habits, nor the prejudices of the king, of the court, nor of any with whom it had to do. It inspired no party, either king or people, with any confidence in its energy or ability; and after holding power for a short time, this national ministry completely failed. The virtues of its leaders, their generous courage, the beauty of their death, have raised them to a distinguished niche in the temple of fame, and entitled them to honorable mention in the page of history; but their political capacities in no way corresponded to their virtues: they could not wield power, though they could withstand its corrupting influence, nor could they achieve a triumph for that glorious cause, for which they could so nobly die!

The failure of this attempt left the English restoration in rather an awkward plight; it had, like the English revolution, in a manner tried all parties without success. The legal ministry, the corrupt ministry, the national ministry, having all failed, the country and the court were nearly in the same situation as that which England had been in before, at the close of the revolutionary troubles in 1653. Recourse was had to the same expedient: what Cromwell had turned to the profit of the revolution, Charles II now turned to the profit of the crown; he entered upon a career of absolute power.

James II succeeded his brother; and another question now became mixed up with that of despotism: the question of religion. James II wished to achieve, at the same time, a triumph for popery and for absolute power: now again, as at the commencement of the revolution, there was a religious struggle and a political struggle, and both were directed against the government. It has often been asked, what course affairs would have taken if William III had not existed, and come over to put an end to the quarrel between James and the people. My firm belief is that the same event would have taken place. All England, except a very small party, was at this time arrayed against James; and it seems very certain, that, under some form or other, the revolution of 1688 must have been accomplished. But at this crisis, causes even superior to the internal state of England conduced to this event. It was European as well as English. It is at this point that the English revolution links itself, by facts, and independently of the influence of its example, to the general course of European civilization.

While the struggle which I have just been narrating took place in England, the struggle of absolute power against religious and civil liberty—a struggle of the same kind, however different the actors, the forms, and the theatre, took place upon the continent—a struggle which was at bottom the same, and carried on in the same cause. The pure monarchy of Louis XIV attempted to become universal monarchy, at least it gave the world every reason to fear it; and, in fact, Europe did fear it. A league was formed in Europe between various political parties to resist this attempt, and the chief of this league was the chief of the party that struggled for the civil and religious liberty of Europe—William, Prince of Orange. The Protestant republic of Holland, with William at its head, had made a stand against pure monarchy, represented and conducted by Louis XIV. The fight here was not for civil and religious liberty in the interior of states, but for the exterior independence of the states themselves. Louis XIV and his adversaries never thought of debating the questions which were debated so fiercely in England. This struggle was not one of parties, but of states; it was carried on, not by political outbreaks and revolutions, but by war and negotiation; still, at bottom, the same principle was the subject of contention.*

It happened, then, that the strife between absolute power and liberty, which James II renewed in England, broke out at the very moment that this general struggle was going on in Europe between Louis XIV and the Prince of Orange, the representatives of these two great systems, as well in the affairs which took place on the Thames as on the Scheldt. The league against Louis was so powerful that many sovereigns entered into it, either publicly, or in an underhand, though very effective manner, who were rather opposed than not to the interests of civil and religious liberty. The Emperor of Germany and Innocent XI both supported William against France. And William crossed the channel to England less to serve the internal interests of the country, than to draw it entirely into the struggle against Louis. He laid hold of this kingdom as a new force which he wanted, but of which his adversary had had the disposal, up to this time, against him. So long as Charles II and James II reigned, England belonged to Louis XIV; he had the disposal of it, and had kept it employed against Holland.* England then was snatched from the side of absolute and universal monarchy, to become the most powerful support and instrument of civil and religious liberty. This is the view which must be taken, as regards European civilization, of the revolution of 1688; it is this which gives it a place in the assemblage of European events, independently of the influence of its example, and of the vast effect which it had upon the minds and opinions of men in the following century.

Thus, I think, I have rendered it clear, that the true sense, the essential character of this revolution is, as I said at the outset of this lecture, an attempt to abolish absolute power in the temporal order, as had already been done in the spiritual. This fact appears in all the phases of the revolution, from its first outbreak to the restoration, and again in the crisis of 1688: and this not only as regards its interior progress, but in its relations with Europe in general.*

It now only remains for us to study the same great event, the struggle of free inquiry and pure monarchy, upon the continent, or at least the causes and preparation of this event. This will be the object of the next and final lecture.

LECTURE XIV.: THE FRENCH REVOLUTION.*

I endeavored, at our last meeting, to ascertain the true character and political object of the English revolution. We have seen that it was the first collision of the two great facts to which, in the course of the sixteenth century, all the civilization of primitive Europe tended,—monarchy on the one hand, and free inquiry on the other. These two powers came to blows, if I may use the expression, for the first time in England. It has been attempted, from this circumstance, to reduce a radical difference between the social state of England and that of the Continent; it has been contended that no comparison could be made between countries so differently situated; and it has been affirmed, that the English people had lived in a sort of moral separation from the rest of Europe, analogous to its physical isolation.

It is true that between the civilization of England, and that of the continental states, there has been a material difference which it is important that we should rightly understand. You have already had a glimpse of it in the course of these lectures. The development of the different principles, the different elements of society, took place, in some measure, at the same time, at least much more simultaneously than upon the Continent. When I endeavored to determine the complexion of European civilization as compared with the civilization of ancient and Asiatic nations, I showed that the former was varied, rich, and complex, and that it had never fallen under the influence of any exclusive principle;* that, in it, the different elements of the social state had combined, contended with, and modified each other, and had continually been obliged to come to an accommodation, and to subsist together. This fact, which forms the general character of European civilization, has in an especial manner been that of the civilization of England; it is in that country that it has appeared most evidently and uninterruptedly; it is there that the civil and religious orders, aristocracy, democracy, monarchy, local and central institutions, moral and political development, have proceeded and grown up together, if not with equal rapidity, at least but at a little distance from each other. Under the reign of the Tudors, for example, in the midst of the most remarkable progress of pure monarchy, we have seen the democratic principle, the popular power, make its way and gain strength almost at the same time. The revolution of the seventeenth century broke out; it was at the same time religious and political. The feudal aristocracy appeared in it in a very enfeebled state, and with all the symptoms of decay; it was, however, still in a condition to preserve its place in this revolution, and to have some share in its results. The same thing has been the case in the whole course of English history; no ancient element has ever entirely perished, nor any new element gained a total ascendancy; no particular principle has ever obtained an exclusive influence. There has always been a simultaneous development of the different forces, and a sort of negotiation or compromise between their pretensions and interests.

On the Continent the march of civilization had been less complex and complete. The different elements of society, the civil and religious orders, monarchy, aristocracy, democracy, have developed themselves, not together, and abreast, as it were, but successively.* Every principle, every system, has in some measure had its turn. One age, for example, has belonged, I shall not say exclusively, but with a decided predominance, to the feudal aristocracy; another to the principle of monarchy; another to the principle of democracy. Compare the middle ages in France, with the middle ages in England; the eleventh, twelfth, and thirteenth centuries of our history with the corresponding centuries on the other side of the channel; you will find in France, at that epoch, feudalism in a state of almost absolute sovereignty, while monarchy and the democratic principle scarcely had an existence.† But turn to England, and you will find, that although the feudal aristocracy greatly predominated, monarchy and democracy possessed, at the same time, strength and importance. Monarchy triumphed in England under Elizabeth, as in France under Louis XIV; but what precautions it was constrained to take! how many restrictions, sometimes aristocratic, sometimes democratic, it was obliged to submit to! In England every system, every principle, has had its time of strength and success; but never so completely and exclusively as on the Continent:‡ the conqueror has always been constrained to tolerate the presence of his rivals, and to leave them a certain share of influence.

To this difference in the march of these two civilizations there are attached advantages and inconveniences which are apparent in the history of the two countries. There is no doubt, for example, that the simultaneous development of the different social elements has greatly contributed to make England arrive more quickly than any of the continental states, at the end and aim of all society, that is to say, the establishment of a government at once regular and free. It is the very nature of a government to respect all the interests, all the powers of the state, to conciliate them and make them live and prosper in common: now such was, beforehand, and by the concurrence of a multitude of causes, the despotism and mutual relation of the different elements of English society; and, therefore, a general and somewhat regular government had the less difficulty in establishing itself. In like manner the essence of liberty is the simultaneous manifestation and action of every interest, every kind of right, every force, every social element. England, therefore, had made a nearer approach to liberty than most other states. From the same causes, national good sense and intelligence of public affairs must have formed themselves more quickly than elsewhere; political good sense consists in understanding and appreciating every fact, and in assigning to each its proper part; in England it has been a necessary consequence of the state of society, a natural result of the course of civilization.

In the states of the Continent, on the contrary, every system, every principle, having had its turn, and having had a more complete and exclusive ascendency, the development took place on a larger scale, and with more striking circumstances. Monarchy and feudal aristocracy, for example, appeared on the continental stage with more boldness, extent, and freedom. Every political experiment, so to speak, was broader and more complete.* The result was, that political ideas—I speak of general ideas, and not of good sense applied to the conduct of affairs; that political ideas and doctrines took a greater elevation, and displayed themselves with much greater rational vigor. Every system having, in some sort, presented itself singly, and having remained a long time on the stage people could contemplate it in its general aspect, ascend to its first principles, pursue it into its remotest consequences, and lay bare its entire theory. Whoever observes with some degree of attention the genius of the English nation, will be struck with a double fact; on the one hand, its steady good sense and practical ability; on the other, its want of general ideas, and of elevation of thought upon theoretical questions. Whether we open an English work on history, jurisprudence, or any other subject, we rarely find the great and fundamental reason of things.† In every subject, and especially in the political sciences, pure philosophical doctrines—science properly so called—have prospered much more on the Continent, than in England; their flights, at least, have been bolder and more vigorous. Indeed, it cannot be doubted that the different character of the development of civilization in the two countries has greatly contributed to this result.

At all events, whatever may be thought of the inconveniences or advantages which have been produced by this difference, it is a real and incontestable fact, and that which most essentially distinguishes England from the Continent. But, though the different principles, the different social elements, have developed themselves more simultaneously there, and more successively in France, it does not follow that, at bottom, the road and the goal have not been the same. Considered generally, the Continent and England have gone through the same great phases of civilization; events have followed the same course; similar causes have led to similar effects. You may have convinced yourselves of this by the view I have given you of civilization down to the sixteenth century; you will remark it no less in studying the seventeenth and eighteenth centuries. The development of free inquiry, and that of pure monarchy, almost simultaneous in England, were accomplished on the Continent at pretty long intervals; but they were accomplished; and these two powers, after having successively exercised a decided predominance, came also into collision. The general march of society, then, on the whole, has been the same; and, though the differences are real, the resemblance is still greater. A rapid sketch of modern times will leave you no doubt on this subject.

The moment we cast our eyes on the history of Europe in the seventeenth and eighteenth centuries, we cannot fail to perceive that France marches at the head of European civilization. At the beginning of this course, I strongly affirmed this fact, and endeavored to point out its cause. We shall now find it more strikingly displayed than it has ever been before.

The principle of pure and absolute monarchy had predominated in Spain, under Charles V and Philip II, before its development in France under Louis XIV. In like manner the principle of free inquiry had reigned in England in the seventeenth century, before its development in France in the eighteenth. Pure monarchy, however, did not go forth from Spain, nor free inquiry from England,* to make the conquest of Europe. The two principles or systems remained, in some sort, confined within the countries in which they sprang up. They required to pass through France to extend their dominion; pure monarchy and liberty of inquiry were compelled to become French before they could become European.† That communicative character of French civilization, that social genius of France, which has displayed itself at every period, was peculiarly conspicuous at the period which now engages our attention. I shall not dwell upon this fact; it has been expounded to you, with equal force of argument and brilliancy, in the lectures in which your attention has been directed to the influence of the literature and philosophy of France in the eighteenth century.‡ You have seen how the philosophy of France had, in regard to liberty, more influence on Europe than the liberty of England. You have seen how French civilization showed itself much more active and contagious than that of any other country. I have no occasion, therefore, to dwell upon the details of this fact; I avail myself of it only in order to make it my ground for using French civilization as the picture of modern European civilization. There were, no doubt, between French civilization at this period, and that of the other states of Europe, differences on which I ought to lay great stress, if it were my intention at present to enter fully into this subject; but I must proceed so rapidly that I am obliged to pass over whole nations, and whole ages. I think it better to confine your attention to the course of French civilization, as being an image, though an imperfect one, of the general course of things in Europe.

The influence of France in Europe, in the seventeenth and eighteenth centuries, appears under very different aspects. In the first of these centuries, it was the French government which acted upon Europe, and took the lead in the march of general civilization. In the second, it was no longer to the French government, but to the French society, to France herself, that the preponderance belonged. It was at first Louis XIV and his court, and then France herself, and her public opinion, that attracted the attention, and swayed the minds of the rest of Europe. There were, in the seventeenth century, nations, who, as such, made a more prominent appearance on the stage, and took a greater share in the course of events, than the French nation. Thus, during the Thirty Years' War, the German nation, and during the revolution in England, the English nation played, within their respective spheres, a much greater part than the French nation, at that period, played within theirs. In the eighteenth century, in like manner, there were stronger, more respected, and more formidable governments than that of France. There is no doubt that Frederick II and Maria Theresa had more activity and weight in Europe than Louis XV. Still, at both of these periods, France was at the head of European civilization, first through her government, and afterwards through herself; at one time through the political action of her rulers, at another through her own intellectual development. To understand thoroughly the predominant influence on the course of civilization in France, and consequently in Europe, we must therefore study, in the seventeenth century, the French government, and in the eighteenth, the French nation. We must change our ground and our objects of view, according as time changes the scene and the actors.

Whenever the government of Louis XIV is spoken of, whenever we attempt to appreciate the causes of his power and influence in Europe, we have little to consider beyond his splendor, his conquests, his magnificence, and the literary glory of his time. We must resort to exterior causes in order to account for the preponderance of the French government in Europe.

But this preponderance, in my opinion, was derived from causes more deeply seated, from motives of a more serious kind. We must not believe that it was entirely by means of victories, festivals, or even master-pieces of genius, that Louis XIV and his government played, at that period, the part which no one can deny them.

Many of you may remember, and all of you have heard of the effect which, twenty-nine years ago, was produced by the Consular government in France, and the state in which it found our country.* Abroad, foreign invasion impending, and continual disasters in our armies; at home, the elements of government and society in a state of dissolution; no revenues, no public order; in short, a people beaten, humbled, and disorganized—such was France at the accession of the consular government. Who is there that does not remember the prodigious and successful activity of that government, an activity which, in a short time, secured the independence of our territory, revived our national honor, reorganized the administration of government, remodelled our legislation, in short, gave society, as it were, a new life under the hand of power?

Well—the government of Louis XIV, when it began, did something of the same kind for France; with great differences of times, of proceedings, and of forms, it prosecuted and attained very nearly the same results.

Remember the state into which France had fallen after the government of Cardinal Richelieu, and during the minority of Louis XIV:* the Spanish armies always on the frontiers, and sometimes in the interior; continual danger of invasion; internal dissensions carried to the extremity of civil war, the government weak, and decried both at home and abroad. There never was a more miserable policy, more despised in Europe, or more powerless in France, than that of Cardinal Mazarin. In a word, society was in a state, less violent perhaps, but very analogous to ours before the 18th of Brumaire. It was from that state that the government of Louis XIV delivered France. His earliest victories had the effect of the victory of Marengo;* they secured the French territory and revived the national honor. I am going to consider this government under its various aspects, in its wars, its foreign relations, its administration, and its legislation; and you will see, I believe, that the comparison which I speak of, and to which I do not wish to attach a puerile importance (for I care very little about historical comparisons), you will see, I say, that this comparison has a real foundation, and that I am fully justified in making it.

I shall first speak of the wars of Louis XIV. European wars were originally (as you know, and as I have several times had occasion to remind you) great popular movements; impelled by want, by some fancy, or any other cause, whole populations, sometimes numerous, sometimes consisting of mere bands, passed from one territory to another. This was the general character of European wars, till after the Crusades, at the end of the thirteenth century.

After this another kind of war arose, but almost equally different from the wars of modern times: these were distant wars, undertaken, not by nations, but by their governing powers, who went, at the head of their armies, to seek, at a distance, states and adventures. They quitted their country, abandoned their own territory, and penetrated, some into Germany, others into Italy, and others into Africa, with no other motive save their individual fancy. Almost all the wars of the fifteenth, and even a part of the sixteenth century, are of this character. What interest—and I do not speak of a legitimate interest—but what motive had France for wishing that Charles VIII should possess the kingdom of Naples?* It was evidently a war dictated by no political considerations; the king thought he had personal claims on the kingdom of Naples; and, for this personal object, to satisfy his own personal desire, he undertook the conquest of a distant country, which was by no means adapted to the territorial conveniences of his kingdom, but which, on the contrary, only endangered his power abroad and his repose at home. Such, again, was the case with regard to the expedition of Charles V into Africa.† The last war of this kind was the expedition of Charles XII against Russia.

The wars of Louis XIV were not of this description; they were the wars of a regular government—a government fixed in the center of its dominions, endeavoring to extend its conquests around, to increase or consolidate its territory; in short, they were political wars. They may have been just or unjust, they may have cost France too dear;—they may be objected to on many grounds—on the score of morality or excess; but, in fact, they were of a much more rational character than the wars which preceded them; they were no longer fanciful adventures; they were dictated by serious motives; their objects were to reach some natural boundary, some population who spoke the same language, and might be annexed to the kingdom, some point of defence against a neighboring power. Personal ambition, no doubt, had a share in them; but examine the wars of Louis XIV, one after the other, especially those of the early part of his reign, and you will find that their motives were really political; you will see that they were conceived with a view to the power and safety of France.

This fact has been proved by results. France, at the present day, in many respects, is what the wars of Louis XIV made her. The provinces which he conquered, Franche-Comté, Flanders, and Alsace, have remained incorporated with France.* There are rational conquests as well as foolish ones: those of Louis XIV were rational; his enterprises have not that unreasonable, capricious character, till then so general; their policy was able, if not always just and prudent.

If I pass from the wars of Louis XIV to his relations with foreign states, to his diplomacy properly so called, I find an analogous result. I have already spoken of the origin of diplomacy at the end of the fifteenth century. I have endeavored to show how the mutual relations of governments and states, previously accidental, rare, and transient, had at that period become more regular and permanent, how they had assumed a character of great public interest; how, in short, at the end of the fifteenth and during the first half of the sixteenth century, diplomacy had begun to perform a part of immense importance in the course of events. Still, however, it was not till the seventeenth century that it became really systematic; before then, it had not brought about long alliances, great combinations, and especially combinations of a durable nature, directed by fixed principles, with a steady object, and with that spirit of consistency which forms the true character of established governments. During the course of the religious revolution, the foreign relations of states had been almost completely under the influence of religious interests; the Protestant and Catholic leagues had divided Europe between them. It was in the seventeenth century, under the influence of the government of Louis XIV, that diplomacy changed its character. On the one hand, it got rid of the exclusive influence of the religious principle; alliances and political combinations took place from other considerations. At the same time it became much more systematic and regular, and was always directed towards a certain object, according to permanent principles. The regular birth of the system of the balance of power in Europe, took place at this period. It was under the government of Louis XIV that this system, with all the considerations attached to it, really took possession of the politics of Europe. When we inquire what was, on this subject, the general idea, or ruling principle of the policy of Louis XIV, the following seems to be the result.

I have spoken of the great struggle which took place in Europe between the pure monarchy of Louis XIV, pretending to establish itself as the universal system of monarchy, and civil and religious liberty, and the independence of states, under the command of the Prince of Orange, William III.* You have seen that the great European fact, at that epoch, was the division of the powers of Europe under these two banners. But this fact was not then understood as I now explain it; it was hidden, and unknown even to those by whom it was accomplished. The repression of the system of pure monarchy, and the consecration of civil and religious liberty, was necessarily, at bottom, the result of the resistance of Holland and her allies to Louis XIV; but the question between absolute power and liberty was not then thus absolutely laid down. It has been frequently said that the propagation of absolute power was the ruling principle in the diplomacy of Louis XIV. I do not think so. It was at a late period, and in his old age, that this consideration assumed a great part in his policy. The power of France, her preponderance in Europe, the depression of rival powers,—in short, the political interest and strength of the state, was the object which Louis XIV always had in view, whether he was contending against Spain, the Emperor of Germany, or England. He was much less actuated by a wish for the propagation of absolute power than by a desire for the aggrandizement of France and his own government. Among many other proofs of this, there is one which emanates from Louis XIV himself. We find in his Memoirs, for the year 1666, if I remember rightly, a note conceived nearly in these terms:—

"This morning I had a conversation with Mr. Sidney,* an English gentleman, who spoke to me of the possibility of reviving the republican party in England. Mr. Sidney asked me for £400,000 for this purpose. I told him I could not give him more than £200,000. He prevailed on me to send to Switzerland for another English gentleman, called Mr. Ludlow,† that I might converse with him upon the same subject."

We find accordingly, in Ludlow's Memoirs, about the same date, a paragraph to the following import:—

"I have received from the French government an invitation to go to Paris, to have some discussion on the affairs of my country; but I distrust this government."

And, in fact, Ludlow did remain in Switzerland.

You see that the object of Louis XIV at that time was to weaken the royal power of England. He fomented internal dissensions, he labored to revive the republican party, in order to hinder Charles II from becoming too powerful in his own country. In the course of Barillon's embassy to England,* the same fact is constantly apparent. As often as the authority of Charles II seems to be gaining the ascendancy, and the national party on the point of being overpowered, the French ambassador turns his influence in that direction, gives money to the leaders of the opposition, and, in short, contends against absolute power, as soon as that becomes the means of weakening a rival of France. Whenever we attentively examine the conduct of foreign relations under Louis XIV, this is the fact which we are struck with.

We are also surprised at the capacity and ability of the French diplomacy at this period. The names of Torcy, d'Avaux, and de Bonrepos, are known to all well-informed persons. When we compare the despatches, the memorials, the skill, the management of these counsellors of Louis XIV, with those of the Spanish, Portuguese, and German negotiators, we are struck with the superiority of the French ministers; not only with their serious activity and application to business, but with their freedom of thought. These courtiers of an absolute king judge of foreign events, of parties, of the demands for freedom, and of popular revolutions, much more soundly than the greater part of the English themselves of that period. There is no diplomacy in Europe in the seventeenth century which appears equal to the diplomacy of France, except perhaps that of Holland. The ministers of John De Witt and William of Orange, those illustrious leaders of the party of civil and religious liberty, are the only ones who appear to have been in a condition to contend with the servants of the great absolute king.

You see, that, whether we consider the wars of Louis XIV, or his diplomatic relations, we arrive at the same results. We can easily conceive how a government which conducted in such a manner its wars and negotiations, must have acquired great solidity in Europe, and assumed not only a formidable, but an able and imposing aspect.

Let us now turn our eyes to the interior of France, and the administration and legislation of Louis XIV; we shall everywhere find new explanations of the strength and splendor of his government. It is difficult to determine precisely what ought to be understood by administration in the government of a state. Still, when we endeavor to come to a distinct understanding on this subject, we acknowledge, I believe, that, under the most general point of view, administration consists in an assemblage of means destined to transmit, as speedily and surely as possible, the will of the central power into all departments of society, and, under the same conditions, to make the powers of society return to the central power, either in men or money. This, if I am not mistaken, is the true object, the prevailing character, of administration. From this we may perceive that, in times where it is especially necessary to establish union and order in society, administration is the great means of accomplishing it,—of bringing together, cementing, and uniting scattered and incoherent elements. Such, in fact, was the work of the administration of Louis XIV. Till his time, nothing had been more difficult, in France as well as in the rest of Europe, than to cause the action of the central power to penetrate into all the parts of society, and to concentrate into the heart of the central power the means of strength possessed by the society at large. This was the object of Louis's endeavors, and he succeeded in it to a certain extent, incomparably better, at least, than preceding governments had done. I cannot enter into any details; but take a survey of every kind of public service, the taxes, the highways, industry, the military administration, and the various establishments which belong to any branch of administration whatever; there is hardly any of them which you will not find to have either been originated, developed, or greatly meliorated, under the reign of Louis XIV.* It was as administrators that the greatest men of his time, such as Colbert and Louvois,† displayed their genius and exercised their ministerial functions; it was thus that his government acquired a comprehensiveness, a decision, and a consistency, which were wanting in all the European governments around him.

The same fact holds with respect to this government, as regards its legislative capacity. I will again refer to the comparison I made in the outset to the legislative activity of the Consular government, and its prodigious labor in revising and remodelling the laws. A labor of the same kind was undertaken under Louis XIV. The great ordinances which he passed and promulgated,—the ordinances on the criminal law, on forms of procedure, on commerce, on the navy, on waters and forests,—are real codes of law, which were constructed in the same manner as our codes, having been discussed in the Council of State, sometimes under the presidency of Lamoignon. There are men whose glory it is to have taken a share in this labor and those discussions,—M. Pussort, for example. If we had to consider it simply in itself, we should have a great deal to say against the legislation of Louis XIV. It is full of faults which are now evident, and which nobody can dispute; it was not conceived in the spirit of justice and true liberty, but with a view to public order, and to give regularity and stability to the laws. But even that alone was a great progress; and it cannot be doubted that the legislative acts of Louis XIV, very superior to the previous state of legislation, powerfully contributed to the advancement of French society in the career of civilization.*

Under whatever point of view, then, we regard this government, we can at once discover the means of its strength and influence. It was, in truth, the first government which presented itself to the eyes of Europe as a power sure of its position, which had not to dispute for its existence with domestic enemies, which was tranquil in regard to its territory and its people, and had nothing to think of but the care of governing. Till then, all the European governments had been incessantly plunged into wars which deprived them of security as well as leisure, or so assailed by parties and enemies at home, that they passed their time in fighting for their existence. The government of Louis XIV appeared to be the first that was engaged solely in managing its affairs like a power at once definitive and progressive, which was not afraid of making innovations, because it reckoned upon the future. In fact, few governents have been more given to innovation. Compare it with a government of the same nature, with the pure monarchy of Philip II in Spain, which was more absolute than that of Louis XIV, and yet was less regular and tranquil. How did Philip II succeed in establishing absolute power in Spain? By stifling every kind of activity in the country; by refusing his sanction to every kind of improvement, and thus rendering the state of Spain completely stationary.* The government of Louis XIV, on the contrary, was active in every kind of innovation, and favorable to the progress of letters, arts, riches—favorable, in a word, to civilization. These were the true causes of its preponderance in Europe—a preponderance so great, that it was, on the Continent, during the seventeenth century, not only for sovereigns, but even for nations, the type and model of governments.

It is frequently asked, and it is impossible to avoid asking, how a power so splendid and well established—to judge from the circumstances I have pointed out to you, should have fallen so quickly into a state of decay? how, after having played so great a part in Europe, it became in the following century so inconsiderable, so weak, and so little respected? The fact is undeniable: in the seventeenth century, the French government stood at the head of European civilization. In the eighteenth century it disappeared; it was the society of France, separated from its government, and often in a hostile position towards it, which led the way and guided the progress of the

European world.

It is here that we discover the incorrigible vice and infallible effect of absolute power. I shall not enter into any detail respecting the faults of the government of Louis XIV; and there were great ones. I shall not speak either of the war of the succession in Spain,* or the revocation of the edict of Nantes, or the excessive expenditure, or many other fatal measures which affected its character. I will take the merits of the government, such as I have described them. I will admit that, probably, there never was an absolute power more completely acknowledged by its age and nation, or which has rendered more real services to the civilization of its country as well as to Europe in general. It followed, indeed, from the single circumstance, that this government had no other principle than absolute power, and rested entirely on this basis, that its decay was so sudden and deserved. What was essentially wanting to France in Louis XIV's time were institutions, political powers, which were independent and self-existent, capable, in short, of spontaneous action and resistance. The ancient French institutions, if they deserve the name, no longer subsisted; Louis XIV completed their destruction. He took care not to replace them by new institutions; they would have constrained him, and he did not choose constraint. The will and action of the central power were all that appeared with splendor at that epoch. The government of Louis XIV is a great fact, a powerful and brilliant fact, but it was built upon sand. Free institutions are a guarantee, not only for the prudence of governments, but also for their stability. No system can endure otherwise than by institutions. Wherever absolute power has been permanent, it has been based upon, and supported by, real institutions; sometimes by the division of society into castes, distinctly separated, and sometimes by a system of religious institutions. Under the reign of Louis XIV, power, as well as liberty, needed institutions. There was nothing in France, at that time, to protect either the country from the illegitimate action of the government, or the government itself against the inevitable action of time. Thus, we behold the government assisting its own decay. It was not Louis XIV only who grew old, and became feeble, at the end of his reign; it was the whole system of absolute power. Pure monarchy was as much worn out in 1712, as the monarch himself. And the evil was so much the more serious, in that Louis XIV had destroyed political habits as well as political institutions. There can be no political habits without independence. He only who feels that he is strong in himself, is always capable either of serving the ruling power, or of contending with it. Energetic characters disappear along with independent situations, and a free and high spirit arises from the security of rights.

We may, then, describe in the following terms the state in which the French nation and the power of the government were left by Louis XIV: in society there was a great development of wealth, strength, and intellectual activity of every kind; and, along with this progressive society, there was a government essentially stationary, and without means to adapt itself to the movement of the people; devoted, after half a century of great splendor, to immobility and weakness, and already fallen, even in the lifetime of its founder, into a decay almost resembling dissolution. Such was the situation of France at the expiration of the seventeenth century, and which impressed upon the subsequent period so different a direction and character.

It is hardly necessary for me to remark that a great movement of the human mind, that a spirit of free inquiry, was the predominant feature, the essential fact of the eighteenth century. You have already heard from this chair a great deal on this topic; you have already heard this momentous period characterized, by the voices of a philosophic orator and an eloquent philosopher.* I cannot pretend, in the small space of time which remains to me, to follow all the phases of the great revolution which was then accomplished; neither, however, can I leave you without calling your attention to some of its features which perhaps have been too little remarked.

The first, which occurs to me in the outset, and which, indeed, I have already pointed out, is the almost entire disappearance (so to speak) of the government in the course of the eighteenth century, and the appearance of the human mind as the principal and almost sole actor. Excepting in what concerned foreign relations, under the ministry of the Duke de Choiseul, and in some great concessions made to the general bent of the public mind, in the American war, for example;—excepting, I say, in some events of this kind, there perhaps never was a government so inactive, apathetic, and inert, as the French government of that time. In place of the ambitious and active government of Louis XIV, which was everywhere, and at the head of everything, you have a power whose only endeavor, so much did it tremble for its own safety, was to slink from public view—to hide itself from danger. It was the nation which, by its intellectual movement, interfered with everything, and alone possessed moral authority, the only real authority.

A second characteristic which strikes me in the state of the human mind in the eighteenth century, is the universality of the spirit of free inquiry. Till then, and particularly in the sixteenth century, free inquiry had been exercised in a very limited field; its object had been sometimes religious questions, and sometimes religious and political questions conjoined; but its pretensions did not extend much further. In the eighteenth century, on the contrary, free inquiry became universal in its character and objects: religion, politics, pure philosophy, man and society, moral and physical science—everything became, at once, the subject of study, doubt, and system; the ancient sciences were overturned; new sciences sprang up. It was a movement which proceeded in every direction, though emanating from one and the same impulse.

This movement, moreover, had one peculiarity, which perhaps can be met with at no other time in the history of the world; that of being purely speculative. Until that time, in all great human revolutions, action had promptly mingled itself with speculation. Thus, in the sixteenth century, the religious revolution had begun by ideas and discussions purely intellectual;* but it had, almost immediately, led to events. The leaders of the intellectual parties had very speedily become leaders of political parties; the realities of life had mingled with the workings of the intellect. The same thing had been the case, in the seventeenth century, in the English revolution. In France, in the eighteenth century, we see the human mind exercising itself upon all subjects,— upon ideas which, from their connection with the real interests of life, necessarily had the most prompt and powerful influence upon events. And yet the promoters of, and partakers in, these great discussions, continued to be strangers to every kind of practical activity, pure speculators, who observed, judged, and spoke without ever proceeding to practice.* There never was a period in which the government of facts, and external realities, was so completely distinct from the government of thought. The separation of spiritual from temporal affairs has never been real in Europe, except in the eighteenth century. For the first time, perhaps, the spirtual world developed itself quite separately from the temporal world; a fact of the greatest importance, and which had a great influence on the course of events. It gave a singular character of pride and inexperience to the mode of thinking of the time: philosophy was never more ambitious of governing the world, and never more completely failed in its object. This necessarily led to results; the intellectual movement necessarily gave, at last, an impulse to external events; and, as they had been totally separated, their meeting was so much the more difficult, and their collision so much the more violent.

We can hardly now be surprised at another character of the human mind at this epoch, I mean its extreme boldness. Prior to this, its greatest activity had always been restrained by certain barriers; man had lived in the midst of facts, some of which inspired him with caution, and repressed, to a certain degree, his tendency to movement. In the eighteenth century, I should really be at a loss to say what external facts were respected by the human mind, or exercised any influence over it; it entertained nothing but hatred or contempt for the whole social system; it considered itself called upon to reform all things; it looked upon itself as a sort of creator; institutions, opinions, manners, society, even man himself,—all seemed to require to be remodelled, and human reason undertook the task. Whenever, before, had the human mind displayed such daring boldness?

Such, then, was the power which, in the course of the eighteenth century, was confronted with what remained of the government of Louis XIV. It is clear to us all that a collision between these two unequal forces was unavoidable. The leading fact of the English revolution, the struggle between free inquiry and pure monarchy, was therefore sure to be repeated in France. The differences between the two cases, undoubtedly, were great, and necessarily perpetuated themselves in the results of each; but, at bottom, the general situation of both was similar, and the event itself must be explained in the same manner.

I by no means intend to exhibit the infinite consequences of this collision in France. I am drawing towards the close of this course of lectures, and must hasten to conclude. I wish, however, before leaving you, to call your attention to the gravest, and, in my opinion, the most instructive fact which this great spectacle has revealed to us. It is the danger, the evil, the insurmountable vice of absolute power, wheresoever it may exist, whatsoever name it may bear, and for whatever object it may be exercised. We have seen that the government of Louis XIV perished almost from this single cause. The power which succeeded it, the human mind, the real sovereign of the eighteenth century, underwent the same fate; in its turn, it possessed almost absolute power; in its turn its confidence in itself became excessive. Its movement was noble, good, and useful; and, were it necessary for me to give a general opinion on the subject, I should readily say that the eighteenth century appears to me one of the grandest epochs in the history of the world, that perhaps which has done the greatest service to mankind, and has produced the greatest and most general improvement. If I were called upon to pass judgment upon its ministry (if I may use such an expression), I should pronounce sentence in its favor. It is not the less true, however, that the absolute power exercised at this period by the human mind corrupted it, and that it entertained an illegitimate aversion to the subsisting state of things, and to all opinions which differed from the prevailing one;—an aversion which led to error and tyranny. The proportion of error and tyranny, indeed, which mingled itself in the triumph of human reason at the end of the century—a proportion, the greatness of which cannot be dissembled, and which ought to be exposed instead of being passed over—this infusion of error and tyranny, I say, was a consequence of the delusion into which the human mind was led at that period by the extent of its power. It is the duty, and will be, I believe, the peculiar event of our time, to acknowledge that all power, whether intellectual or temporal, whether belonging to governments or people, to philosophers or ministers, in whatever cause it may be exercised—that all human power, I say, bears within itself a natural vice, a principle of feebleness and abuse, which renders it necessary that it should be limited. Now, there is nothing but the general freedom of every right, interest, and opinion, the free manifestation and legal existence of all these forces—there is nothing, I say, but a system which ensures all this, can restrain every particular force or power within its legitimate bounds, and prevent it from encroaching on the others, so as to produce the real and beneficial subsistence of free inquiry. For us, this is the great result, the great moral of the struggle which took place at the close of the eighteenth century, between what may be called temporal absolute power and spiritual absolute power.

I have now arrived at the end of the task which I undertook. You will remember, that, in beginning this course, I stated that my object was to give you a general view of the development of European civilization, from the fall of the Roman empire to the present time. I have passed very rapidly over this long career; so rapidly that it has been quite out of my power even to touch upon everything of importance, or to bring proofs of those facts to which I have drawn your attention. I hope, however, that I have attained my end, which was to mark the great epochs of the development of modern society. Allow me to add a word more. I endeavored, at the outset, to define civilization, to describe the fact which bears that name. Civilization appeared to me to consist of two principal facts, the development of human society and that of man himself; on the one hand, his political and social, and on the other, his internal and moral, advancement. This year I have confined myself to the history of society. I have exhibited civilization only in its social point of view. I have said nothing of the development of man himself. I have made no attempt to give you the history of opinions,—of the moral progress of human nature. I intend, when we meet again here, next season, to confine myself especially to France; to study with you the history of French civilization, but to study it in detail and under its various aspects. I shall try to make you acquainted not only with the history of society in France, but also with that of man; to follow, along with you, the progress of institutions, opinions, and intellectual labors of every sort, and thus to arrive at a comprehension of what has been, in the most complete and general sense, the development of our glorious country.* In the past, as well as in the future, she has a right to our warmest affections.†

THE END.

*

This dispute turns upon the greater or less extension given to the term. Civilization may be taken to signify merely the multiplication of artificial wants, and of the means and refinements of physical enjoyment. It may also be taken to imply both a state of physical well being and a state of superior intellectual and moral culture. It is only in the former sense that it can be alleged that civilization is an evil.

Civilization is properly a relative term. It refers to a certain state of mankind as distinguished from barbarism.

Man is formed for society. Isolated and solitary, his reason would remain perfectly undeveloped. Against the total defeat of his destination for rational development God has provided by the domestic relations. Yet without a further extension of the social ties, man would still remain comparatively rude and uncultivated—never emerging from barbarism. In proportion as the social relations are extended, regulated and perfected, man is softened, ameliorated, cultivated. To this improvement various social conditions combine; but as the political organization of society—the state—is that which first gives security and permanence to all the others, it holds the most important place. Hence it is from the political organization of society, from the establishment of the state (in Latin civitas), that the word civilization is taken.

Civilization, therefore, in its most general idea, is an improved condition of man resulting from the establishment of social order in place of the individual independence and lawlessness of the savage or barbarous life. It may exist in various degrees: it is susceptible of continual progress: and hence the history of civilization is the history of the progress of the human race towards realizing the idea of humanity, through the extension and perfection of the social relations, and as affected, advanced or retarded, by the character of the various political and civil institutions which have existed. II.

The term "civilization" has two distinct meanings, signifying either a force at work upon and among mankind, or a particular condition or state of human society. In the former sense it denotes the forces by which and the process through which mankind as a whole, or in some of its branches, is uplifted and developed in its internal spirit and external relations. It sums up all the humanizing forces that have raised man and are now carrying him higher in his thoughts, his deeds, his aspirations. In its other meaning the word is used to denote an advanced condition of humanity or human society, marked by political, social, and industrial order and organization, and a high degree of knowledge and culture. In this sense we may properly compare and contrast different civilizations, meaning thereby different conditions or types of human society.

When the author speaks of the "progress of civilization," he is thinking of civilization as a force or group of forces. When he examines civilization as it was at the downfall of the Roman empire, he is regarding it as a particular condition or state in which European society was at that epoch, as a product of previously operative forces. When we speak of the civilization of to-day we may mean either the actual state of mankind and society to-day as the product of past tendencies, or the forces and tendencies themselves which are to-day operative and which will produce a different and more advanced condition of human society hereafter. It is only by keeping both ideas in mind that the student will get the full force of the author's lectures. The history of civilization is obviously a history of the various causes and forces—intellectual, moral, political, social, industrial—which, working in the past, have made man and society what they are to-day; it is more than a mere account of the successive conditions or states in which past generations of men have lived.

*

In this passage the author seems, for the moment at least, inclined to make the term "civilization" almost synonymous with "intellectual development." Mere intellectual advancement, especially where it is found only among a limited group, or peculiarly favored class, where its effects and influence do not extend downwards through the masses, does not necessarily indicate the highest type of civilization. The progress of civilization, as the author in other passages appreciates, must always be marked not merely by the intellectual and moral advancement of the individual, but also by improvement in his environment, in his social, political, and industrial condition and possibilities.

To-day civilization must be judged not merely by its best features and products, but by its bad features and results. The half century since these lectures were written has made it more evident than ever before that the progress of man can only be continuous when society—the social state, as M. Guizot calls it—is progressing, and that social conditions can only be permanently improved by the advancement of the individual.

*

It is true that Christianity was addressed primarily not to the social condition of man, to the social class relations, but to "the interior condition of man"; yet it has from the very first, by the fundamental principle on which it is based—the law of love—demanded justice as between classes and individuals. It has ever insisted on justice and charity by the rich towards the poor, by the strong towards the weak.

†

"It is impossible not to feel the incompleteness of any statement of the influence of Christianity upon civilization. Some of the more obvious and apparent results can be mentioned, but its full work cannot be traced. . . . Its operation lies in the realm of the silent and unobserved forces which act upon the individual character and the springs of action, but which can, in the nature of the case, leave no record of themselves for later time."—Adams, Civilization during the Middle

Ages,.
*

Opinion de Royer Collard, sur le Projet de Loi rélatif au Sacrilége,.
*

Man can be comprehended only as a free moral being, that is, as a rational being: but as a rational being it is impossible to comprehend his existence, if it be limited to the present world. In the very nature of human reason and of the relations of the human race to it, lies the idea of the destination of the race for a supermundane and eternal sphere. Reason is the germ of a development which is not and cannot be reached here below. To doubt that it is destined for development, and that there is a corresponding sphere, is contradictory: it is to doubt whether the fruit, unfolding from the blossom, is destined by its constitution to ripen.
Herein, while the delusion of certain philosophical theories respecting Human Perfectibility is made apparent, may be seen nevertheless the correct idea of man's earthly life. It is that of a continual progress, a reaching towards that perfection, the notion and desire of which lies in the nature of his reason.
Humanity in all its social efforts has always been governed by the idea of a perfection never yet attained. All human history may in one view be regarded as a series of attempts to realize this idea.
As individual man can attain the ideal perfection of his nature only as a rational being, by the harmony of all his powers with his reason; so it is equally clear that humanity can realize the idea of social perfection only as a rational society, by the union and brotherhood of the human family, and the harmony of all individuals with the Divine reason. How far it may be in the intentions of Divine Providence that the human race shall realize this perfection, it may be impossible to determine. Certain it is, that it can never be brought about by any mere political institutions, by checks and counterchecks of interest, by any balance of international powers. Only Christianity can effect this universal brotherhood of nations, and bind the human family together in a rational, that is, a free moral society. H.
The last half century is filled with suggestive facts and tendencies bearing on this point. If one examines merely external conditions and phenomena, he may think that classes have become more sharply defined during that time, and that the clash of supposed interests between classes and countries has become fiercer. It is, however, easy to note the prevalence as never before of a deep concern for the "common interest of humanity." The spirit of philanthropy, the increasing effort to put an end to strife, to substitute reason for force of arms in the settlement of international disputes, to reconcile rather than set in antagonism the social and industrial classes—all these are evidences of the consciousness that the true civilization of the individual is attained only in the advance and betterment of society—the human family. The solidarity of the human race is recognized to-day. The universality of human brotherhood is more and more seen to be the only basis for that civilization which is the ultimate aim of individual and society.
*

It is impossible completely to separate these two parts of the history of civilization. Political institutions and social facts and forces are always in part the product of intellectual conditions, while the intellectual development of a people, hence of individuals, is always dependent on political, social—even at times industrial—environment. Institutions and ideas are not completely separable. The subsequent lectures are conclusive evidence of this.
*

"There is a pleasure in viewing from the shore the difficulties of another tossed on the sea in the

tumbling waves and howling winds."
*

The theocratic form of government was common in the early days of the human race. Its characteristic principle is the superhuman or divine nature of the ruler or ruling class in the state. Usually a priestly caste held the highest rank and exercised the supreme authority, political as well as religious, though often there was a king, who was at the same time chief priest, ruling in the name of the gods, or by virtue of his descent from the gods. In Egypt, for example, the kings were held to be of divine descent, and all power was in their hands and those of a priestly caste. In Ethiopia, Persia, and India other types of theocracy existed in ancient times. The Mosaic law established a pure theocratic government over the Jews. In some of the Asiatic states theocracy still exists. The complete subordination of all other classes to the priest-king, or priestly caste, has nowhere produced marked intellectual or political advancement. For a good description of theocracy, see Bluntschli's Theory of the State.
*

The essence, the strength of Greek civilization lay in the domain of the intellect. The Greek mind was speculative, as is shown by her philosophy, and æsthetic, as is abundantly proved by her literature and her art. On the practical side the Greeks were deficient. The Greek power and the Greek state disappeared under the rising power of material, practical Rome, while the Greek civilization was taken over into and made a part of the Roman. In a word, the Greek state fell, but Greek civilization lived on.
*

Modern civilization is the product of what has gone before it. Each age, each institution, each civilization preceding, has contributed some idea, force, or fact which finds place in our civilization. Greece, Rome, Christianity, the barbarian, even the Orient, has had a share in this. The varied sources explain in part the diversity so strongly emphasized by the author. The widened intellectual range of to-day also permits, in fact demands, a greatly diversified activity. This diversity must not be mistaken for discord. The unity of modern civilization, so far as its purpose and ideal are concerned, is not less perfect than that of the ancient. Allowance must also be made for the fact that we are so far removed in point of time from the ancient world that only the larger, the dominant ideas of that age, impress us; while of the later civilization we see and hear all of the varied movements and thoughts, and in contemplating these separate and partial phases of the life of to-day we do not always correctly note their relations to the whole movement—the civilization of the age.
*

This statement may easily be misunderstood. During the middle ages, and especially during the so-called dark ages, from the sixth to the tenth century, civilization was "in a state of progression" only in the general sense that it was not absolutely stagnant. There were many changes, but little actual progress. During these centuries the chaos in which Europe was seemingly left by the barbarian inroads was becoming less chaotic, the darkness less black. Professor G. B. Adams says: "It is a transition age. Lying as it does between two ages, in each of which there is an especially rapid advance of civilization, it is not itself primarily an age of progress. As compared with either ancient or modern history, the additions which were made during the middle ages to the common stock of civilization are few and unimportant. . . . Progress, however much there may have been, is not its distinctive characteristic."—Civilization during the Middle Ages,.
*

Diocletian, a. c. 284, must be regarded as the first who attempted to substitute a regularly organized system of Oriental monarchy, with its imposing ceremonial, and its long gradation of dignities, proceeding from the throne as the center of all authority and the source of all dignity, in place of the former military despotism, supported only upon, and therefore always at the mercy of, the pretorian guards.

This system was still further perfected by Constantine the Great, ad 306—337, who introduced several important changes into the constitution of the empire.

He divided the empire into four great prefectures; the East; Illyricum; Italy; and Gaul.

The four pretorian prefects created by Diocletian were retained by Constantine; but with a very material change in their powers. He deprived them of all military command, and made them merely civil governors in the four prefectures.

He consolidated still more his monarchical system by an organization of ecclesiastical dignities corresponding with the gradations of the civil administration. This system continued substantially unchanged at the division of the empire, ad 395, and was perpetuated after that period.

Each of the empires was divided into two prefectures, and the prefectures into dioceses, in the following manner:

Prefectures.   Dioceses.
EASTERN EMPIRE. I. THE EAST. 1.   The East.
2.   Egypt.
3.   Asia Minor.
4.   Pontus.
5.   Thrace.
II. ILLYRICUM.   1.   Macedonia (all Greece).
2.   Dacia (within the Danube).
WESTERN EMPIRE. I. ITALY.   1.   Italy.
2.   Illyria (Pannonia, etc.).
3.   Africa.
II. GAUL.   1.   Spain.
2.   The Gauls.
3.   Britain.

Rome and Constantinople constituted each a diocese by itself.

Each of these dioceses was divided into provinces, of which in both empires there were one hundred and twenty; and the provinces into cities.

Imperial Administration.

Household.—The court officers were: the Grand Chamberlain; two Captains of the Guard; Master of the Offices; Quæstor or Chancellor; Keeper of the Privy Purse (comes rerum privatarum), whose functions are to be distinguished from those of the Minister of the public treasury.

Provincial Administration.—In each prefecture a Prefectus pretorio, at the head of the civil administration. In each diocese a Vicar of the prefect. In each province a President. The cities were governed by Duumvirs and a Defensor.

Military Organization.—After the Guards and Household troops, ranked the legions and the auxiliaries. These were commanded in each prefecture by a Major General of the Militia; a commander of the cavalry, a commander of the infantry; military dukes and counts, legionary prefects, etc.

Judiciary.—Cases of special importance reserved for the emperor were decided by the quæstor; ordinary matters by various magistrates, according to their relative magnitude. An appeal lay from the defensor to the duumvirs, from the duumvirs to the president, from the president to the vicar, from the vicar to the prefectus pretorio.

Finances.—The revenues were passed, by the collectors of cities, into the hands of the provincial receivers, and thence, through a higher grade of treasurers, to the minister of the public treasury. H.

For fuller accounts of Constantine's innovations, consult Bury's History of the Later Roman Empire; Gibbon's Roman Empire, chapters xiii and xvii. Duruy's History of the Middle Ages has also a brief account.

*

Vienne, the two Aquitaines, Novempopulana, the two Narbonnes, and the province of the Maritime Alps.

†

Constantine the Great was singularly partial to Arles; it was he who made it the seat of the prefecture of the Gauls; he desired also that it should bear his name; but custom was more powerful than his will.

*

Petronius was Prefect of the Gauls between 402 and 408.

†

The municipal corps of the Roman cities were called curiae, and the members of these bodies, who were very numerous, curiales.

‡

Constantine the Second, husband of Placidia, whom Honorius had taken for his colleague in 421.

*

The researches of later scholars have brought to light some facts and views slightly at variance with those of the author. By the middle of the third century before our era (bc 266) Rome had extended her conquests over the entire Italian peninsula. The cities of Italy were not, however, made mere subject municipalities, paying tribute to a city in whose privileges they had no share. Most of them were left in control of their own local affairs, while their residents were given full or partial rights of citizens of Rome. Whenever they were present in Rome they participated as fully in the affairs of the government of Rome as did the resident. This was strictly in harmony with the prevalent idea that Rome was the mistress of Italy, and not merely the capital of a state embracing all Italy. The social war (bc 90) was a revolt of the Italian cities against Roman domination, and resulted in the granting of complete Roman citizenship to all the Italian citizens. A little later this was extended to the citizens of southern Gaul. From this time forth, while the municipalities retained their separate life and laws as hitherto, the political union of Italy was in large degree a fact, and there was at least a partial identity of interest between Rome and all the cities of Italy.

It was manifestly more difficult to extend a system of this sort over the provinces outside of Italy with any certainty that the bond would be a strong one. The establishment of a central representative government at Rome, to which each of the provinces and cities should send representatives, was never tried—probably never thought of—by the Romans. During the period of the republic the provinces were governed for Rome by proconsuls and proprætors, over whom she herself had no real control while they were in the provinces, and whom, on the other hand, the provincial municipalities could not control. The irregularities of these governments raised the

necessity for some sort of government over the cities which should stop the disintegration which was setting in. When the empire was established came a real head for the state, and a growing centralization of the provincial municipalities in the hands of officers responsible to the emperor alone. Gradually the provincial cities and towns lost more and more of their local rights, including that of choosing their own magistrates. They were all united to Rome through the prefects and other representatives of the emperor. When the empire fell the bond was broken that held them together, but the local governments were revived or continued in the municipalities. For further discussions of this subject the student may with profit consult Arnold, Roman Provincial Administration; Guizot, History of Representative Government in Europe, Lectures XXII and XXIII; Adams, Civilization in the Middle Ages, chap. ii; Woodrow Wilson, The State.
*

It was something more than the mere "remembrance of the empire" that survived its downfall. The idea, the possibility of a world-empire was created by the attempts of Rome at such an empire; the influence of this idea was felt throughout the early middle ages, and there is a constant recurrence to it. It gave the motive for Charlemagne's policy; it found expression in the later Holy Roman Empire. It sunk only when the establishment of national states instead of one world-empire became the creative idea of European statecraft. During the chaotic centuries of the early middle ages there seems little doubt that the memory of the Roman empire, and of the political unity which it at one time implied, was a conservative force in preventing the complete disintegration of political society.
*

It is impossible to state with positiveness what were the differences, if any, between the functions of the πρεσβύτεροι and the ἐπίσκοποι, in this period.
†

Upon almost no point connected with the history of the Christian church is there a wider difference of opinion, and a greater mass of controversial literature, than upon the form of the early Church organization. The whole subject is wrapped in mists which are rather increased than dissipated by the statements and counterstatements of various partisans who too often, upon a slender basis of known fact, build a vast superstructure of doubtful theory. The statements of the author contain one theory as to the organization of the Church. The theory most radically opposed to this—and the student will always remember that there is but one set of facts underlying all of these theories—maintains that from the very beginning there has been a definite organization of the Church, authoritatively, almost divinely, established, and consequently there has been no period of the Church without its established constitution and government. The early Christians attached themselves to this organization, which was created and ordained as to its forms as well as its beliefs by an outside, superior authority.
The other view—that presented in the text—represents the Church organization as an evolution, growing in distinctness and completeness and definiteness of official stations and powers, as the adherents increased in numbers, and necessity demanded. All the members of the early groups of Christians had a voice in determining the forms and discipline of the Church.
The origin of these differences of view, which no amount of argument at this day can probably reconcile, is easily explicable. Of the three periods or states of the early Church, as indicated by the author, the boundaries are shadowy. The first certainly did not extend beyond the middle of the first century, while the third had been entered upon by the close of the second century or early in the following. As to the general constitution and organization of the Church in the third period there is substantial agreement, because the facts are known. Of the status of affairs during

the first two periods far less is known, hence there is room for dispute as to whether what was true in the third period was also true in the preceding, or whether the third was merely the orderly evolution from the more primitive organization of the first two. Absolutely to prove either theory is impossible unless new facts are disclosed. Many of the wide differences in the organization and polity of various branches of the modern Christian church are due to the controversy above indicated.

Whatever may have been the organization of the primitive Church, by the time of Constantine there was a distinctly marked separation of the clergy from the laity, and a gradation of the former into various ranks and classes, while the laity possessed little, and thereafter continually less, voice in the administration of the Church or the selection of its officials. The Church had, in fact, become a vast organized system—an institution.

It must be remembered that at the outset Christianity was the religious belief of but a few uneducated persons; that it spread quietly but rapidly throughout the empire, but hardly touched the upper and official classes; that by the second century the adherents of this faith had become so numerous as to provoke persecution at the hands of the pagan emperors. The last of these systematic persecutions was that ordered by Diocletian at the close of the third century. In 311 the Emperor Constantine became an adherent, or supporter, of Christianity, and in 312 it was given complete toleration throughout the empire, while under Theodosius (379-395) it became the only religion allowed in the state. Between the middle of the third century and the fall of the Western empire the Church was the recipient of much wealth and many favors from the empire, and the ecclesiastical officials came into many positions of power and influence in municipal affairs.

*

The laws of the Roman Government, embodied in treatises and decrees running back over several centuries, were first codified in the fourth century in the Gregorian and Hermogenian codes, which were made by private individuals and were very imperfect. In 438 was published the Theodosian code, compiled under authority of the emperor by a commission of lawyers. This contained most of the statute law, or imperial decrees, down to that time.

The last and most important of the codifications of the Roman law was the Justinian Code, made in 528-529. This was a collection, in condensed form, of all the decrees and edicts then in force. This constituted the statute law of the empire. In 533 appeared the Digest, or Pandects, which was a collection of legal opinions, not unlike in nature the decisions of modern courts and the treatises of legal writers. In the same year appeared the Institutes of Justinian, a text-book for law schools, containing a summary of the principles of Roman jurisprudence. Lastly came the Novellæ, or decrees of Justinian issued after the code had been published.

The Justinian Code, Pandects, and Institutes, with the Novellæ, constitute the Corpus Juris Civilis, or Roman Civil Law—"the last will and testament of Roman jurisprudence." This highly developed system of law was thus preserved during the dark ages, and forms the basis of the system of jurisprudence in most of the continental European states of to-day. It is one of the most important contributions of Rome to modern civilization. See Encyclopædia Britannica, articles on Justinian and Roman Law, and the authorities there cited.

*

The student will note that the author is here discussing the influence of the ecclesiastical system, the governmental machinery of the Church as an organization.

Christianity as a religious belief, permeating society in the closing centuries of the ancient world, gave to mediæval, and hence to modern, civilization certain ideas that have had a tremendous influence both on man and on society. A new conception of the nature of God and of man's direct and personal relation to him; a new ideal of life as typified in Christ, the attainment to which was the supreme law of conduct; the future life as dependent upon character and conduct in this world; the equality of all men from the Divine standpoint—all these ideas, fundamental to Christianity, have been forces the power of which has not been relaxed in the subsequent ages. All took their beginning in these early centuries.

The author's opinion that the preservation of the Christian religion in these troublous times was due to the power of the Church as an organization in the fifth century merits a word. That the Church defended, protected, and promoted the Christian religion is of course true; that was its purpose; but that the religious belief, already in the fifth century so widespread, would have disappeared had the ecclesiastical organization been less powerful, it would be difficult to maintain.

For an excellent statement of the additions made to civilization by Christianity, see Adams's Civilization in the Middle Ages, chap. iii.
*

In the earlier centuries of her history the Christian church labored for the separation of the spiritual and temporal authority, in order to protect herself from the control of the state. The older religions were a part of the state, and the Church now protested against the idea that the temporal rulers should control the religious and ecclesiastical affairs of Christianity. In this protest she was successful. Later, when the Church itself had become powerful and the state weaker, she attempted to assume control over the temporal affairs of Europe, and to establish her position as supreme temporal as well as ecclesiastical and spiritual ruler. These two seemingly inconsistent attitudes of the Church on the relation of the spiritual and temporal authority were separated by a considerable interval of time.
*

Since these lectures were delivered, a flood of light has been poured upon early Teutonic society by the researches of scholars, especially of the Germans. Waitz, Maurer, Sohm, Arnold, and others in Germany, Stubbs and others in England, have made valuable contributions to our knowledge on this subject.

Brief accounts, based on these researches, are given in Lewis's History of Germany, Church's Beginning of the Middle Ages, Emerton's Introduction to the Middle Ages, Duruy's History of the Middle Ages. Andrews's Institutes of General History contains suggestive bibliographies. One of the best and most trustworthy accounts in English of both political and social institutions is in Stubbs's Constitutional History of England, chaps. ii and iii.
*

The influence of at least two of the political ideas or institutions of the Germans has been especially marked in our later civilization. These two are the elective monarchy, based on the right exercised by the freemen of the German tribes of electing their leader or king, and the public or popular assembly, in which the freemen met for legislative and judicial purposes. See Stubbs's Constitutional History, as cited in the last note.
*

The custom or institution referred to here is the comitatus. This was a band of warriors united by voluntary bonds of fidelity to a military chieftain, whom they were bound to follow to war whenever called upon. They lived with their leader and were equipped and maintained by him. The bond was purely a personal one, and might be dissolved at pleasure. The great body of the military forces of the Germans was composed of these bands. This was a forerunner of the feudal system, but is not generally regarded by the best modern authorities on feudal history as in any important sense the source or origin of feudalism.

*

The fall of the Roman empire is dated in 476, when the last emperor was deposed. For five centuries the Romans and the Germans had been in conflict. At first the Romans had striven to conquer the Germans, later they struggled to defend their own borders from the inroads of the barbarians, and finally they were overcome on Roman soil by the conquering hordes.

In the last century before our era Julius Cæsar extended the Roman boundaries to the Rhine, and expelled the Germans from Gallic territory. During the reign of Augustus expeditions were made into the territory of the Germans, until in 9 ad the German leader Hermann (Arminius) defeated the Romans and practically freed the German soil from Roman hold. In the middle of the second century the Marcomanni attempted to cross the upper Danube into Roman territory. The Roman empire was now on the defensive. The invaders were defeated, but during the next hundred years German irruptions were frequently made. The Roman troops were kept busy guarding the long stretches of the imperial frontier from the incursions of a people whom overpopulation and the lack of room for the primitive agricultural methods of the time were impelling to seek larger areas for habitation.

At that time all of Europe north and east of the Danube and the Rhine was occupied by the German tribes, save in the northeast, where the Slavs dwelt. The Germans included the Saxons in the northwest, the Franks along the Rhine, the Alemanni in the valley of the upper Rhine, east of them the Burgundians and Marcomanni, and still farther east the Goths divided into the Visigoths and Ostrogoths, the latter on the lower Danube and along the Black Sea. The Goths had set up a kingdom about the middle of the fourth century, and were the most advanced and dangerous foes of the empire.

Towards the end of the fourth century the Teutonic peoples were forced upon the empire by the pressure of a race until then unknown in Europe—the Huns, a Mongolian or Tartar race from the north of Asia. In 376, the Huns, invading Europe, fell upon and subdued the Ostrogoths, established a kingdom of their own, and attacked the Visigoths, who begged and received admission into the Roman empire south of the Danube, where they were assigned a definite territory. Trouble soon arose, and in 378 the Visigoths revolted, and at Adrianople defeated the Roman army and killed the Emperor Valens. This German victory over Roman forces was the beginning of the end. The next emperor, Theodosius, checked the Visigoths by leaving them in possession of the Danube valley and treating them as allies. At his death, in 395, the Visigoths under Alaric again attacked the empire, ravaged Thrace, and took possession of Greece, from which they were induced by the Roman general Stilicho to withdraw to Illyria. In 400, Alaric invaded Italy, but was defeated by Stilicho in 402. The movement of the barbarians along the border was now general. In 406 the Vandals and Suevi burst into Gaul and pushed on into Spain, while the Burgundians settled in eastern Gaul. In 408 Alaric again invaded Italy, and sacked Rome (410), but died shortly after. His successor allied himself with the Romans, went north into Gaul and Spain, subdued the other German invaders except the Vandals, and founded in Spain the kingdom of the Visigoths. This ended the Roman dominion in Spain.

In 429 the Vandals crossed from Spain into Africa, overran the northern coast, plundered the Mediterranean, and in 455, under Gaiseric, crossed into Italy, and took and sacked Rome, whence they retired again to Africa.

The Huns north of the Danube, in 449, under the leadership of Attila, advanced into northern Gaul. There they came into contact with the combined Roman forces and German tribes, were

defeated in 451 at the battle of Chalons, which freed western Europe from fear of Hunnish
conquest. In 452 Alaric invaded Italy, but was turned back, and on his death, in 454, the Hunnish
power, which had precipitated all the movements of the barbarians for nearly a century,
disappeared.
In 410 the Romans abandoned Britain, and in 449 the Anglo-Saxons began to take possession of
the island.
Thus by the middle of the fifth century all the provinces were lost to the empire, while Italy itself
was in the hands of German mercenary troops, who were her only protectors. After the death of
the Emperor Valentinian III, in 455, a series of puppets were set up and deposed by the leaders of
the army. The last one, Romulus Augustulus, was deposed in 476 by Odoacer, leader of the
German mercenaries (Heruli). Odoacer decided to appoint no new emperor, but to rule himself as
representative of Zeno, the Eastern emperor, though the latter declined to recognize him as such
representative. In 493 Odoacer was slain by Theodoric, king of the Ostrogoths, who established
the Ostrogothic kingdom of Italy.
Thus at the downfall of the Roman empire the territory was in the actual occupancy of several
fairly well-defined kingdoms or groups of Germans, some of which had been in possession for
many years. The Vandals were masters of Africa; the Suevi, of a part of Spain; the Visigoths of
the rest, together with a large part of Gaul; the Burgundians, of that part of Gaul lying on the
Rhone and Saône; the Ostrogoths of nearly all Italy; while the Franks under Clovis had begun
(481-496) the career of conquest, which in the next and following centuries resulted in the
overthrow of those kingdoms, the establishment of the Frankish dominion, and the formation for
a time of a new center of gravity for Europe under Charlemagne.
The dominant people everywhere were Germans. The problem of the middle ages was to settle
whether all former civilization should be overturned by the German, or the German people
should be Romanized and Christianized. Modern civilization is the result of the interplay of these
forces.
The best account in English of the conquest of the Roman empire by the Germans is Hodgkin's
Italy and Her Invaders. Gibbon's Decline and Fall of the Roman Empire is, of course, of great
importance. Emerton's Introduction to the Study of the Middle Ages, and Adams's Civilization
in the Middle Ages, contain excellent brief accounts of the conquest.
*

Henri de Boulainvilliers (1658-1722), an eminent French historical writer.
†

Jean Baptiste Dubos (1670-1742), a prominent student of politics and law, and an historical
writer.
‡

Gabriel Bonnot de Mably (1709-1785), a French historian.
*

The oldest and smallest independent republic in the world; situated in eastern central Italy. Area
thirty-three square miles; population about eight thousand. It dates from the fourth century.
*

By political legitimacy is meant the right of a government to exist and to exercise the powers
which it undertakes to wield. What constitutes the true source of legitimate government is a
matter of contention. The prevalent American theory, for example, is, for America at least, that
all government, to be legitimate, must be founded on the consent of the governed, either
expressed or implied. The longer a government continues in existence, the greater the

presumption of its legitimacy, no matter what may have been the actual circumstances of its establishment. Those governments which have been clearly established by force, or have been founded on a political revolution, have subsequently justified their lawfulness not by the manner of their establishment, but on the acquiescence of the governed in the acts of authority, and on their recognition as lawful by other governments.

*

These terms are applied to those who, under the custom of the comitatus, already described, attached themselves to another person to whom, by virtue of their oath of attachment, they owed certain services. According to Secretan (Essai sur la Féodalité), antrustion was the name given to members of the king's comitatus, while fideles and leudes were terms applied to members of the comitatus of a nobleman. It must be remembered that the author is here attempting to describe the society of a period five centuries in length, and his descriptions are of necessity not exactly applicable to the entire period, for society and institutions were constantly changing.

*

Allodial proprietors held their lands in absolute ownership, subject to no control by a superior. The term benefice was applied to lands granted to another, to be used and enjoyed by the grantee on condition of performing certain specified services for the one granting the land. The term appears first to have come into frequent use after the Carlovingian dynasty was established over the Franks (752).

†

The formal beginning of the right of inheritance as applied to benefices is usually traced to an edict of Charles the Bald in 877. It is too much to affirm, as the author does, that there was nothing like regularity in the terms for which benefices were granted. In the earliest period they were almost certainly not hereditary; in the later period they were rarely for a limited term of years. Researches made since M. Guizot wrote have overthrown several statements in this and the following chapter.

*

The student will no doubt easily recall periods in mediæval history concerning which these statements seem hardly exact.

*

The following chronological indications may assist in recalling a more distinct view of the invasions, conquests, and revolutions of this stormy period:

[486.   Clovis, king of the Salian Franks, and real founder of the Frankish empire, defeats Syagrius, the Roman general, at Soissons, and extends the kingdom to the Loire, where it touches the kingdom of the Visigoths.]

507.   Clovis adds to his former acquisitions the conquest of the Visigothic kingdom. Dies, 511. Kingdom divided between his four sons, but ultimately united under one of them, Clotaire I, 558.

530.   Thuringia conquered and annexed to the Frankish dominions.

534.   Conquest of Burgundy by the Franks.

554.   Ostrogothic kingdom destroyed by Narses.—Italy becomes a province of the Eastern Empire.

560.   Gepidæ destroyed by the Lombards and Avars.

568.   Kingdom of the Lombards established in Upper Italy.—Southern Italy continues an exarchate of the Eastern Empire.

628.   Dagobert I (son of Clotaire II) king of the Franks. Invasion of the Slavonians (Wendi). Mayors of the palace control the royal authority.

687.   Pepin of Heristal, mayor of the palace [dictator of Frankish kingdom].
711.   The Saracens appear in Europe; conquer Spain; cross the Pyrenees; checked on the Aude,
712; invade France; beaten by Eudes, duke of Aquitaine, 721; driven beyond the Aude, 725.
715.   Charles Martel mayor of the palace.
726.   Leo (Iconoclastes), Emperor of the East, issues an edict against image-worship; the
people of Rome and Naples revolt; exarch of Ravenna murdered by the people, and the city
yielded to the Lombards. A sort of republic under the authority of the Pope established at Rome;
including the territory from Viterba to Terracina, and from Narni to Ostia. Commencement of the
temporal power of the Popes. The Pope and the republic of Venice (founded 697) unite to drive
the Lombards from Ravenna.
732.   Saracens invade France; defeated by Charles Martel at the Battle of Tours.
752-757.   Pepin the Short, mayor of the palace; deposes Childeric, the last of the
Merovingian kings; recognized king by the Pope; founds the Carlovingian dynasty.
Exarchate of Ravenna destroyed by the Lombards; the Pope and the Romans refuse submission;
invite the aid of Pepin, who invades Italy and forces the Lombards to give up the exarchate of
Ravenna and the Pentapolis, which he bestows upon the Pope. Commencement of the relations
between the Popes and the German princes.
768.   Charlemagne king; conquers Aquitania, 769; overthrows the Lombard kingdom of Italy,
774; first war against the Saxons; drives them beyond the Weser, 772-774; defeats them again,
777; war against Spain, 778; second war against the Saxons, 778-785; subdues all on the south of
the Elbe, compels them to receive baptism. The Lombards (of Beneventum), the Greeks, and
Avari, league against him—defeated. Avari subdued and Christianized, 791-799.
800.   Charlemagne restores the Roman Empire of the West; receives the imperial crown from
the Pope; Saxons on the Elbe subdued and dispersed, 812. [The subjugation of the Saxons had
cost Charlemagne thirty years war.] War with the Wiltzians and other Slavonian tribes. Maritime
incursions of the Northmen on the ocean coast, and of the Saracens on the Mediterranean.
814.   Death of Charlemagne. This event was followed by the dismemberment of his empire,
and the formation of the three great states of Germany, France, and Italy; also of three secondary
kingdoms, Castile, Aragon, and Navarre.
The death of Charlemagne and the breaking up of his vast system likewise opened the barriers of
the empire to the incursions of the Saracens, the Northmen, the Slavonians, and the Hungarians:
it was not until the close of the tenth century that the barbarian invasions can be said to have
definitely ceased.
H.
*

It must not be forgotten that "the Germans, at the time of their emergence from their original
seats and their occupation of the Roman lands, were not mere wandering groups of freebooters,
but well-organized nations, with a very distinct sense of political organization" (Emerton). The
earlier writers have misrepresented the Germans in this regard, and even the statements and
implications of the author are not entirely reconcilable with modern views.
One great fact of mediæval history was, however, that the dominant people, the Germans, were
not at the beginning of the era sufficiently civilized to appreciate, take up, and carry forward the
political and social ideas which Roman civilization had produced. During the dark ages
civilization was waiting while the German peoples fitted themselves to carry forward the work.
Time was needed for this, and until that time had elapsed the state of Europe was not far
removed from barbarism.

*

Most of these codes were written out, within a century of the conquest of the Roman empire, in the Latin language. They cover civil and criminal law, and, in general, the relations of man to man. Like the Roman codes which undoubtedly inspired them, they contain little new legislation, but bring together the customs and usages and edicts which up to that time had been unwritten. The legal system which they embody was not that "of a society which no longer existed," for many of the German legal ideas found in these codes influenced the social and legal order of Europe almost till modern times. Of these codes the Salic and the Visigothic are among the most mportant. They have all been published with annotations by German scholars during the past half century. A good brief sketch is given in Emerton's Introduction to the Middle Ages, chap. viii, where a bibliography is also given. See also the Encyclopædia Britannica, vol. xxi, article "Salic Law and Other Barbarian Laws."

The later laws and proclamations of the Frankish kings were known as capitularies, and are of the highest importance in tracing the legal development of the Frankish government and customs. They have been published in Pertz, Monumenta Germanica, and elsewhere. An excellent analysis of their contents is given in Guizot's History of Civilization in France, Lectures XXI and XXV.

Among the peculiarities by which most of these laws are distinguished from modern legislation, the most striking is perhaps the fact that all offences were punished with fines, This is significant of the barbarian sentiment of individuality, of personal independence. The barbarian will not suffer his life or liberty to be affected by his actions.

*

The code of the Visigoths, as sanctioned by the Council of Toledo in 633, was only a revision and amendment of the code of Alaric, published in 506.

*

Theories as to the origin of the feudal system have been radically reconstructed since these lectures were written. While there is not yet complete agreement upon all points, it is no longer maintained by the most careful investigators that the feudal system was entirely due to the Germanic element, and "was the offspring of German society." The forms of feudalism were essentially Roman, the spirit German. See note at the end of Lecture IV.

†

In this lecture the author had in mind the entire period from the fifth to the tenth century, and his statements are based on the general character and import of the whole time. In order to an appreciation of the discussion it is essential that the events of this chaotic period be well known. The chronological suggestions already given will serve as a help to those familiar with the general outlines. The student will find excellent sketches of the period in Duruy's History of the Middle Ages, and in Emerton's Introduction to the Middle Ages. For the reign of Charlemagne, consult Eginhard's Life of Charlemagne, and Mombert, History of Charles the Great.

The important factor in Europe during this period was the Frankish kingdom. Of all the Germanic kingdoms set up during the era of the invasions and wanderings it alone developed such stability and approach to unity as made it markedly influential in both that and later periods. Established on a firmer basis by Clovis, it absorbed the Alemanni (496) and the Visigothic kingdom in Gaul (507). Clovis himself was baptized into the orthodox Catholic faith in 496, and thereby brought the kingdom into friendly relations with the pope, between whom and the other Teutonic kingdoms there was discord, owing to their adherence to Arianism, a theological heresy of this period. The Franks with far less difficulty than the other Teutons seemed able to combine the three elements, Roman, barbarian, Christian, the fusion of which has in large measure produced modern civilization. At the death of Clovis, in 511, the Frankish kingdom was a decently ordered barbarian state. Under his successors family quarrels weakened the kingdom, but in 530 Thuringia, in 534 Burgundy, and a little later certain territory east of the Rhine, was annexed. The kingdom was several times divided among sons of the rulers, but in 613 was reunited under Lothaire II, and during the reign of his son, Dagobert I (628-638), the Merovingian family attained its highest power. During all of this period there had been a division, now openly indicated by separate rulers, now nominal, between the eastern part (Austrasia) and the western part (Neustria) of the kingdom. Austrasia was more Teutonic, less centralized; Neustria more centralized and more Roman.

Under the weak successors of Dagobert the real power in each branch of the kingdom was wielded by the chief officer of state, the mayor of the palace. In 687 the Austrasian mayor of the palace, Pippin of Heristal, leading the nobles of his country, overcame the king and mayor of the palace of Neustria and became the real dictator of the entire kingdom. His victory was in one sense the ascendancy of the Teutonic over the Roman ideas in the kingdom. The office of the mayor of the palace continued in Pippin's family until in 752 the last of the Merovingian kings was set aside and Pippin the Short was crowned by the pope king of the Franks, thus establishing the Carlovingian dynasty.

Under the weak Merovingian rulers the Frankish nobles had assumed a virtual independence, and the Carlovingian mayors of the palace had striven to rebuild the central power thus weakened. The alliance between Pippin the Short and the pope gave the new Frankish ruler the moral support of the papal authority.

In 768, Charlemagne, the greatest of the Carlovingians, came to the throne. Two motives seem to have guided his acts: to strengthen the central government of the kingdom, and to revive the Roman empire by consolidating Christian Europe into a single government. His conquests in Germany and Italy, his coronation in 800 as the emperor of the Holy Roman Empire, were the carrying out of this idea. Though his statesmanship was broad and his acts were wise, his attempt did not suit the conditions of Germanic Europe, nor did his effort at a strong central government accord with the growing independence of the landed nobility throughout the continent. With his death it became evident that only the personal force and statesmanship of a strong ruler could make headway against these disintegrating tendencies. His immediate successors were unequal to the task, and though the name of the empire continued, it was unable to maintain the position established for it by Charlemagne. The family quarrels between his descendants, sons of Louis the Pious, culminated in the treaty of Verdun in 843, by which Lothaire, with the title of emperor, received Italy and a strip along the Rhine to the North Sea, Louis the German received the territory from the Rhine to the Elbe, and Charles the Bold received France west of the strip given to Lothaire. This was the beginning of modern France as a separate kingdom, the throne of which was held by the Carlovingians till 987, when Hugh Capet, Duke of France, one of the feudal nobility, took the throne and founded the dynasty that ruled France till the present century. At this time France was hardly more than a group of separate sovereign states, under the nominal suzerainty of the king. Germany also soon became split into several large districts, each under the control of a practically independent duke, while in Italy the government rapidly disintegrated after the treaty of Verdun, already mentioned.

Thus, in the course of two centuries after Charlemagne, the Holy Roman Empire had so declined that, except under Otho I (962) and a few of his successors, it represented an idea rather than a fact. At the same time lines of cleavage, linguistic and governmental, were becoming apparent, substantially those marking the later nationalities of the Germans, the French, and the Italians. A turbulent, chaotic state was again prevalent over Europe, but it was not the rude, barbarous chaos of the fifth century. Some advance had been made; but the Teutonic peoples were not yet by the tenth century fully ready for the restraint of orderly government, which meant, as they felt, a lessening of that individual liberty which was so strong a trait in the German life. The feudal system was first to have its course before political order should overcome unrestrained personal independence.

An appreciative brief study of the real significance of Charlemagne's reign and the first centuries of the Holy Roman Empire is contained in Adams's Civilization during the Middle Ages,. Of very great value is also Bryce's Holy Roman Empire.

*

The detailed accounts of the origin and character of feudalism given in Hallam's Middle Ages and Guizot's History of Civilization in France, second course, were for a long time the only ones available in English. The views of neither of these writers, especially as to the origin, are now accepted as satisfactory, though the student who desires to know the earlier theories will always consult them. Adams's Civilization during the Middle Ages, chapter ix, is highly valuable; hardly less so are chapter xv of Emerton's Introduction to the Middle Ages, on the origin, and chapter xiv of the same author's Mediæval Europe, on the character of the feudal institutions. Andrews's Institutes of General History, chapter vi, is suggestive as a summary, and contains an excellent bibliography. Stubbs's Constitutional History of England, chapter ix, may also be profitably consulted. All of these later works are based on the researches and conclusions of the German scholars and historians, Waitz, Roth, and Brunner, whose works may perhaps be considered the ultimate authority to-day.

*

Even when feudalism was at its height, and disunity in the state seemed the greatest, the theory was preserved of a central power, the king, exercising the sovereign authority to which all other elements in the feudal state were directly or indirectly subject. This idea never entirely disappeared, however faint and obscure it may seem at times to have been.

*

This little group is the unit, but the "feudal system" included also the idea of a bond connecting the various units or groups. Each possessor of a fief was bound by personal and property ties to the person from whom he held his fief, and in turn often had other lesser vassals attached to himself by a similar tie. Between vassals of the same suzerain there was always much of common interest. To speak of a single group, such as is described in the lecture, as constituting or typifying the "feudal system," is not entirely accurate.

*

It must always be understood, of course, that all of the importance and power that attached to him was by virtue of his proprietorship of the fief, and disappeared with the loss of the fief.

*

The primitive Germans undoubtedly had an extremely high respect for women, though it cannot be shown that they surpassed other races of the Aryan family in this regard.

*

When the system became generally established these duties and obligations were definitely fixed. The vassal owed service; the lord owed protection. The vassal's duty consisted in military service, personally and with a definite retinue, for a fixed period, not usually exceeding forty days; attendance upon the lord's court and council; the payment to the lord for particular

purposes, of certain special sums of money, known as "aids," "fines," and "reliefs." Refusal or omission by the vassal to fulfil these duties rendered the fief liable to forfeiture. The obligations of the lord were to protect the vassal from outside enemies, to refrain from violence against him, and to grant him lawful justice. Failure in these obligations released the vassal permanently or temporarily from his allegiance.
*

Each possessor of a fief, of course, "had the power to enforce his will upon others"—i. e., his villeins and serfs; but over these possessors themselves, who were at once vassals of those above and suzerains of those below them, there was no one powerful enough to assert and enforce his will. The weakness of this central or general power in the state was the strength of feudalism. When the central political and social force arose the feudal system fell.
*

The fundamentals of chivalry are traceable to the early German ideas of personal bravery, fondness for feats of arms, and respect for woman, together with regard for the oppressed and unfortunate, inculcated by Christianity. It became a formal institution wherever feudalism existed, while the Crusades aided its development by giving opportunity for its practice. Sons of noblemen were trained in its ceremonies and ideas, and at the age of twenty-one were knighted. Its bad feature was that it fostered aristocracy, and that its external forms covered many excesses and vices. Its spirit, its ideal of life, manners, and character, have had a large subsequent influence in the development of modern manhood.
*

To say that the progress of society was opposed by feudalism is but to affirm that the German peoples of the ninth, tenth, and eleventh centuries were not ready for more advanced political and social institutions, for the establishment of any government that would materially lessen their individual liberty. The feudal system gave scope for that liberty; it was suited to the condition of the people. On the other hand, centralized government was not an original Teutonic institution. The Teutonic mind had to be made ready for it. That very process of preparation constituted social progress. The feudal system was not so much an obstacle to the progress of society as it was a necessary intermediate stage before the more evident and rapid progress toward orderly government and society that came in the following centuries.
*

The feudal system as a fully organized institution was hardly found outside of the limits of the empire established by Charlemagne, which included France, Germany, and Italy; it was carried, with modifications, into England. In France and Germany it attained its fullest development, and its effects continued there longer than elsewhere. From the ninth to the twelfth century it flourished in its completest form, but the germs of the system are found several centuries earlier. Feudalism was a governmental and social system based upon three essential ideas, and marked by one universal peculiarity. The latter was the absence of any strong central power in the state; the former were: a peculiar kind of land tenure, a peculiar personal relation existing between different classes in society, and special rights and powers of government and sovereignty exercised by the holders of land over those residing on it. The first two of these are separately traceable to a far earlier period; their union was the special characteristic of the feudal system. The disorders of the eighth and ninth centuries in the Frankish monarchy and the Holy Roman Empire gave cause for the establishment of feudalism. Royalty could not fulfill the duties which it undertook, and the protection which the nominal head of the state could not give was sought elsewhere. On the verge of complete disintegration society seized hold of certain customs that had existed for centuries, organized them into a rough system, and thus established a new kind of government. The absence of a strong central power occasioned the feudal system. Until that central power was made strong, feudalism lasted; with its upbuilding, feudalism fell. The two were incompatible.

The real basis of the system was the form of land tenure upon which were built certain rights, duties, and powers of individuals. The origin of the fief, as an estate held by feudal tenure was called, is found in the Roman custom, by which, in the later days of the empire, the owner of a small estate surrendered it to a more powerful neighbor, and received it back without rent and for an indefinite period, on a sort of lease that was terminable at the will of the owner. This tenure was known as the precarium, and later as a benefice. Under it, while the title of the occupant was not that of an owner, he was yet more amply protected against violence in turbulent times and secured in his occupancy by the superior influence and power of the one from whom he held the land. The German conquerors, in overrunning the empire, took a large part of the soil to their own use and granted it to their followers. In doing so they applied this Roman custom of the precarium, which they found in the territory. At the outset and for a long time thereafter this land tenure carried no personal relation, and involved no obligation of personal service in return. The second feature in feudalism was the personal relation between different classes—the relation between lord and vassals. The vassal was bound to render fealty and personal service to the lord in return for protection on his part. This relationship, which was a voluntary one, seems also to have been traceable to a Roman institution, that of patron and client, the patrocinium. According to that custom, the wealthy and powerful patron took the weak and landless client under his protection, his patronage, in return for services rendered by the client. The relationship was purely a personal one of protection and service, not altogether unlike that of the German comitatus already described. So long as these two independent customs, traceable to Roman originals, continued separate, as they did for two or three centuries, feudalism was not established. When, however, the holder of a benefice became also a vassal; when the relationship growing from the landholding was united with that growing out of personal fealty, the feudal tenure became established.

During the time of the Merovingians it does not appear that the two ideas were joined, so that while the factors of feudalism existed the system itself had not been produced. Under the Carlovingians many lands were granted as benefices, or fiefs, and these appear to have been made hereditary before the close of the ninth century. During the same period many of the administrative officers, such as dukes and counts, appointed by the kings, impelled thereto by the weakness of the central power, claimed their offices as hereditary, and their respective duchies and counties as fiefs, thus splitting up the state. In these same confused and anarchical times many free proprietors of allodial estates, for the sake of the protection of a stronger authority, since the central government was unequal to the task, gave up their lands to more powerful neighbors and received them back as fiefs. The Church, which had become possessed of vast estates, granted and held many of its lands and offices in this way.

It was during the Carlovingian period, or at least while the Carlovingians were mayors of the palace, that the idea of personal service was connected with the holding of fiefs. Large armies were needed, and in the absence of state revenues the habit grew of granting benefices on condition of military service rendered in return.

Finally, in the same period, the custom was established of granting to the holders of great fiefs complete jurisdiction or sovereignty for civil purposes over their estates. This was commonly done by grants of immunity, as they were called, by which the owner of a fief took the place of the officers of state on his own domain, and administered laws and dispensed justice as an almost independent sovereign. Probably, also, many strong feudal lords usurped the sovereignty without the formality of a grant from the nominal king. When this had become general, and when the custom of subinfeudation had been adopted, a general decentralized system of government built on land tenure had been substituted for the centralized monarchy which Charlemagne had attempted.

It is now possible to see that the essential forms of feudalism were derived from Roman originals, but the force that applied them, modified them, and organized them into a system was the German spirit of independence, and love of individual liberty. Instead of building up a strong central government, the Germans aimed at the establishment of a social system based on the personal relation of man to man, that should permit the fullest freedom to the individual members so far as they possessed land.

The good features of feudalism were beneficial to the feudal lords only, while, as indicated in the lecture, the villeins and entire body of the lower classes were harshly treated. Had a strong, united, central government been possible, feudalism would have been unnecessary; its merit was in keeping society from complete disintegration in theory and in fact, at a time when the tendency was all in that direction.

It began to lose force in the eleventh century, but continued in England until the Wars of the Roses, in Spain till the fifteenth century, while many remnants were left in France till 1789, and in Germany until the present century. The causes of its downfall were the growth of royalty, and of the cities, the development of trade and commerce, and the modification in methods of warfare; in short, it disappeared when civilization advanced beyond the feudal stage. Cf., note.
*

A brief sketch of the organization of the Church, and of its growth from the fifth to the twelfth century, is given in the note appended to this lecture,.
*

This phrase signified the conferring or bestowing by a bishop upon one of the lower order of the clergy of a position, such as the charge of a parish church, to which was attached a fixed income payable from Church funds or lands. Such a position was an ecclesiastical benefice; the act of conferring it was the collation.
*

The distinction between the power of conferring the authority to exercise the spiritual functions of an ecclesiastical office, and the right of designating the person upon whom the authority shall be conferred for any particular place, should be borne in mind. The former, by the established constitution of the Church and by universal practice, always belonged exclusively to the bishops: they alone ordained the inferior clergy; they alone consecrated the bishops. In regard to the latter the practice varied: sometimes, the person designated was elected by the clergy and people, which was the primitive mode; sometimes by the clergy; sometimes by the temporal sovereign. But in no case did the people or the prince imagine themselves competent to consecrate, to confer upon the person they had selected for bishop, the spiritual powers pertaining to the functions of the see or benefice. This was always referred to the bishops, with whom it rested to confer or withhold those powers, without which the designation by people or prince was of no effect. This remark, of course, applies only to the sacred or spiritual orders; the authority of priors, abbots, etc., was derived from their election.
H.
*

The doctrinal belief or dogma of the Church had at that period to be accepted by all without question, and almost without examination. "Belief was in the middle ages not a matter of choice or of conviction, but of duty. The individual had no rights in the matter, but must submit himself without question to the dictates of the Church."—Emerton, Mediæval Europe,.
*

Many of the leaders of early Christian thought were opposed to compulsion in matters of faith. Heresy was treated and punished as a civil offense only after the Christian religion came to be the official religion of the Roman empire. St. Hilary (301-366), St. Martin (319-400), and St. Ambrose (340-397) were, as the text states, opposed to persecutions, while Augustine (383-430) was among the early advocates. Theodosius I, Emperor of the East (379-395), issued decrees against those who would not accept the orthodox faith. The usurping Emperor Maximus (383-388) was the first to put any one to death for heresy. From that time till the seventeenth century punishment for heresy was common. Noted thirteenth century instances were the persecutions of the Waldenses and Albigenses.
*

The term "heresy" admits of various definitions, but its usual application is to doctrines held by nominal Christians in conflict with one of the articles of faith or fundamental doctrines of the Church. No age in Christianity has been without sects and heresies, from the Gnostics, Manichæans, Novatians, Donatists, to the Waldenses, Albigenses, and Protestant Reformers. Still, the very fact that the holders of these so-called heretical views were usually driven out of the Church, or punished, shows that there was not room in the Church for the free exercise of individual reason.
†

Four grades of councils were recognized in the early and mediæval Church: Diocesan, composed of all the clergy under one bishop; provincial, consisting of all the bishops in one ecclesiastical province, under the metropolitan or archbishop; national, where all the bishops of a nation met under the patriarch or first metropolitan; general or œcumenical, at which the whole Church was regarded as represented. The famous Councils of Nicæa, Constance, and Trent are examples of the last, of which there have been but twenty to the present time, as recognized by the Roman Catholic Church.
*

There are several things in the foregoing paragraphs not quite accurately put.
The assumption of the right, or the exercise of the power to coerce faith, to punish physically for religious opinions, cannot indeed be too strongly condemned. It was a monstrous tyranny exercised by the Church at this period. The right of separating from its society such as rejected the fundamental articles of its constitution, is entirely a different thing—being a right inherent in every association, not to advert here to any grounds on which the obligation to do so was thought to rest.
Again, in regard to the authority of the Church and the "rights of individual reason"—here undoubtedly, in the corrupt ages of the Church, monstrous abuses grew up; yet these abuses should be distinguished from the primitive principle, from the perversion of which they sprang—the principle which required implicit faith in all matters divinely revealed. . . .
Nor, again, does the Church deserve the praise given to it in the text of acting in its councils in opposition to its principles. In the councils, the Church no doubt exercised to a certain extent the right inherent in all ordinary associations of legislating for itself. In all matters relating to rites, ceremonies, and doctrines, not considered to be definitively settled by Divine appointment, these

councils exercised the power of determining by their own authority. In all such matters there was scope for "discussion, deliberation," and arbitrary preference. But when the question was concerning any fundamental article of faith, the statement that "one might fancy one's self in the midst of the philosophical schools of Greece," is anything but true. They never dreamed of settling any such question by excogitation, speculation, reasoning. The appeal was to the sacred Scriptures as the ultimate and absolute authority. It was a matter of interpretation. If the sacred writings were not clear and decisive in themselves of the point in question, the next and only inquiry was, what could be historically ascertained to have been the interpretation sanctioned by the universal consent of the Church from the Apostolic age downwards,—and that was held to be decisive. Such was always the theory of the Church as to the authority of its councils: it was never imagined that the ascertained consent of the Church universal from the primitive age, in regard to a question of interpretation bearing on an article of faith, could be set aside, by any discussion or vote, by any speculation or reasoning.

Thus, from not distinguishing things quite distinct, the author's censure on the one hand, and his praise on the other, may convey an erroneous impression. H.

*

Some of the barbarians had embraced Christianity before their invasion of the Roman empire. Among these were the Goths, converted in the fourth century by their bishops Theophilus and Ulphilas; the Heruli, the Suevi, the Vandals, and perhaps the Lombards. They were converted by Arian missionaries, and embraced that form of Christianity. In the sixth and seventh centuries the Suevi, Visigoths, and Lombards adopted the orthodox faith; the Heruli, Vandals, and Ostrogoths adhered to Arianism.

The remarks of the text can therefore be applied literally only to the Burgundians, Franks, etc., by whom the first conquerors of the empire were swept away. Still, the Church had much to do even in bringing under her full influence the first barbarians. H.

†

The introduction of the imposing ceremonial and spectacular display in the worship of the Church was not merely to attract the "barbarians" into the Church, but also due to the influence of the barbarians and their customs and ceremonials on the Church after they entered it.

*

See note at the end of this lecture.

*

The quarrel respecting investitures between Gregory VII and the Emperor Henry IV arose from the former's attempt to establish the complete supremacy of the pope by destroying the control of feudal lords and princes over the lands and offices of the Church. Gregory's decree was that no officer of the Church should do homage under the feudal system to any temporal lord for his office or estate, but that he should receive the symbols of his investiture from the pope. As these officers of the Church possessed at the time under feudal tenure more than one third the lands of Europe, the significance of the papal claim can be understood. After a long struggle the quarrel on this particular point was compromised. Stephen's Hildebrand and His Times may be consulted with profit on this contest.

*

We have seen (note) that by the fifth century the Church had become a vast institution with an organized government, constituting a regular hierarchy. The clergy had become separated from the laity; over the clergy of a city, with its outlying territory, was a bishop, elected, in the early days, by the clergy and people, the bishop in the chief city of a province ranking above the others, and known as the metropolitan (later archbishop), while in the West the Bishop of Rome and in the East the Bishop of Constantinople had come to outrank all others in the Church. The supremacy of the Bishop of Rome had been built up by several forces: the pre-eminence of Rome as the one time mistress of the world; the fact that the Church at Rome was the only Apostolic Church in the West; that she had sent out and planted many churches; that her bishops had maintained a neutral attitude in the doctrinal controversies of the third and fourth centuries; that by the Council of Sardica, in 343, appeals were allowed to the Bishop of Rome in certain cases.

To reinforce these influences were the greatness of one or two of the bishops of this period (notably Leo I and Gregory the Great), and the theory by that time definitely held that the Bishop of Rome was the successor of Peter, and that, as Peter had had supremacy by divine authority over other apostles, so the Bishop of Rome had authority over other bishops and churches. After the time of the Emperor Constantine the connection between Church and state was close, and the emperors exercised considerable control over ecclesiastical affairs, although the removal of the capital to Constantinople left the Bishop of Rome a great degree of independence.

In 445 the Emperor Valentinian III declared the Bishop of Rome the supreme judicial and administrative officer of the Church in the empire. Thus, by the time of the downfall of the Western empire not only had the organization of the Church become well established, but the supremacy of the pope was well recognized. After the fall of the empire (476) the Church alone, and the pope as its head, represented the unity for which the empire had stood.

At this time it was that the Church and the pope, in order to protect themselves against the barbarians, as indicated by the author, set up the principle of the complete separation and independence of Church and state, of the spiritual and temporal power.

Pope Gregory I (590-604), the foremost incumbent of the papal chair during the early dark ages, appears at the head of the ecclesiastical organization, directing its movements, extending its force, guiding its clergy. When the Lombards had conquered northern Italy, and the Exarchate of Ravenna only feebly upheld the authority of the Eastern emperor in Italy, the Bishop of Rome had, of necessity, assumed and exercised temporal powers in the city, and this power was augmented by Gregory, who ignored, or claimed superiority over, the exarch. Thus began the authority of the pope as a temporal ruler.

During the sixth, seventh, and eighth centuries the most important event in the history of the papacy and the Church was the alliance between the pope and Pippin the Short, Mayor of the Palace under the Merovingians. The pope was in danger from the Lombards; he invited the protection of the Franks under Pippin. Pippin wished to become King of the Franks by the overthrow of the Merovingians; he wished the sanction of the religious power for his usurpation. The alliance was easily struck; the Carlovingian dynasty in France was established and the position of the pope was much strengthened.

We have seen the establishment of the Holy Roman Empire by Charlemagne. His conquest of the Lombards freed the papacy from absorption by the Lombards, and the coronation of Charlemagne as emperor by the pope established a close relationship between the two powers. Its exact nature was in doubt during the entire middle ages. On one hand it seemed to imply, by the act of coronation, the supremacy of the pope over the temporal ruler—"the bestowal of the empire by gift of the Church." On the other hand, the imperial idea was that the emperor was the successor of the former Roman emperors to whom the pope, as Bishop of Rome, had been subject. The struggle of the middle ages was between the two ideas—the papacy and the empire—to settle which, if either, was supreme, or whether both were equal—joint rulers of God on earth, one spiritual, the other temporal. The Church had forgotten or now ignored its contention of the fourth and fifth centuries for the separation and mutually complete independence of spiritual and temporal power.

The weakness of the empire after the death of Charlemagne, its decline until the coronation of Otho I (962), the Donation of Constantine and the Pseudo-Isidorian Decretals—two remarkable documents whose genuineness was accepted for several centuries, though now proved to be baseless forgeries—and the talents of two or three strong men, who in the ninth century occupied the papal chair, established the theory of papal supremacy over the empire. During the tenth century, the squabbles of Italian politics and the corrupt characters of the popes lost the papacy power and respect, while in the last half of the century the empire was revived by Otho I and his two successors; so that the year 1000 saw the world-monarchy, represented by the Holy Roman Empire, and the world-church, the Holy Catholic Church, again claiming position as joint rulers of the earth. But a bitter struggle was again imminent, since neither power was long willing to admit the supremacy or indeed the equality of the other.

In the eleventh century, Gregory VII sought to carry into effect his idea of the supremacy of the pope in all temporal as well as spiritual affairs (see). He sought to reform the Church within and to destroy the feudal authority of laymen over ecclesiastical vassals, and thus to make the Church in all its parts independent and dominant.

The struggle between Gregory and the Emperor Henry IV added to the papal prestige, and during the twelfth and thirteenth centuries the authority of the pope reached its height, with nearly all the kings of Europe acknowledging fealty to him for their possessions. About the middle of the thirteenth century, the temporary ascendency of Frederick II was followed by the unrivaled papal domination for a time. In the fourteenth century the rise of independent states, the removal of the papal seat to Avignon, the great Schism, resulting in two popes, two capitals, and a divided Church, practically destroyed the temporal power of the pope save in central Italy, and weakened his spiritual authority.

For an excellent detailed account of the papacy and its relation to the state, its rise and downfall as a temporal power, see Emerton, Mediæval Europe; Bryce's Holy Roman Empire is also especially valuable.

*

The legislative body of France, the States-General, was not summoned between 1614 and 1789. During that time the laws were mere royal edicts. The term "parliament" in French usage means not a legislative body, but a law court.

*

In the fifth century the schools of the Roman empire, modeled on the secular schools of earlier pagan Greece and Rome, were swept away. In their place the Church established schools in connection with cathedrals and monasteries. These taught only what was needed for the clerical and monastic life. Until the eighth century there were no schools for the education of the laity, as indeed there was little opportunity for the use of education by a layman. In England and France, in the eighth and ninth centuries, there was a revival of education due largely to Alcuin and the fostering care of Charlemagne and Alfred the Great. Both monastic and cathedral schools were improved, while new schools were established. Amid the anarchy of the tenth century there was again a relapse, from which came a revival in the eleventh century leading to the establishment of the mediæval universities. Cf. West's Alcuin and the Rise of the Christian Schools; Mullinger's Schools of Charles the Great.

*

The rise of Christianity improved the condition of the slave by inculcating more humane ideas regarding his treatment. The Roman emperors under the influence of the Church softened many of the harsh features of the system, and the clergy at the same time advocated manumission as a religious duty. During the middle ages the attitude of the Church was pretty steadily that of opposition to slavery. It must not, however, be a matter of surprise that an institution so closely connected with the industrial life of the world was not removed until a change could be made in general economic habits. It has even been held by some that the amelioration of the condition of the slave and serf without manumission, was better for society and the slave than complete emancipation would have been during some portions of this period.

*

The wager of battle was an appeal to arms to determine the truth as between two parties, in the belief that divine power would give the victory to the right man. The ordeals were of various kinds—lot, walking over hot iron, immersing the hand in hot water. If an accused person appealed to one of these and escaped injury, he was cleared. Under the oath of compurgation, the accused was freed if on oath he declared himself innocent and produced a certain number of other persons to swear that they believed his statement. All through the middle ages the Church was endeavoring to replace these and other Teutonic laws with laws and ideas drawn from the old Roman law. Consult the admirable account of the German legal ideas in Chapter VIII of Emerton's Introduction to the Middle Ages.

†

The Roman law had never entirely disappeared from use in Europe. It influenced the formation of the canon law, and some of its principles had early modified the Teutonic law. With the rise of the universities its study was renewed, and gradually it supplanted German law in continental Europe. While the Church did much to preserve and to spread the principles of Roman law, it is too much to affirm that but for the Church it would have perished. One of the two great gifts of the ancient world to the modern was the Roman law.

*

Penance included sorrow for sin, reformation, and the doing of expiatory works. The sacrament of penance in the Church embraced the granting of forgiveness of sins, by the absolution of a priest, to those who repented, confessed, and performed satisfaction. In the early days public confession and penance was common, but after the time of the crusades almsdoing, fasts, and pilgrimages were usually enjoined in place of public penance.

*

See especially Bentham's Principles of Morals and Legislation, chaps. xii-xiv.

†

The Truce of God was a regulation of the Church enjoining the suspension of all private warfare from Wednesday evening to Monday morning in each week, also during the seasons of Advent and Lent, and on the great feasts. It was also binding at all times in certain places, as churches and convents, and for the protection of certain classes, as pilgrims, women, bishops, monks, clerks, merchants. This regulation appears first to have been introduced at a synod in Roussillon, in 1027, whence it spread over Aquitaine, France, Germany, Italy, Spain, and England. It was enjoined by numerous councils of the Church. Excommunication and banishment were its penalties. Its greatest force was in the twelfth century. Emerton, noting that many churchmen wished to do away entirely with private warfare as a means of settling differences, adds, "The demand not to fight at all was too much for mediæval human nature." The Truce was all that was

practicable in that period.
*

It must not be forgotten that true advance in knowledge and in scientific methods came only in opposition to, and by the breakdown of, the authority of the Church over the intellect. Independent thinking even in philosophy was not permitted in the middle ages. The influence of the Church and also of the scholastic system was to train and develop the intellect, but not to add to knowledge.
†

What is stated in this paragraph is more exactly true of the influence of the Christian religion—of Christianity as an uplifting force than of the Church as an institution. The true spirit of Christianity and the authority and influence of the organized Church have not always pointed or moved in one and the same direction.
*

These barbarians, it will be remembered, followed the Arian heresy, both those who embraced Christianity before the invasion of the empire and those who did so after that event. The Burgundians, converted by Arian missionaries in 433, adopted the Catholic faith about 517. The Franks, following the example of Clovis, embraced the orthodox faith in 497.
H.
*

It cannot be truly affirmed that the Church as a whole had any such object. This is too sweeping a generalization.
†

Gregory of Tours (540-594) was the father of mediæval French history. His Historia Ecclesiastica Francorum covers the fifth and sixth centuries, and is almost the only source of information for this period. His avowed aim was to recount "the wars of kings with hostile nations, of martyrs with pagans, of churches with heretics."
*

Monasticism, or monachism—a life of religious retirement—is of pre-Christian origin, and is found in connection with most of the leading religions. St. Anthony of Egypt, born in 251, is generally regarded as the founder of Christian monachism. He lived, a hermit, in the Egyptian desert, whither many, attracted by his holiness, followed and adopted the ascetic life. Pachomius of the Thebaid built a monastery in the fourth century where the ascetics dwelt together cœnobites); he was the first to form rules for the organization, thus giving a government to the system. St. Basil in the same century spent several years in monastic life, and after he became Bishop of Cæsarea published a code of rules for the regulation of the cœnobitic monachism, substantially as they remain to-day for the Greek Church.
Among the earliest communities of monks in Gaul was that established about 375 by St. Martin of Tours, at Marmoutiers, where he built a convent. About 415 John Cassian founded a large monastery near Marseilles, and by his writings did much to spread through the West a knowledge of Eastern monachism.
The first regular order with monastic vows and a complete organization was established by St. Benedict of Nursia, who in 529 founded the famous convent of Monte Casino near Naples, whence went forth the order of the Benedictines. The strict rules laid down by him were adopted in all the European convents. The monks were to take the vows of poverty, chastity, and obedience; their rules of discipline required them to devote their time to study, and to manual labor, mainly agricultural. Asceticism of a moderate type was enjoined.

By the influence of Gregory the Great monasticism first entered upon the field of missionary work among the barbarians. During the dark period from the sixth century to the ninth the monks rendered great services to the cause of religion, letters, and civilization. By their industrious hands waste forests and barren lands were converted into rich and productive gardens; in the convents were preserved all the remains of ancient learning; there missionaries were educated. At first monks were laymen, but before the tenth century they formed a class of the clergy. During the earlier period the monasteries and their inhabitants had been subject to thebishop of the diocese, but by the twelfth century they had been made immediately subject to papal jurisdiction.

Reverence for these institutions, and gratitude for the benefits they conferred, led to gifts and endowments on the part of the pious laity, until at length the monasteries became as notorious for riches, luxury, and corruption, as they were at first for simplicity, devotion, and industry.

*

Gregory VII (Hildebrand) succeeded Alexander II in the papal chair in 1073. He virtually governed the Church during the time of his predecessor, and was indeed the real author of the decree of Nicholas II, 1059, by which the power of nominating and confirming the pope was taken from the German emperors and vested in the cardinals. His whole life was devoted to aggrandizing the power of the Holy See. His talents were great, and his energy indomitable. He died in 1085. For the rise and progress of the papal power, see Hallam's Middle Ages, chap. vii; Ranke's History of the Popes; [Bryce's Holy Roman Empire; Duruy's History of the Middle Ages; and Emerton's Mediæval Europe.]

The papal power was at its height from the time of Innocent III, 1194, to that of Boniface VIII, 1294, after which it sensibly declined. H.

*

The reform of Cluny started from the establishment of a monastery at Cluny, in Aquitaine, in 910. Here the Benedictine rules were vigorously enforced, and monastic life brought back to its power form of extreme asceticism. Beyond this, however, was the idea that monasticism had a wider mission in reforming the outside world. Other monasteries in Europe caught the idea, and an association was organized known as the Congregation of Cluny, that included numbers throughout all Europe. The Abbot of Cluny was regarded as the real head of the organization. The influence of this movement was to give a purer tone to all monastic life, and to affect the religious life outside the monastery. Hildebrand (Gregory VII) was a monk at Cluny, and his reforms were in line with the "Cluny movement." Later, but, in many respects, not greater, was the reform of St. Bernard, and the founding by him of the Cistercian community at Clairvaux (1115).

*

Abelard was one of the most prominent founders of Scholasticism. The significance of the quarrel between Abelard and St. Bernard was that it exemplified the whole struggle between freedom of thought and inquiry, and the authoritative rule of the Church as enforced by the extremists.

*

The centralization of the power of administering local affairs in France, begun in the thirteenth century, was completed under Louis XIV (1643-1715). An agent of the king, the intendant, was absolute ruler in each of the provinces into which France was divided; in each town or commune within the province there was a subagent of the intendant, who exercised by authority of the king all the powers of local government. In many communes the people ceased even to elect local officers, either legislative or administrative. In others they continued to elect, but the power and activity of the king's subagent left nothing for the elected officers to do. Thus all local government was centered in the king.

All this was swept away by the Revolution of 1780. Today, the residents of each commune and city elect a council, and the council chooses the mayor and his assistants. The local government is vested in and exercised by the council and mayor, but the latter is responsible to the central government of France and is removable by the President.

*

Of these, Frederick Karl von Savigny (1779-1861) is the only one of first rank. As a university professor in Germany and a writer on Roman law and institutions he exercised a great influence. His most important work in this connection is Geschichte des römischen Rechts im Mittelalter.

*

In the Roman municipality the curia, or senate, whose membership was based on a land qualification, deliberated on the affairs of the city and chose the magistrates.

†

These statements must be taken as only approximately exact. Conditions differed widely in different parts of Europe. In Italy and southern France the old municipalities appear to have retained during this entire period much of their old form and vitality. Further north the cities succumbed more readily to the mediæval influences, and lost power and activity; indeed, almost disappeared between the fifth and the tenth century.

*

The most potent cause of the revival of the old cities and the planting and growth of new ones in the tenth, eleventh, and later centuries, was the revival of industry and of commerce. So long as the unsettled life of the dark ages continued, so long as agriculture was almost the sole occupation, there were few reasons for the existence of cities. As soon, however, as the trade and commerce which had been wiped out by the barbarian inroads began again to be demanded by the improving civilization, cities sprang into life everywhere, and not least in northern France, in Germany, and in England, where in ancient times there had been few. Some of the monasteries had been granted the right of holding annual or more frequent fairs or markets, to which merchants resorted from wide distances. Gradually around such monasteries where market rights existed arose cities of artisans and traders. Again, on the feudal domains were artisans dependent upon the lord or suzerain, to whom the product of their labor belonged. These artisans grouped themselves in communities and villages, organized themselves into industrial associations (craft or artisan gilds), which came in various ways to exercise powers over industrial matters and to protect its members. The exact relation of these gilds to the towns and cities is not entirely clear, nor was it uniform throughout Europe. It is certain, however, that whether the gilds became in time cities, or remained subordinate to the municipalities, the towns and cities were a part of the feudal system in the eleventh and twelfth centuries, and were subject to feudal exactions and dues.

Thus industry and trade account for the revival of city life, the planting of new cities, and the growth of old ones. The causes for this development were substantially the same throughout western Europe. The reasons and the methods of their enfranchisement were widely variant in different countries.

The growth and enfranchisement of the cities, and especially the industrial organization and its connection with municipal life, have been the subject of the most scholarly investigations during recent years. Most of these studies are unavailable for English readers. The following contain

brief accounts of value: Duruy, History of the Middle Ages; Emerton, Mediæval Europe; Ashley, English Economic History; Gross, The Gild Merchant; Cunningham, English Industry and Commerce; Stubbs, Constitutional History of England.
*

The continuity of city life and municipal institutions from Roman time to modern was not so great, in all probability, as is assumed in the lecture. The rise of the free city was rather the rise of a new institution than the restoration of an old one, save in southern France and Italy.
*

To describe the exact relations of the cities to the feudal lords would demand too much space. In general it may be said that the inhabitants were individually or collectively liable for all the services and obligations which were due from vassals to their superiors, including allegiance, tribute, and aid. The burdensome nature of these exactions, the desire for more power over their own lives and affairs, led to the insurrection, the successful outcome of which constitutes "the enfranchisement of the towns."
*

It was mainly in France that the enfranchisement of the cities was attended with great violence and war. In Germany, England, and even in Italy while the results attained were similar, the process involved more of purchase and less of war. See, note.
*

Like all other treaties of peace, they stood until broken by one or both parties. The charters were frequently violated by the lords, or revoked by the king, in order that, as the price of their renewal, large payments of money might be obtained from the cities.
†

The first French commune was at Le Mans (1067), which was abolished after two years. After this, Cambrai (1076), Noyon, Beauvais, St. Quentin, and Laon (1106) followed in the order named, though they did not obtain charters until dates slightly later.
*

The apparent vacillation in the policy of the French kings until the latter part of the twelfth century was due in large degree to their uncertainty of their own power; they hesitated to favor the enfranchisement of the cities at the risk of the hostility of the large feudal lords, including especially the Church. Later, the policy of the monarch was consistently favorable to the cities.
*

There was great variety in the charters, but the privileges granted to the cities in the middle ages were in general these: the right of corporate property; a common seal; exemption from the more ignominious or oppressive tokens of feudal subjection, and the defined regulation of the rest; settled rules as to succession and private rights of property; and lastly, and of the greatest value, exemption from the royal jurisdiction, as well as from that of the territorial judges, and the right of being governed by magistrates of their own, either wholly, or (in some cases) partly chosen by themselves.
H.
*

The class here referred to is the great middle class—the bourgeoisie of France and the continent generally, the commons of England—made up of the merchants and traders, distinguished on the one hand from the nobility, on the other from the laborers and peasants.
*

See et seq.

*
There were two general types of government in the cities, communal and consular. In the former, the government was vested in a select body of from twelve to one hundred citizens. This body was probably elected by the citizens. It chose from its own number the chief executive officer of the commune, who, with the select body, exercised the administrative and judicial power of the city, subject to such control as still remained in the feudal lord whose vassal the commune was. In the consular cities a board of twelve consuls wielded the executive power, assisted by a council of not more than one hundred. For special purposes a larger assembly representing the entire body of citizens was summoned. The cities of Italy and southern France were of the latter class; those of northern France and parts of Germany were of the former. Many points concerning these governments are still buried in obscurity. M. Guizot's discussion throughout the lecture has special referrence to the French communes and cities.
*
The origin of these "trading companies"—the merchant and artisan gilds—and their exact connection with municipal life is still somewhat obscure, notwithstanding recent researches. The student may with profit consult Brentano's History and Development of Gilds, Gross's Gild Merchant, or Lambert's Two Thousand Years of Gild Life.
*
As the population of a town or city increased, the desire for and tendency towards self-government were natural. In France, as already stated, this was obtained, as a rule, only after a struggle between the city and the feudal lord upon whose domain the city stood. Later, the cities often obtained their charters or gained additional rights by purchase or on the gift of large sums of money to the suzerain or king. Whether it came as the result of war or of bargain, the end attained was the same: the commune or city received a charter from the feudal lord, by which the future relations of the lord and the commune were determined. Usually a regular, fixed payment by the commune was substituted for the irregular feudal exactions, and the amount and character of the military service due from the commune was fixed. Thereafter the lord's dealings were with the commune as a corporation, and not with the individual inhabitants. On the other hand, the commune gained the right of managing in great degree its own affairs. The charters varied, however, in the grant of powers. In some there was a mere substitution of corporate for individual relations to the suzerain, in others almost complete freedom from demands of the lord. Each communal or city charter was a grant of rights; to just the extent that the city gained power and privilege, by just so much was the authority of the lord diminished. This diminution of the power of the feudal baronage was welcomed by the king. Hence the cities often found ready aid from the monarch, in the twelfth and early thirteenth centuries. Note especially the policy of Louis VII (1137-1180). Later, however, the king, having established his own power more firmly, began to break down that of the cities by imposing upon them his own judicial and administrative officers. Thus, in France, the communes helped to break down feudalism, gained some rights of self-government, but instead of becoming and remaining entirely self-governing in their local affairs, were left in the end closely dependent on the monarch.
In Italy, so far as the enfranchisement was involved, much the same course was run by the cities. There was, however, no strong central government in Italy, hence the cities were able to take one step further and establish their complete independence, forming the city-republics that occupy so prominent a place in the later mediæval and early modern history of Italy. By the middle of the twelfth century the cities of Lombardy, with Milan at their head, had become extremely rich and powerful; they formed a confederation among themselves—the Lombard League—and

maintained an obstinate struggle for more than thirty years with Frederick Barbarossa, Emperor of Germany, which terminated in 1183 by the treaty of Constance, wherein the emperor renounced all legal privileges in the interior of the cities, acknowledged the right of the confederated cities to levy armies, erect fortifications, exercise criminal and civil jurisdiction by officers of their own appointment.

In Germany, the majority of the cities were of mediæval origin. Their development and enfranchisement resulted as in Italy. In the absence of any strong central power in Germany which could either compel their allegiance or protect their interests, they were obliged to rely on their own resources for defence.

Among the German cities, confederations were also formed; of these the most celebrated was the Hanseatic League, which originated in 1239-1241, from a convention between Lübeck, Hamburg, and one or two other cities, by which they agreed to defend each other against all oppression and violence, particularly of the nobles. The number of towns united in this league rapidly increased; it included at one time eighty-five cities. Regular diets were held every third year at Lübeck, the chief city of the confederacy. This league was at various times confirmed by kings and princes, and in the fourteenth century exercised a powerful political as well as commercial influence. It made treaties with other states, and maintained a fleet to protect its commercial rights. The league was dissolved in the seventeenth century. The League of the Rhine was a similar confederation. During the later middle ages the majority of these cities were absorbed into the states near them.

In England the feudal system never held so complete sway, and the cities gained rights of self-government by a more orderly process of development, through purchase from the lords of the manors and by charters from the kings, beginning with that of London.

The influence of the crusades in all these countries facilitated the enfranchisement of the cities. The literature of the subject in foreign languages is abundant. In English it is mainly confined to special chapters in general works. In addition to those already cited, see Adams, Civilization during the Middle Ages, chap. xii. Hallam's Middle Ages has been made less valuable by later researches. Zimmern, The Hansa Towns, contains some useful information.
*

On the history of the crusades the following may be consulted: Cox, The Crusades; Michaud, History of the Crusades; Gray, The Children's Crusade; Pears, The Fall of Constantinople; Von Sybel, The History and Literature of the Crusades; Mombert, A Short History of the Crusades.
*

A. G. P. de Barante, Histoire des Dues de Bourgogne de la Maison de Valois, 1364-1477. This work, in eight volumes, has never been translated into English. Other and later works dwell on the same facts. The turbulence noted was not mere disorder, but was in large part a struggle for the realization of better ideals and forms.
*

In the third period society utilized and gave definiteness and form to what had been begun in the second. In this sense the second period did produce something "durable"; it laid the foundations of modern government and society.
*

By the victory of Charles Martel at the battle of Tours (732).
†

Later scholarship has proved the stories of the visions and sufferings of Peter the Hermit to have been the invention of a later age. The pope, not Peter the Hermit, was the moving influence

towards the first crusade. It is doubtful if the latter was in the Holy Land before the first crusade.
*

One should remember, also, as a possible additional cause, that pilgrimages were a Christian duty, and a recognized
*

The chronicles of William of Tyre and James de Vitry are of the highest value for the thorough study of this period.
*

Mémoires sur les Relations Politiques des Princes Chrétiens avec les Empereurs Mongols. Deuxième Mémoire,.

"Many men of religious orders, Italians, French, and Flemings, were charged with diplomatic missions to the court of the Great Khan. Mongols of distinction came to Rome, Barcelona, Valentia, Lyons, Paris, London, and Northampton; and a Franciscan of the kingdom of Naples was archbishop of Pekin. His successor was a professor of theology in the university of Paris. But how many other people followed in the train of those personages, either as slaves, or attracted by the desire of profit, or led by curiosity into regions hitherto unknown! Chance has preserved the names of some of these. The first envoy who visited the King of Hungary on the part of the Tartars was an Englishman, who had been banished from his country for certain crimes, and who, after having wandered over Asia, at last entered into the service of the Mongols. A Flemish friar, in the heart of Tartary, fell in with a woman of Metz, called Paquette, who had been carried off into Hungary; a Parisian goldsmith and a young man from the neighborhood of Rouen, who had been at the taking of Belgrade. In the same country he fell in also with Russians, Hungarians, and Flemings. A singer, called Robert, after having travelled through Eastern Asia, returned to end his days in the cathedral of Chartres. A Tartar was a furnisher of helmets in the armies of Philip the Fair. Jean de Plancarpin fell in, near Gayouk, with a Russian gentleman whom he calls Temer, and who acted as an interpreter; and many merchants of Breslau, Poland, and Austria, accompanied him in his journey into Tartary. Others returned with him through Russia; they were Genoese, Pisans, and Venetians. Two Venetians, merchants, whom chance had brought to Bokhara, followed a Mongol ambassador, sent by Houlagou to Khoubilaï. They remained many years in China and Tartary, returned with letters from the Great Khan to the pope, and afterwards went back to the Khan, taking with them the son of one of their number, the celebrated Marco Polo, and once more left the court of Khoubilaï to return to Venice. Travels of this nature were not less frequent in the following century. Of this number are those of John Mandeville, an English physician; Oderic de Frioul, Pegoletti, Guilleaume de Bouldeselle, and several others. It may well be supposed, that those travels of which the memory is preserved, form but a small part of those which were undertaken, and there were in those days many more people who were able to perform those long journeys than to write accounts of them. Many of those adventurers must have remained and died in the countries they went to visit. Others returned home, as obscure as before, but having their imagination full of the things they had seen, relating them to their families, with much exaggeration no doubt, but leaving behind them, among many ridiculous fables, useful recollections and traditions capable of bearing fruit. Thus, in Germany, Italy, and France, in the monasteries, among the nobility, and even down to the lowest classes of society, there were deposited many precious seeds destined to bud at a somewhat later period. All these unknown travellers, carrying the arts of their own country into distant regions, brought back other pieces of knowledge not less precious, and, without being aware of it, made exchanges more advantageous than those of commerce. By these

means, not only the traffic in the silks, porcelain, and other commodities of Hindostan, became more extensive and practicable, and new paths were opened to commercial industry and enterprise; but, what was more valuable still, foreign manners, unknown nations, extraordinary productions, presented themselves in abundance to the minds of the Europeans, which, since the fall of the Roman empire, had been confined within too narrow a circle. Men began to attach some importance to the most beautiful, the most populous, and the most anciently civilized of the four quarters of the world. They began to study the arts, the religions, the languages, of the nations by whom it was inhabited; and there was even an intention of establishing a professorship of the Tartar language in the university of Paris. The accounts of travellers, strange and exaggerated, indeed, but soon discussed and cleared up, diffused more correct and varied notions of those distant regions. The world seemed to open, as it were, towards the East; geography made an immense stride; and ardor for discovery became the new form assumed by European spirit of adventure. The idea of another hemisphere, when our own came to be better known, no longer seemed an improbable paradox, and it was when in search of the Zipangri of Marco Polo that Christopher Columbus discovered the New World."
*

More exact would it be to say that the feudal barons as a class lost their importance as a political factor. Feudalism as a system did not long survive the crusades. The king, on the one hand, notably in France, and the people—the Third Estate—on the other, succeeded to the feudal power. The crusades re-enforced the influence of the cities in breaking down feudalism.
*

Probably the greatest direct effect of the crusades was the stimulation given to commerce, through the knowledge they brought to Europe of Oriental and other products. With the knowledge came the desire to possess. The cities of Italy date their commercial importance from this time. They retained it until the discovery of oceanic routes to the Orient carried the stream of commerce away from the Mediterranean.
*

One of the outgrowths of the crusades is worthy of note here. Between the first and second crusades were formed in the Holy Land three great military orders: the Knights of St. John or of the Hospital, the Knights of the Temple, and the Teutonic Knights. The first was organized to care for and defend sick and wounded pilgrims; the second, to defend the pilgrims to the Holy Land; the third, to succor German pilgrims. Their services to Christianity made them the recipients of large estates, and other wealth, to be used for the purposes of the order. After the era of the crusades they established themselves in Europe, where they obtained great wealth and influence. See Woodhouse, Military Religious Orders of the Middle Ages.
*

The following chronological table may serve to put before the student's eye a connected outline of the principal facts. Eight crusades are enumerated.
First Crusade—ad 1096-1099. Urban II, Pope.
1094. Peter the Hermit, by direction of the pope, preaches a crusade throughout Europe.
1095. Council of Clermont in France. (A previous council had been held at Piacenza.) Attended by the pope and an immense concourse of clergy and nobles. The crusade proclaimed; great privileges, civil and ecclesiastical, granted to all who should "assume the cross"; a year allowed to prepare. Peter the Hermit, not waiting, sets out at the head of a vast rabble of undisciplined fanatics and marauders, who perish by disease, famine, and the sword, in Asia Minor.
1096. An army of 200,000 or 300,000 mounted and mailed warriors, and men capable of

bearing arms, and a multitude of monks, women, and children, depart from Europe and assemble on the plains of Bithynia, east of Constantinople. Principal leaders of the expedition, Godfrey of Bouillon, with his brothers Baldwin and Eustach; Robert, Duke of Normandy; Robert, Count of Flanders; Raymond of Toulouse; Hugo of Vermandois; Stephen de Blois; Bohemond, Prince of Tarentum, with his nephew Tancred.

1097. Nicæa taken by the crusaders.

1098. Antioch and Edessa taken.

1099. Jerusalem taken; a Christian kingdom, on feudal principles, established; the crown conferred on Godfrey of Bouillon.

Interval, 1100-1147. Baldwin I succeeds his brother Godfrey as king of Jerusalem. A new army of crusaders destroyed by the Saracens in Asia Minor, and the remnant of the first army cut to pieces at Rama. Acre (Ptolemais), Berytus, and Sidon taken. Later, the Christian army unsuccessful; Edessa taken by the Turks in 1144; continued ill success of the Christians leads to a new crusade.

Second Crusade—1147-1149. Eugene III, Pope.

Leaders of this expedition, Conrad III, emperor of Germany, and Louis VII, king of France, who set out separately on their march. Both armies destroyed in Asia Minor by famine and the sword. The fugitives assemble at Jerusalem. Conrad, Louis, and Baldwin III, king of Jerusalem, lay siege to Damascus; the enterprise fails; Conrad and Louis return to Europe.

Interval, 1149-1189. Saladin takes possession of Egypt and founds a dynasty in 1175. Makes war upon the Christian kingdom of Jerusalem; defeats Guy of Lusignan at the battle of Tiberias; Guy taken prisoner; Acre and Jerusalem taken (1187). Conrad of Montferrat lays claim to the crown of Jerusalem, and rallies the remains of the Christian forces at Tyre.

Third Crusade—1189-1192. Clement III, Pope.

Leaders, Frederick I (Barbarossa), emperor of Germany, Philip Augustus, king of France, and Richard I, of England.

Frederick departs first with an army of 100,000 men, which is entirely destroyed in Asia Minor. The emperor himself is drowned in Cilicia, 1190. His son Frederick of Swabia afterwards killed at Acre.

1190. The kings of France and England embark by sea, and pass the winter in Sicily; the armies embroiled by the artifices of Tancred, usurping king of Jerusalem, and by dissension between the kings.

1191. The armies of France and England, with the Christian princes of Syria, take Acre. Philip Augustus returns to France, leaving a part of his army with Richard, who displays his bravery in some useless battles, but is unable to regain Jerusalem.

1192. Richard concludes a truce with Saladin and returns to Europe.

Fourth Crusade—1202-1204. Innocent III, Pope.

Leaders, Baldwin IX, Count of Flanders; Boniface II, Marquis of Montferrat; Henry Dandolo, Doge of Venice, and others. The kings of Europe could not be aroused to engage in this crusade, notwithstanding all the urgency of the Holy See. The chief command was conferred by the crusaders on Boniface of Montferrat. This expedition, however, never reached the Holy Land, but engaged in putting down a usurpation at Constantinople, which finally led to the taking and plundering of that city by the crusaders, and the division of the empire among the conquerors, of whom Baldwin was raised to the imperial dignity. The Latin empire of Constantinople was destroyed in 1261 by Michael Paleologus.

Interval, 1204-1217. Meantime the Christians in the East, though despoiled of most of their possessions, and weakened by divisions, bravely defended themselves against the sultans of Egypt. They continually invoked aid from Europe; but more powerful interests at home made the European princes regardless of their calls. Only those of more exalted imaginations could be influenced. There was a crusade of children in 1212.

Fifth Crusade—1218-1221. Honorius III, Pope.

Three kings, John de Brienne, titular king of Jerusalem, Andrew II, king of Hungary, and Hugh of Lusignan, king of Cyprus, united their forces at Acre. The king of Hungary was soon recalled by troubles at home; Hugh of Lusignan died; and John de Brienne went to attack Egypt alone. In 1221 the crusaders, after many reverses, submitted to a humiliating peace; John of Brienne, returning to Europe, gave his daughter in marriage to Frederick II, emperor of Germany, who thereby became titular king of Jerusalem.

Sixth Crusade—1228-1229. Gregory IX, Pope.

Leader, Frederick II. This emperor had taken the vows of the cross five years before, and, though anathematized by the pope, had failed to fulfil his engagement. At length he set out, and the Sultan Kameel yielded Jerusalem to him by treaty without battle. Frederick crowned himself king of Jerusalem. Threatened with the loss of his Italian dominions, he returned to Europe.

Seventh Crusade—1248-1254. Innocent IV, Pope.

Leaders, St. Louis (IX) and the French princes. The king of France engaged in this crusade in consequence of a vow made during a dangerous illness. Most of the princes of the blood and great vassals accompanied him. He turned his arms first against Egypt, and took Damietta in 1250; but his army, surprised by a sudden rising of the Nile, and carried off in great numbers by pestilence, was surrounded, and Louis himself, with 20,000 of his army, was made prisoner. He obtained his liberty, by payment of a heavy ransom and the surrender of Damietta. He remained four years in Palestine, repairing the fortifications of the towns which yet remained in the hands of the Christians (Ptolemais, Jaffa, Sidon, etc.), and mediating between the Christian and Mohammedan princes.

Eighth Crusade—1270. Clement IV, Pope.

Leaders, Louis IX; Charles of Anjou; Edward, prince of England, afterwards Edward I. This expedition was first directed to the coast of Africa; Louis deparked before Tunis and laid siege to that city; but the army was cut down by the plague, to which Louis himself and one of his sons fell victims. Charles of Anjou, his brother, made peace with the Mohammedans, and renounced the expedition to the Holy Land. This was the last crusade. H.

*

The nobility of England had been much weakened by the Wars of the Roses in the fifteenth century, and with the accession of Henry VII, the first of the Tudors (1485), was begun the policy of upbuilding the power of the king by breaking down that of the nobles, and by rendering the commons subservient. This policy characterized the entire Tudor dynasty (1485-1603). Respect for the public authority was greatly increased during this period.

*

Henri Benjamin Constant de Rebecque (1757—1830), French publicist and statesman, an ardent admirer and advocate of constitutional government, and especially monarchy; the author of many political essays and pamphlets in favor of constitutionalism, which were published collectively under the title Cours de Politique Constitutionelle.

†

The constitution of Brazil, sworn to by the first emperor, Dom Pedro I, March 25, 1824, was variously modified during the ensuing ten years.

*

The present century has witnessed a decided tendency away from monarchy towards even extreme democracy. The necessity of a strong central administrative power in each government is admitted, but that this must take the form of monarchy is not claimed by modern political scientists. That the legislative power should be in the hands of the people is generally conceded. Possibly it may be affirmed that at present (1896) there is a slight tendency towards reaction from extreme democracy.

*

See, note.

†

Nevertheless the right to elect whomsoever they pleased remained in the people—the tribe. The establishment of hereditary succession in a given tribe depended more upon the personal character of the descendants in a family once elected, than upon any deliberate change of custom on the part of the tribe.

*

It was in form rather than in reality that even the first emperors ruled as representatives of the people. Myers, in his History of Rome, has the following neat statement of the matter: "Octavius carefully veiled his really absolute sovereignty under the forms of the old republican state. The senate still existed, but so completely subjected were its members to the influence of the conqueror, that the only function it really exercised was the conferring of honors and titles and abject flatteries on its master. All the republican officials remained, but Octavius absorbed and exercised their chief powers and functions. He had the powers of consul, tribune, censor, and Pontifix Maximus. All the republican magistrates—the consuls, the tribunes, the prætors—were elected as usual, but they were simply the nominees and creatures of the emperor. They were the effigies and figure-heads to delude the people into believing that the republic still existed. Never did a people seem more content with the shadow after the loss of the substance."

*

See, note.

*

Forum judicum, i, lib. 2; tit. i, l. 2, l. 4.

*

The Merovingian dynasty, 481-751.

†

Marcus Aurelius Cassiodorus (468(?)-568), Roman historian and statesman, whose writings, Variarum Epistolarum Libri XII, are the principal source of information on Italy and the Ostrogothic kingdom in the sixth century.

‡

The Church Councils of Toledo constituted the legislative assembly in the Visigothic kingdom. See.

*

See, note, and 90, note.

*

Louis VI (the Fat) came to the throne in 1108.

*

Suger was Abbot of St. Denis and minister of Louis VI (the Fat). His idea of monarchy is well, if not completely, expressed in his own words: "It is the duty of kings to repress, by their power and the innate right of their office, the audacity of the nobles who rend the state by ceaseless wars, desolate the poor, and destroy the churches."

*

This is true of constitutional monarchy, but hardly of such forms of monarchy as existed on the continent of Europe prior to the nineteenth century. The monarchy of Louis XIV was a revival of the fact, if not of the theory, of imperial monarchy, which centered in the rulers all powers by absorption, not by any representative functions.

†

For a good account of the facts of French history underlying this lecture, consult Duruy's History of France.

*

See.

*

See Lectures V and VI.

*

See et seq.

*

See.

*

This was especially true of the Gallican church. The statement as it stands is too broad. For some of the more important disputes between the councils and the popes, see et seq.

*

See.

÷

The reference here is to the Dictatus Papæ, a document among the papers of Gregory, containing a brief statement of his theory of the papacy and its superiority to all other earthly powers. There is, however, no evidence that this document was ever made public in Gregory's time, hence the statement of the lecture is not well founded. For a copy of this document, see Matthews, Select Mediæval Documents, or Emerton's Mediæval Europe,.

×

There is abundant room for difference of opinion here. Certain it is that during the next century the papacy most nearly attained the supremacy which it sought. That this was due in great part to Gregory VII is generally admitted.

†

The Hohenstaufens occupied the imperial throne from 1138 to 1254. Frederick I (Barbarossa), 1152-1190, and Frederick II, 1212-1250, were the most noted members. Under Pope Innocent III, 1198-1216, the papacy reached its height, and the Hohenstaufens were humbled, though the empire temporarily recovered under Frederick II.

*

Louis IX (St. Louis) reigned in France from 1226 to 1270; during this time the royal power was greatly increased. The Pragmatic Sanction referred to, bearing date March, 1268, is now commonly believed to have been a later forgery. However that may be, St. Louis was strenuous and persistent in upholding the independence of the king in temporal affairs, and in its right to supervise ecclesiastical matters in France. See Guizot, History of France, chap. xviii.

†

The term Pragmatic Sanction is commonly applied to four ordinanees published at a subsequent

date: 1. That of Charles VII, of France, issued at Bourges, in 1438, by which the papal power
was limited, and the independence of the French Church in various particulars declared—
conformably to the canons of the Council of Basel. This council commenced in 1431 and closed
in 1449. It passed a great many canons declaring the pope subject to the decrees of general
councils, limiting his powers, and decreeing the reformation of various abuses and corruptions of
discipline and practice. The history of this council, as well as that of the earlier council held at
Constance in 1414-'18, is deeply interesting. 2. The decree passed by Charles VI, emperor of
Germany, in 1439, confirming the canons of the Council of Basel, is also called a Pragmatic
Sanction. 3. The decree of Charles VI (1713) respecting the succession to the imperial throne. 4.
The law of succession proclaimed by Charles III, of Spain, in 1759. H.

‡

The attempt of Boniface VIII (1294-1303) to interfere in the government of France was met by
the denial and nullification, from the French monarch (Philip the Fair) and States-General, of the
pope's supremacy over the state.
A bull of Boniface VIII (1296), Clericis Laicos, forbade the clergy to pay taxes to the secular
power. Edward I outlawed all clergy in England who undertook to obey the bull. The statute of
mortmain in England (1279) was also aimed at the power of the Church.

*

Ostrogothic kingdom, 493-555; Lombard kingdom, 568-774.

*

The struggles with the emperors of Germany began with the reign of Otho I (936-973), who
revived the Holy Roman Empire and again extended its authority over Italy.

*

Professor Emerton gives the following admirable summary of Italian institutional history:
"Under the Carolingian system the city became in Italy the natural unit of administration. It fell
under the control of the count, and most often this person was also the bishop. . . . From the
eleventh century on, an organized popular movement is visible and becomes more and more of a
force until it displaces the episcopal government and puts in its place a democracy with elective
magistrates, and a strong aristocratic element. From the thirteenth century we notice the rise to
power within the democracies of this aristocracy based upon certain well-marked families. From
the fifteenth century some one among the great families in each community forces its way to
leadership, and produces a series of tyrants who carry on the business of the state, until they
finally bring it out into the petty 'legitimate' monarchy of the sixteenth and seventeenth
centuries."—Mediæval Europe,. For the history of Italy during the period covered by the lecture,
consult Hunt, History of Italy, or Sismondi, History of the Italian Republics.

*

Since this lecture was delivered the unification of Italy has been accomplished, so far as outward
form goes, and the process of actual fusion of the various states that existed in Guizot's time into
one real Italy is rapidly progressing. One of the marked characteristics of the present century has
been the tendency to consolidation and unification of national states, and Italy is a conspicuous
example.

†

It is, of course, obvious that Guizot does less than exact justice to republican government here, as
he does more than justice to monarchy in the preceding lecture. That a republic is likely to
exhibit less fixedness of purpose and policy, and less firmness and force in administration, than
is a monarchy, is true; but that the idea, the principle, of monarchy is essential to orderly

government, the present century seems to have disproved.
*

The crusade against the Albigenses was twofold in its cause and its purpose: first, religious, to put down a growing heresy or tendency against conformity to the beliefs of the Church; second, political, to destroy the power of the lords of the south, notably Raymond of Toulouse, in whose territories the Albigenses were. That there was wide diversity of interest between the north and the south of France; that the municipalities of the south were numerous, prosperous, and powerful; that the outcome of the crusade was the absorption of the southern regions into dependence on the crown—all this is true. To regard the movement, however, as primarily or fundamentally a crusade against republican institutions as typified in the municipalities of southern France, is to miss much of its meaning.
†

According to the formerly accepted story—which seems to have been adopted by Guizot—the confederacy of the Swiss cantons took its origin in the united revolt (1307) of the three forest cantons, Uri, Schwyz, and Unterwalden, against the encroachments of Albert of Austria, a Hapsburg ruler. This account, first found in documents written at least two centuries after the supposed event, is now regarded as unhistorical. The essential known facts are these: The three cantons were in the twelfth and thirteenth centuries substantially in feudal dependence on the non-resident Hapsburg counts. Throughout the thirteenth century they were seeking to release themselves from this dependence. In 1231, Canton Uri, in 1240, Schwyz, were granted charters by the emperor releasing them from Hapsburg domination, and establishing their direct feudal dependence on the empire. In 1291 these two cantons and Unterwalden formed a permanent league; in 1309 their charters were confirmed by the Emperor Henry VII; in 1316 these charters were recognized by Emperor Ludwig. During the fourteenth and fifteenth centuries the confederation grew, and the authority of the empire weakened. After 1340 no representative of the empire remained regularly in the cantons. The establishment of the independent republican governments was thus not a sudden process, but a gradual growth.
*

The first States-General of France, in the proper meaning of the word, as including the clergy, nobility, and commons or deputies from the towns, was convoked by Philip the Fair in 1302. The feudal nobility had before this time submitted to the appellant jurisdiction of the crown, exercised by the royal tribunals; they had also lost the legislative supremacy in their fiefs; and now, when the commons became a co-ordinate branch of the national legislature, they lost their last privilege of territorial independence. H.
*

The cities of Castile were early invested with chartered privileges, including civil rights and extensive property, on condition of protecting their country. The deputies of the cities are not, however, mentioned as composing a branch of the Cortes or general legislative council of the nation until 1169, and then in only one case. But from the year 1189 they became a regular and essential part of that assembly. Subsequently, through the exercise of the royal prerogative in withholding the writ of summons, and through the neglect of many cities in sending deputies, the representation became extremely limited, and the privilege itself was gradually lost; so that in 1480 only seventeen cities retained the right of sending representatives. The concurrence of the Cortes of Castile was necessary to all taxation and grants of money, and also to legislation in general, as well as to the determination of all great and weighty affairs. The nobles and clergy formed the two other estates of the Cortes; but they seem to have been less regularly summoned than even the deputies of the towns.

In the kingdom of Aragon, no law could be enacted or repealed without the consent of the Cortes; and by the "General Privilege," a sort of Magna Charta, granted in 1283, this body was to be assembled every year at Saragossa—though it was afterwards summoned once in two years, and the place of assembling left to the discretion of the king. The Cortes of this kingdom consisted of four estates: the prelates; the commanders of military orders, who were reckoned as ecclesiastics; the barons; the knights or infanzones; and the deputies of the royal towns. This body by itself, when in session, and by a commission during its recess, exercised very considerable powers, both legislative and administrative. Valencia and Catalonia had also each its separate Cortes both before and after their union with Aragon. See Hallam, Middle Ages, vol. i, chap. iv. H.
*

For the history of the period covered by this lecture, see Duruy's Middle Ages, and special histories of the several countries.
*

The Hundred Years' War (1336-1453) between France and England was a contest due to rivalry over certain feudal possessions in France and Flanders, and to the claim of the English king, Edward III (1327-1377), to the French throne. The first period (1336-1360), in which the English gained victories at Crecy (1346) and Poitiers (1356), ended in the treaty of Bretigny, by which Edward obtained feudal possession of Aquitaine and a few other provinces, and gave up all claim to the French crown. In the second period (1360-1420) Aquitaine was overrun by the French, the war renewed by Henry V (1413-1422) of England, and the French humiliated through internal quarrels and English victories, notably Agincourt (1415). By the treaty of Troyes (1420) the crowns of the two countries were to be united on the head of the English king after the death of the reigning French sovereign (Charles VI). The war was renewed (third period, 1420-1453) because the French people refused to carry out the treaty, and on the death of Charles VI (1422) recognized his son, Charles VII, as king. The French, inspired by Jeanne d'Arc, finally drove out the English, who at the end of the war, in 1453, retained on the Continent only Calais.
*

Philip VI, the first king of the house of Valois, came to the throne in 1328. H.
*

The insanity of Charles VI, the dissensions among the nobility, and the success of the English in the Hundred Years' War, were all contributory causes to this.
*

The general term taille, or tax, seems here appropriated to the particular tax made perpetual in the reign of Charles VII, who frequently levied money by his own authority. In general the kings did not claim the absolute prerogative of imposing taxes without the consent of the States-General; though they often in emergencies violently stretched their power. The taille was commonly assessed by respectable persons chosen by the advice of the parish priests—a privilege of importance to the tax-payers, who were allowed some voice in the repartition of the tax. This is, however, entirely distinct from that consent of the people to the tax which the theory of the French constitution made requisite. It is asserted that this perpetual taille was granted by the States-General in 1439, but this does not appear in the terms of any ordinance.

One thing is certain, that this tax, whether at first established with or without the concurrence of the States-General, was perpetual, and managed without any check upon the crown. The two acts of the reign of Charles VII, the establishment of a standing military force, and a perpetual tax for its support, were the great events of the period, and fatal to the liberties of France. There was henceforth but little check to the increasing power of the crown. The nobles lost their political influence; the people gained nothing. The precedent was improved by succeeding monarchs, until the absolute despotism of the crown was completely established.

H.

The taille was a land tax, but, instead of falling uniformly on all lands, was levied only on land held by commoners.

†

The parliament of Grenoble was established in 1453; that of Dijon in 1479. The term parliament in French history denotes always a judicial and not a legislative body. For a long time there was but a single parliament, that of Paris, the organization of which was defined by Philip the Fair in 1302. The first division came when the provincial parliament at Toulouse was created in 1443. The other provincial parliaments are indicated above.

*

Charles the Bold, Duke of Burgundy, was defeated and slain at Nancy (1477), and Burgundy was annexed to France, thus ending a long rivalry and contest.

÷

For an excellent sketch of French history during the period of this chapter, see Duruy's History of France,.

*

The Inquisition was an organization under authority of the Church for the detection, punishment, and suppression of heresy. The idea that it was a duty of the Church to ferret out and punish heresy had been common from the early days. The outburst of heretical ideas in southern France in the twelfth and thirteenth centuries—for example, the Albigenses—occasioned a more definite organization of inquisitorial processes. The name was borrowed from the duties of certain civil officers of France touching taxation. A formal tribunal was created, and by papal authority it soon became the special function of the Dominicans to carry on the work. It found strongest foothold in Spain. There it had a political function in part, but only because the unorthodox in matters of religion—the Jews, the Moors, and, later, the Protestants—were also usually independent in their political thinking, and hence were regarded as a menace to the government.

*

The house of Hapsburg (Austria) occupied the throne of Austria and of the Holy Roman Empire of Germany from 1438 to 1740.

†

The Hundred Years' War, 1336-1453; the Wars of the Roses, 1455-1485.

*

See, note.

*

The same idea is recognized in the constitutions of all free republics. The treaty-making power, and the conduct of international and diplomatic business, are placed in the hands of the executive. The attempt of the people, or even of the legislature, to dictate or guide matters in this field generally produces confusion and international discord. When, however, the question of war and its expenses is involved, modern ideas demand that the people, or their representatives, should be consulted.

*

Allowance should be made for the fact that the parliament did not have full confidence in James,

and that he did not give unqualified assent to their desire for war.
*

The quarrel between Boniface VIII (1294-1303) and Philip IV of France resulted in the election of a Frenchman as pope in 1305 (Clement V), who transferred the papal throne to Avignon (1309), where it was under the domination of the French king until 1376, when it was restored to Rome. During this period of "Babylonian captivity" the papacy lost authority with other nations, and even, at last, with some of the clergy. In 1378, upon the death of Gregory XI, a dispute arose between the French and the Italian cardinals over the election of his successor. Each party elected a pope, one of whom sat at Rome, the other at Avignon. Two popes, two capitals, and a divided Church were fatal to papal authority.
*

See, note. This Pragmatic Sanction recognized the authority of general councils as superior to that of the pope, restored to churches and abbeys the right of electing their heads, forbade the payment of annates, and permitted the reception and publication in France of papal bulls only after the king's approval.
*

The Concordat increased both papal and kingly power by placing the selection of bishops and abbots in the hands of the king, by giving the pope the annates or first year's revenue of every ecclesiastical benefice within the king's nomination. The principle that the pope was subordinate to the general council was given up.
†

The Jansenists and the Gallicans differed on points of theology, but were at one in opposing the claims of supremacy in the Church contended for and exercised by the pope.
‡

These propositions, drawn up by Bossuet, were decreed by a convocation of the French clergy assembled by Louis XIV, in 1682, and are called the Quatuor Propositiones Cleri Gallicani. They declare that power and authority are given by God to the Vicar of Christ in spiritual, but not in temporal things; that this power is limited and restrained by the laws of the Church and general councils; and that the sentence of the pope is not unchangeable unless sanctioned by the Church Catholic; [and that the rules and usages received in France and in the Gallican Church shall remain unchangeable]. These decrees are the foundation of the independence of the Gallican Church. H.
*

The fundamental feature marking the views of Huss was the placing of the Scriptures above the ordinances and dogmas of the Church as a basis for theological opinion. This, carried to its logical conclusion, was necessarily a repudiation of the final authority of both Church and pope as interpreters of theological belief.
*

The influence of the revival of learning on the subsequent civilization of Europe is too important to be discussed in a few words. The fact that the lecturer at the outset limited himself to "the history of the exterior events of the visible and social world" is his excuse for not tracing the development of the human mind during these momentous centuries. The revival of classical study was but one phase of the Renaissance. It is possible to trace the development of the movement. The nature and various stages in the progress of the revival are seen in the Arabian schools in Spain, scholasticism, the growth and spread of schools and universities in the twelfth and thirteenth centuries, the rise of modern languages and literatures of Europe, the humanists and the revival of classic learning, the spread of Greek learning after the fall of Constantinople, new scientific methods, printing, and the spread of literature.

*

Pietro Bembo (1470-1547), Italian scholar and cardinal; loose in his life; princely in his method of living; a devotee of literature, and a writer of pure and classic taste. See Symonds, Renaissance in Italy, ii,.

*

This act may be considered as the logical consequence of social forces set in motion by the posting of the ninety-five theses in 1517. For a carefully prepared translation of these theses, and of other documents connected with this period, see Translations and Reprints from the Original Sources of European History (University of Pennsylvania), vol. ii, No. 6.

*

Henry, Duke of Guise, organized the Holy League (1576), of which the ostensible purpose was to resist the Huguenots, but the real purpose was to aid the duke in gaining the crown. His death, and also that of the king, in 1589, not only dissolved the league, but made certain the accession of Henry of Navarre.

*

Consult Lecture XIII.

†

Richelieu's policy in the Thirty Years' War was dictated purely by political motives.

‡

The Fronde, a political party and insurrection whose chief aim was to stir up strife against the government, bears a superficial resemblance to the Great Rebellion in England. They were alike so far as both made absolutism the prime object of attack, but utterly different in the spirit underlying each. The religious element was entirely wanting to the Fronde.

*

See.

*

Especially was this the case in Germany. In England and Spain, commerce and colonization are prominent facts of the period, while in France the upbuilding of the monarchy stands out in high relief.

×

See, 310ff.

÷

The reappearance of the religious reform movement connects itself closely with the revival of learning, the two chief phenomena of which are the founding of universities in Germany and the multiplication of books. These factors forbade the dissolution of reform ideas. Books preserved the thoughts of Wycliffe and Huss. The printing press disseminated those of Erasmus and Luther.

÷

It is manifestly impossible within the space of a brief note to attempt any historical sketch of this great period. A good knowledge of the events is, however, essential to the appreciation of M. Guizot's discussion. In addition to the brief accounts given in the general histories ordinarily accessible, the following works may be used with advantage by the student who desires a more comprehensive idea of the scope and meaning of the period: Seebohm, Protestant Reformation (contains a brief but good bibliography); Ranke, History of the Popes; Häusser, The Period of the Reformation; Fisher, History of the Reformation; D'Aubigne, History of the Reformation (intensely Protestant); Spalding, History of the Protestant Reformation (strongly Roman Catholic); Köstlin's Martin Luther will also be found of value. Fisher, Outlines of Universal History, and Andrews, Institutes of General History, give brief bibliographies. (that is, of the confession and satisfaction which are performed under the ministry of priests)."

"The penalty thus continues as long as the hatred of self (that is, true inward penitence); namely, till our entrance into the kingdom of heaven."

"(35) They preach no Christian doctrine who teach that contrition is not necessary for those who buy souls out of purgatory or buy confessional licenses.

"(36) Every Christian who feels true compunction has of right plenary remission of punishment and guilt, even without letters of pardon."

"(81) This license in the preaching of pardons makes it no easy thing, even for learned men, to protect the reverence due to the pope against the calumnies, or, at all events, the keen questionings of the laity." Translations and Reprints, vol. ii, No. 6.

*

The sale of indulgences in general, and by Tetzel and his colleagues in particular, constitutes a most important feature of the movement. The theory of indulgences as preached by Tetzel is shown in a pattern sermon to be used by the priests in his district around Leipzig: "With these confessional letters you will be able at any time in life to obtain full indulgence for all penalties imposed upon you, in all cases except in the four reserved to the Apostolic See. Throughout your whole life, whenever you wish to make confession, you may receive the same remission, except in cases reserved to the pope, and afterwards, at the hour of death, a full indulgence as to all penalties and sins, and your share of all spiritual blessings that exist in the Church militant and all its members. . . . Are you not willing, then, for the fourth part of a florin, to obtain these letters, by virtue of which you may bring, not your money, but your divine and immortal soul, safe and sound into the land of Paradise?"

That the practice was grossly abused at this time admits of no question. Tetzel's appearance at Jüterbogk, but a few miles from Wittenberg, aroused Luther to action. His views (subject to revision on convicion) are expressed in the following, among the ninety-five theses: "Our Lord and Master, Jesus Christ, in saying 'Repent ye,' etc., intended that the whole life of believers should be penitence.

"This word cannot be understood of sacramental penance

*

With the rise of scholasticism there sprang up independent, free associations of students, after the ancient Greek order. These free associations became formal organizations afterwards, with a single recognized head, called the "rector." Municipalities and princes, as well as the papacy, granted them charters, and they became permanent institutions equally with the monasteries and communes. Each school had its specialty, as: Paris, theology; Bologna, law; Salerno, medicine. Later, other faculties were added to each, and modern universities were born.

*

The Edict of Nantes (1598) guaranteed to the Huguenots liberty of conscience; freedom of worship; right to all public offices equally with Catholics; exclusive political control for eight years over Nîmes, Montauban, La Rochelle, and a few other towns; and the right to assemble by deputies every three years in order to present to the government their complaints. The latter clause, constituting them a veritable imperium in imperio, afforded a sufficient pretext for the revocation of the entire edict by Louis XIV.

†

Jacques Bénigne Bossuet (1627-1704), a famous French orator and Roman Catholic theologian, author of several books in exposition of Roman Catholic doctrines. Jean Claude (1619-1687), a prominent French Protestant preacher and theologian. Bossuet and Claude were engaged in frequent theological controversy; in 1678 occurred their noted conference or discussion on the authority of the Church; both claimed the victory. This freedom of discussion ceased with the revocation of the Edict of Nantes.

*

Climatic conditions as well as political considerations must not be overlooked.

†

This statement is more exact than the passage on, with which it is not easily harmonized.

No doubt the assertion of this principle of absolute independence, or the unlimited right of private judgment in religion, became and has continued to be the great characteristic result of the religious revolution. But the Reformation did not at the outset (any more than many other great revolutions) generalize itself, define and enunciate the principles on which it proceeded. It began with opposition to special abuses and corruptions. Neither Luther nor his associates comprehended at first how far they should be carried. It was only in the sequel that the right of private judgment in religion was brought out, asserted, and contended for as a principle. Luther himself and the earliest reformers did not contend for it as an absolute principle. This is evident from the continual offers of Luther to submit himself implicitly to the decision of a general council. It is evident, moreover, from the fact that the reformers, just as much as the papists, held it right to inflict coercion, physical pains, and death upon those who denied what they regarded as the essential faith.

*

From the point of view of our age, the inconsistency of the Reformation is glaring, when one recalls the intolerance of the reformers.

Now whether the principle of independence of all authority, the absolutely unlimited right of private judgment in matters of religious faith, be or be not a correct principle, it will not be disputed at the present day that absolute independence of all human authority, and so far forth the unlimited right of private judgment, is a correct principle, and that all coercion or physical punishment is a monstrous absurdity and a monstrous crime. Yet nothing is clearer from history than that the reformers did not understand, did not act upon this principle; it was a century and a half before Protestants learned definitively that they had no right to inflict death, imprisonment, stripes or fines upon heretics, and no right beyond that of simply separating from their communion.

*

Intellectual authority is doubtless included, respect for which rests on the double basis of recognition of equality and superiority in others, and a profound regard for the truth as revealed in the experience of others.

*

Rose, Ignatius Loyola and the Rise of the Jesuits, may be consulted. An excellent sketch of the rise of the Jesuits is given in Sir James Stephens's essay on Loyola, in his Ecclesiastical Essays. The literature of the subject is abundant.

*

Since the time of Henry VIII the power of the Church over legislation and administration has been gradually decreasing. Since Archbishop Laud (1645), the advisers and ministers of the sovereign have, almost without exception, been laymen.

*

The French revolution of 1789.

†

Perhaps there is no epoch in the world's history where one can find more diversified interests and conflicting motives than in the Reformation. It has a separate history for each nation and a separate history for the various classes of society. To the German peasant it seemed to offer an escape from the burdens of feudalism; to the noble, an opportunity for gain; to the emperor, another force to check the the papacy; to the scholar, it meant intellectual emancipation. The Reformation cannot be separated from the period which preceded it. The new spirit, which in Italy produced its magic effects in art, literature, and culture, in Germany awoke the religious fervor of the people. As one has said, "This new spirit in Italy emancipated the human intelligence by the classics; in Germany it emancipated the human intelligence by the Bible." The struggle was between Teutonic freedom and Latin authority, between the spirit of Saxon and Roman law. It was, in fact, the last Germanic invasion of the sacred soil of Rome. It prepared the way for the political revolutions which followed.

*

A distinction may be made between the reigns of Henry VIII and Elizabeth and those of James and Charles; the former rested on the fact of power, the latter on the pretense of prerogative. The reigns of Edward I and III, on the other hand, were based on a constitutional right. They recognized the king as a part of the nation; the Stuarts sought to be the state.

*

The wholesale dissolution of monasteries and gilds restored about one fourth of the lands of England to individual ownership, while the breaking up of the three-field system and the inclosure of the commons produced a revolution in methods of agriculture. See Cunningham's Growth of English Industry and Commerce.

*

The formation of the House of Commons dates from the first appearance of the third estate as a permanent factor in legislation. This was in the Model Parliament of 1295.

†

The Acts of Parliament leading up to the separation of the Church of England from the Church of Rome are: Act of 1533, prohibiting appeals to Rome; Act of 1534, ordering all payments to Rome stopped; Act of Supremacy, 1534, declaring Henry the supreme head on earth, under God, of the Church of England. By the Act of the Six Articles, 1539, Parliament sanctions the first creed of the new Church.

*

The division of parties as given in the lecture is somewhat arbitrary.

*

His name at this time was Edward Hyde; he was created first Earl of Clarendon by Charles II.

*

The Grand Remonstrance (1641) shows, perhaps better than anything else, the formation of party lines in England. This document, drawn by Pym and Hampden, had, as its object, an appeal to the nation to support the parliament against the king. Its two hundred and six clauses may be divided into, the political clauses which asserted the power and prerogative of parliament, and the religious clauses which advocated, in indefinite terms, the "peace and good government of the Church." The former were subscribed to even by Falkland and Hyde, while the contest over

the latter was so fierce that it threw the Episcopalians into the ranks of the Royalists, and thus left the Presbyterians as the champions of the parliamentary principles. Later, however (1647), the Presbyterians were divided by the excesses of the radical element (Independents), and the right wing was driven to join with the Royalists.
*

The cause of this success was rather the possession of military power than the promulgation of popular principles.
*

Views are apt to differ widely in making comparisons. Following is that of Goldwin Smith: "The chief (Cromwell) was not a Cæsar; much less was he a Bonaparte, an unprincipled soldier of fortune, vaulting on the back of a Revolution to make himself an emperor. The relation of Cromwell to the English Revolution was not that of a Napoleon, but, if it is not blasphemy to mention the two names together, that of a Robespierre. The chief of the Rousseauists was the leader of the most religious and the deepest part of the French movement."
*

Cromwell's fondness for power may well be admitted, but not to the extent that it was his "darling ambition." That he desired "to place the crown on his own head and keep it in his family" is without historic proof. Although he was privately and officially pressed to take the title of king, his answer was final: "I cannot undertake this government with the title of king. And that is mine answer to this great and weighty business." The sincerity of his refusal can be judged only by his other acts.
*

Cromwell's vigilance, as well as the success he attained, disarmed opposition and prevented the formation during his lifetime of any organized effort for his overthrow.
*

The Restoration was a restoration of Parliament as well as of monarchy. The years which followed brought about a combination of the two, which culminated in the Bill of Rights (1687).
÷

The title Prime Minister was first applied to Robert Walpole, but was not used in any official document until the Congress of Berlin (1870).
*

Two causes working together account for the fall of Clarendon: The inherent weakness of his political theory; his outspoken disapproval of the king's conduct and life. The latter cause initiated his dismissal, the former made it popular.
*

The Cabal ministry consisted simply of a few members of the Privy Council, whom the king chose as his advisers. They did not constitute a ministry in the modern sense, since they were responsible to the king and not to parliament. Their sole bond of agreement was religious toleration. The statements in this passage of the lecture are too sweeping to be exact.
*

By the treaty of Nimwegen (1678), the integrity of Holland was practically guaranteed, and the dream of France of a boundary on the Rhine partially realized.
But to Louis the treaty was only a truce. He continued his armies on a war footing and strengthened his fortresses. By the words of the treaty, the ceded towns were to be surrendered "with their dependencies." Courts, called Chambers of Reunion, were organized by Louis (1679) to adjudge what territories in Alsace, Franche-Comté, and the three bishoprics were included in

the term "dependencies." These courts were well instructed. They awarded all of Alsace, Zweibrücken, and Saarbrück to France. With Alsace went Strasburg, through the influence of French arms and money. This alienated the emperor, as the occupation of Zweibrücken alienated Sweden. A quarrel with the pope turned many Catholics against Louis, as did the revocation of the Edict of Nantes (1685) the Protestants. Poland, Spain, and the Turks were alienated. The result was the secret formation of the League of Augsburg under the leadership of William of Orange for the maintenance of the Treaty of Nimwegen. Two years later William landed in England, unhindered by France. French troops were then moved to the Rhine and the Palatinate occupied. War was now begun along the whole frontier. The expulsion of James gave William the power and support he sought to fight Louis. At first the victories were all with the French. In 1696 the tide began to turn. England regained control of the sea. France was exhausted. "Half the kingdom," Vauban wrote, "lived on the charity of the other half." Peace was made at Ryswick, 1697. William III was acknowledged as King of England; all conquests made by France since 1678, with but few exceptions, were restored to the empire; and the Dutch were allowed to garrison the barrier fortresses between France and Holland. Thus did Louis XIV renounce his claim to be the dictator of Europe, and the Protestant succession in England was made secure.
*

Louis's policy towards England accounts in large measure for the success of Charles II and for the failure of James. Towards Charles, Louis played a double game, furnishing money in vast sums to secure a dissolution of parliament when it seemed inclined to peace with Holland (as in 1674 and 1682), and assisting the opposition party to attack the king if he became too independent.

Towards James his tactics were altered somewhat. James's open avowal of Catholicism made it certain in Louis's mind that James would not ally himself with Holland, but would find sufficient employment with parliament at home. Consequently French gold flowed less and less frequently northward, and Louis made up the lack in "moral support." Parliament, however, which had been greatly strengthened by the conduct of Charles, saw in Catholic Louis the dictator of the royal policy and religion for England, and looked to William of Orange as their deliverer at once from Catholicism and from foreign corruption.
*

The following summary of the events in this period may be helpful:

1625.   Charles I becomes king. He married Henrietta Maria, sister of Louis XIII of France, which involved him in war with Spain. This, in turn, made him dependent upon Parliament for financial support, and enabled the issue to be raised whether the granting of supplies should precede a redress of grievances. Political principles are paramount. Parliament continuously victorious. The First Parliament votes supplies for one year only, and is dissolved.

1626.   The Second Parliament takes steps to impeach the king's favorite, the Duke of Buckingham, thus declaring the principle of responsibility of king's advisers to Parliament, and is dissolved without granting subsidies. War with Spain develops into war with France. Charles has recourse to forced loans and impressment of seamen, and billets soldiers on the people.

1628.   The Third Parliament, led by Wentworth and Pym, draws up the Petition of Right, asking that certain grievances be redressed. Charles consents.

1629.   Charles dissolves Parliament, and attempts for eleven years to rule alone, with Wentworth and Laud as his advisers in political and religious affairs respectively. Public opinion is repressed by the Courts of Star Chamber and High Commission; revenue raised by levies of ship money (1634).

1637. The attempt to force the Prayer Book on the Scots results in the Solemn League and Covenant (1638), signed by the Scots, preserving the Presbyterian form of Church government in Scotland. War follows between Scotland and Charles, and forces the latter to call a Parliament.

1640. The Long Parliament summoned.

1641. The Triennial Act was passed, providing that more than three years should not elapse without the summoning of a Parliament. Parliament declares that it shall not be dissolved without its own consent. Parliament proceeds to undo, so far as possible, the illegal acts since 1629, impeaches the ministers, abolishes the Court of Star Chamber, and forbids ship money and other abuses. The Protestants become divided, on the Root and Branch Bill for the abolition of Episcopacy, into two hostile parties: Episcopalians and Presbyterians. The resolve of Parliament to obtain redress of all grievances results in the resistance of Charles, and his attempt to override and outmanœuvre Parliament results in an open break.

1642. Both Parliament and the king prepare for war, and the English nation is divided into two hostile camps: the king's party, of Royalists, Catholics, Episcopalians, and conservative republicans; the parliamentary party, comprising all Protestant dissenters from the Church of England, and the republicans. In general, the north and east are for the king, the south and west for Parliament. The towns stood with the latter and the country with the former.

1642-1649. Civil war. The most important results were the defeat of the king, the attempt to establish Presbyterianism as the State religion in England, the division between the Parliament, which was largely Presbyterian, and its army, which was composed of Independents, the expulsion of the Presbyterian majority from Parliament by the army, the trial and beheading of Charles (1649) by order of the Independents, who alone, by this time, are left in the Long Parliament.

1649-1653. The Commonwealth. Power in the hands of the army, which is republican in politics and independent in religion. Fairfax, lord-general, Cromwell, lieutenant-general of the army.

1653. The Instrument of Government is drawn—a Constitution for England, defining and describing the government in its administrative features. Cromwell is named Protector.

1653-1659. The Protectorate. The legislature, at first in one branch, is in 1657 made to consist of two. Cromwell is offered and refuses the title of king, but is allowed to name his successor. In all but name the monarchy is re-established.

1658. Cromwell dies. Richard Cromwell inaugurated Protector, but resigns after a few months.

1659. Movement set on foot by the leaders of both parties to restore the king. Writs issued assembling a Convention. Charles invited to return.

1660. The monarchy is restored, and Charles II becomes king. Appoints Clarendon his chief minister. General amnesty granted, with few exceptions.

1662. Final division between the Church and Dissenters marked by the passage of the Act of Uniformity.

1664. Clarendon's Code passed against non-conformity.

1667. Clarendon's fall. Rise of the Cabal (Clifford, Arlington, Buckingham, Ashley, Lauderdale). Foreign policy reversed. Triple alliance between Holland, Sweden, and England.

1669. Secret treaty of Dover negotiated through Charles's sister Henrietta. Chief provisions were: Charles should declare himself a Catholic, and receive from Louis £ 80,000 in money and the aid of six thousand troops; that Charles and Louis should make a joint war on Holland.

1673. The Test Act, requiring officers to take the sacrament according to the Established Church, overthrew the Cabal, and Danby becomes chief minister.

1674.   William of Orange marries Mary, sister of the king. The Habeas Corpus Act passed.
1685.   James II succeeds to the throne without opposition. He declares himself a Catholic. Louis sends, proof of his support, the sum of £ 67,000. The king appoints Roman Catholic officers in the army, and later to the ministry. Finding his policy unsafe, he seeks an alliance between Catholics and non-conformists by the Declaration of Indulgence (1687).
1688.   The second Declaration of Indulgence issued. All parties invite William of Orange to come over and declare for a free Parliament. William publishes his declaration that he goes to England as the husband of Mary, to secure a free and legal Parliament by the decision of which he would abide. In September, James attempts conciliation; dismisses Catholics from office, restores charters, and dissolves the Ecclesiastical Commission. In November, William lands in the west of England. James marches with an army against him, but soon, seeing his cause lost, escapes to France. William enters London. A Convention Parliament is called, which finally drew up.
1689.   The Declaration of Right. This is accepted by William and Mary, and they become King and Queen of England, February 18. By an act of Parliament, the Declaration of Right was turned into the Bill of Right. This closed the struggle between the king and Parliament. The effect of the revolution was fourfold: It destroyed the Stuart theory of the divine right of kings; it reasserted the fundamental principles of the constitution; it enthroned Protestantism in England; it ushered in the reign of Parliament.

Authorities on this period are numerous and easily accessible. Ranke, Hallam, Gardiner, are standard works. The Epochs of Modern History are handy and helpful, while Montague, Elements of English Constitutional History, supplies information on many of the constitutional points. Bright, History of England, Green, Short History of the English People, and Ransome, History of England, are among the best of the shorter histories.
*

This lecture might perhaps with greater appropriateness be termed either Absolute Monarchy in France or The Philosophical Revolution.
The following works will help the student more fully to comprehend the lecture: Kitchin, History of France; Duruy, History of France; Perkins, France under Richelieu and Mazarin; Perkins, France under the Regency; Buckle, History of Civilization in England, chap. viii-xiv.
*

See Lecture II.
*

Such development, when clearly successive, is usually revolutionary. The contemporaneous growth of varying elements in the same general society indicates a more steady form of progress.
†
One must not forget that the communes and free cities of France had, by the twelfth and thirteenth centuries, made a decided break in the feudal system and an encroachment upon the sway of feudalism.
‡
This is one of the author's sweeping statements on a point where there is room for difference of opinion.
*

One notable exception to this is England's experiment in constitutional monarchy. A liberal view would assert that this began with the reign of Edward I (1272), and, with the exception of the period of the Tudors (1485-1603), when a relapse occurred, has been continuous to our time. The more conservative view would show constitutional monarchy, broad and substantially complete, from the seventeenth century.

†

It may be doubted whether such names as those of John Locke (1632-1704) in political philosophy, Isaac Newton (1642-1727) in mathematics, or Edward Gibbon (1734-1794) in history (to whom M. Guizot is largely indebted), will not always be ranked with those of the great continental writers.

*

Comparing the statement in the text with what the author says on, one is led to think that England in the latter half of the sixteenth century had attained as influential a spirit of free inquiry as France in the early part of the seventeenth century. The influence of Locke in political and Bacon in speculative philosophy made the advance of French philosophy in Europe possible.

†

The cause for this is, in part, the language. French having taken the place of Latin as the common language of courts and schools, it was but natural that it should become a medium for science and philosophy. The fact that Louis XIV was a great patron of arts and letters also accounts for much. This does not, however, necessarily denote the leadership of French thought in Europe.

‡

The lectures of M. Cousin on philosophy, and of M. Villemain on French literature, delivered at the Sorbonne, in Paris, at the same time with the lectures of M. Guizot, constituting the present volume.

*

From 1795 to 1799 the government of the Directory was in power in France, but during its later years became weak and inefficient. On the 9th of October, 1799, Bonaparte returned unannounced from Egypt. On the 16th he was in Paris; on the 22d his brother Lucien was elected President of the Council of Five Hundred; and on the 9th of November (18th Brumaire), by a coup d'état, the execution of which was left to Bonaparte, the government of the Directory was swept away, and Bonaparte was master of the situation. A provisional government of three consuls was agreed upon. A committee, headed by Sieyès, was appointed to draw up a constitution, which, after important modification by Bonaparte, was accepted by the people of France by a vote of 3,011,107 to 1,567. The Consulate was proclaimed on the 24th of December, with Bonaparte as First Consul. The internal policy of the Consulate was one of general reconciliation of all the warring elements under the Directory; general amnesty and freedom for those who had emigrated during the previous years; enforcement of the Constitution; restoration of credit; the codification of the law. The external policy was war with Austria; feigned friendship with Russia. The effect of both policies was magical in restoring confidence and order.

*

The death of Richelieu occurred in 1642, six months before that of his sovereign, Louis XIII (1643). Louis XIV was but five years of age. His mother, Anne of Austria, became Regent, and appointed Cardinal Mazarin as her prime minister. Abroad, Mazarin showed unmistakable signs of genius; at home, his political dishonesty clouded every good he accomplished. Spain, an hereditary enemy, encouraged uprisings in the provinces and formed alliances with ambitious generals, like Prince Condé. The uprising of the Fronde disturbed the country; the Parliament of Paris, though primarily a judicial body, undertook to turn back the tide flowing towards centralized monarchy, and finally, in 1652, the king, then barely fifteen, declared he "forbade the

assumption by Parliament hereafter of any cognizance of the general affairs of the state and of the direction of the finances." Thus Louis, at the age of fifteen, was on the high road to absolutism.
*

Battle of Marengo, fought against the Austrians June 14, 1800, is one of Bonaparte's most brilliant successes. In the short space of five weeks, it is said, he transported thirty-five thousand men, with artillery and baggage, across the Alps, defeated the enemy, restored French supremacy in northern Italy, and returned to Paris.
*

The states of Italy were, during the years 1494 to 1516, the prey of France and Spain. Charles VIII, as a member of the house of Anjou, revived its claims to the throne of Naples. The time was ripe. The other European powers were otherwise engaged. Turin, Genoa, Pavia, Florence, and Rome opened thir gates as if to a deliverer. Ferdinand II, king of Naples, was defeated. Charles was crowned king. Possession of the kingdom was soon lost; was regained by his son Louis XII in 1501, and again finally lost in the same year.
†

Charles V's expeditions to Africa (1535 and 1541) were rather expeditions sent against pirates in the pay of the Porte; and since Charles was at war with the Sultan, these expeditions seemed as necessary as they were unsuccessful.
*

The Franco-Prussian War of 1870-'71 restored Alsace to Germany.
*

See.
*

Algernon Sidney, beheaded for conspiracy in 1683.
†

Ludlow was one of the few who were not pardoned by the Act of Grace of William III (1690).
*

He was ambassador to England during the reign of James II, and was ordered to leave by William of Orange.
*

"The dominating trait of the government of Louis XIV was an immense effort to bring back into the hands of the prince all the forces of the country, doubtless to dispose of them in the interest of the country, but more especially for the interest of the king. Hence, that excessive centralization which enveloped the commerce, the industry, the political life, even the moral life, of France; and the thousand bonds of a minute regulation, so that the initiation of the ministers was almost universally substituted for individual and communal action."—Duruy, History of Modern Times,.
†

Without Colbert and Louvois, Louis XIV would probably have lacked the two essential elements on which he relied, namely, money and arms. Colbert's fame rests on his administration of finances. He created the budget, and shifted 22,000,000 francs from the shoulders of the peasantry to the privileged nobility, and increased the revenues by 27,000,000; instituted a protective system (1667), drained marshes, built roads, encouraged manufactures of wood, tin, crockery, etc.; established councils of arbitration and boards of trade; encouraged commerce by granting privileges to five great trading companies; built up a vast merchant marine and a navy;

expanded the colonial power by settling old and acquiring new colonies. France to-day enjoys the fruits of Colbert's great work. Louvois was almost equally great in military administration. He created corps of engineers, schools of artillery, cadet schools; reformed the army throughout; introduced a regular order of promotion; published new tactics; and established hospitals, notably the Hôtel des Invalides in Paris.

*

"These ordinances are the greatest work of codification which was executed, from Justinian's time to Napoleon's. A portion of them are still in force; the ordinance of the marine composes almost all the second book of the present French code of commerce."—Duruy, History of France, Translation,.

*

Sometimes the character of a sovereign colors a reign and defines its history. The character of Philip II stands in strong contrast to that of Louis XIV. The former was phlegmatic, melancholy, and mastered by a fatalistic passivity; the latter was full of restless activity.

*

In the war of the Spanish Succession (1701—1714) the aim of Louis was to secure for his grandson Philip, Duke of Anjou, the throne of Spain. Charles II of Spain died without issue, leaving the throne of Spain vacant. Leopold I of Austria, cousin of Charles, claimed it; while Louis, by right of his wife, the eldest sister of Charles II, claimed it for his grandson Philip. Charles, just before he died, made a will, naming Philip as his heir. Leopold would not consent, and war was inevitable. England, the Netherlands, Prussia, and Portugal were drawn in against France for reasons connected mainly with the maintenance of the balance of power, and the Grand Alliance was formed against Louis. France was thoroughly humiliated and weakened in the war, but by the treaty of Utrecht (1713) Philip was permitted to ascend the throne of Spain.

*

The lectures of Villemain and Cousin are meant.

*

See, note.

*

Voltaire, Montesquieu, Rousseau, Diderot, D'Alembert, Condillac, Helvetius, Mably, Condorcet, etc., are the great philosophic speculators of the eighteenth century in France.

*

This expectation was fulfilled. Consult the author's History of Civilization in france.

†

The author stood, perhaps, too near the eighteenth century to judge correctly the relative influence of French and English civilization. Duruy, in his Modern History, takes an opposite view. He leaves the impression that the "free mind" of the period arose in England. Voltaire himself said, "I went to England to learn how to think," and he brought back to France the ideas of Locke, Newton, and Shakespere. Diderot freely acknowledges his obligation to Bacon, as Condorcet does to Locke.

Made in the USA
Columbia, SC
19 September 2020